Praise for

Against the Current

CANADIAN WOMEN TALK ABOUT
FIFTY YEARS OF LIFE ON THE JOB

"A must read for every young woman today."

The Hon. Judy Erola
President, Canadian Pharmaceutical Association
Former Minister, Status of Women

"The strong images and words of these women remained with me long after I finished reading. As with a good movie, insightful scenes from these women's lives often flash through my mind as I encounter workplace dynamics in the '90s."

Susan Meredith
Principal, Briarwood Junior Public School

"This book demonstrates that through women's struggles, perseverance, gutsiness, and a strong belief in themselves, they can make a difference."

Esther Greenglass
Professor of Psychology, York University

"Every parent and every teacher should give a copy of Judith Finlayson's highly readable book to their young daughters and students."

Senator Sharon Carstairs

"The woman's place is no longer in the home, and the Canadian home is no longer what it used to be."

Herbert Marshall
Chief Statistician
Dominion of Canada
1954

Against the Current

CANADIAN WOMEN TALK ABOUT FIFTY YEARS OF LIFE ON THE JOB

Judith Finlayson

To Helen enjoy the company of women Judith Finlayson

Doubleday Canada Limited

Canadian Cataloguing in Publication Data

Finlayson, Judith
    Against the current: Canadian women talk about fifty
    years of life on the job

ISBN 0-385-25543-8

1. Women—Employment—Canada. 2. Sex role in the work environment—Canada. I. Title.

HD6099.F55 1995   331.4'0971   C95-931357-5

Jacket design by Tania Craan
Text design by Heidy Lawrance Associates
Printed and bound in the USA on acid-free paper

Published in Canada by
Doubleday Canada Limited
105 Bond Street
Toronto, Ontario
M5B 1Y3

*To Bob, who sustains the present,
and to Meredith, the future.*

CONTENTS

Chapter 3: CLERICAL AND SECRETARIAL   81

Chapter 4: BUSINESS AND PERSONAL SERVICES   103

Chapter 5: COMMUNITY SERVICES   131

Chapter 12: THE ARTS

ACKNOWLEDGEMENTS

Against the Current could never have been conceived, let alone completed, without the wonderful community of women which is the backbone of my life. To all the women across Canada who trusted me with their stories, I'm extremely grateful. Every story was valuable in its own way and cast a unique light on women's collective experience. It's with regret that due to the practical considerations of producing a book, I include less than half of them here.

I also owe an inestimable debt to the many people who suggested women for me to interview. Several, with very busy lives of their own and precious little time to spare, sat down at their keyboards and produced pages of typewritten suggestions, including relevant commentary. Others picked up the phone and called colleagues around town and across the country in pursuit of possibilities. Quite simply, I could not have produced this book without their help and would like to express my sincerest thanks to, among others: Penny Allderdice, Doris Anderson, Mona Bandeen, Donna Baptist, Eleanor Barr, Ted Barris, Lois Browne, Sarah Colguhoun, Marjorie Cohen, Laurel Dempsey, Anne Derrick, Anne Drozd, Mary Eberts, Maria Eriksen, Sharon Fraser, Ros Friend, Diann Graham, Sharon Sparling-Graham, Fran Gutman, Rosalind Halverson, Trish Hennessey, Joan Jones, Lenna Jones, Marilyn Keddy, Dorothy Krouskie, Georges Laberge, Janine Lahaie, Betty Lee, Mary Lynk, Shelagh M'Gonigle, Maureen McDonald, Sandra Hunt McDonald, Lorraine Michaels, Marg Miekel, Paddy Musson, Edith Nee, Laurel Ritchie, Jane Robinson, Elizabeth Rose, Rebecca Rosenberg, Nancy Ruth, Sharon Sawchuk, Annie Scoot, Barbara Sears, Gail Singer, June Skea, Carol Anne Soong, Mary Stikeman, Brenda Taylor, Saeko Usukawa and Joan Wallace.

I would also like to thank Barbara Schon, not only for contributing the index, but also for those many days when walking our dogs in the park provided a cherished social break from solitary work. Madeline Koch pitched in when the transcribing became overwhelming, and her encouraging comments on the stories contributed early feedback. Alexandra Horsky and Joy Williams of the Canadian Women's Foundation were enthusiastic about the book before they'd read a word, and their confidence was reassuring.

I am also indebted to John Pearce, Editor-in-Chief at Doubleday Canada for signing the book. My editor, Susan Folkins, offered sensible and con-structive criticism and engaging marginalia, and was always a pleasure to work with.

My husband, Bob Dees, who has always been a great support in work and an equal partner in marriage and parenting, deserves special thanks, as does my daughter, Meredith, who brings much laughter, insight and patience to my life.

Introduction

In 1975, when the federal government was searching for a catchy slogan to promote International Women's Year, they settled on the provocative question, "Why Not?" At best a backhanded way of promoting equal opportunity for women, the campaign struck some as remarkably out of touch. Economic equality had played a prominent role on the public agenda for years, likely reaching a pinnacle in 1967 when the Royal Commission on the Status of Women was launched. Its report, published three years later, became a hotly discussed best seller which one *Toronto Star* columnist christened "a call to revolution."

Actually, by the time the commissioners published their incendiary document, the revolution had been under way for almost 30 years. In 1942, the Mackenzie King government established the Women's Division of the Selective Service Agency to register women for recruitment into the war effort. At that point, the shadow of labour shortages loomed ominously over a Canadian society struggling to meet the demands of wartime production. Since just over 20 per cent of women worked for wages, women constituted the last supply of potential workers to be drawn into employment. Mobilization of this reserve army of labour initiated the influx of women into the paid labour force, which many observers believe to be the greatest social change since the Industrial Revolution.

By 1944, the pinnacle of wartime employment, one-third of adult women were working for wages, a level that wasn't surpassed until 1967. Lured by government inducements such as tax breaks and publicly funded child care, not to mention awesome salaries, at least compared to low-paying "female" jobs, women marched into foreign territory with little more than an inkling of what lay ahead.

Traditional wisdom suggests that women's love affair with paid work was a temporary phenomenon that ended when "the boys" came home. But working for wages gave women a sense of power and freedom they were unwilling to relinquish, and many were resentful when they were booted out of the work force to make way for the returning men. Speaking in the House of Commons in 1944, Dorise Nielsen, a Saskatchewan member of Parliament, mocked public attitudes towards women's contribution to the war effort. "Well, girls, you have done a nice job; you looked very cute in your overalls, and we appreciate what you have done for us. But just run along; we can get along without you."

Although the 1950s have been closely identified with so-called traditional values, from the mid-1950s on, women's participation in the work force increased dramatically. In 1951, only 24 per cent of women worked for wages. By the end of the decade, that ratio had increased to almost 30 per cent, closing in on wartime levels.

The rapid expansion of the clerical, retail and service sectors fuelled the demand for new workers, just as the war had done a decade earlier. As the first wave of baby boomers reached school age, teachers were suddenly in short supply, and married women constituted the last labour reserve that could be called into action. The new consumer society was also compelling women into the work force, and many took jobs to buy the products aggressively marketed on television shows such as "Ozzie and Harriet" and "Father Knows Best," both of which, ironically, celebrated the joys of "traditional" family life.

Today, the myth of the 1950s domestic bliss has overtaken the reality of the postwar years, but members of the contemporary media recognized the currents of their age. As one *Financial Post* writer reported in 1957, "This is a woman's world and getting more so. More and more married women are going to work and they are quickly being snapped into jobs."

By the mid-1960s, fuelled by widely read books such as Simone de Beauvoir's *The Second Sex* and *The Feminine Mystique* by Betty Friedan, the so-called second wave of feminism emerged. Women's right to meaningful, well-paid work is at the heart of the report by the Royal Commission on the Status of Women, published in 1970. The development of the contraceptive pill and its widespread availability enabled women to plan childbearing alongside careers. As a result, between 1975 and 1990, almost twice as many women entered the labour force as men, and during that time, women's labour-force participation jumped from 44.4 to 58.4 per cent.

Today, almost 60 per cent of Canadian women work for wages (compared to 73 per cent of men). Moreover, by 1992, when Statistics Canada prepared a report on dual-earner families, women had clearly pulled out the rug from under the stereotype that identified them, however wrongly, as "pin-money" workers. At that point, females were either the major or equal breadwinners in almost a quarter of Canadian husband-wife families of working age.

In 1992, 50 years had passed since women first invaded the labour force en masse. For all intents and purposes, women's recruitment into the war effort signalled the start of a major demographic shift. Prior to 1942, most women worked as agricultural workers or in the home. Since then, more and more have moved into salaried jobs, many of which were previously held by men.

Although pieces of the story have been told, this 50-year influx has never been documented as a whole or in the words of women themselves. Individual women, like men, may not be able to write their history but, I believe, they know it intuitively. People feel life through their fingertips and often understand that their experiences are historically significant, even though they may not grasp the meaning themselves. If this book takes one small step towards capturing history in the words of the women who made it, and measuring the depth of change that has occurred over the past 50 years, then my objectives are met.

I began work in the fall of 1992 and subsequently travelled across Canada, from the Gulf Islands in British Columbia, to Newfoundland in the east and as far north as Yellowknife, interviewing approximately 200 women. All the interviews were conducted between March 1993 and December 1994. Although my experience as a journalist had taught me that women are eager to tell the truth about their lives, and that they don't shy away from revealing troublesome details, I was often surprised by the frankness I encountered.

Even so, a number of women had second thoughts after being interviewed and asked that their stories not be used. Some women agreed to be interviewed only if I guaranteed them anonymity. Occasionally, women asked me not to use specific information, often of an intimate nature—for instance, about domestic violence—in deference to children who weren't aware their fathers had been violent. But often, when I double-checked about painful incidents, the response was, "Use it if it helps other women," although on a number of occasions, I chose not to use authorized information that I felt might be potentially harmful to the woman involved.

Finding subjects wasn't difficult. In fact, I left each place I visited with the names of many women I wanted to interview, but was unable to meet for one reason or another. I've been blessed with a magnificent network of women across the country who suggested women in their communities, who, in turn, suggested others, and so on and so on.

From these lists, I selected subjects that met my own criteria. In every place I visited, I tried to interview a wide range of women, from those with intimate knowledge of the social safety net, to those who customarily walk the corridors of power. I interviewed some women because I sensed a meaningful story in the barebones description of their experiences. Others seemed like pioneers and their stories historically significant, making them touchstones against which a half century of change could be assessed. Some were chosen because they strengthened themes that were emerging, and others for the opposite reason—because they seemed unusual and would broaden the scope of the book.

I began this project with the assumption that every woman has a story and was hoist with my own petard. The first draft of the manuscript was twice as long as my publishers expected, and at that point difficult choices had to be made. I had always known that a representative sample was far beyond the scope of this book and that my best effort would be candid snapshots, catching the essence of the past 50 years. The final selections were made painfully, and with that end in mind.

These cuts, combined with the number of women who decided against allowing their interviews to be used, meant that the stories of over a 100 women were omitted. Often these stories expanded on the themes that emerged in the interviewing. They also helped to establish the subtext of the book in my mind and, consequently, I perceive them as integral to my research. For that reason, I've used points from some to elucidate the introduction, rather than repeating stories that appear later in the book. The themes I highlight in the introduction appear in the index, which directs readers to women whose stories address relevant topics.

Organizing the material into a structure was as troublesome as selecting the stories, since women's work lives rarely slip into ready-made compartments. Unlike men, whose right to work is taken for granted, women are likely to enter, or leave, the work force reactively. They may take jobs because their families need the income, or return home to care for children or other family members. Beverley Butler of St. Mary's, Newfoundland, who left school in Grade 10 to work in the local fish plant, provides a case in point: "After three years, I quit to get married. Eight years and three children later, I went back to the fishery because we needed the income."

Socialization likely holds pride of place in explaining why women's work lives so often take unexpected twists and turns. I was struck by the number of women who began their stories with the statement, "When I began to work, women had three options: teacher, nurse or secretary." While many women embraced "traditional" female jobs and found them fulfilling, others soon discovered that their interests and abilities lay elsewhere.

Career transitions were a repeatedly struck chord in women's lives, and although they were helpful in highlighting social currents, they played havoc with my need to organize my material. I needed to distil this mixed brew of women's lives into chapters, and I could see the difficulty in pigeon-holing women whose employment histories often zigzagged in surprising ways.

Ultimately, I decided on a makeshift sectoral approach to categorizing the stories, while recognizing its shortcomings. The interviews often appear under the initial occupation of the subjects. Sometimes, though, the entry-level position was so incompatible with the work life as a whole, that I used the job that seemed to define best who the woman was.

The title, *Against the Current*, came out of my interview with the late Grace Hartman, who, in 1975, became the first woman president of a Canadian union when she was elected to head the Canadian Union of Public Employees. In the course of our conversation, she described herself as a woman who, like others, was prepared to "swim against the current" in an effort to improve the workplace for members of her sex. This image of swimming upstream epitomizes the message that emerged from the interviews, one of quiet determination and perseverance, rather than militancy. Interestingly, my publishers and I spent months spinning our wheels and agonizing over a title. One day, Grace's line, which had been there all the time, jumped out at me from the page. It was a wonderful moment of serendipity.

As my interviewing progressed, certain subjects came up repeatedly. I was startled at how often government-grant programmes and special events such as International Women's Year, figured in women's stories. Even though the community of women has been a mainstay of my own life, I was also surprised at how frequently women reflected on the importance of other women as a source of support and necessary information. Unhappily, a number of women who balanced work with raising children also spoke negatively of other women's devaluation of their child-rearing role.

In 1952, Ontario became the first province to pass equal pay for equal work legislation, and by the end of the decade, similar legislation had been passed in all provinces except Quebec and Newfoundland. Even so, some women reported that in contravention of the legislation, men were paid more for doing the same work. More commonly, the legislation was circumvented by denying women access to better-paying or higher-status jobs. Those who tried to move beyond stereotypical images of women's proper place often reported opposition. For instance, in the early 1970s, one woman remembered being "turned against" and threatened with dismissal when her superior realized she had management ambitions. Another, who trained as a nurse, recalled her father saying, "What more could you want? You're already a nurse," when she enrolled in university to work towards a bachelor of arts.

Lip service to the contrary, there's still an undercurrent of resistance to female ambition, to some extent because it clashes with our most cherished assumptions about womanhood. While some women forged ahead despite this impediment, others internalized the conflict, which often works itself out in the twilight zone that accommodates the push-pull between work and family life.

One 50-year-old Montreal businesswoman, who married during her final year of a liberal-arts degree and reluctantly became a teacher to put her husband through medical school, found her hopes to further her own education once he graduated dashed by an accidental pregnancy. "After our daughter was born, I went through a rough period," she remembers. "I hated staying home and felt robbed of my career, so I found a part-time job, teaching at a high school. But when I came home and the baby was crying, I'd get the guilts. So, after six months, I quit." Then she entered a period where, she says, she tried to be perfect: "I became a gourmet cook, took piano lessons, learned to play tennis, entertained beautifully. I think I needed to prove myself because I was so embarrassed I was staying home." She identifies this as "another story of the '60s and early '70s." Like many of her friends, she felt "torn and unhappy." In retrospect, she thinks they were all depressed and recalls getting together at the end of the day to drink wine to "get through the next few hours."

The influence of convention is powerful and the idea that "real" women will meet Prince Charming, marry, have children and be totally fulfilled by marriage and motherhood is a trenchant myth that often influences women's experience of work. "I've never forgiven Rock Hudson because I believed those movies he made in the '50s and '60s—Doris Day and the happily ever-after machine," comments Donna Chow, a Winnipeg research scientist, whose long-term position was recently terminated. "Today, I understand that being a good little girl and following the rules cost me heavily in my career."

Now in her late '40s, Dr. Chow earned an honours degree in math, physics and chemistry at the University of Toronto, but after she married, followed her husband around for many years as a faculty wife. "I didn't go back to school until after my son was born and I was going crazy at home," she recalls, pointing out that although she eventually got her doctorate and did the appropriate post-doctoral work, her "time out" on the family track left her eight years behind in her career. "I've been over the age limit when I applied for all my awards, which meant I had to break age barriers as well as any related to gender," she reflects. "The funding agencies don't consider that women are having children when they're about 26 or 27, just after they get their Ph.D.s. That's when you need to do your post-doctoral work, and God help you if you get pregnant!"

While women who are moving up through the hierarchy often feel the work-family conflict because of inequities built into the system, many women experience the clash more directly when they encounter problems with child care. Beverley Butler, mentioned earlier, went back to work at the fish plant in St. Mary's when her youngest child was two, and remembers that finding child care in a small community was difficult because everyone wanted to work in the fish plant. Her problems were exacerbated by shift work. "If the catch was in, I'd often have to work until two or three in the morning, which played havoc with child care," she recalls. Even though three-quarters of the plant workers were female, child care was never negotiated by her union—to some extent, she thinks, because there weren't many women leaders.

Throughout the 1980s, the popular media dwelled on the high-achieving career women with husbands and children who were "having it all." By the sobering '90s, it became obvious that many women who juggled children and work were collapsing from the strain of "doing it all." In fact, the stress of the so-called second shift has been identified as one of the greatest health hazards facing women today, and it was often mentioned by the women I interviewed, particularly those who were single parents. This is not the easy route to social assistance preached by family-values evangelists but, rather, a failproof recipe for what psychologists call "role overload," the state of being overburdened by responsibilities.

Most often, the single parents I interviewed were the product of divorce, and if they had to access the social safety net, they did so reluctantly. "I've been a single parent for nine years and only went on social assistance once, for three months, when I was out of work," recalls Donna Bonner of Halifax. A secretary for 17 years, she encountered difficulty finding employment when she made the switch to "non-traditional" work and apprenticed as a carpenter. "Social assistance was the hardest call I ever made. I felt there were people worse off than me. I still had food in the cupboard."

Inevitably, the women who were single parents did whatever was necessary to keep their families intact, often at great cost to themselves. I can't help thinking about one west-coast secretary who lost both her legs beneath the knee in a tragic accident. She attributes her remarkable recovery—with dual prostheses, she learned to walk well enough to pass for full-bodied—to her need to care for her two children. Like most women, she received no financial support from her former husband. "I had to work to ensure a good lifestyle for my kids, and I soon realized I had more luck getting jobs if employers didn't realize I was disabled," she comments.

But children aren't the only family responsibilities that have an impact on work. Margaret Evans, a clerical worker from Thunder Bay, Ontario, told me a story which exposed a gaping hole in the social safety net. Laid off from her job, she was called back to work the same day her mother, an Alzheimer's victim, was found living in chaos and physically deteriorated. Since no one else could care for her mother, she couldn't return to work. Some time later, she received a letter saying she wasn't entitled to unemployment insurance because she didn't accept the call-back. Moreover, she was being fined for violating the Unemployment Insurance Act since she'd received payments she wasn't entitled to. With the help of a legal-aid clinic, she successfully appealed the fine, although she couldn't return to work for "four years of hell" until she got her mother into a home. Throughout this time she remained ineligible for unemployment insurance.

Several women were very critical of how they were treated by male Unemployment-Insurance-Commission counsellors, particularly around family-related issues. Some with children were made to feel like criminals because the counsellor didn't believe they were really looking for work, even when they provided evidence to the contrary. Another remembered being pressured to return to work before her 17-week maternity leave was up. The perception of hostility coloured some women's experience of the workplace as well, often showing up as various forms of harassment.

One engineer still has vivid recollections of being harassed at a conference in 1971. "I asked myself if I was giving this guy any signals because I didn't mean to," she recalls. " I didn't wear make-up and very little jewellery, so it really threw me when he started to come on to me." That experience influenced her approach to dressing and affected her sense of herself as a woman for the rest of her career. "I learned to be very careful. I wear nice suits, but I make sure that I don't look sexy. People should only see me as a good engineer, not as a woman."

Such fractures in female identity can lead to feelings of fraudulence and a sense of not belonging, which often came up in the interviews. Women who are "doubly disadvantaged" by race, ethnicity, disability or sexual preference may actually experience this alienation as threatening.

One Western lawyer told me a compelling story about applying for an articling position in the late 1970s at a firm that was uneasy about hiring women. Towards the end of the interview, during which she'd been very uncomfortable while the guys told jokes for their own entertainment, she was asked in an off-hand way, "You're not a Jew or a homosexual are you?" Although she hadn't been raised as a Jew, a Jewish grandfather and her emerging lesbianism made her vulnerable on both counts. "I was living with a woman and some of my friends knew about it," she recalls. "But I was afraid of not being accepted in a work situation if that information came out—not without reason since I knew this firm had recently ditched a guy who was gay." Luckily, someone arrived at the door and asked the group for lunch, rescuing her from a response. In the end, she took the position anyway simply because she needed the job. "I can't believe I worked for those people," she comments in retrospect, revealing how the need to gain credentials often outweighs idealism, and echoing a situation common to many victims of sexual harassment.

The split between masculine and feminine values and the desire to bring one's own identity to the workplace, as a female or as a member of a disadvantaged minority, are topics that surfaced in a myriad of ways. For instance, Dorothy Grant, a fabric artist based in Surrey, British Columbia, is trying to redress the devaluation of Haida culture through her work. Several years ago, she began making clothing featuring Haida art designed by her husband, Robert Davidson, a well-known artist. "We're a team and we work together as a co-operative couple, following Haida tradition, where the men did the designs and the women did the appliqué and the design of the piece," she comments.

On a similar note, the artist Joyce Wieland talks about finding her voice as a woman while living in New York in the 1960s, where the art world was very male dominated and intellectual. "I found this very troubling," she remembers. The message was that if women wanted to be taken seriously as artists, we had to deny our experience and identity as women." Once she recognized this conflict, she began to search for ways to make her femininity part of her work. "I made a film about being trapped in a kitchen. Then I began to work in cloth. By introducing these elements of domesticity, I was desperately attempting to legitimize my work in terms of my own experience." Gradually, she realized that quilts might be a medium with the potential to transform women's experience into art. So, in 1969, when she was invited to stage her own show at the National Gallery in Ottawa, she exhibited quilts. "It was a bold move and I was terrified," she remembers. Happily, the show was a great success.

Unfortunately, few women, particularly those working in large corporations with strong "masculine" cultures, can afford a comparable gamble. They risk being identified as "flakey" or, worse still, subversive. In fact, I found that senior corporate executives were the group of women most unwilling to talk candidly about their experiences. "I've got too much to lose," says one member of the Calgary "oil patch," who refused to be interviewed. "I've spent years getting to where I am. Now the guys think I'm more or less one of them and I'm able to accomplish most of my objectives. If I start talking frankly about the price I've paid to get here, I'd be dead in the water."

The sense of being in foreign territory coloured the experience of work for many women, and a number lamented the absence of mentors and role models to help them navigate these uncharted regions. They regretted not having other women who could advise them on matters such as workplace skills, or even how to dress. Recognizing the need to keep their feelings to themselves, they emphasized another downside of advancing in the hierarchy: loneliness.

Even so, a strong sense of positivism underscores the stories. Most women want to make the best of what they have. Many feel the obstacles they encountered because of their sex weren't insurmountable. Sometimes, they even proved to be advantageous by provoking the proverbial "click" of recognition that inaugurated a craftier approach towards dealing with the workplace.

Actually, many women felt that being female made them better equipped to succeed, although they also recognized that institutions were slow to view them as the asset they knew they were. Women's empathy, ability to think holistically, to listen, to work collectively and develop businesses because of their willingness to start small, were just some of the factors they identified as being particularly valuable. Clearly, some women felt that the masculine way of doing things was a style whose time had passed.

Although I intended initially to limit the scope of this book to paid work, the importance of volunteer work surfaced so often in women's stories that I decided to include it. Many women volunteered for the traditional reasons: involvement in their communities and the satisfaction derived from "doing good." But others saw volunteerism as additionally advantageous to their careers. For politicians, the links are obvious. Shirley Dysart, Speaker of the House in New Brunswick, feels that volunteer work is a "stepping stone to a career in public life" because it creates a profile at the community level. Other women see volunteer work as a vehicle for learning skills to which they were denied access in their jobs. Several women who identified their organizations as old boys' networks, with a blind spot towards them as managerial material, had been able to upgrade their skills through volunteering. "Volunteer work is a great training ground," comments Gabrielle Matern, a Montreal flight attendant, who has been active in volunteer arts-related organizations, and remembers being dismissed by her male boss as "just a flight attendant" when she disagreed with him. "Everybody is appreciative because the work is for free, and they'll usually teach you things because you're there to support them."

When I began this book, one of my objectives was to capture some of the diversity that exists among women. Over the years, I've become increasingly irritated when I hear women referred to as a homogeneous mass and then criticized because we don't think alike or share similar beliefs. Comparable assumptions would never be made about men, whose basic differences and right to disagree with each other are taken for granted. Women, like men, are divided by factors such as background, experience, ethnicity, race and socio-economic circumstances. These differences influence how we perceive and feel about the world and, to some extent, how we are treated.

So it's not surprising that there are women who've encountered major obstacles to advancement and those who haven't, women who've been sexually harassed and those who've escaped it, women who've buckled under the pressure of family responsibilities and those who've taken them in stride. These experiences are all fragments of the female mosaic and are equally valid in defining where women are today.

The fundamental question is, of course, have women progressed since 1942 when we were first recruited into the work force? In my opinion, the answer is an emphatic yes, although that statement isn't as black and white as it may seem. Actually, I think we've been following a circuitous route, "Two steps forward, one step back."

While discrimination is rarely as overt as it was when women were openly paid less than men for doing the same job, women's wages still trail those of men by approximately 25 per cent. Some analysts attribute this wage gap to women's loss of productivity during their childbearing years, but statistics show that earnings of even the youngest men are almost 15 per cent higher than those of their female counterparts, who are unlikely to have had children.

One of the factors contributing to women's reduced earning power, which surfaces from time to time in the interviews, is the gender segregation of the work force. Most women still work in low-paying "women's" jobs, and those who try to move into "non-traditional" occupations often encounter resistance. Like it or not, stereotyping remains a pervasive barrier to women, and even the most successful suffer from misconceptions about what women can, and should, do.

Similarly, equality in the work force will remain an illusion until men share equally in the family workload. Studies show that women with families still work, on average, 15 hours more a week than their male counterparts, an extra duty that is damaging to women's health as well as to their ability to succeed. Recent government cuts to social programmes, which thrust more community and care-giving responsibilities onto the family, will increase this already-heavy burden on women.

More subtly, the need to adapt to a workplace model based on long and inflexible hours and developed for men, with full-time domestic partners, leaves women particularly vulnerable to being identified as a "poor fit," particularly for higher-status positions. Herein, I think, lie the strong underpinnings of the so-called glass ceiling, women's recognized inability to rise above certain levels in the hierarchy.

As intruders rather than native sons, women are often the "last hired and the first fired." In these days of the lean-and-mean corporation, cutbacks in full-time employees have meant substantially more part-time and contract work for women. Less pay, fewer—if any—benefits and virtually no access to job promotion are now the reality for this labour pool, 70 per cent of whom are women.

Fifty years ago, it was acceptable to restrict a woman's employment opportunities on the basis of her marital status. Today, the barriers are less visible and in some ways more difficult to circumvent. Influenced by political correctness, much of the bias against women has gone underground. So while the surface often suggests a gender-neutral agenda, sexism often lurks beneath the veneer.

There have always been a few females who struggled to positions of power and, often inadvertently, played the role of exceptions to prove the rule that there was in fact nothing holding women back. Today, the sheer number of women advancing through the hierarchy has dramatically altered the dynamics of the workplace. Some men are extremely threatened by this spectre of female power and the backlash against women's rights, which surfaced in the 1980s, reached new levels with the '90s' anti-equity efforts, which have been dubbed "the revenge of the angry white male."

Even so, I doubt that women will retreat to the mythical world of "traditional values." Most families need a second income to survive. In fact, a report published by the National Council on Welfare in 1994, and based on Statistics Canada figures for 1992, concluded that in that year women's wages were all that prevented over half a million Canadian families from falling below the poverty line.

Economic necessity notwithstanding, virtually all the women I interviewed wanted to work outside the home. They took pride in doing a good job and recognized the importance of employment to their sense of self-esteem. Again, Beverley Butler of St. Mary's, Newfoundland, provides a case in point. A former fish-plant worker unemployed as a result of the moratorium on cod fishing, she deeply resents being deprived of her work which, she feels, gave her a sense of purpose and the feeling she was making a contribution. "They talk about people being on the package sitting around collecting money for doing nothing. That makes me mad," she comments. "I would have earned the money I'm getting as compensation if I'd been allowed to keep my job. I've been 14 years in the fishery. They took my livelihood and I want it back."

1

Education

Pearl Walpole
Mississauga, Ontario

"I did have a few flurries with the male principals. But, in the end, everything worked out because I was older than they were, and since I'd been principal of my own eight-room country school, I had experience they couldn't challenge."

In 1932, at the age of 18, Pearl Walpole began her teaching career in a one-room country school. When she retired in 1974, she was co-ordinator of primary education for the Peel Region of Ontario.

When my husband and I moved to Toronto in 1941, I applied for a position as a supply teacher at the neighbourhood school. I only received a minimal amount of work, but the following year, one month after our daughter was born, the principal phoned to say his last man had been called up for military duty. I found a neighbour to take care of my daughter and went back to work.

In those days, married women were forbidden to teach. When the superintendent learned that I was married and also had an infant, he said they were getting to the stage where the schools wouldn't be able to function unless they hired married women. He clearly felt they were scraping the bottom of the barrel.

After six months, I quit. I had promised to work only from January to June and, at some level, felt I shouldn't be working since I was married. I had my second child, a son, and didn't teach again until my daughter started school. In 1948, I was asked to become a supply teacher at a school so desperate for staff that the principal's wife offered to take care of my son.

Because the class was hard to discipline, they had trouble getting a supply teacher. The principal told me I was the first supply teacher who was able to keep the students under control. Of course, I could keep discipline because of my experience as a principal.

Once I got back into the school system, it wasn't long before I had a permanent position. During this phase of my career I had one serious conflict with a male teacher. We clashed at a board meeting where he argued there should be a differential between men's and women's salaries because men had families to support.

I was outraged. I argued that teachers should be paid for what we did, not according to our sex. I was particularly annoyed because this teacher had been so pleased with my work as a supply teacher that he'd left a note for the principal, which had been passed on to me.

But a completely different person appeared before the board. This teacher became very insulting—so much so that he was asked to leave the room and told not to come back until he apologized. When he returned, he mentioned my work as a supply teacher and concluded that I might be "one of the few women who should be paid as much as a man." I said I wouldn't accept the apology under those terms, because I was no different from any other woman. We were all working just as hard as the men. I'm pleased to say, he didn't win his case.

About 12 years later, after I became a supervisor and he was a principal, we happened to leave a meeting together. He grabbed me by the arm and said, "Pearl, did you ever think there would be a day when you and I would be walking arm in arm down a path?"

I said, "Why not? You finally saw the light."

I've often said I was able to accomplish so much because I was in the right place at the right time. I got back into the school system as a married woman because of the war. Then, in the postwar period, they needed all the teachers they could get because of the population growth. So being a woman wasn't a disadvantage. I was able to give teaching my best, and it was good to me.

Margaret Fulton
Vancouver, British Columbia

"The higher I went, the more prestigious the levels of the education system I functioned in, the more I found restrictions on me as a woman—what I was supposed to say and how I was supposed to behave."

Dr. Margaret Fulton began teaching in 1942, in a rural Manitoba school. After teaching high school for many years in Ontario, she earned a Ph.D. in English literature, became dean of women at the University of British Columbia (UBC) and, in 1978, president of Mount Saint Vincent University in Halifax, where she stayed until 1986.

I started teaching in a one-room school in 1942. I had no degree—only a Grade 12 education and then a certificate that allowed me to teach. But I was in charge and it never occurred to me that it wasn't appropriate. Most of my teachers had been women and my role models were all strong women, like my mother, who took no nonsense from anybody.

I was happy and it was certainly good training in taking responsibility. I had to design the curriculum, deal with the school board and educate about 30 kids who were scattered from Grades 1 to 9. I wasn't introduced to inequities in the work force until I moved to a consolidated school where male teachers with identical qualifications were paid more than female teachers at the same level.

My teaching career coincided with the baby boom so I never had trouble getting jobs. In my early days, they only really wanted to know if you could keep discipline. I kept taking courses and, eventually, was offered a job teaching health and physical education in a high school in Fort William, Ontario. Although I got a huge increase in salary, I was still teaching on a permit, and my female colleagues urged me to take my degree to avoid becoming a second-class citizen.

So in my late 20s, I arrived at the University of Manitoba. I was a mature female student, very much an oddity, and they didn't know what to do with me. But I stuck it out and went back to Fort William Collegiate Institute to teach Grade 9 and 10 English and coach the girls' teams. I had an excellent record as a coach. We won everything.

At this point I began to wonder if I wanted to spend the rest of my life running around in a gym suit. I had no notion of myself as a scholar, but I'd done rather well teaching English, so I decided to get a master's degree and went West when the University of British Columbia offered me a teaching fellowship. After I got my master's, I became an instructor, teaching first- and second-year English but, again, my women colleagues warned me that I would be a second-class citizen without a Ph.D.

The problem was that I had been paid so poorly as a teaching fellow, I didn't have any money to continue my education. So when Fort William Collegiate Institute offered a better salary than UBC would have given me, even with a Ph.D., my old prairie-depression complex took over. I said to myself, "It may be very prestigious to be at a university, but I have to look after myself."

I taught Grade 13 in Fort William for a number of years, but after awhile, I could see the system was breaking down. We were working primarily to get the kids through the departmental examinations at the end of the year. When Lakehead College offered me a job, I heard the voices of my women mentors saying I needed a Ph.D., so I enrolled at the University of Toronto.

That's when the scales really began to drop from my eyes. It was the early 1960s and women couldn't enter the senior common room. The men had offices, but the women didn't. Before I arrived, the dean of graduate studies was quoted on the subject of female scholars: "Well, gentlemen, we're scraping the bottom of the barrel."

I wanted to do my thesis on diaries and letters as a literary genre, using Jane Carlyle. When I went to see the dean, he said, "You will not do Jane Carlyle. You'll do Thomas Carlyle." So, that was that.

Our bibliography courses were given in Massey College, an all-male bastion. As women, we had to enter through the basement, and to get into the dining room, we had to be invited by a male and escorted by him. The feminist movement was just beginning, and we picketed the college to get this changed.

While I was doing my doctorate, I was a don at Whitney Hall, a women's residence. This experience convinced me that the permissiveness of the '60s was boomeranging on women, who were given the message that they had to be sexually active even when they didn't want to be. They were socialized in a way I had never been. Growing up on a farm and seeing my mother function as a co-manager of the economic union gave me a strong sense of women's abilities. Also, the stigma of getting pregnant when you weren't married was a tremendous deterrent for most of the women of my generation. You were jolly careful, and you stood up to men in a way that later generations didn't.

I'm not trying to pretend I had a lot of opportunities to marry, but somehow or other one does come close every now and again. In the final analysis, it didn't seem worth it. I felt I might as well keep my freedom and keep on the move since I was always interested in learning.

I had been invited to teach at Lakehead College once I got my Ph.D., but in the three-year interval they hired a new department head who was antagonistic to women. So the position I'd been assured of didn't material-ize. I found a job at Wilfrid Laurier University in Guelph and stayed there long enough to get tenure, then moved to UBC to become dean of women.

A dean of women never had the status of a dean of any faculty, but the role had influence and it was exciting. I had a wonderful advisory commit-tee composed of the senior women on campus, and because there was a group of us, we were able to bring about changes. No woman could have done it on her own.

In the '70s, the tendency was to treat women like cloned males. People said women had the same opportunities as men. But the opportunities were to function as men in a male environment in traditionally masculine ways. If they didn't do that, then the only other option was to play the depen-dent woman and get a boyfriend. I could see that women were giving up their academic prowess, particularly if their boyfriends were in the class. I fought to get more counsellors and supervision in the residences because I knew, from my experience as a don, it was important for young women to have a place where they could draw strength from each other and come to grips with who they were as women.

In 1978, I became president of Mount Saint Vincent University in Halifax. The university environment was extremely hierarchical, and even though its student body was predominantly female, Mount Saint Vincent was no exception. One day, I remember saying in a fit of pique, "I don't know why you people don't put pips on your shoulders and wings on your sleeves and salute each other in the halls as you pass by. This is a para-military structure."

I found working in that structure very difficult because I had enjoyed my freedom since my one-room school days. I tried to behave nicely, but I knew, without articulating it, that unless I had qualifications equal to those of the senior men, I wouldn't be able to accomplish anything. Once I had my doctorate, though, I could look any dean in the eye and know that my qualifications were as good as his, so I could take my equality whether he wanted to give it to me or not.

I got trapped at times and knew I had to go along with the way the men were playing or I'd end up with nothing. It was a struggle, but when I left, the school was far less male than when I came. It's easy to forget that we're fighting thousands of years of tradition, and change won't come overnight.

Marie Hamilton
Halifax, Nova Scotia

"My first school had 80 children and me. No white teachers would take the job and the school had been closed for six months before I arrived."

In addition to teaching for 25 years, since 1929, Marie Hamilton was very active in her community and received many awards, including the Person's Award and the doctor of humane letters from Mount Saint Vincent University. She died in 1993, at the age of 83, not long after this interview.

In my day, it was unusual for a black person to finish high school. I watched other black women working so hard—my aunt, for instance, who left home very early in the morning and cleaned house late into the night—and I felt there must be a better way. I wanted to be a nurse, but I wasn't admitted to nursing school because they wouldn't take black women. They said if I was the only one, who would board with me? So after I graduated from high school, I went to normal school and became a teacher.

I worked in rural areas for 25 years and now, when I look back, I'm glad I became a teacher because I was able to accomplish so much. In those days, very few black women taught—most were domestics. I'll never forget my first day. The students were standing around the classroom and all eyes were focused on me. I thought, what am I going to do? We said the Lord's Prayer and continued from there. I divided the school into two groups—primary to Grade 4 attended in the morning, and Grades 4 to 7 attended in the afternoon. Since I had come from the city, I naively asked where the library was. But there was no library. I was expected to teach with only the one or two books on my desk.

I never said a word about the conditions. I just decided to do what I could. Since I didn't have books, I had to invent some practical methods for teaching the children. I knew the families cut kindling to sell at the market, so I said, "This is our math lesson. When you go home, tell me how many sticks you put in the large bundle and how many in the small." Then, I'd ask them to tell me how much money their parents received for the different-sized bundles when they sold them. It worked very well.

I knew that the Department of Education issued a trustee's manual, which listed the supplies schools were entitled to, so I asked my trustees if they'd ever thought of requesting things like books. They said no, because they assumed they'd never get them. I got them to apply and gradually we started getting resources.

In those days, the trustees of country schools collected taxes directly from homes to pay the teacher's salary. Sometimes people didn't have much money, so it took awhile to amass the whole sum. Teachers in rural areas taught for three months before they got paid, and before my time, there were teachers who, on occasion, never got paid at all.

It was pretty rough, but I enjoyed it. I remember, for instance, that in North Preston the roads were ploughed in the white areas but not in the black part of the community. During my first few years of teaching, I boarded in North Preston so this wasn't a problem. But once I married, I moved to Beechville and had to drive every morning. If there was a snow-storm, I couldn't get to the school and I'd have to turn back. This would have been true for an ambulance driver or a doctor, as well.

The school in Beechville, where I worked later, was in very poor con-dition, but it was clean. It was heated by a wood stove, but the janitor made the fire very early, before he went to work, so when I arrived, I often had to light it again. The public-health nurses never visited the school, so I called a doctor I knew and asked him to come out for a day to vaccinate the chil-dren. He vaccinated many of the women in the community at the same time.

I taught for 25 years without interruption and had six children in the process. In the rural communities, you didn't find the same restrictions on marriage or pregnancy that existed in the cities. I'd teach until the eighth month, then I'd find someone—not necessarily a licensed teacher —to take over the class. I'd take a month and a half off and go back to work. I man-aged to nurse all my children. I'd pump my breasts, fill up bottles, and leave them for the baby-sitter.

Either someone in the community looked after my children or I took them to school. Black people support each other so child care was never a problem. In rural communities, especially, there were large extended fam-ilies and everybody looked out for everybody else. It wasn't as difficult for women, then, as it is today.

In my 25th year of teaching, I was asked if I'd work as a house-mother in Veith House, an orphanage in Halifax. I accepted the offer. It was my job to see that the children were up and dressed every morning. Then I'd march them down for breakfast and send them off to school. It was diffi-cult because some of the children had lived in three or four foster homes, and they had chips on their shoulders. But once I started working with them, I became very involved. After supper, I'd help them with their school work, and sometimes I wouldn't get home until 9:30 or so at night. My son would have the kettle on so I could make a cup of tea.

One day, when I was working at Veith House, a lady came in to see the supervisor. While she was waiting, she said to me, "My, your floors are beautiful." She assumed I was the scrub woman. I kindly directed her to the housekeeper.

On another occasion, at a time when my daughter, Sylvia, was working at the radio station, I happened to be travelling to Veith House in a taxi. The radio was on and I heard Sylvia reading the news. When the taxi driver commented on the clarity of the report, I said, "That was my daughter."

He almost ran the car off the road. "You must be kidding," he said.

"Well, I wasn't kidding when I had her," I replied. He simply couldn't believe that my daughter, a black, could be a reporter.

I worked at Veith House for three years, then it closed and the building became a community centre. I continued working at the community centre part time, but I remember having to pass a brewery every day and certain men heckling me. Eventually, I got tired of this and one day left for work 10 minutes early so I could talk to someone at the brewery office about it.

"I'd like to find out why, when I pass every morning, the men on the roof heckle me," I said. "I'm a private citizen, I'm respectable and I'm not doing anything wrong. I'd like to be able to walk by here in peace. Can you do something about it? Otherwise I'll take action."

"I'll guarantee that won't happen again," the man in the office said. And sure enough, it didn't.

After I retired, when I was in my late 50s, I went back to university and took courses in early-childhood education and sociology. I set up an early-childhood programme in the old Veith House building and then was asked to organize a preschool, which is still going today. At that point, early-childhood development became a major part of my life. I'm 82 years old and I still teach a course from September to June every year.

Phyllis McAlpine
Winnipeg, Manitoba

"**B**ecause I was competing in the system, I had to overlook the fact that I had rights."

After earning her doctorate in London, England, Phyllis McAlpine returned to Canada to do post-doctoral work and, in 1972, accepted a job as a research associate at the University of Manitoba, where she is now head of the Department of Human Genetics. She also chairs the Nomenclature Committee for the International Human Genome Organization.

I graduated from the University of Western Ontario with an honours degree in zoology in the early 1960s. I couldn't afford to proceed to a master's programme, so I taught high school for a year in Woodstock, Ontario, and soon realized I wanted to attend graduate school. By a great stroke of luck, instead of meeting with the head of the department at Western, I was introduced to a wonderful woman, Dr. Helen Battle, who became my mentor.

Dr. Battle took a genuine interest in the female students. She adopted a motherly role and introduced us to other women who were her friends. Without her help, we probably wouldn't have succeeded in science. When I arrived in her office in 1964, Dr. Battle recommended me to her friend, Dr. Margaret Thompson, at the Hospital for Sick Children, who was looking for a graduate student. The rest is history.

With hindsight I can see that Peggy protected me, too. In my second year, I shared an apartment with a woman whose supervisor was a man, and she seemed to have a much harder time because he threw the students into the deep end of the pool and told them to go at it. Peggy had a real interest in who I was and what I was doing—in me as well as my work.

I've remained friends with both Peggy and Helen. They're both a part of me I don't want to give up. I come from a rural background. My family didn't have personal experience with science so these women helped me in important ways. Now I make an effort to help other women in science as they helped me.

I did my master's in genetics in 1966, but there were no jobs, so Peggy arranged for me to go to England to do a Ph.D. After I got my doctorate, I accepted a job at the University of Manitoba as a research associate.

In my 30-year career, I've encountered lots of discrimination. My younger colleagues refuse to believe that things are actually better, but they are. Shortly after I came to Winnipeg, I remember attending a meeting where a potential hiring was being discussed. The maximum salary available was $18,000 and the man who was my department head said, "You can't expect a married man with a family to live on that."

"Well, that's what you're paying me," I remarked. My comments were dismissed as irrelevant.

When the first contract was signed between the university and the faculty association, I was one of the people whose salary was below the floor. While I was waiting to discuss my position, I discovered that the man who was head of my department had completed the paperwork without bothering to ask if the terms were acceptable to me.

Once I got my Ph.D., I had to decide between having children and having a career. In those days, you weren't able to do both. I have to admit I have a certain amount of resentment about this—not so much the choice itself, or the end result of the choice, but the fact that I had to make the choice.

I think the real difference between myself and my colleagues, who are 10 years younger, involves what I was forced to accept, without being able to recognize, and certainly not express, as discriminatory. I had to be one of the boys. I couldn't reveal my own personality because then they wouldn't let me participate. Playing the game by their rules, I often had to deny my female reactions.

I think we've reached the point where if you have the courage to raise male-female issues, institutions can't deny them. For instance, if a male chair of a meeting disallows a concern that's primarily of interest to women, he's risking trouble because he'll be seen as anti-women. Often these messages have to be presented by senior women who have established the credibility to speak their minds without having their career paths distorted. I now see myself raising issues of equality and fairness, not only for women, but also for visible minorities, whose experiences are probably about 20 years behind those of white women.

Even so, there have still been instances where I've lost out because I'm a woman who spoke her mind. The trouble is, I can't keep my mouth shut when I see something that is grossly unfair and, as a result, I'm often not invited to be on high-level committees because I'm perceived as a "shit disturber."

These days, my professional interest lies in the mapping of human genes. My profile in the gene-mapping world comes from work I've done in the United States. I couldn't get money out of the Canadian system because my work isn't in laboratory research: it's in evaluating information, prior to publication. I was the only person naming genes, but few people in power defined my work as important, possibly because I'm female.

Being a single female has also been problematic. There's an aspect of how you do business from which I've been excluded. For instance, when you want to do new things, it's useful to get people together informally so you can become acquainted and establish your alliances. Because the married men won't invite a single female home for supper—if you're invited it's as one of a crowd—I've been excluded from much of that potential. Between 9 a.m. and 5 p.m., I know hundreds of people at the university. Between 5 p.m. and 9 a.m., I don't know very many.

When I started in science, the game was different, but that's the game I learned to play. Younger women think it's legitimate to explain the problems and get the rules changed, but they couldn't do that unless the women of my generation had gone ahead and prepared the way. I'm the third female department head in the medical school in 110 years. My generation got a wedge into the power structure, which was no easy task.

The women who are 20 or 30 years younger than me are dealing with different issues. For them, it will be considered normal to have children and be less productive for a period of time. But other problems will emerge. I think it's important to be aware that we can't accept what we have now as enough. Change is a dynamic process, and we still have a long way to go.

Joan Baril
Thunder Bay, Ontario

" Teaching, like nursing, was seen as a profession for bright high-school girls. Few went to university. Those who weren't as bright went into clerical."

A teacher in the elementary-school system since the 1950s, Joan Baril now teaches a variety of subjects at Centennial College in Thunder Bay.

I graduated from teachers' college in 1953, when I was 18. Although I didn't know it at the time, I was among the first group of women teachers in Port Arthur who didn't have to sign a blank letter of resignation when they were hired. Previously, once a woman teacher married, the date on her letter was filled in and her resignation became effective.

This policy produced a very strange staffing arrangement. The majority of teachers were young, single women who stayed only for a few years, which meant the schools were, for the most part, staffed by young, relatively inexperienced people. There were some older women—we called them "old maids"—maybe, one or two male teachers, as well as a male principal and vice-principal. Few men went into elementary-school teaching, and those who did expected to move up quickly. They usually had to wait only two or three years until they became vice-principals.

No one seemed to think this was odd, but by 1953, it became obvious that the system had to change to accommodate the baby boom. Surprisingly, instead of calling back the experienced married teachers, they first tried dropping the qualifications. For a few years, teachers were able to get their certificates with only a Grade 12 diploma and a six-week summer course. It doesn't make sense now, but in those days, when married women weren't supposed to work outside the home, it seemed logical. However, even this didn't meet the demand, and around 1955, they started to bring back married women.

Another amusing thing I remember about my early days is that the schools had separate male and female staff rooms. The young men used the male staff room where they had access to the principal and the vice-principal as well as their mentoring. They made quite a clique together. All the women were relegated to the women's staff room, removed from the decision making. But since we clearly weren't going anywhere, I guess it didn't matter.

In the women's staff room, there wasn't any real antagonism between the young women and the older ones, but there was a gulf. Nobody asked the older teachers for the benefit of their experience. It never occurred to us that some might be single by choice, so we felt sorry for them. And the possibility of lesbianism never crossed our minds.

Once, I remember going into the staff room and finding one of the older women crying. She had taught for many years and had recently applied for a vacant vice-principalship. Naturally, she was turned down. A young guy with one year's experience got the job instead. I wasn't the least bit sympathetic. In fact, I was surprised she wanted the position.

When I told other people this story, they felt that vice-principals had to be male to keep the big boys in line. They believed a woman was incapable of disciplining the students. But this particular teacher had an upper grade and she could handle the boys. Interestingly, nobody seemed to notice that nuns were principals in the separate-school system and that they did fine.

Overall, it was a very authoritarian structure. The purpose of staff meetings was to let you know what had been decided, not to solicit your opinion. In 1956, when I was teaching in an air-force school in Trenton, Ontario, I led a revolt. The principal was initiating a complicated way of surveying the children in the school yard, and everybody thought it was stupid. I announced my intention to speak up at the staff meeting, and everybody said they would support me. Well, when I spoke up, they weren't behind me at all, because it was absolutely unheard of to oppose the principal's directive. Instead, my friends fell into a fit of giggling, probably because the situation was so stressful. Naturally, I got shot down.

Although married women were able to teach throughout the '50s, they still had to quit when they became pregnant. The rationale was that the children shouldn't see you showing because this was unseemly. You were supposed to quit by the third month, but you could only leave at Christmas or in the summer. I remember one teacher who was pregnant when she returned in September. She managed to hang on until Christmas by dodging the principal. No one ratted on her because she was very young and we thought she needed the money.

When I started teaching I earned $1,800 a year. I got married in 1957 and our first apartment cost $100 a month. It was a low salary, but the men could expect to be fast-tracked into administration. They also made more as teachers. In 1958, I discovered that there was an equal pay for equal work law in Ontario. So when I heard that a male teacher who had started a year after me earned $200 a year more than I did—that was a substantial amount, roughly 10 per cent of my salary—I foolishly went to the principal. With hindsight I realize I should have gone to the union. The principal told me that our jobs weren't equal because the male teacher gave out the ping-pong balls at recess.

I remember going to union meetings where the discussion revolved around how to raise teachers' salaries and the answer was that we had to raise our qualifications. We shouldn't expect to get a decent wage with only one year of training. The arguments then took the turn that it wasn't reasonable to expect women to spend three or four years getting a degree because they were going to get married, have children and not be able to teach. People would also say that if you allowed married women to continue teaching, you'd take jobs away from the single ones.

In 1962, when my son was born, I took a year off and then went back to work. My husband was an army officer and I was the only army officer's wife who worked outside the home. I didn't have any trouble finding a full-time housekeeper because she was a married woman and had difficulty finding work.

By that time the pattern had changed in the schools. Women teachers worked until they got pregnant, then they stayed home with their kids and came back when they were older. I was one of the few who returned when my kids were young. The reason was simple: my husband was a spendthrift and we needed the money.

I travelled around the country a great deal with my husband and never had difficulty finding teaching jobs. Starting the first of March, *The Globe and Mail* would run pages and pages of classifieds looking for teachers.

After my husband died, in 1968, I came back to Thunder Bay and got a job in elementary teaching. At this time the college system was exploding and many jobs were becoming available. The male elementary-school teachers walked right into the high-paying administrative jobs in the colleges. I considered myself lucky to get a job teaching English as a Second Language. I'd never taught the subject before, but they couldn't find anybody else.

Bernice Shrank
St. John's, Newfoundland

" **O**ver the years, I've been attacked personally. I've been denied merit awards and subjected to various kinds of harassment. I also think I was singled out in terms of salary discrimination."

Bernice Shrank is an American expatriate who arrived in Newfoundland in 1969. She's a tenured professor of Anglo-Irish studies at Memorial University.

When I first arrived at Memorial University, via New York where I grew up, and Wisconsin and England where I functioned as a young scholar, I was full of myself and ready to take on the world. But Newfoundland exists in a time warp and feminism hadn't happened here. People saw me as a noisy, cosmopolitan, highly competitive person.

There was only one other woman Ph.D. in the university. She had earned her doctorate very late and was regarded by her colleagues as a clown. She wasn't a clown—she was an utterly conservative Catholic woman with a very generous spirit—and she became a dear friend, even though we were totally different. But in terms of my goals, which were to make a huge name for myself as a scholar, she didn't have a clue because nobody had given her the space to develop. She used to say that the best route to success was to be "the pineapple of politeness."

Over the years, many things have happened to me. One day, an older colleague walked into my office. "Hello, Bernice," he said, grabbing me by the boob and squeezing. I thought, isn't that odd. The poor fellow is losing it. Many years after he died, I learned that he was well known as a sexual harasser, but the light didn't come on at the time.

I found it very difficult to establish myself as a scholar because I didn't know the ropes. For whatever reason, my thesis supervisor declined to play a mentoring role, and the network of mentoring that might have helped simply didn't exist. So I learned by hard knocks, which is a great pity because I wasted a lot of time.

Basically, I ran into gatekeepers who didn't want to let me—or any other upstarts—in. It was painful to accept that people who didn't even know me were prepared to block me. I discovered how to circumvent certain men and how to get published with great difficulty.

In the beginning, the structure at Memorial was very paternalistic which, in many ways, suited me. I was young and my relationships with the older men who were in charge went pretty well. It wasn't until they passed the mantle to the younger men that the fault lines appeared. It was difficult for them to order me around because I was no longer in my 20s and they weren't 60.

Many of my women colleagues, particularly in the early days, weren't academically credible. One of the painful things about being the only woman at your level is that it's lonely. Even though there was a great discrepancy in our credentials, all the women were supposed to rub shoulders, but I think many found me threatening. I had three children and only took maternity leave for one. I had a career, and a career profile across Canada. I had started to publish and I made demands about how I wanted to be treated.

In addition to being an academic, I'm an agitator and a defender of the rights of individuals. That has gotten me into trouble. I walked into a university with little tradition of individual rights and outspokenness on the part of faculty. What I am, today, is a product of what I was when I arrived and the pressures I found when I got here. Because I was excluded at the university, I found my place within the faculty association. I might not have become involved with union activities if I hadn't found things that needed to be addressed. I might have been content to make my statement.

I think these things happened because I was an outspoken, arrogant woman who wanted to make her mark on academia. I'm very committed to a view of a university in which the search for truth is unfettered. Many of my colleagues, even after tenure, find themselves terrified of opening their mouths.

Recently, I was asked to chair the Canadian Association of University Teachers' Academic and Tenure Committee which is, essentially, the national grievance committee for academics. I find that work fascinating and very, very important.

The association recently offered to buy out my time at the university to do grievance work. This is common and several men from the university have done it. In January, I was told it was OK but, in June, I found out there were problems. Naturally, I'm wondering why it was OK for the men, but not for me? Could it be because I'm female and a "shit disturber?"

Last fall a committee was struck to look for a new department head. It had no senior people, and when some of us confronted the administration, the dean said, "We don't want the senior women. They're axe grinders." We wrote to the vice-president but, so far, it hasn't been sorted out.

I think, perhaps, my bitterness comes from the feeling that this university, and many universities, are not particularly tolerant or open places. Because the stakes are so limited, the passions are intense and the judgements vicious and nasty. I've kept records of my battles and I'll write about them someday.

I don't think I've experienced a hatchet job. I think it's been done in codes, along the lines of "You know what she's like. She'll be so much trouble." It's nothing you can defend against. It's more like a small dart consistently placed in one's back.

A certain amount of it probably has to do with being the "dirty dark stranger from somewhere else," the unwillingness in provincial circumstances to accept an outsider. Really, though, it's another form of gatekeeping. The game is to keep people out.

I'm a very productive member of the university. I take home a lousy salary and teach six courses like all my non-productive colleagues. My husband is an economist who's routinely consulted on sex differences in salaries in universities. He calculated that I've subsidized the university to the tune of $60,000 during my tenure, which represents the accumulated difference between my salary and that of the average male at the same rank.

I'm at another stage of dealing with how I've been treated. I'd like the university to recognize that they have a problem. I'm very reluctant to escalate when it might be done nicely. My work and my personal life are better if I'm not in a state, and they win if they can stop me from working.

I have a rich family life and another side of me is very fulfilled through reason and research. Also, I have many great students. Sometimes I ask myself, "How much more is there?" If the administration doesn't like me, does it really matter? I guess it bothers me because it's wonderful to be stroked, but I don't think that will happen here.

Lois Reimer
Winnipeg, Manitoba

"How could I reconcile my position as a responsible administrator, which is certainly how all my colleagues saw me, with advocacy and even activism?"

Lois Reimer graduated from the University of Manitoba with a bachelor of arts degree and began her career teaching on a permit in 1953. After a brief career as a teacher, she "fell into" academic administration at the University of Manitoba, moving to the University of Toronto (U of T) in 1959. She retired in 1992 and returned to Winnipeg to care for her aging mother.

After I returned from my grand tour of Europe in 1966, my career moved breezily along. I had two superb mentors, men who promoted, helped and supported me, and gave me opportunities to shine even when they didn't have to. I later realized that was quite wonderful. Gender didn't seem to enter the picture.

When I was appointed head of student affairs at the University of Toronto in 1967, someone pointed out that I was cheaper than the man I replaced. In those days, I was so stupid I didn't realize that was a function of gender. He was older, a retired army type, and I probably thought his salary was greater because he brought so much more to the job, even though I knew he hadn't.

As director of student awards, I sensed that many parents were surprised to find that I was the man in charge. But, again, that didn't bother me. I knew I was different. There weren't many of me.

From student awards I moved on to general student services, and in 1984 became an executive assistant to one of the vice-presidents. Then my office was reorganized out of existence, which presented a bit of a problem. I was holding a fairly senior position, was too young to be retired and hadn't committed any major gaffes. But I just had my old B.A., which meant increasingly less, and certainly less at the upper echelons of university administration. I was seen as not easily transferable.

In 1984, the university celebrated the 100th anniversary of the admission of women, and interest in women's issues was renewed. A grass-roots group approached the president with the suggestion that some kind of women's advisor be appointed. Well, gee, here was old Lois, soon to be out of a job because her office had been reorganized out from under her, and she was the right sex. Needless to say, I got the job.

I would not have described myself as a feminist at that point. In fact, I'm not even sure I knew what it was. Now, I've learned that the term covers a broad spectrum, but in those days I had a fairly radical image in my mind and I knew it didn't represent me. Recently, someone reminded me of a very funny story, which I'd completely forgotten. I'd been in the job about six months and was still madly meeting people. When this woman came into my office, I rose, went around the desk to greet her, shook her hand and said, "I'm Lois Reimer and I'm not a feminist."

Funnily enough I went into the job with a fair amount of support. I think some of the women liked and trusted me, and they knew I could do a good job. The more astute among them probably thought, this is the best we're going to get. And that was true. I got the job because I was a trusted servant of the university who knew the place, worked hard and wouldn't do anything silly or irresponsible.

I recently came across an interview I'd given to the student newspaper shortly after I took the job. Essentially I'd said, "Well, gosh, I've got a lot to learn." That was true. "But if there really are inequities, then we'll root them out." Little did I know.

About that time, we had our first sit-in to support a women's centre on campus. The women's centre coalition qualified as the far-left category of feminism, which I didn't think had anything to do with me. Their banners said things like, U of T Administration Hates Women. I was advising the president who hoped that I'd get these people to go away. Well, damn it all, not only did I not get them to go away, I said we should have a women's centre.

That was my first experience with what the job was really going to mean. It was also the first time that some of the women began to think I might not be in the president's back pocket, and the first time the president thought, what have I done, who is this person?

I started off being very conservative. I'm still a conservative person— I don't think anyone would quarrel with that. But after a few years in the job, I became much more of an activist, not only because I had to, but because I was seeing a lot that I simply hadn't perceived before.

For instance, for many years the chairman of the English department said in public that a woman would never be appointed to the tenure stream as long as he was head of the department. Nowadays, the dinosaurs are more subtle, but just as effective and harder to deal with. Now the catch words are excellence and academic integrity. We can't get too involved in women's studies. If it's important, it will be taught and researched in our existing curriculum. Initially, I didn't believe statements like this were a problem. Now, I have too much evidence not to believe it.

I soon began to sort out the perennial complainers, those who approached every new appointee with a catalogue of grievances, from those voicing the many legitimate concerns that had been swept under the carpet for so long. I became angrier and angrier. Not powerful—I never had any statutory power. But I did have political power as people began to see they could get my ear and I could channel information to my senior colleagues.

The job was a radicalizing experience and I had a lot of help. To counterbalance the fact that I was part of a very conservative institution, I was fortunate enough to have the ready support and friendship of many wonderful women whom I would never have known otherwise. The university had some very bright, experienced and committed women who were always at the other end of the phone when I said, "Good grief! What do I do about X?" Instead of saying, "You jerk, you should have done something about that years ago," they helped me deal with the situation at hand.

I really felt I was lucky and I still do. I think being thrust into that job was the best thing that ever happened to me. I was fortunate, not only because of how it changed me, but also because it gave me an opportunity to draw on my background and on my years of experience at the university. I had been there long enough that I could call in numbers when I needed a favour. I knew the good guys from the bad guys.

I was enough of a team player—I had been that all my life—to recognize that certain things would take a great deal of time and that raising hackles all over the place wouldn't advance things. I knew I had to be persuasive, and that I'd have to present data. The men really liked numbers, graphs and charts, and they would always ask for statistics when all you had to do was look around. In the end, my actual figures turned out to be so much worse than the anecdotal evidence that I was told we couldn't publish them.

In 1992, I decided to retire. Eight years was too long to do that job, although there's no question I was getting more effective every year. But I was also getting very tired of fighting the same battles over and over again, even though I was enjoying it.

Also, as the universities downsized, a Ph.D. became essential for a high-level career in administration. In the past few years I talked about wanting a change, but the opportunities weren't there. When some family things came together—my brother was very ill and my mother, who was almost 90 and living on her own, required attention—it made sense to change. I was approaching 60 and I had gone as far as I could go at the U of T. I could afford to retire.

I came back to a family which, I'm sure, is proud of me and thinks I've done well, but has absolutely not the slightest comprehension of what I was doing, or why. It's very, very funny. My upbringing is very conservative and my family is unaccustomed to women holding professional positions. But my mother, bless her, made a remark that made me think we have crossed over. Referring to a woman in a certain position, she said, "Of course, she won't get any further because women don't."

For awhile I thought of myself as the classic late bloomer, but I'm not classic, if indeed there even is such a thing. I don't think anybody's life fits a particular pattern; it's more common to experience some kind of difficulty and to grow from there. Looking back on my career, I think I would have advanced more quickly if I'd been a man. I know there are males with my background and experience who have gone further, and they can't all be better than me. So I think I experienced an element of gender discrimination, although I wasn't aware of it at the time.

But it was an exhilarating experience to have reality thrust upon me when I was in my early 50s, and I wouldn't have missed it for the world.

Monette Malewski
Montreal, Quebec

"Although I loved teaching, the union job opened up new areas for me. I learned skills, such as negotiating, which I would never have learned in the classroom."

Monette Malewski began teaching in the 1960s. After working as an administrator in education and community services, she is enjoying a new career in financial planning.

I'm a woman of the '50s and '60s. I believed I had to be my own person, but I always put marriage and family first. That's why I entered teaching: so I'd have holidays when the children weren't at school and would be able to buy extras without being the breadwinner. Teaching also enabled me to put my husband through law school.

For me, teaching was a career not a job. I enjoyed it, and I knew even if I had children I wouldn't stay home. I was elected president of my union in 1969. It was a volunteer job in the sense that it didn't pay until towards the end of my tenure in 1981, but not in the challenges it involved and the hours it required.

My daughter was born in 1971 and the flexibility of teaching was a great asset. Until she was about three, I was able to teach from 9:00 until noon, then do my union work. In essence I had a part-time teaching job and a full-time union job, as well as a new daughter.

In 1980, I separated from my husband. Once I was on my own, I thanked my lucky stars that I hadn't quit my job. My daughter was 9½ when we split and I had full custody. My ex-husband is a lawyer, but I didn't want any money for myself, although with hindsight, I see I should have been compensated for putting him through law school and helping him advance his career. I just wanted enough to share our daughter's expenses in proportion to what we earned. My main concern was that the divorce wouldn't change her lifestyle.

In 1981, I was asked to apply for the job of director-general of the Association of Jewish Day Schools, an umbrella organization that lobbies various levels of government. The association had negotiated against me and thought I was good. I was surprised to be asked, but I decided it was a great opportunity.

Taking that job was a major turning-point. It helped me through my divorce which, no matter who you are, throws your whole being and who you are into question.

The main difficulty was being a single mother since it wasn't a 9-to-5 job. So I spent some time looking at different ways of making sure that my daughter was taken care of.

I was particularly fortunate because I have wonderful parents and an older brother who became kind of a father-figure to my daughter. My daughter would probably say I didn't spend enough time with her, and I'd acknowledge that. I may not have been there as often as she would have liked, but I believe I was always there when she needed me.

She was my priority and I put a lot of energy into making sure she was well provided for. I didn't provide myself with many frills. There were things we couldn't buy because I sacrificed to keep her in private school. For instance, we didn't have carpets and I drove an old car. At one point she suggested that she go to public school so we could buy carpets, and I said, "No way."

In 1986, I was approached by the government to take on a major responsibility on an important commission. It was tremendously exciting, but I had just started a relationship with a wonderful man which looked like it might be serious. The job involved a lot of travel, so I chose not to take it because I felt the relationship was more important.

Even so, the offer made me aware that my dollar value on the job market was much greater than my current salary, and I used it to negotiate a major increase. Because of that experience, I'd tell other women to examine their worth and fight for it; otherwise they'll be taken advantage of. I wasn't prepared to be taken advantage of any more.

In 1987, I got married. There was no question of my leaving work. My husband is older and he wasn't challenged by my career, unlike some of the younger men I had dated. I was earning as much as, or more than, some, and I could feel it threw their sense of self-worth into question. They had difficulty with a woman who asserted herself, who had made it in a career and had a good reputation. I needed to feel secure that my job wasn't a threat to my marriage and that's the kind of man I found.

In 1989 the YM-YWHA (Young Men's-Young Women's Hebrew Association) approached me about a job in human-resource development. Initially I wasn't interested, but the idea grew on me. The money was better and it would add another piece to my career. I spent three years at the Y, and I loved it. But when the recession hit, they couldn't afford the position and I found myself without a job.

That was a big blow. I had experienced difficulties in my personal life, but never in my professional life. In many ways, unemployment is like divorce. Even though you know, logically, it's not your fault, it makes you question your self-worth.

Since I'm a good negotiator, I achieved a suitable compensation package. I argued that they had come after me and had hired me away from a good job, and that during a recession it would be difficult to find a comparable position. The package gave me the freedom to breathe. So I said to myself, "You've got the money. Take some time to think about what you want to do."

Basically, I treated my unemployment as a job. I got up every morning and went to a support group for jobless executives. Then, I started to network. My goal wasn't to find myself a job immediately, but to discover what I wanted to do. Over the years I had met lots of people, so I used those contacts to gather relevant information.

Three things were important to me: to maintain my professionalism, to be challenged and to work with people. But beyond that I was ready to take on anything. And, of course, when people know you're out there and they know your skills, they have great ideas for you.

For instance, I was approached about running for political office. I weighed that, but decided against it because there's no time for family life and that's important to me. Also, the political system doesn't allow you to be your own person.

Things didn't really gel until last year when we were on vacation with some friends. One of the men suggested that I think about going into business with my husband, who's in financial planning. "You have all the attributes," this fellow said. "You're an educator. You know how to deal with people. You know how to negotiate, you have a huge network and you'd be your own boss for a change."

When I asked my husband what he thought, he said he'd love to have me join him. I learned that teachers do well in the field, so I decided to give it a try even though I had been offered another job in the meantime. I was still in my 40s and willing to take a risk, so I went back to school and took courses.

My involvement in the company is gradually changing the way my husband does business. We're doing many things he wouldn't have done on his own—such as presentations, which I'm good at because of my teaching experience.

Roslyn Kunin
Vancouver, British Columbia

"The theory is, if you do well enough on visiting appointments, they'll put you in a tenure-track position. So I absolutely killed myself."

Roslyn Kunin began teaching in the 1950s. In the 1960s she earned a doctorate in economics, but she had difficulty finding a tenured position at a university and eventually took a job with the government. After a distinguished career as a labour-market economist, she recently retired from the federal government to work as an independent economic consultant.

When I finished school in the 1950s, having a career was something to fall back on. In my family, a woman with aspirations could be a teacher, librarian, secretary or nurse, and a nurse wasn't too desirable because you had to handle bedpans.

I went into teaching because in those days you could teach with one year of college, and my family didn't have the money for an extended university programme. Academically, I led the college, but I was only 16 when they put me in a classroom with 17-year-old juvenile delinquents who were a head taller than me. I wiped out.

One day, I saw an ad in a magazine for a correspondence course that promised a good job and better pay. I taught myself bad typing and worse shorthand—in those days you could easily get a job with those skills—and became a secretary. I went back to university at night, mostly for the social life. It certainly satisfied that need. By the time I graduated in economics, at the top of my class, I had a husband, a baby and another on the way.

Then I started job hunting. It was the early '60s and I encountered things like: "We won't consider a woman for a man's job." A man's job was market research. When I applied for a position with a bank, they said, "Sorry, you don't have the right kind of shorthand." They wouldn't even consider me for an economist's position. Men who hadn't done nearly as well at university were getting into management.

I ended up working in an office again because it was the only job I could get. I think I deliberately failed to mention my degree so they'd hire me. I also failed to mention that I was pregnant with my second child. At that time my husband was a student, we had a growing family and I needed to work.

I was living near my family, and my mother and grandmother looked after the children. But when my husband enrolled in graduate school, we moved to Waterloo, Ontario, where I had no support systems. My one rule was that I wouldn't leave my kids with strangers before they could talk. After that they would be able to tell me if something was wrong. So I stayed home for a year with two little babies and went squirrely. Brilliant as my children were, I needed someone older than three to talk to.

My husband was a student and we were supporting a family of four on $2,000 a year. We lived on Catelli Dinner because it was cheaper than Kraft. There were no jobs in Waterloo that would pay more than the cost of a baby-sitter, so I decided to go back to school to get a master's degree. I got a scholarship, which I think covered my baby-sitting costs, but I had to commute 90 miles a day to McMaster University in Hamilton in a beat-up old Volkswagen.

It was hectic, but we managed. In a small town like that, there were always women who were willing to baby-sit. Our biggest problem was keeping the cars going. I finished my master's degree and got my first "visiting appointment"—euphemism for "we don't want you around too long"—at the University of Guelph. I taught there for two years, but they made it clear there were no long-term prospects without a Ph.D.

That brought us to the West Coast. At that point, UBC, which had the fifth-best economics department in the English-speaking world, offered me a better scholarship than any other university. My husband had just finished his master's degree in philosophy. Since I had followed him to Ontario, we decided it was his turn to follow me.

I got my Ph.D. and another visiting appointment at one of the universities out here. I taught graduate and undergraduate courses, did research and published during the teaching term, and sat on all their lousy committees. I even went out in snowstorms to buy beer for the seminars. At the end of two years of working from semester to semester, as they dangled a contract in front of me, the head of the department called me into his office, closed the door, sat me down and said: "Ros, you're a married woman and we're never going to waste a permanent job on you. We'll always have something for a semester or two, but there won't be a permanent position." This to a person they called two weeks before the semester began and said, "Ros, can you teach the master's course," and I said, "Of course!"

So I got another visiting appointment at another university and worked even harder because they, too, had a tenure-track appointment opening up the following year. I published a book during the teaching term, brought in far more than my salary in research grants, got scholarships for my students, got the department more publicity than it had ever received, taught graduate and undergraduate courses, and at the end of the year, they gave the position to a man with no teaching experience who hadn't finished his Ph.D.

They did take me out for a farewell dinner. My husband, who was pretty miffed, ordered far too much expensive wine, drank most of it and confronted the head of the department. "She's done more than anyone else in this department. Why didn't you give her the job?" The only reason they could come up with was that they weren't sure I'd be able to work that hard again.

It would have taken years of my life, and a fortune in legal fees, to fight. I also knew I'd get a reputation as a troublemaker. I applied to the Government of Canada and was offered an astounding amount of money compared to what I'd been making, so I left for Ottawa.

Despite the culture shock of moving from academia to bureaucracy, I enjoyed it. But my husband, who came East for the summer, hated Ottawa with a passion. We both knew when he returned to British Columbia the odds were good that he wouldn't be coming back. To make a long story short, I got lucky and the government moved me back to Vancouver and into a very nice job where I stayed for 20 years.

2

Health Care

Mary Bergland
Ignace, Ontario

"I didn't have a doctor's knowledge, though I often had to do a doctor's work, and sometimes I'd lie awake at night worrying if I'd done the right thing."

For 25 years, beginning in 1939, Mary Bergland substituted for the resident doctor in Ignace. The Mary Bergland Community Health Centre is named in her honour.

Ignace was a railroad town and we had a railroad doctor, who enlisted when the war started. Since I'd trained as a nurse in the early 1920s, I had to take over when he left.

Luckily, I had bought some instruments earlier through someone who worked in a pharmacy. The doctor was an old man when I first came up here, and since you never know what's going to happen, I had been trying to prepare for an emergency.

Acting as the doctor, I got called out for all kinds of things: delivering babies, sewing up cuts, illnesses and so on. I got summoned to quite a few accidents on the highway, and if any deaths had occurred, it was my job to notify the authorities.

My memory is not as strong as it used to be, but I can vividly recall one incident when a railroader was hurrying to get off the tracks as the train was coming. He got his foot caught, and the train cut his leg off just below the knee. If it weren't for my instruments, I don't know what I would have done. I clamped off the artery and stopped the bleeding so we could get him to the hospital in Dryden, where he eventually recovered.

Another time, a woman who was expecting twins came to my house when she was in labour. I sensed something was wrong and recommended we drive to Dryden immediately. After a few miles her pains got worse. I delivered a baby boy in the back seat of the car and wrapped him in my sweater.

The mother continued having labour pains, but the second baby wouldn't come. We were 70 miles from a doctor and it was pretty scary, but in the end we reached the hospital in time for the second baby to be born by Caesarean. I was so relieved the mother hadn't died! One of those boys is still living and working in Ignace.

When I trained as a nurse, I never thought I'd be dealing with these types of emergencies, but I never expected to live this long, either: I'm 91! I was the eldest of eight children, so that taught me a lot. Also, I'd been nursing in Fort William for a few years before I came to Ignace, so I'd seen a few things.

Some of my patients died. It was inevitable. When things were serious, I'd phone Fort William or Dryden for advice, and the doctors there were very good about helping me.

I usually charged a dollar or so, but people were hard up in those days, so often I worked for free. That happened a lot before public-health insurance. I never thought much about it because my mother was quite religious and we were brought up to help others.

It wasn't easy. My family needed to be looked after and times were tough, so in addition to being the doctor, I had to do the housework. When you're bringing up three kids and there isn't much money, you need to be pretty resourceful. I made the children's clothes to save money. Sometimes I'd rip up my husband's old pants and use the best parts to make pants for the boys. We also picked berries and made preserves. There I was, a nurse with a family who had to become a doctor.

I always worked out of my house, mostly in the kitchen, but I did some of the suturing in the bathroom. My husband's niece worked in the confectionary store attached to the house, so in an emergency she'd look after the children. Other people would help me, too. Often I was working around the house when I got called, so if I was busy with something, people would sometimes finish my work. I was fortunate because I had good friends.

Quite a few years ago—I can't remember exactly when—we got a doctor and I retired. I missed working, but it was also nice to be able to go to bed at night without worrying that I'd be woken up for an emergency.

I didn't expect to be doing many of the things I did, but if you were asked to do something unexpected and it meant quite a bit, you'd still do it, wouldn't you?

Barbara Bromley
Yellowknife, Northwest Territories

"Nursing was my chosen profession, although I suppose I could have made more money from hardware."

Barbara Bromley worked in the North as a public-health nurse on and off for more than 40 years. In 1967, she took over a family hardware business, which she ran for seven years, before returning to public health in 1975.

I arrived in Yellowknife in 1948, as a bride, having graduated the week before with my degree in public-health nursing. Basically, I went from high school to university to marriage without working except for summer jobs in the post office. In Yellowknife, the population was about 1,200 and there was a small hospital where I found my first job as a relief nurse. Then, I had four children in seven years and didn't nurse full time again until 1963, when my youngest started Grade 2.

Public health was new in the North, and I was the only nurse with a degree in the field. Once we got started, we organized well-baby clinics, handled immunization, treated patients with tuberculosis and venereal disease and did school-nursing over a huge area, travelling by dog team, snowmobile, plane or canoe. Our other big job was Medevac.

Nursing stations were scattered across the Arctic, but at that time there was only one nurse per station. If someone was very ill, the nurse would communicate with the doctor in Yellowknife, who would make the decision to bring the patient out.

I particularly remember one call from the priest on Holman Island about an Inuit man who had had a heart attack. It was about 9:00 p.m., and the only available aircraft—well, the only one that happened to be going to Holman Island in the dead of winter—was a Hercules. My husband was terrific when I got called away. He'd stay with the kids and make me a Thermos of coffee.

I had to sit on the floor in the back of this Herc along with the drums of gas it was transporting. We landed about midnight, but since it was winter, it would have been dark at any time. The patient lived in an igloo—

the only igloo I've ever been in. I had to get down on my hands and knees and crawl through the entrance. Outside it was very cold, but inside it was like a sauna. The family had a seal-oil lamp—a piece of soapstone with oil and a wick—which they also used for cooking.

The old fellow was lying on a bed of caribou hides, and his daughter was sitting beside him. I took his blood pressure and pulse and felt his skin. He was a bit clammy and his blood pressure was up, so I decided to move him to the hospital.

He started talking to his daughter in Inuktitut and became very agitated. The daughter talked to the priest in Inuktitut, with the odd English word, and the priest translated to me. As this went on, it became clear that the father didn't want to leave. If he was going to die, he wanted to die in his home.

Prior to this, there had been an epidemic of TB across the North during which numerous Inuit were brought to sanatoriums and hospitals in the South. Not only did many of them never return, their families never learned what had happened to them. The Inuit didn't have what we would call proper names, and they weren't listed anywhere, which made them difficult to trace.

Anyway, this gentleman's wife, the girl's mother, had been taken out with TB a couple years before, and they'd never heard from her again. They didn't know if she was alive or dead. So, understandably, he didn't want to leave. I don't think he even knew the priest had sent for us.

I don't remember the time—it seemed like an eternity—when, finally, I said to the priest, "I'm not going to remove this man from his igloo. I think it would be more damaging to put him on that horrible Herc and take him to Yellowknife where no one speaks Inuktitut." The priest was a little angry, because he was doing his job, too. So I said, "I take full responsibility."

All the way back in the Herc with the empty gas drums popping—they do that at high altitudes and they sound like a rifle shot—I worried about what I was going to tell the nurse in charge. How could I explain that I'd come back without the patient? Fortunately, she agreed with my decision.

We tried to keep in touch with the man, and I know he recovered from that particular episode. How long he lived, I can't remember.

In 1967, after I'd been working full time for four years, I lost my husband in a tragic canoeing accident. He was with a family friend and our 16-year-old son, and they were only 80 miles from the Arctic coast when their canoe capsized in an unmarked rapid. Our son got to shore, but the other two were lost.

Suddenly, I had to quit nursing and take over our hardware business. When somebody is lost in an accident, you have to wait seven years until they're officially declared dead. That meant everything was frozen. We could carry on with the store and put the money into a separate account from that day on, but we couldn't touch the assets. That was a problem because we were in the middle of constructing a building in the new town. When the Federal Business Development Bank, which had financed the project, was notified of my husband's death, everything ground to a halt. They decided they couldn't continue the loan because I was a woman with no business experience.

The truth is, I helped my husband run the hardware store, and I'd been involved in developing the plans for the building. But if you'd asked me, I would probably have said I knew very little about either.

So there I was, alone with four kids, the youngest of whom was 11. I didn't have time to grieve. We had an excellent manager in the store, a woman, and I don't know what I would have done without her. The RCMP (Royal Canadian Mounted Police) did a search and found no trace of the canoe or the men and, after a few weeks, my lawyer recommended we have them declared legally dead.

That was my entrance into the next phase of my working life. It was an ordeal to get the Federal Business Development Bank on side, but thanks to the help of the store manager, my lawyer and the regional manager of the bank, we got the loan continued. We never missed a payment and I went on to build another building, across the street. But now I know how hard it is for women to get into the business world, and I can sympathize with those who have similar struggles.

The manager and I didn't have any real problems running this business as two women, but as time went on, I began to feel we needed a man. We sold heavy oxygen and acetylene and wire rope, and some of our customers clearly preferred dealing with a man. "We have a manager who knows as much about this as anybody," was my response.

I don't know whether I was weak and selfish and only thinking of myself, but I decided to hire a man. I talked it over with my manager, who wasn't so sure a man was necessary, but I went ahead and hired a chap I knew. It was probably the worst mistake of my life. He was all right—he was fine— but he and the manager didn't get along, and within two years she left. I was very sad about that, although she and I have remained good friends.

I managed to keep the business going for seven years, even though my heart wasn't in it. In 1975, when my youngest son turned 18, I had a round-table conference with the kids and told them I wanted to return to nursing. The store was a very big business at this point, and I said that if any of them wanted to take it over when they finished their education, I'd keep it going. They had pulled together for all those years, but now they wanted to do other things, too.

Once the business was sold, I took a refresher course and went back to public health. When my husband was alive, I didn't mind working in the store with him and I would have been glad to continue on that basis. But while I was running it myself, I always felt I was working to keep the family together, to keep us intact, with food in our mouths. Once the kids said they weren't interested in the business, I wasn't either. I wanted to get back to nursing, a pleasure compared to hardware, which I viewed as a necessity.

Dr. F. Marguerite Hill
Toronto, Ontario

"The first time I saw the role of women threatened was when they tried to merge Women's College Hospital with the Toronto Hospital. The people who were going to take us over were men, and that wasn't right."

After earning a master's degree in psychology from the University of Toronto, Dr. F. Marguerite Hill enlisted in the Canadian Women's Army Corps (CWACs) in 1942, and served overseas. She graduated from medical school in 1952 and had an illustrious career which included many "firsts," before retiring in 1988.

I was born in Toronto in 1919 and grew up in this city. There were no boys in the family, and I never had any doubts about wanting a career, even though my mother worked at home—perhaps because my parents always expected me to pay my way.

I wanted to go into medicine, but my step-sister, who was a nurse, said medicine was no career for a woman, so my family refused to fund me through medical school. In any case, I won an arts scholarship, which covered my fees. I decided to major in psychology, because it was the nearest thing to medicine.

In 1941, after earning my master's degree, I started working as a school psychologist. The following year my old psychology professor, at that point an army colonel, recruited me for the war effort. I went through officer training, into the Canadian Women's Army Corps, and worked in personnel selection.

I ended up in Kitchener, Ontario, where the new recruits were assessed and trained. They'd be given intelligence tests, then I'd interview them and recommend placements. I quickly learned to send young and pretty women to work with the men because these women were more likely to get promoted into officer training than those who were capable but plain.

In 1944, I was sent overseas. The boat we sailed on was so small that when I first saw it, I thought it was a ferry to take us out to the ship. But it was extremely comfortable. A steward ran our baths and poured us hot whisky before we went to bed. There was a good library so I read my way through Jane Austen.

We sailed with 12 women and 88 medical doctors, all of whom were men. By the time we docked, the men had drunk all the alcohol on board, including the silver polish. D-Day occurred while we were in the mid-Atlantic.

I ended up in Leicester, placing English recruits. It was a good learning experience, but we certainly weren't in the front lines. Still, there was a great sense of camaraderie among the women, and we all felt we were part of the war effort.

When I returned to Canada, I was able to go to medical school, as the veteran's programme paid my way. I don't regret starting medicine late. In fact, I think having more life experience and a strong background in the arts, particularly psychology, made me a better doctor.

There were over 200 students in my class, 10 of whom were women. I don't recall any problems and I was lucky with my postgraduate training. I was always able to get the position I wanted. I think both my army experience and my age helped. I was probably as old as some of my teachers.

I did five years of postgraduate study in internal medicine and was a gold medalist in my year. It was quite a coup when I became the first female chief resident at Toronto General Hospital. I think I got the position because I was good. I worked hard and wasn't married so I didn't have anything to distract me from my work.

I guess I was a bit spoiled because, in 1957, when I finished, I went to the Women's College Hospital where they were looking for women. When they hired me, they promised me I'd be made physician-in-chief. Since I knew I was going to get pushed up through the hierarchy, I didn't have to worry about fighting for promotions.

Women's College has a long history of pioneering women in medicine, but the main appeal was the chance to run things. I was made physician-in-chief in 1968 and held that post until 1984, when I retired at the age of 65. In 1961, four years after I started, we took the first two men on staff. Now we joke that we're the only gender-equal institution in the country because the sex ratio is 50-50.

After I retired, I ran a private office for five years, but I pretty well stayed out of the picture until late 1989, when there was a threatened merger between Women's College and the larger, male-dominated Toronto Hospital. A group of people banded together to battle the proposal, and I became actively involved.

This was a real change for me. In 1952, just after I had graduated in medicine, I drove out West. One of my stops was Banff, where the Federation of Medical Women was having a convention, which I attended. As far as I could see, the women spent all their time arguing about petty issues such as the fees to pay for stamps, so I didn't join.

In those early years, I had felt that a woman should get wherever she was going on her merits, not on her sex, and I didn't like anything to do with women's rights. But when the battle about the merger came up, I realized my point of view had gradually shifted. As women, we may not have had as many opportunities as men, but at least we did our job and nobody stopped us. Now, someone was trying to stop us and that was unacceptable.

Women's College was the one place where we could give women real responsibility and foster their development. I also felt that the hospital provided better patient care and that we gave the students something different from the bigger teaching hospitals. Basically, Women's College was defined by a caring approach because it was run and staffed by women. Looking at my female colleagues in family practice, I see that the majority are much more concerned than their male colleagues about their patients as people and are more sensitive to their needs. They don't rustle them through the office as fast as the men, a fact that has been proved statistically. Of course, this is also a generalization. There are good male and bad female doctors.

When I was physician-in-chief, I had a cast of residents to teach, and women often created problems. On several occasions, women got pregnant and I was very cross with them, especially with one who knew she was pregnant when she first arrived and didn't tell me. The men had to cover for women who were on pregnancy leave and I didn't think that was fair.

In my day, the majority of women had children and most took two weeks off to have a baby. Now, it's four months and that makes a difference. Of course, times have changed. Recently, one of the very good male doctors took four months of paternity leave.

I've always felt torn because I recognize that women often have two jobs. But I don't hold it against the men that women have family obligations and, as a result, can't be promoted as quickly. I think that's our choice. Someone like me, who didn't have ties at home, could go farther and take on more responsibilities, but most women can't.

I had an engrossing career and I focused on it. I also broadened my base from Women's College and was active with many other things.

In 1968, for instance, I was asked to be the first woman board member of the Canadian Imperial Bank of Commerce (CIBC). The chairman and his wife were friends of mine, and I guess he knew me well enough to feel I wouldn't do anything to embarrass them. By that time, I'd been on many boards and I was used to being the only woman at meetings, so I wasn't intimidated. Even though I didn't know much about the business world, I thoroughly enjoyed it. The other board members came from across Canada and were all chairmen of this and that, and several helped me to figure out what was going on. They told me the language of the meetings improved when I arrived, although I had no idea what it had been like before.

I resigned from the CIBC in 1984. By that time the loans were so large —the board had to vote on them—that I thought it was ridiculous to have me there. I don't think a board member had ever resigned before, and they were quite surprised.

In 1988, I retired from medical practice. It was no adjustment at all. I closed my office and came home, although I still have four patients—old friends who've tried other doctors, but weren't satisfied. I thought I'd have lots of time to read, but I don't. I'm on the board of Women's College Hospital, and I have many interests, such as gardening, the theatre, ballet and travel, which I've always enjoyed. I have no regrets.

Dr. X
Hamilton, Ontario

"You wouldn't hear a man criticized because he interacted well with nurses, but this is the subtle message I've been given."

Dr. X, is a 33-year-old surgeon. After completing a residency in her surgical sub-specialty at McMaster University, she accepted a one-year contract position at a hospital she prefers not to identify.

I was born and raised in Toronto. My father wanted me to become a pharmacist because he thought it would be flexible in terms of raising a family. But my brothers felt that if I had the marks to get into pharmacy, I'd be better off going into medicine.

Initially, I wasn't keen to go to medical school, but I applied anyway. I was on the waiting list all summer and only got in when another student fainted looking at a cadaver. My ambition wasn't to be a family doctor, but to be a specialist and possibly do a bit of research.

Forty per cent of my class was female so I didn't have a sense of being different. In my fourth year I decided surgery would interest me as a speciality. I did some electives and applied to a number of centres, but wasn't accepted anywhere.

It was the first time I felt being a woman was a major disadvantage. The male candidate from my school, who was accepted at the school of my choice, was definitely inferior to me. He had done a rotating internship with only two or three months of surgery, whereas I had done a full surgical internship. He also showed a lack of responsibility and his general-knowledge base wasn't outstanding. People would stop me and say how terrible it was that he'd been accepted instead of me.

I spent the year doing a master's programme in research science and the following year was admitted to the general surgery programme at McMaster, which has more women than almost any programme in Canada. I enjoyed it. I'm a practical, pragmatic person and I like to solve problems. Surgery is also very exciting in terms of intellectual stimulation.

Surgeons have the reputation of being uncaring, but I've always been told that to be a successful surgeon you need the three A's: affability, availability and ability. Surgeons usually will make sure their patients are happy because they're relying on the referrals of family physicians. If the patient isn't happy, they won't get the referrals.

That said, I don't think you'll ever find a surgeon who looks forward to the office, myself included. One of the things that's attractive about surgery is that your patient is asleep. Still, I need a bit of human interaction, which is why I didn't do pathology, which also interested me.

I think many women are reluctant to apply for surgery because the training is very time-consuming and it doesn't lend itself to part-time work, unlike some other specialties. As you go through training, you gradually realize the implications of being a woman because the more senior you are, the more your sex becomes a issue.

When you're training in surgery, the discrimination is very subtle. For instance, it's up to the staff man to decide how much of the operation he'll let you do. I was technically very good and felt I got my share, but other women haven't had the same experience. And if you don't get the experience, your skills don't develop as quickly as they should.

During my third year of surgery I started thinking about getting into my subspecialty. I applied and wasn't accepted. I don't think being female helped. They had one female before who, the story goes, didn't have the technical skills they expected so that coloured their response to other women.

It took awhile, but I finally got a spot and spent two additional years training. When I finished I still didn't have a job. The stories circulate: how so and so had a bad experience with a woman because she took time off to have a family and he had to work more than he expected. As a result, he's wary of hiring a woman again. The problem is that you don't hear those stories until it's too late.

Even though I couldn't get a position in my subspecialty because I was qualified to do general surgery in a community setting, I looked at a position in Saskatchewan. It was excellent from a work point of view since they were very supportive of women. They already had a female general surgeon, who was a single mother with an eight-year-old and managing very well. Her success benefited other women as they identified her as a kind of role model and asked me to meet with her. I turned the position down because I grew up in eastern Canada and wanted to take a chance on staying here.

Then a hospital in Ontario started looking for both a new division head and a junior person. When they didn't find the head, they hired me on a one-year contract with the incentive that if I made a good impression, I'd have an advantage over the other candidates. Most people said, "Go for it.

You've got your foot in the door. Once you're there, they'll realize how good you are."

Although nobody disputes that I've done a very good job, when the new division head arrived, he chose someone else to take my place—a fellow with 12 years' experience—despite the fact that the chief of surgery felt they needed younger people to replace doctors who were aging. The other surgeon's 12 years notwithstanding, my piece of paper says I'm equally qualified.

Not being offered this job came as a shock, not only to me but also to my co-workers, from the nursing staff to the other physicians in the department. In fact, the nurses were so upset they sent a letter to the new division head stating, basically, that I was a vital team member and they felt strongly he had made a decision they didn't support.

Interestingly enough, the new division head wrote me a very good letter of reference. The message that I get along very well with the nurses and do an excellent job looking after patients comes through very strongly. However, it doesn't stress that I'm a good surgeon and, as a result, reading between the lines, the letter diminishes me professionally. Being known as a doctor who gets along well with nurses links me with staff who are lower down in the current hospital hierarchy. It also implies that my patients do well because the nurses take better care of them. They do well because I did a damn good operation, but that gets lost.

I was seen on the ward a lot, and the nurses didn't hesitate to call me, although it took them awhile to get used to the idea of asking me directly, since things hadn't been done like that before my arrival—often, I believe, to the detriment of patients.

I think some of my problems have had to do with style of practice. I practise medicine the way my colleagues did at McMaster, which emphasizes patient care. Here, surgeons delegate the responsibility to other people. For instance, I started writing discharge letters for all my patients, which, before I came, was done by internists. That may have been perceived as encroaching on their territory.

I also developed a standard orders sheet that made things more efficient. Patients now have their orders documented and the nurses can give them their medication right away rather than chasing after me for two hours while the patient suffers. If a man did that, he'd be described as optimizing efficiency. I, on the other hand, am described as caring for my patients, which damns with faint praise.

I think many of my problems revolve around the fact that I'm confident of my ability and have definite ideas about how things should be done. When they hired me, they knew they were getting a single female who had no commitments and could come on a couple of weeks' notice. I was able to set up practice and get going in three days. But when I arrived and started demanding my rights as a fully qualified surgeon who said, "This is how I want to do things," I was labelled as not being a team player. Basically, I don't think they expected criticism from a woman.

I think I could fight this on legal grounds, but I recognize that it would be bad for my mental health. If they don't want me, it's not a wholesome situation.

Some of the men who brought me on are sad to see me go and they've been very helpful. The woman issue may not be central, but you can't help noticing it. They don't have many women specialists here, even though quite a few are coming through the schools.

Now I'm looking for another position, which will be difficult because of my specialty. My field is overcrowded in the States. If I were a family physician,they'd welcome me with open arms. I can't sell myself as a researcher or a teacher. In addition, the medical system is in the throes of radical change and nobody knows what will happen, so people are reluctant to hire until things settle down. Still, I'm optimistic something will come up.

From a personal point of view, I'm seeing someone now, which means I think about when it would be a good time to have a family, if that's what I decide to do. For a female doctor, there's no good time. Will I be starting a new position pregnant? That won't impress people, particularly if it's not a good pregnancy. Stories about women physicians who've messed up get circulated and work to your disadvantage. For instance, the one about the surgeon who got pregnant and needed five months of bed rest: the other surgeons had to take her calls and felt betrayed.

Now, because I'm almost 34, the option of having a family is condensed into a few years. It's not like 10 years ago, when it wasn't a pressing issue. Meanwhile, to get a job, I have to jump through all kinds of hoops. Universities have unrealistic expectations now, but that's not their problem because they can find people who will meet them.

I don't regret going into medicine, but if I had it all to do over again, I'm not sure I would. In terms of choosing a specialty like surgery, I'd take a lot more time deciding whether it was worth the price. I'd think longer and harder about the alternatives, and I don't know if I'd make the same decision. On the other hand, I enjoy what I do and I know I'm good at it, so wherever I go they'll get a good deal.

Mavis Hairs
Montreal, Quebec

"I gave the hospital a lot of unpaid time. Eventually, I learned you don't do things like that."

Since 1975, Mavis Hairs has held various hospital jobs, as a dietary worker, cafeteria cashier and in the purchasing department. Due to illness, she is currently living on disability insurance, although she would love to get back into the work force.

I started working as a student nurse in Jamaica, but I got pregnant in my third year and wasn't able to graduate. I was terribly naïve. No one had told me, "If you're going to have sex, protect yourself."

So I had my baby, and in six months, I was pregnant again. It wasn't such a lovely thing. Shortly after I had my second child, my husband started to gamble. He was also a little violent. It got to the point, after our third child was born, that whatever I earned, he wanted. So one day I just walked out. Fortunately, I was able to immigrate to Canada.

In 1974, when I first arrived, I worked as a domestic. I was sponsored by a family who felt they owned me. Working as a maid really bothered me, but I told myself it was only for a year and things would get better.

If I wasn't careful, I was working 10 to 12 hours a day, and I wasn't allowed to eat anything unless it was given to me. One day, when my employer went out, I ate a tin of pickled herring for lunch and she was furious because she said it was expensive. So from then on, if she had to leave the house at lunch-time, I wouldn't eat. One day she came back and asked if I had eaten, and I said, "No, you don't want me to touch anything." She was ashamed of herself.

Her children were quite nice, though, and we became good friends. They knew I was an educated person. One of her daughters was a teacher, and she would talk her problems over with me. But the mother, excuse my language, she could be a bitch.

After that, I went to work in a hospital as a dietary worker. Everyone was surprised it was my first job in the field because I had such a good grasp of what I was supposed to do. I never experienced problems there.

The one thing that continued to bother me was that I had left my children in Jamaica. When I think about it now, I can still feel the pain. I felt so awful every Christmas that I wouldn't have Christmas dinner with my friends. Because of one thing and another, it was six years before I could bring them here.

After my spell as a dietary worker, I became a cashier in the hospital cafeteria. Then the problems started. I had enrolled in school and was working on my bachelor's degree in education. One of my supervisors didn't think this was right. I don't know why. I wasn't going to school during working hours. But this supervisor was giving me such a hard time that I reported her to the director and she had to apologize.

When I went to work in the general-stores department, I began to have even more serious difficulties. It was a big job. I picked up the mail, answered the phone and received all the food and medicine. I had to correct any mistakes the purchasing department made and worked closely with finance. It was a mess when I started. I was told that some companies hadn't been paid for years.

The problem was, my supervisor didn't like me. He tried to get me fired during my probationary period, but I went to the union and they backed me. I decided to show them that I was the most competent person for the job and I worked very hard. After six months, the manager said to me, "You know, Mavis, you're a genius."

But the supervisor still didn't want a woman in that job, and with the support of the other men, he started subjecting me to stress. Sometimes I'd arrive to find that the purchase orders I had sorted and checked the day before were all mixed up. Then someone would tell the manager that I wasn't doing my job. Although I didn't recognize it at the time, I was also being sexually harrassed. The supervisor would come and look down my dress. Another man who called me "Chocolate" or "Cocoa" would try to hold me.

I decided it was my job, and since I needed work, I wasn't going to let them drive me crazy. But that meant that I was often working 12 hours a day to keep up. When I came home in the evening, I used to jog to work off the stress.

Finally, the manager couldn't take it any more and she left to take a lesser-paying job. They gave her job to a male nurse. In the meantime, my vacation had been approved. But three days into my holiday, someone phoned and asked why I wasn't at work. I told them my vacation had been approved. Five days later I was fired because they said I was stressed out. They offered me a degrading job instead, which I refused to take. Now the case is in the courts. My experience at the hospital has made me much wiser.

Afterwards I applied for lots of jobs, many of which I was qualified for. But I never got them. Sometimes I wondered if I wasn't hired because I'm black. I received my bachelor's, then my master's degree in education. When I went to work in general stores I had more education than the manager and the supervisor. A black woman pulls together a department in ruins. You'd think I'd be able to get what I wanted. But I had to take what was given.

I've always been a fighter, but there are certain things I don't fight because you just never know. For much of the time I was working in the hospital, I had three kids and they had to go to school. I couldn't make myself vulnerable. I had to survive and, let me tell you, you have to be tough to survive, even in a mediocre position, because there's always someone else who wants your job.

I don't think it's as easy to find a job now as it was when I first came to Canada, in 1974. And I don't speak French. Nowadays, you really need it. People ask me, how can you live in Quebec and not speak French? But I was raising three children, working full time and going to school. How could I learn French at the same time?

My mother died when I was 17 years old. So I'm a woman who has been struggling all her life. But my children have grown up OK. I always say, "The good Lord knew I was going to be a single mother and He gave me good children." Some people come here and they're looking for too much in the way of material things. My priority has always been my children and their education.

Some time ago, I started a little business in catering, plant service, house cleaning etc., but then I got sarcoidosis and had to quit. I'm living on disability insurance now. The last time I saw my doctor, I told him "I want to work," but he said I wasn't well enough. I'm 52 years old and I still have quite a bit to offer. I'm anxious to get going. I try to believe things will get better.

Arlee Hoyt-McGee
Fredericton, New Brunswick

"I did a lot of invisible work, as do most nurses, and we didn't get reimbursed. Worse still, these things were never identified as nurse's skills."

Arlee Hoyt-McGee began her nursing career in 1953, following a short stint teaching in rural New Brunswick under a special licence. In recent years, her interests have moved in the direction of patients' rights, and she has researched and written two nursing histories.

Many nurses believe they only had three career choices: teacher, nurse or secretary. I wasn't particularly interested in being a nurse. I would have liked to become a journalist or a writer. But growing up in rural New Brunswick, I didn't know any women writers and I certainly didn't know about journalism courses. Nursing was a logical choice because it was an acceptable profession for a woman. Also, my parents didn't have the money to send me to university. I had a high academic standing, but at my school the scholarships went to the boys.

So I enrolled in a traditional three-year nurses' training programme. When I trained, nurses made $6 a month the first year, $8 the second and $10 the third. That covered broken thermometers and extra books, as well as personal things such as nylons and sanitary napkins. It was difficult for those of us who didn't come from affluent backgrounds.

Domestic work was a big part of first-year training—jobs like making beds and so forth, which aren't done by nurses today. Courses were even given in flower-arranging. Student nurses did more than supplement staff. The hospitals wouldn't have existed without their free labour.

After I graduated, I went to work at a small hospital with 30 beds. The matron used to attend church every Sunday morning when, it seemed, every expectant mother went into labour. Because I was on my own, I delivered the babies when I couldn't find a doctor.

In those days, the fact that hospital nurses delivered babies single-handedly wasn't recognized. The doctors would take credit and get paid for the delivery. Also, doctors were credited for things like giving anaesthetics, being first assistant in the OR and removing sutures, which were done by nurses. I call this "invisible work."

Early on, I recognized that the focus on patients' physical needs, which characterized my training, wasn't broad enough. So I applied for a government grant to study psychiatric nursing at the University of Western Ontario. When I returned to New Brunswick, I worked in a hospital with one psychiatrist and taught the student nurse how to give shock treatments, which we did on an out-patient basis. We prepared the pentothal, assisted with shock treatments and sent the patients home in a taxi. This was common procedure. In 1955, nurses didn't have liability insurance. Surprisingly, we had no problems. There were no back fractures, just short-term memory loss, which may have been a good thing.

After I married and had two children, the hours I worked became important. As a young home-owner, I needed to provide an income, so I started doing shift work as a private-duty nurse. Besides working nights and tending children by day, the dreadful part of that job was that doctors would order the nurse with no way of guaranteeing you'd be paid. In several cases I was out the money. I particularly remember one stroke patient who was very difficult to lift. I was tiny—around 5 foot 1—and caring for this patient was three weeks of gruelling work for which I never received any money.

For some time I also worked as a nurse in a doctor's office, where I interpreted the doctor's directions, relayed messages and comforted patients. I supplemented what the physician didn't have the time, or insight, to do. Again, like other nurses who work for physicians, invisibility was an issue. I performed many of the doctor's tasks—for example, the Department of Transport tests for pilots—and he signed the form and collected the fee.

Despite these problems, in the '50s, nurses probably had more credibility than they do today. I felt important in my role even if it wasn't reflected in my salary. And I was able to work autonomously. But, gradually, I realized I needed a more flexible environment to maximize my potential as a nurse.

A nurse educator, Kathleen McLaggan, encouraged me to apply for a job in public health. Since you had to be able to drive, I lied and got my husband to give me a crash course in driving. I went out on a trial visit with a supervisor who must have known I couldn't drive, but she was very kind and gave me the job anyway.

For five or six years, during the 1950s, I had my own territory in public health. It was a wonderful experience. I called the people in the district "my families." I was exposed to situations you'd expect to find in the Third

World—for instance, homes with mud floors. Once, I found a number of infants who were sick from diarrhoea and vomiting. I had the water tested and found it to be the cause. It doesn't take a genius to do these things but they make a real difference to the people affected.

I often travelled with one nurse and we broke the rules to do benevolent things. We found a little girl who wasn't attending school because she didn't have any clothes, so we bought her things to wear. I think this was the beginning of my career as a maverick and my life as a risk taker.

Once I found a total of 17 children in homes throughout my district who would be considered developmentally handicapped today. They were in wheelchairs or had some other deformity that prevented them from functioning in the school system, and they couldn't attend school because there was no busing.

I proposed the idea of a home-visiting teacher, and after much lobbying and planning, the school board bought the idea. But when a home-visiting teacher was hired, the concept was credited to education, even though it came from public health. Nurses do many innovative things, but they don't always get recognized for their contributions. Still, even though most of my services were anonymous, being an agent of change gave me a great deal of personal satisfaction.

I also worked in the province's only polio clinic. That was a unique period. Some children spent their entire adolescence in the clinic, often in an iron lung. Again, I was often asked to do non-nursing functions. The Sister Kenny hot packs (an Australian nurse's revolutionary, for the time, method of treating the symptoms of polio) were hard to apply and the building was very primitive. We suffered from heat in the summer and froze in the winter.

In 1976, when I was in my 40s, I decided to take my bachelor of nursing degree. My son was at university at the same time. We used to drive to school together, but on campus I respected his privacy and we barely spoke.

That was a difficult time for me. My young colleagues were outspoken and accustomed to doing research and giving papers. I was the product of a school system in which you raised your hand to go to the bathroom and didn't speak out. I didn't even know how to use the library.

I didn't think anyone understood my needs so I struggled along, embarrassed to ask my nursing peers for help. My biggest support came from a professor in the sociology department. He encouraged me to write, and co-authored some papers with me, one of which was published internationally. He was also recognized by other students and given an award.

After I graduated, I became the first nurse in the province to specialize in alcohol and drug abuse, a serious problem that wasn't addressed in medical training. Eventually, I was the first anglophone woman appointed to the first alcohol- and drug-dependency commission in New Brunswick. For seven years, I travelled around the province helping the commission to set up treatment centres and establish support programmes for families.

I worked hard and provided thorough documentation, unlike some members who just came to rubber-stamp policies. Often when I gave my reports, the men would ignore the issues and read newspapers or go to the bathroom. One day, I got angry and said, "I'm not giving this report. When you put your papers down and sit here and listen, then I'll tell you what I have to say." That got their attention for awhile.

I also served on a national board which travelled across the country, but I was only paid a per-diem fee. Extra jobs on committees meant hours and hours of extra work, researching papers, policies etc., for which I was never reimbursed, but, more significantly, for which nursing wasn't credited.

For most of my career, I've worked in a role that's difficult to describe: as a freelancer with an emphasis on "free." My family benefited from a second income, but if worse came to worst, we could survive on one. Having a supportive husband allowed me to be selective about my career path. But throughout my 40 years as a nurse, unlike my nursing sisters who chose a more traditional route, I received few benefits, and when I retire, I won't even receive a pension.

In the 1970s, I started documenting incidents where patients' rights were violated. I received letters from all over Canada, and my phone rang day and night. I decided to write a consumer guide that eventually became a reference book in New Brunswick schools. I received probably the largest grant a single nurse has ever received, $46,810, from Monique Bégin, then the minister of health.

My patients'-rights work led me into law. I applied for a Beaverbrook Scholarship, which is very difficult to get, to attend law school. The interview was a rare experience. You sit at a long table facing a group of prominent men, and you're queried about why you want to do this. Seven of the 41 who applied got scholarships. At the time, I was about 50 and the oldest female recipient.

Law school was not what I expected and it was probably my demise. Everything was based on grades and the stress was phenomenal. Because it was so intense, the students played hard on the weekend, doing everything to excess, whether it was relationships or substance abuse. I got into a nurturing mode and tried to help them with their problems. In the meantime, I was a wife and mother and continuing with some independent nursing practice while trying to grasp subjects like property law, in which I had little interest. I found two or three people at the law school who were understanding but, basically, it was a chauvinistic place. Women's concerns were just starting to be noticed and specialty law courses were not offered.

After successfully completing my junior year, I left. It was the first undertaking I didn't complete, to some extent because I felt I was learning things that weren't of use to me, and since I was older, I wanted to change things immediately. I only wanted to know the aspects of law that were relevant to patients' rights. Also, it was very hard on my marriage. Although we had no major difficulties, I studied from 4 a.m. until 12 midnight.

In 1980, I prepared an article, "The Fight for Patients' Rights," for *Reader's Digest* which was nominated for a National Magazine Award. I didn't win, but the piece generated great response from people across Canada who felt their rights had been violated or ignored. I was able to help many resolve their concerns, but, again, my work was invisible, confidential and free.

After that, I focused on being an independent practitioner in employee assistance. I had a good practice and I liked my work, but clients called at all hours of the day and night. Finally, I recognized that I gave as much as I could. I won't use the word burn-out—it's too nebulous to describe what happens to nurses who get exhausted.

In 1988, when I was 56, I returned to university to get my master's degree. Since there was no master's programme in nursing at the University of New Brunswick (UNB), I completed my thesis in English.

Over the years, I've recognized a pattern in nursing history: women's work and the invisible services of nurses. So, as I phased out of my client practice, at 61, my mission became clear. I researched and wrote two nursing histories: one on the Victoria Public Hospital in Fredericton, the other on the history of the Nurses' Association of New Brunswick. I voluntarily started the first nursing history research centre in Eastern Canada to preserve and promote nursing history. I'm writing a course for the nursing faculty at UNB that involves the collection of some 500 slides reflecting images of nurses. These things should help to enhance nurses' visibility. I can only hope.

Margaret Drummond Page
Thunder Bay, Ontario

❝The other day I was at the university talking to a couple of male colleagues. When I said I had to leave for a meeting at the art gallery, where I'd just been made president of the board, one of the professors looked at me with astonishment and said, 'But, Margaret, you're just a nurse!'❞

Margaret Drummond Page graduated from nursing school in 1941 and became a public-health nurse in 1945. Although she has worked in Africa and Asia, most of her work life has been spent in Northern and Northwestern Ontario.

I graduated as a nurse during World War II. My aim was to become a nurse on an ocean liner and sail around the world, but since the war was waging, there were more important things to do.

I started working in the Westminster Hospital in London, Ontario. Much of the hospital had been taken over by the military and some of our patients had been injured in the war. I particularly remember a regiment that survived Dieppe. I worked nights and the men talked about how committed they were to fighting for Canada. I learned a lot from those conversations.

I left the hospital in 1944, after hearing an inspiring speech about the importance of public health. I immediately went home and told my room-mate I was enrolling in the public-health programme at the University of Western Ontario. I wanted more interaction with the community than the closed structure of the hospital could provide, and I got a real sense of that in my first posting in Timmins, Ontario.

Then the supervisor came along and told me they needed a nurse in Cochrane. I wasn't too enthusiastic, but she said, by way of convincing me, that they had a beautiful lake in the middle of the town. Three men interviewed me and I still maintain all they were interested in was my religion and what I looked like.

I spent 2½ years in Cochrane on a one-nurse assignment and enjoyed it enormously. I made great friends, and since it was a small community, I learned the importance of confidentiality. I was privy to information about pregnancies, family difficulties and so on. Once I found a man in bed with a dozen dogs. People were poor in the rural areas. But they were nice, and they were trying to do their best for their children.

In 1948, I was recruited by the Ontario Society for Crippled Children, which is now Easter Seals. Although I liked what I was doing, their offer was very good, so I decided it was time to widen my scope. They sent me up to Kirkland Lake to open an office, and once I got that nicely settled, they transferred me to Cobourg. Working with families who had physically-handicapped children gave me a new perspective.

A big part of my job was getting money out of civil servants for services. One day, when I was particularly busy, I had to go to Peterborough to see the town clerk. In those days women wore hats, and I always wanted to look my best since getting money from these fellows wasn't easy. I was in such a rush that I put on two hats, one on top of another. Fortunately, I stopped for breakfast in a restaurant and someone politely raised the subject.

In 1951, I was transferred to Fort William where I worked until 1958, when I got married. If you were planning to get married, you had to give the society six months' notice, and once you were married, you couldn't work any more. So I left.

After that I did a number of different things in related areas, then, after my husband died suddenly in 1967, I took a position as associate director of the school of nursing at Lakehead University. At that point nursing wasn't an integral part of the university, and often the schools gave the message, "You're nice little girls; you can't go out and get into trouble." I felt we needed to broaden our scope and I took a lower salary to accomplish this objective.

In 1984, as I was approaching the end of my career in Canada, I finally indulged my taste for international travel, when I took a position as principal of the school of nursing at the University of Malawi. I had intended to go for two years, but I loved it so much I stayed for five. In 1989, I worked in Pakistan with the McMaster University School of Nursing.

Nursing isn't an easy profession, but I think I've had a rich and interesting life, both professionally and as a volunteer. Through my volunteer work I've been able to work with different groups of people, which has helped me to see more facets of the world. For instance, I've served in the naval reserve for 15 years and currently hold the rank of honorary lieutenant colonel.

Although I'm officially retired, I've actually just moved onto other things. I've always made a point of changing my goals every 10 years. I feel you have to do that to be excited about what you're doing, and I was fortunate that I could.

Anne Ross
Winnipeg, Manitoba

"I'm a bit of a rebel but never without a cause and that's what the clinic gave me."

Anne Ross ran Winnipeg's Mount Carmel Clinic for 36 years, beginning in 1948, and received the Order of Canada in 1985.

When the war broke out, I was a young bride whose husband suddenly disappeared into military service. I couldn't live on the seventy-two dollars a month I received from his pay, so until my baby was born in 1944, I did private-duty nursing to support myself. Then I quit and stayed home.

I was gung-ho to be a mother with a capital M. In those days, you didn't work outside the home when you had babies. I didn't really believe staying at home was necessary, but you know how things are. Shortly after our son was born, my husband was shipped overseas.

In 1947 my daughter was born, and I stayed out of the work force until 1948. Then, I ran into a doctor who asked me what I knew about the Mount Carmel Clinic. I said not a heck of a lot. He told me it was going under and nobody seemed to care.

Mount Carmel was started as a Jewish clinic that mostly served poor immigrants. They couldn't afford an X-ray or lab technician. They could only afford a nurse, and barely that. He suggested I could do all three.

My husband and I talked it over, and he said, "If that's what you want, go ahead." Although I loved being a mother, I realized I was bored out of my skull, so I agreed to take the job on the condition I got full-time help for my children, who were four years and 14 months, respectively. By happenstance, I found a terrific woman and went to work.

When I walked into the clinic, my heart sank. It was dark and dreary. There were no patients. I didn't know why I was there and I was only earning $70 a month. I walked the neighbourhood streets and saw poverty, neglect, abuse—the works. Meanwhile I had no doctors, no dentists, nothing. All I had were students and I was supposed to teach them to do X-rays.

I started to visit homes and practically begged people to come. I managed to get a doctor here, a doctor there. Since medicare didn't exist, they had to give their time voluntarily, so it often took a lot of persuading.

Anyway, to make a long story short, I was finally able to introduce new programmes.

One of my first projects was a day hospital for neglected children. These kids suffered from running ears, asthma, impetigo from head to toe—you name it, they had it. Many were also abused. In those days you didn't think about sexual abuse, but it existed.

I wanted to establish a day hospital because I realized we treated the children and sent them home to the same conditions that created the problems. We'd give them penicillin or whatever, and they'd return even sicker. So I started visiting homes to see what was wrong. I saw such poverty and deprivation that I felt compelled to do something. We gathered up the children, half naked in filthy diapers, and brought them to the clinic, where they were bathed, treated, fed nourishing meals and given clean clothes which we collected from the community. Then we took them home. This was the origin of a day hospital for children, which is now known far and wide.

I really believe the clinic would have died if we hadn't reached out into the community and responded to the needs that were there. I've been credited with being a pioneer in the development of community clinics, but to me it was common sense.

Birth control, which wasn't legalized until the late 1960s, was another issue. Families would arrive with eight, nine, 12 children. Often none was being well looked after, and I believed we had to help the parents with family planning. Why weren't they getting the information they needed? Because they were poor?

I called a meeting of doctors, health workers etc., and we decided to start a family-planning clinic. A couple of lawyers were on the board, and one said to me, " Anne, you'll go to jail." My airy retort was: "So, you'll bail me out."

The birth-control clinic took off like a firecracker. We even had a Catholic monseigneur who sat on our committee on the condition that we taught the rhythm method. That was OK with us. The women said their husbands wouldn't use condoms. The birth-control pill had been discovered in 1956, and I asked a doctor I knew if we could get it for the clinic. He wanted to know if we could afford to purchase it and, of course, we couldn't, but I started asking the pharmaceutical salesmen who came around how we might get the pill for free. At that point nobody wanted to touch oral contraceptives because they thought they were unsafe. However, one salesman said he could get the pill for us if we agreed to do a study. The study took up a lot of time and I hated it, but it got us the pill and also helped to build the new clinic.

Around this time I started getting invitations to speak—mostly at schools and universities. The principals didn't like me. I remember one who sat in on a lecture, then said, "You weren't bad. I thought you'd be worse."

In 1969, abortion became legal in Canada and we set up a pregnancy-counselling service, the first anywhere, as far as I knew. We'd counsel the women first and talk about the options, such as adoption.

Winnipeg General Hospital was the only hospital in town doing abortions, and it was even difficult to get one there. Suddenly the clinic became inundated with requests and I couldn't get the services our people required. We were told things like the abortion committee will be meeting in three or four weeks. No woman who wants to terminate a pregnancy could wait that long, so I said, "To heck with that nonsense." I had heard that legal abortions were being performed in New York so I flew down to investigate. I watched an abortion being performed and everything seemed to be fine, so I began referring patients there.

Then, in 1971, out of the blue, a cabinet minister in Manitoba wrote a letter to the United Way telling them to cut funds for the clinic because Anne Ross was "pimping" for abortionists in New York. He said I should be fired although he'd allow them to investigate me first. In his opinion, I was a party to murder.

He wrote to the mayor and the attorney general urging them to investigate the clinic. He called our patients immoral tramps and even suggested they be spayed like dogs. We knew we weren't doing anything illegal so we kept silent at the clinic, but when he continued to attack me personally, the patients organized and went to the cabinet. He was forced to resign. It was the first of the pro-choice protests that have become so common today.

I don't want to be considered a heroine about the abortion issue. I had no conviction. I was just answering a need that existed in the community. That's how I built the clinic. People would say, "Mrs. Ross, we need an abortion and we can't get it." I thought, they're entitled to it. They have a right, and who is he to tell them what to do?

But behind that I had a profound belief that children should not be brought into the world unless they were going to be looked after. I saw too many who were rejected and abused. In those days we kept quiet and shame on us. But, in fact, there was nothing we could do. Since parents had a right to do anything they wanted to their children, nobody thought of raising these issues with police.

In the process of answering the needs of the people in the community, we developed the concept of treating a person as a total entity—physically, emotionally and socially. We felt that poverty was often the main culprit underlying health problems, so in addition to treating ailments, we became advocates for better living conditions. We organized tenants' associations, gave free milk to pregnant mothers and worked as a team—nurses, doctors, counsellors—to affect change in people's lives who, by and large, had a multiplicity of often immobilizing problems. We believed in early intervention, prevention and maintenance of health. Now it's a stylish concept, but it wasn't then.

I'm an idea person, but ideas are difficult to sell. They might cost money or offend someone. Basically, people are afraid of new things. So I've been attacked and maligned by some, helped and cheered on by others.

I retired in 1985, after 36 years at the clinic. During that time, I'd say that medicare was the single greatest change in health care. Before that it was horrendous. Although I've written two books on teenage pregnancies and had a career as an open-line talk-show host, the Mount Carmel Clinic has been the focus of my professional life.

Nita Chaudhuri
Toronto, Ontario

"I'm interested in the multidisciplinary aspects of health—that is, not looking at health as just a medical model, but in its entirety, which includes social and economic relations."

At the time of this interview, Nita Chaudhuri was 30 years old. She has worked for the World Health Organization in Switzerland, at UNICEF in New York and at a health clinic in Spanish Harlem.

When I was working on my master's degree in international planning and nutrition, I went to Bangladesh to do fieldwork. I was hoping to improve my language as well, since my family speaks Bengali. I had no family there —my parents came to Canada from India in 1959—and was completely alone in the village, although my appearance gave me a lot of social access. I was born and raised in Ottawa, so it was interesting to see how blatantly the women in Bangladesh were treated as second class.

While I was working in Bangladesh, I had a long-distance relationship with the man I eventually married, who lived in Switzerland. For five years, I travelled between Switzerland, Canada and Bangladesh keeping that relationship alive. I think I experienced greater culture shock in Switzerland than in Bangladesh because I didn't expect such backwardness. Women didn't get the vote until 1973, and it still isn't acceptable to work outside the home after marriage. After my husband and I married, we moved to Toronto because, as a female and a member of a visible minority, I didn't want to live in Switzerland.

Our first year in Canada, I worked 150 per cent. I taught a course in public health, wrote policy and worked in community outreach. Then I decided I wanted to work in the community full time, so I took a job as an environmental health promoter in a health centre. Since this position doesn't exist anywhere in Ontario other than Toronto, to some extent I'm setting a precedent for what a job like this might involve.

I look at environmental health in the context of the south Riverdale area of Toronto. The neighbourhood is heavily industrial so there are many problems. During the 1970s, many kids became very ill, which they traced back to lead poisoning emanating from a smelter. This awareness sparked extensive community action. The first battle won a pollution-control system on the smelter. Then, when it was discovered that the children were exposed to the lead through the soil, that was replaced at a cost of $11-million.

Volunteers raised most awareness around the lead. My job is to continue that work in a professional capacity, to build community action around environmental issues and to advocate around them.

As environmental issues have become popular, it's been interesting to see how competitive the field has become. In many ways, environmentalism is now dominated by white middle-class males. This plays itself out in Toronto in terms of who shares the power and who has the contacts. Although more women are moving into the field, I've been at many meetings where I'm the only person with tinted skin and also the only female.

The interesting thing is that most of the grass-roots activists in the environmental movement have been women. The bureaucrats view them as screaming housewives, but they're the ones who have pushed the issues. The other type of environmentalist, let's say male, has been somewhat co-opted and now does a lot of consulting. There's nothing wrong with that, but they're not activists who are centred on protecting the next generation.

My focus is environmental health, which means a myriad of things, but basically how physical environment is a determinant of health. I'm currently working on several issues, including a sewage plant which is slated for expansion. The women in the community have collected a great deal of information about alternative approaches to sewage treatment. They've been very active in the public-consultation process because they're concerned about the impact on their children's health and they're not stoic.

I don't believe I got this job because I'm a woman from a visible minority. First of all, I'm very well qualified. Also, I don't have an accent, which makes a big difference. When you look at me, you see a minority, but when I start to talk, you hear an English Canadian. Because I was born and raised here, I know how to move through the system.

I think tokenism is more likely to show up with regard to, for example, sitting on committees. Yesterday, I was called and asked to suggest someone to sit on a committee on palliative care. I mentioned one of my co-workers and the woman on the other end of the line asked if she was white. When I said yes, she hesitated and said, "I'm looking for somebody to represent...."

There may be some discrimination in the workplace at the social level —I haven't worked long enough to know. It's hard to tell what's race and what's personality.

I guess when I want to do something I go for it. I'm not 100 per cent confident all the time—nobody is—but I usually won't let things stop me. It's very helpful when your family is proud of its origins and has no inferiority about its culture. I come from a culture that's 5,000 years old. My parents are both physicians and our family is very academic. Those class values are instilled in you. My family is also very socialist—the élite sort of socialism you see in Toronto. When you come from an élite but you have a socialist view it can be very confusing.

The first time I admitted to gender difference was when I took a Women in Development course for my master's degree. I think you define yourself by the issue that most oppresses you, and I defined myself by race, not by gender. At first, the emphasis on gender seemed odd, and then I realized it was right on and very relevant, personally.

I used to have an ideal notion of women, but I've certainly lost that. I don't know if men do it, but women's gossiping and back-stabbing can be very destructive. Maybe things will change, but as far as I can see, women are as competitive, power-hungry and manipulative as men. After recognizing the validity of gender inequality, it was quite depressing to accept this, although I will say that both women and men have helped me equally in my career.

My work is very important to me and that creates a constant struggle with my husband. Although we don't have children, he's afraid that the family isn't enough of a priority for me. I think that's what women struggle with today: do they sacrifice the quality of life at home to have a fulfilling career? My husband says he believes I should work, but he often prevents me from doing things I need to do for my career.

I gave up a lot of career opportunities to be married. My husband works in banking so he wanted to stay in the West, whereas I wanted to work in the developing world. I was moving in that direction, but when I got married, I cut off my contacts in the United Nations' system. I'm not sure my husband will ever really understand the sacrifices I've made. He made sacrifices, too, leaving his country to come here, but he's only here for a short time. Then, he says, we're going back to Switzerland.

Another aspect of women's work is the nurturing and emotional support we give men. I don't think men recognize how much of that they get in a relationship. My husband often tells me I'm not domestic enough. He's happiest when I'm cooking—I suppose because my career is very important and I'm not the kind of woman who's constantly baking. But it's interesting to see how my invisible emotional support isn't recognized. It's the physical things, like baking, that are acknowledged.

3

Clerical
and
Secretarial

Claire Culhane
Vancouver, British Columbia

"I'm seventy-five years old and I suppose you could say I've had a colourful life, even though most of my jobs have been in offices, which are usually considered quite tame."

Claire Culhane was born in Montreal on Labour Day, 1918. A political activist for most of her life, she supported herself and her family by doing office work.

One of the reasons I've had such a keen interest in social justice is that I've experienced discrimination myself. I wanted to be a doctor, but my brother was studying dentistry and my parents couldn't afford to send both of us to university. As a boy, his education had priority.

So, in 1935, when I was 17, I applied to the school of nursing at the Montreal General Hospital. The head nurse told me I'd be admitted even though, in her opinion, "Jewish girls didn't make good nurses." I interpreted that to mean I'd never last beyond the probation period so I enrolled at the Ottawa Civic Hospital instead. Although I did well academically, I was suspended for not being respectful enough of authority. At that point, I realized I wasn't cut out to be a nurse in that kind of environment.

I returned to Montreal, took a business course and got an office job in my uncle's dress factory on St. Catherine Street. Most of the office workers were women and we worked long hours—from nine to six, six days a week. I earned six dollars a week, which was good money in those days. The head bookkeeper probably made 15, but the women working on the machines were making 10 cents an hour, which didn't seem right to me so I joined the Office Workers' Union.

The union shared space with the Retail Clerks' Union, whose president was a young Irishman named Garry Culhane. He was separated from his wife and children, but there were no divorce laws in Quebec at that time. When we started to live together, my parents sat shiva for me, a Jewish tradition which meant that in their eyes I was dead.

I joined the Communist party in 1937, and when Mackenize King declared it illegal in 1940, Garry and I became criminals in the eyes of the law. I didn't dare go to work and we were forced underground. Avoiding the police meant living in rented rooms that cost $2 a week, and moving from boarding-house to boarding-house. A couple of times we ended up in a rooming-house, not realizing it was a brothel.

When war broke out, Garry and I were living in a tent near Lachine (Quebec). Soon after, we decided to try our luck at getting employment in British Columbia. It was a good decision because, as the war geared up, there was a boom in shipbuilding. Garry soon found work in the shipyards, and I was hired as a secretary at a lumber company.

A few months after we arrived, Garry was offered a better job in Victoria and we moved. He had always dreamed of owning a fishing boat, so we used the $300 I'd received from an insurance policy my parents had taken out for me to buy a dirty, stinking, 32-foot gill-netter. We moored it at the public docks, which were free, but we only fished for a few months. Experienced fishermen can spot greenhorns and soon edge them up on the reefs to cut their lines. We didn't have money for more lines, but we did have a boat to live on, rent free, as it were.

There was nothing romantic about living on a boat. We had a bucket for a toilet and when it rained, the water leaked on our bunk. I found work as a secretary in the navy dockyard, which meant I had to look respectable. That was no easy task since my clothes reeked of diesel oil and my hands were covered with tar from catching driftwood to keep the fire going. Clean water was a problem as we tried to pump a sufficient supply to avoid making extra trips. We'd fill up one basin, which we used first for cooking, then for washing ourselves, then for washing dishes, then for the laundry and, finally, for washing the floor.

We had friends who offered a standing invitation for dinner every Saturday night. I was feeling the need to be much cleaner than our living conditions permitted so, after dinner, while everyone else was sitting around talking, I'd excuse myself and go to the washroom. It took me about eight minutes to fill the tub, have a bath and be back downstairs. That meant that at least I'd have a weekly bath.

Garry and I lived on my wages so he could send his earnings to his wife and kids. It wasn't an easy life. Things improved in 1944 when he found a job with the Boilermakers' Union in Vancouver, and I was hired as the union secretary.

In 1945, when I was 26, I had my first child. I loved her dearly, but caring for a husband and a child and holding down a full-time job was difficult. I'd take my daughter to nursery school before I went to work. In the evening, I'd pick her up, buy groceries, cook dinner and do the chores. But, like most women I still thought it was my husband who was struggling to keep the home fires burning.

In 1950, I had my second daughter, and around that time I began to wonder if my marriage was a mistake. Garry and I disagreed constantly and I could see that our fighting was affecting the children so, in 1954, I left him and returned to Montreal. At that point I realized I'd have to forego political activity to concentrate on caring for my family.

In the 1950s, I was a single mother trying to raise two young children on my own and to advance in my profession. I soon found work as a medical-records librarian at a hospital in east-end Montreal. I was excited about the opportunity, despite the long bus trip, which took 1½ hours each way, and the problems created by full-time employment. Since there was no day care, I lied about my younger daughter's age to enrol her in school a year earlier than the legal age. My older daughter, who was only 10 at the time, was responsible for her after school and she resented it. Even so, there was nothing else we could do.

While I was working at the hospital, I learned about bursaries for professional upgrading and enrolled in a two-year correspondence course to become certified as a medical-records librarian. One requirement was first-year university. I managed to get a scholarship from a Jewish women's organization to pay my tuition at Sir George Williams University, but that made my work schedule horrendous, even for me. In addition to my full-time job, the correspondence courses and evening courses two nights a week at Sir George, I was also bringing typing home to earn extra money, since Garry never sent financial support for the children.

Just before I finished my first year of the course, Garry showed up in Montreal, asking for a reconciliation. Although I had reservations, my daughters liked the idea and I caved into their desire for a "normal" family life.

In 1957, we moved to Ireland so Garry could set up a boat-rental business. It was like going back to the Middle Ages. I looked for work, but there was no employment for married women and no one had ever heard of a medical-records librarian. Finally, I found a five-week clerical job at a Dublin hospital. I remember there was a staff party at Christmas that I wasn't invited to because I was a foreigner: Canadian and Jewish!

Garry's business wasn't going well, and after much discussion, we decided the only alternative was for me to return to Montreal to work at two jobs—the usual typing in the evenings in addition to my work as a medical-records librarian—so I could send him money for the business. Since the children were settled in school, we decided they should remain in Ireland. My most vivid memory of that period is people blaming me for walking out on my family. That was the assumption. Nobody bothered to dig deeper to discover that I had left to continue as the principal breadwinner, which was the only way the family could survive economically.

Within six months, I returned to Ireland, but it soon became clear that the marriage was over. In 1960, I returned to Montreal with the children to work as a medical-records librarian. I continued to avoid political involvement until 1967, when I read about a Canadian medical-aid project in Vietnam. I realized I wanted to do something more meaningful with the rest of my life, and since my daughters were grown by then, I went to Vietnam as administrator of a Canadian civilian TB hospital. But that's another chapter in my life.

Grace Hartman
Toronto, Ontario

"**W**orking and seeing discrimination turned me in the direction of feminism, not the other way around."

Grace Hartman was active in public-service unions since joining the municipality of North York as a clerk-typist in 1954. In 1959, she was elected president of her local and, in 1965, was elected one of the five general vice-presidents of the Canadian Union of Public Employees (CUPE). In 1975, she was the first woman to be elected president of CUPE, a position she held until she retired in 1983. She received a number of awards and honorary degrees, including an honorary doctor of laws from York University. She died in 1993, not long after this interview was conducted.

I started working in 1954 for the municipality of North York, as a clerk-typist, to help supplement our family income. I worked in the planning department, and because I had some shorthand skills, was gradually promoted to stenographer. At that time, work was clearly designated by sex and jobs were posted as male or female.

Around 1960, a new job was posted. By then I was doing parts of the planners' jobs and had a good knowledge of the department, so I applied, as did a man. He was capable, but he was a Monday and Friday absentee, and I had more seniority, which was a significant point since we had a collective agreement.

They mulled over the applications and, finally, decided not to fill the position. Of course, I knew why. Although I had the qualifications, in their eyes it was a man's job. I would have grieved if they had given it to him, so they didn't give it to either one of us.

Months later, the job was posted again. This time, it required a university education and work experience couldn't be substituted. That was a common strategy.

I had been elected president of my local in 1959, and in the 1960s, I remember negotiating and being asked by the mayor why women wanted equal pay since men were the heads of the family.

"Do you have any idea how many women are heads of families?" I asked. When he said no, I gave him a figure, which I knew because so many women shared their financial problems with me. Still, women were often treated as temporary employees. When Metropolitan Toronto was formed in the late '50s, for instance, women weren't admitted into the pension plan nor did they have equal benefits.

Like many of the women I worked with, I had young children. So I knew about the work women had to do at home, in addition to their 9-to-5 jobs. I got a lot of help from my husband with things like cooking and cleaning, but it was still tough to hold down a job and raise young children. Sometimes I had to iron when I got home so that my kids would look good for school, because in those days they didn't wear T-shirts. Our local tried to set meetings to accommodate working mothers. At first we scheduled them for 5:30, but when the husbands complained that they had no dinner, we ended up having them at 7:00.

The job came first as far as the employer was concerned, and you could never use children as an excuse. There was no day care so people relied on neighbours—a woman across the street looked after my boys. Despite what people said about kids whose mothers went out to work, mine were pretty normal.

I recognized that women didn't have much chance to advance into management, no matter how capable and dedicated they were. And I saw the union as the only practical instrument for helping women to overcome these barriers—in pay, as well as status. I didn't set out to take up women's causes. My husband made me aware of discrimination by drawing my attention to things he thought were wrong—such as, men earning more than women. He was a unionist, too, although not an active one, so I was the one who did battle.

Although the unions provided a vehicle to make changes, often the male unionists didn't want to hear our proposals. They weren't interested in women's issues and often saw us as obstacles to customs like having their meetings in a pub.

Even so, I was elected to my union positions by men, as well as by women. In those early days, women didn't go to conventions, and if they did, they were targets because men thought they were there for one reason. Those of us who were prepared to struggle against this bias, to swim against the current, began to encourage the wives of union members, as well as women unionists, to come to conventions in order to improve the environment.

In 1967, I temporarily became secretary-treasurer of CUPE. At that point, I talked to my sons about the implications of taking on these added responsibilities. They both said, "Go for it. We're not babies, we can look after ourselves."

Although I was acclaimed, it was a very political convention. I had a particularly bad week because of interference, and it was clear the president wasn't prepared to work on equal terms with a woman. I came home and announced I wanted to quit. One of my sons said, "Is that so? It was a family decision that you go, and it will be a family decision that you quit." I felt so ashamed that I stayed.

In 1975, I was elected president of CUPE. There were no other female presidents of a Canadian union—likely of any union in the world—although the year before Shirley Carr had been elected executive vice-president of the Canadian Labour Congress. That put two vocal women from the same union on the executive committee of the labour congress where women, or public-sector unionists, had never been before.

I don't think they liked having women at the top, but the public-sector unions were growing rapidly, which meant taking a significant number of women into membership. By the time I retired in 1983, the membership of the national executive board was in proportion to the membership of the union. Now the two top officers are women.

It's much easier for women union leaders today, I'm sure. Shirley and I didn't have other women to support us. It was just the two of us, and we were both so busy we didn't have time to spend with each other.

The loneliness made it difficult. When I travelled to meetings, the participants were predominantly male. They'd invite me to join them, but I knew they hoped I'd refuse. Anyway, sitting in a bar wasn't my idea of how to spend an evening, so I'd go back to my room and read, knit or do needlepoint to keep my sanity. It was lonely in another way, too. Because I was so busy, I often missed family events such as weddings, birthdays and funerals.

Still, we were able to make changes over the years, at first on a small scale and then on a much broader basis. That, I think, made it all worthwhile.

Joan Jones
Halifax, Nova Scotia

"My impression is that white women have made progress in leaps and bounds by using the strategies and methods of the civil rights movement. But black people and people of colour are fighting the same issues we were fighting 30 years ago."

Joan Jones entered the work force in the early 1960s as a secretary. She became a high profile political activist in the late 1960s and since that time has been an entrepreneur, a temporary clerical worker and a wharf inspector. At the time of this interview, she was a support-service worker for legal-aid recipients.

I started work straight out of high school for the Singer Sewing Machine Company as secretary to the assistant manager. It was around 1960, and this was probably one of the most horrendous work situations I've experienced, although nobody thought it was peculiar at the time. They made the rules and you followed them.

For instance, women were not allowed to smoke at their desks, but the men were. We used to go to the bathroom and smoke—that was allowed —which meant there were times when virtually all our desks were empty. The man I worked for would knock on the bathroom door and ask whoever answered to send some girls back to their desks.

We also had this crotchety boss who would get into fits and scream at people. There was one male secretary. He was an older man and obviously the last of a dying breed—remember, the first secretaries were male. He managed the secretaries, but I don't think he had it any easier than we did, except that he could smoke at his desk.

I stayed at Singer for three or four years until my daughter, Tracey, was born. There was no maternity leave in those days so I worked until about two weeks before I gave birth. Nobody seemed to care that I was pregnant. They were more interested in my productivity.

I don't think there was any racial discrimination at Singer. I was the only black, and often if you're the only one, you're not perceived as a threat. But I've had jobs where racism existed. In one job interview with someone I knew fairly well, I was asked how I'd get along with white people. I got very angry. I said, "I've survived. Doesn't that answer enough?" I don't know if the interviewer realized what he was asking. He's a judge now.

During the late '60s, when we were still living in Toronto, my husband and I became politically active. When we moved to Halifax our reputation preceded us. We were instrumental in bringing people like Stokely Carmichael and some of the Black Panthers to Halifax, and became very well-known as political activists. We also became very much avoided in terms of employment.

It got to the point where neither one of us could find work. Since I could sew, I made my husband a leather jacket which he liked. He suggested I do some sewing for a living. To make a long story short, my husband learned to make sandals and I started making leather clothes. Eventually that developed into a store called the Nile and a second store called the Blue Nile. It was hard work, but it kept us alive for awhile.

Somebody recently suggested that if I became unemployed, I should start another business. But being in business taught me that having your mom-and-pop shop isn't all it's cracked up to be. You make a subsistence living working 12 to 15 hours a day. I remember days when I made 25 dashikis. I could probably still do it, but I don't want to.

The one great thing about having a business is that you can control your own destiny as long as you're selling your product. By the time we opened the store, we had three children and we couldn't afford a baby-sitter. I used to take the kids to work with me and they'd nap on mats.

After we closed the business, I started getting temporary government work. We were still high-profile activists and almost untouchable in terms of employment, so I never told people who my husband was. I also made sure I didn't get identified that much in the media. He was the known commodity, but they weren't quite sure about me.

I was happy to be working, although not necessarily happy in temporary work. My longest stint was 3½ years, which I question because it means they like your work but they have the option of letting you go. It used to bother me. If I'm that good, why can't the job be permanent?

One racist incident I vividly remember occurred when I was working as a wharf inspector. The first time I went out to a wharf with an engineer was in February, and we were inspecting a log skidway, which was iced up and ran into the water on a steep angle. The engineer went down and looked under the wharf, then he came back and said, "You do it."

I said, " I don't think so."

He repeated the command and, again, I refused. At that point, he started getting angry.

The second wharf we visited was extremely high. He went over the side and down the ladder and swung under the wharf. Then he said, "You do it."

"I don't think so," I repeated. I'd never been told what I was supposed to be looking for, nor had I been given any training in how to do this safely. When he asked me again, I said, "No fuckin' way." I was very upset, but I was determined not to do anything that wasn't safe.

Six months later, when I got my evaluation, it said, "Unco-operative going under wharfs." By then I could go under any wharf and climb any ladder, so I told them I wouldn't sign it. When they asked me why, I said, "Because the information isn't correct. It's based on the first time I went out." When I explained the situation, my supervisor said I hadn't been expected to go under the wharf at that point, so they deleted it.

I think the engineer behaved like that partly because I was a woman and partly because I was a black woman. Sometimes there's nothing you can put your finger on. You just have a sense of it.

I became a wharf inspector because someone approached me and asked if I'd like the job. To be perfectly honest, I wasn't inspired, but I said yes because I needed work. I had to wear a white construction hat which gives you a lot of power, but it embarrassed me because it sent the message that as a representative of Public Works I could stop the job. I found that intimidating. I knew the guys working on the wharf knew far more about construction than I did.

They were pretty rough-edged guys—most feminists would call them male chauvinist pigs—and they liked to whistle at nice-looking women, but when it came to getting down to the gist of things they were absolutely wonderful. They were more than willing to show you what they were doing and answer all your questions. I had no problems with them.

Seven years ago I got this job which involves helping legal-aid clients with all their non-legal problems. I like it, but if there are budget cuts, there's a possibility it will end. I'll be the first to go because I'm not involved with the legal end of things.

I feel frustrated because I'm still working on issues I've been struggling with for almost 30 years. When you struggle, as we all do, to make life better for your children and realize that your grandchildren are experiencing the same things you did, it makes you feel terrible. Even when I'm employed, it's been proven that as a black woman, I'll be paid less. I'm an example of that and, right now, I feel tired and depressed.

Shirley Brodt
Montreal, Quebec

" **B** eing a single parent and holding down a full-time job hasn't been easy, but leaving my marriage was the first thing I did that made me realize I had strength."

Shirley Brodt entered the work force 12 years ago as a secretary. Now she co-ordinates word-processing services for a large community agency in Montreal.

I'm 42 and have four children. I've been divorced for 14 years. When I got married, 23 years ago, women didn't have careers. I was young and dumb. I loved school. I loved writing exams and essays, but I never thought ahead. My motivation was to escape home and have a baby. When my marriage ended, I had four kids, seven and under, and no job skills.

I had done my BA while I was married, so when I left, I decided to go back to school and got my master's in library science. Then I discovered there were no jobs unless I moved out West, which I wasn't prepared to do. I was pretty desperate so I decided to work in reverse. I opened up the newspaper, saw that secretaries were in demand, went to secretarial school and landed the job I have now.

I would have taken any job as long as it allowed me to be there for my kids when they came home from school. My mother was still alive when my marriage broke up so she helped out with child care, but it was still quite stressful. Even so, when people tell me how difficult it must have been, it wasn't, really. My point of comparison is that staying married would have been more difficult.

My husband pays support—the same amount since we separated—so I'd be destitute without a job. I think a lot about what I'd do if he stopped paying. I've got one kid in university and three kids to go. I'd have to move into a much smaller apartment. There's not much I can cut back on other than cigarettes. I don't have a car. I don't have cash hidden away. I guess I'd have to get a second job, although I haven't the foggiest notion what that would be.

I've been lucky because I found the right strategy for dealing with my work environment. I come and go early and work through my lunch hour to be home for my kids. I'm overcompensating, but I'm doing it because if my kids get sick or there's some other emergency, I don't want anyone saying, "Look at her and her four kids. She's causing problems." I want people to say she works above and beyond.

That was the only way I could see of juggling things so both my company and my children would be satisfied. I'm able to be home relatively early to make supper and help my children with their homework. Now that they're older and the need is no longer there, I'm still doing it.

I've managed to set it up so my kids are alright and my workplace is happy, but I'm a complete wreck! I get up at 6:00, am usually at work by 8:00, and leave at 4:30, so I can do the shopping on the way home. I make supper, wash the dishes, wash clothes, maybe iron if I'm in the mood. I try to squeeze in some reading here and there and go to bed around 10:00 or 10:30.

It's straight work from the time I get up. After supper I sit with my legs up on a chair, and I can't move for about 10 minutes. But then I get my second wind and do whatever needs doing. My ex-husband has the kids on alternate weekends, when he doesn't have anything else planned. On the weekends they're not with me, I stay home and read. Reading is my emotional recuperation.

When the kids are with me, we hang around and play games if they want, or we read together. We might go for a walk. Sunday is usually a cleaning-up or shopping day. Sounds exciting, doesn't it? Sounds like a single mother.

I don't know at what point one can say that raising four kids as a single parent is an accomplishment. I think 20 years from now, if I'm still alive, if anyone says that to me—and my kids are emotionally healthy— I'll accept it.

My kids are good people. I've often thought I was lucky because they're very gentle. If they weren't my children, I'd choose them as friends. That, I think, has helped me a lot over the years. Many parents have horrid problems with their children. I was very fortunate.

Now that the kids are getting older, I sometimes think about what I'll do when they're gone. I'll keep working and maybe I'll go back to school. I may be reaching a turning-point in my own life. It's harder now, not easier. I'm emotionally exhausted. I'm finding the isolation difficult, and that never bothered me before.

Jessie McCartney-Filgate
Toronto, Ontario

"I got all my jobs through friends. In those days, women grouped together to help each other."

Jessie McCartney-Filgate started working as a doctor's receptionist in the mid-1950s, and recently retired.

I was living in Ottawa in the mid-1950s when I applied for a position as a doctor's receptionist. The equivalent of Canada Employment sent me, although they said they didn't expect me to get the job because I stuttered so badly.

The first thing the doctor asked was if I knew how to make a cup of tea. I stammered through the explanation. Then he asked me to walk across the room because, he said, he wanted to look at my legs. Then he announced I had the job.

"I need someone of medium intelligence, who has good legs and knows how to make a decent cup of tea," he declared. "I can tell from your résumé that you know how to type."

I said I couldn't possibly take the job because I couldn't talk on the phone and I'd embarrass him. He said, "If people are embarrassed by your stammer, there's something wrong with them. "

Such a thought had never occurred to me and I felt like a great stone had been lifted off my back. I had never had a job where I was required to speak before and I began to talk. I haven't stopped since.

I still had a hard time getting work, though. When I went for interviews, people would look over my shoulder, up at the ceiling, anywhere but at me.

About 10 years after I stopped working for the doctor, an old friend hired me to work at an educational film company. One Saturday morning, she asked me to go in to look at some films. The man who owned the company came in, too. He ordered me to go into his office and to have sex with him, then and there. When I said I couldn't, he said, "We're talking about your job. You do it with the man you're living with; why not me?"

In those days, the mid 1960s, there was no recourse for this sort of thing. I knew he'd fire me and I really needed the job because I was supporting two kids, basically by myself. But I still couldn't, so I said no.

On Monday morning, he ordered my friend to fire me. When she refused, he ordered the office manager to do it. He said he would fire her, too, if she didn't. The three of us talked about the problem, but none of us knew exactly what to do. Then one of the other women said, "A good friend of mine is the personnel manager at a big company. I'll see if she'll help us out."

She made a call and sent me over to meet this woman, who gave me a typing test. I was so upset I was shaking and I know I did badly. But she knew exactly what was going on and she took my hand. "Your hands are really cold," she said. "When can you start?"

It was just before Christmas. I said I could stay where I was until the New Year. "Don't be silly," she said. "Why don't you start tomorrow? That way you'll get paid for the holidays."

In those days, there were lots of women like that and I don't know what we would have done without each other.

Wilma Sharp
Vancouver, British Columbia

"You weren't let go when you got married, but you certainly didn't advance. And women were aware of this."

Wilma Sharp worked for a large life-insurance company, as a stenographer and correspondent, between 1954 and 1964. She stayed out of the work force for 20 years while raising her four children. She is currently upgrading her skills while working as a clerk at a university.

I started working for a large life-insurance company, based in Ontario, at the age of 17. I had completed the equivalent of Grade 12, plus a year of business college.

I was one of "the girls," which meant you were expected to work for a few years, get married and leave. I was unmarried for seven of the 10 years I was there; and as long as you were unmarried—and young—you had a bit of opportunity. I became a correspondent which meant I had my own dictaphone and a girl who did my typing. But once I got engaged, the promotions stopped.

At one point, I started taking the management association exams. By the time I'd passed three, I realized I wasn't going anywhere. In contrast, even the guys who failed were getting promoted. I gave up on the exams and took night courses in tailoring. My tailoring certificate came in much handier than the exams because it meant I could make clothes for myself and my kids.

My most vivid memory of the insurance company is its paternalism. For instance, they provided a rest room where women could go for naps, and if you were suffering from menstrual cramps, the nurse would give you a little white pill. It turned out the pill was phenobarbital. I didn't know what I was taking, but it made me fly. It also made me aggressive and I'd do things that were out of character.

Once I wrote a very sharp letter to another office and offended their manager. A letter came back demanding an explanation. Nobody could understand how quiet-and-submissive Wilma could do such a thing. It certainly wasn't in her nature. I knew why, but I couldn't tell my boss I was flying on their medication for menstrual cramps.

Another of their "perks" was a full-course meal in the staff cafeteria that cost 25 cents. I was told they brought this in because the girls earned so little money that many weren't eating properly and were becoming sick. When I started, I earned about $18 a week, which had to cover my shelter and food. This worked out to less than I grossed at my high-school summer job at a resort, which included lodging and board.

Every year you marched down on your anniversary and got a small, set raise. After I'd been there about four years, I realized the company would never pay me what I was worth so I decided to look around. When someone who'd interviewed me called for a reference, I was immediately summoned into my boss's office and given a raise. They knew it would take two people to replace me.

I'd also say they never bothered to get to know me as a person. Eventually, I left because my husband finished his MBA and got a job in Vancouver. At that point, I applied for a $5000 insurance policy costing $70 a year. Although I'd been in and out of this man's office for years, he advised me that I might be making a mistake because I couldn't afford it. He knew I was married but he probably thought I'd married a farmer, not an MBA. They didn't treat you like a responsible adult.

In 1964, the dean's graduating address to the wives of the MBA class, which, of course, was all male, emphasized our duty to follow our husbands to wherever they were offered jobs. Many of these women, like me, had supported their husbands through school.

After we arrived in Vancouver, I stayed out of the workplace for almost 20 years, raising kids and doing volunteer work. I went back in 1982, partly to help my husband because his company was having difficulty during the recession. At that point I felt lucky to get four hours of work a day, five days a week, which I did for over five years. Now, I feel that like many things, that job was sort of forced on me.

I've always felt cheated because I didn't have the opportunity to go to university, even though I was at the top of my class in elementary and high school. In the mid-1980s, I started taking business courses at the British Columbia Institute of Technology, but I found the classes too big. So, at age 53, I took re-entry training with a view towards getting into personnel. Going out on placements was my introduction to ageism. The firms didn't know what to do with me. They were excessively polite and treated me like somebody's aunt. It made me realize I'd never get hired because they were looking for younger, more glamorous people.

I'm taking courses part time, although sometimes I wonder why. By the time I'm finished, nobody will hire me as a manager. I'm also working at the University of British Columbia in a clerk position. Everybody was surprised I could do the job so well, which made me laugh. I was doing the same kind of work when I was 17. There's no challenge and it doesn't reflect what I'm capable of. If I'd known I was going to be in the work force at this point, I would certainly have done things differently.

Yvonne Manzer,
Halifax, Nova Scotia

"**D**uring the eight years I was with that company, all the sales reps were men and all the support staff were women. When I asked about getting into sales, or a higher-paying position, management never gave me much encouragement, although I received excellent job evaluations."

Yvonne Manzer began working as a receptionist in 1974. She has held a variety of secretarial and administrative jobs, has worked at a transition house for battered women and part time with an escort service. She is currently administrative co-ordinator for the Elizabeth Fry Society in Halifax.

I'm 40 years old. When I was growing up, it never occurred to me that I should plan for a career because my parents made all the decisions. I graduated from high school in Saint John, New Brunswick, then went to secretarial school because that's what my mother told me to do.

My first job was as a receptionist. After a year, I was promoted to secretary. Then I went to work for a multinational company as a secretary before being promoted to a junior administrative position.

My boss used to say that when he got transferred to Halifax, he'd take me with him. He constantly asked me personal things—about sex. I felt uncomfortable answering, but it never occurred to me that he was off limits. I guess I was very naive. When I told him, in response to his question, that I had started to sleep with my boyfriend, he was furious. He said that meant he couldn't take me along to Halifax. What would people think now that I was having an affair?

The company eventually transferred me to Halifax, and while continuing in my job, I briefly worked part time for an escort service. I was about 26 when I saw an ad in the paper that read: "Do you enjoy going out for dinner? Do you want to make some money?" I discussed it with a woman I worked with who had done a similar thing and she said it was great. Since she hadn't run into any problems, I called.

The guy who ran the service worked for a taxi company. He came to pick me up after work and we talked about the job. He said he often picked men up at the airport who were in town for business, and he'd ask them if they wanted company for dinner. If so, they paid $100 and I got $50.

I decided to give it a try, not only for the money, but also because I've always been curious about people. I'd meet the guys in a bar or restaurant and we'd have dinner. I did it six times and only two guys made an untoward advance. The last time I went out with a guy, we were at a club and he asked me to go back to his place. He kissed me two or three times and I left.

I stopped doing it because the guy I worked for started to make me feel uncomfortable. When he paid me, he'd ask how it went. Soon he was really starting to pry. One day, he called and said he'd met some guys who wanted to go on a cruise to Florida. Would I like to go? I said no. Then he started to suggest other weird situations and I sensed he might be trying to break me in for sex. So I stopped.

About eight years ago, I went to work at a transition house for battered women. I really enjoyed that. It was difficult when a woman came, but after a few days, you could see the change. There was a lot of camaraderie among the women and I received a lot of validation that my work was worthwhile.

I spent a total of four years at the transition house, in two segments, and it was one of the best work experiences I've had. The relationship between the staff and the board was terrible, but even so, I met a lot of incredible women and I grew a lot.

I also worked for a year with Kitimavic, a federal youth program. When I returned from a month's retreat, I discovered I was pregnant. After my son was born, I went back to work at the transition house. At first I took him with me and that went quite well. When a distressed woman came in and wanted to make a connection, having the baby helped if she had kids, too. But after a year the board changed the rules and children couldn't come to work, so child care became a problem.

After I left there, I had several different jobs. One was as bookkeeper and administrative co-ordinator at a company that analyses the environment. That was a terrible experience. I was putting in lots of overtime, for starters. Then the boss told me that he didn't like the way I dressed and he wanted me to look more businesslike. At that time I didn't have money to buy new clothes, so I went to the Salvation Army and bought some business outfits.

Then the guy who was training me put in a bid to do my work and they contracted out half my job. I was shocked. I had never been treated like that. I was called into an office and told, "Half your work has been contracted out. Here's your new job description and you'll be paid less." So I left.

Now I'm administrative co-ordinator for the Elizabeth Fry Society. It's a women's collective and, finally, I feel my personal life and my work life are integrated. I'm getting paid to do a job I'd do for free. I'm able to be creative and work on social change with, and for, women. Feminist theory about the benefits of non-hierarchical structures is being put into practice here.

One thing I'd like to say is that it's very difficult being a single parent. I live in a housing co-op where my son is the only child and I'm often put in the position of having to apologize for him.

Also, I've had very little help. No one has ever said anything like: "I have a free night. Would you like to go to a movie?" My son asked me if any of the men in the co-op could spend some time with him, but when I asked about this in the co-op meeting, one of the men attacked me for being manipulative. There's so little support for single parents. It doesn't seem like children are welcomed in this society, sometimes even in so-called alternative environments.

However, in my current job I can bring my son to work if I choose. Also, child care is paid for if I have an after-hours meeting. I hope all workplaces will start demonstrating similar respect for the demands of motherhood.

4

Business and Personal Services

Helen Bugler
St. John's, Newfoundland

"I had been a chameleon in my work history. If you wanted to pay me, I'd be an interviewer, a bookkeeper, I'd wash windows, whatever. Someone was paying and I was being. But working with the Women's Institutes made me realize there was a whole world I never knew existed—a world where I, perhaps, might make a difference."

Helen Bugler, who first entered the work force in 1948, raised her six children between 1952 and 1965. She has had a varied work history since then, mainly focused on market research and other kinds of interviewing. She currently runs a part-time business in market research and works as a school counsellor.

In 1948, when I was 15, I quit school and got a job in a book bindery that paid $10 a week. A year later, I was married and four months' pregnant. The baby died when it was 3½ months old. After this experience, I got a job in a store selling ladies' dry goods. In 1952, my next child was born and I didn't work for wages again until 1965. During that time, I had six more children, plus a miscarriage, so I didn't have time to do much else.

My husband was an auto mechanic and steadily employed, but there was never enough money to cover eight people's needs. Even though I knit or sewed all the children's clothes, we still weren't getting anywhere.

I decided to take a job selling Fuller Brush products. In those days, at least in Newfoundland, it was inconceivable that a women would go door to door, carrying mops and brooms and a heavy case. Even so, I was very successful. But after three months, my husband got sick of having me busy on Saturdays and made me quit.

He's a demanding man. At that time, everything had to revolve around his work which meant I had to make breakfast for the family, get the kids off to school, tidy up, do my sales and be back in time to cook him a hot lunch for one o'clock. While I had no problem succeeding in the man's world of Fuller Brush, I found it difficult to fit my work around my husband's schedule.

Without the freedom to work at certain times, I couldn't take a 9-to-5 job so I worked as an interviewer for Stats Canada for seven years, off and on. When I wasn't doing that, I did market research and anything else that turned a dollar, as long as I could be home in the morning, for lunch and for the evening meal. I'm a very industrious person. I did anything to turn a dollar.

I often worked at night. Sometimes, on a cold, wet night, I'd be knocking on doors and I'd ask myself, "Do you really need to eat this badly?" At that point there wasn't much joy in my work. I worked only for money, not for pleasure; and not even because I was unfulfilled at home. In fact, in my own little household I was very fulfilled.

In 1971, when I was 39, I got pregnant again. I wasn't earning big money with Stats Can. My week's work paid $80 and if I kept busy with other little jobs, I could usually get my income up another $250 to $300 a month. But when you consider that the most my husband ever earned was $9,000 a year, I made a significant contribution to the household. We always had a car and even bought a house—not a great house, but a decent one.

Since I didn't want to be knocking on doors with a big belly, I decided to quit work. In December, I started knitting mitts and socks. By the middle of January, I missed my job because I had become used to a very fast pace. Also, in those days, there was no unemployment insurance for pregnant women so the lack of income was worrisome.

Although I sometimes hated interviewing, I was very good at it, and as a result, many opportunities came up. When a woman I knew asked me to do a campaign soliciting memberships in the Chamber of Commerce, I said no because I was pregnant, but I agreed to meet her anyway. She told me I didn't show, so I worked until the day before my son was born.

When I came out of the hospital, I nursed my baby and went back to work with Stats Canada. I soon found that managing a new baby and a job with no support was too hectic, so I set myself up in a little business doing contract work which included research projects at the university. I always kept a nest egg of $300 or $400 dollars. Since the January sales were on and I had a project lined up, I decided, on the strength of that job, to spend a bit of money on things we needed for the house. The project was delayed until February 15, and on February 10, 1975, my husband had a heart attack.

The doctor said my husband couldn't work and only $110 was left of our nest egg. It was nine weeks until we received any benefits! By juggling we managed to survive without asking for help, which was important to me.

When I started at the university our mortgage was $430 a month, our total income was $582 and we had six kids to feed. I had to earn more money, so I returned to Stats Canada. All the interviewers were women and we were on the lowest level. Our running joke was, "A woman will never be a man in this place," which meant we wouldn't get the office jobs in the higher categories. If I'd been a man, I might have made the jump because I had a lot of abilities.

A three-month contract with the Ministry of Energy, Mines and Resources was one of my first good jobs. I went to Ottawa for six weeks to train, and things started to change at home. Although my husband would never say I was the breadwinner, I had started to do work that didn't fit around his schedule. Instead, he ended up rearing our youngest child.

After I returned from Ottawa, I drove a van around the province making presentations. I'd leave home Sunday afternoon and wouldn't return for eight or nine days. My kids lived on chicken soup for the first year until my husband learned to cook. He never bought groceries. He'd prepare what I purchased before I left. As a man who had never poured his own tea or helped with the children, he didn't feel competent in the grocery store. But that was the norm for our generation.

The job with the ministry lasted 18 months. It was one of the most successful programmes of its kind in Canada and I did many media interviews. But, once again, when I finished, I couldn't get unemployment insurance benefits because I was a contractor.

I had absolutely no money. Never being able to get a job that was insurable was a hardship. This wasn't uncommon for women at the time and it meant that when a job ended, you had that desperate falling-off-a-bridge feeling.

In 1979, I applied to be a project manager at Statistics Canada. For two months I heard nothing. Then they called and said I had the job.

It was a year's contract, and when it was up I was eligible for U.I. (Unemployment Insurance) for the first time. I had always said when that happened I'd take a rest. I was only off work for a week when somebody called to tell me about a job involving Women's Institutes.

I have to admit I'd always been sort of anti-woman. I found women who just sat around all day gossipy and small-minded, and I didn't want anything to do with them. When I went to work for the Women's Institutes, those feelings changed. The institutes aren't a militant group. They started in Newfoundland in 1929 when a tidal wave did some drastic damage on the south coast. A group of rich women got together to help women recover by using what they had. They taught sewing, canning, recycling clothes and so on. During the long winter nights without work the women took it further, making beautiful mats, knitwear and other crafts. This is the source of Newfoundland's strong craft culture.

Anyway, the Women's Institutes wanted someone to go into the communities and promote educational programmes. This was my first introduction to women as individuals and it was a turning-point in my life. Seeing how much these women supported each other was a revelation. The programme, which I designed with another woman, was a great success. I was almost 50 years old and she was the first woman I ever really got to know.

I was good at my work because I had enough experience to empathize with the women. I'm a good listener. I think I have an innate ability that allows people to feel at ease, and in feeling at ease, to either learn from something I've said or tell me things that will enable them to help themselves. I felt this job was a niche for me. And, for the first time, I recognized I wasn't just working for money. I was gaining a sense that my own experience was valuable.

Over the next few years I did more work for the Women's Institutes in conjunction with Status of Women. At one point, I went to work at the university for a woman geneticist who said, "Helen, you're getting older. You're getting jobs but you'll find it harder and harder. You must go back to school."

I had left school in Grade 8. No one in my family had ever been to university, but many of the people I worked with had degrees and I was always competing with them.

I really didn't want to go to university, but the woman I worked for kept at me and I figured in order to shut her up I'd better go. I registered for first-year biology and second-year psychology and got the shock of my life. I'm a brave soul with the courage to tackle anything, as my job history shows, but when I listened to the biology prof, I couldn't understand a word.

I started having hot flashes. The doctor said, "Helen, you're not having hot flashes. You're having anxiety attacks." There were 72 students in the class. Half quit and another quarter failed. When I passed, I felt I could do anything.

Within the next year I did 21 courses because I wanted to graduate. I was 55 when I started. By the time I was 57 I had my BA. I started applying for jobs and everyone laughed at me. They said I wouldn't get anything at my age. I wrote four applications and received three job offers. I took a job counselling older adults who were going back to school. It lasted three years and ended when the funding was cut.

When I started to work, I felt the effects of gender and now I'm experiencing ageism. I recently applied for a job and know I was screened out because I'm 61. Now I'm faced with unemployment. My husband is 64 and he hasn't worked for 18 years. He has trouble understanding my commitment, but I know I don't live when I'm not involved. We've had quite a few quarrels over it. I'm made to feel guilty because he thinks he might be dead in a year or two and all I do is work.

I finished my master's in June and I'm proud of it. But I'm not going to the convocation because my husband is so uptight about it. He didn't marry a university graduate, and when he gets bitter, he says things like that—not that he's a mean person.

I've also registered in the faculty of social work and I'll have that degree next year. I'm good at counselling, but I need a piece of paper that acknowledges that skill. Since I need to keep employed, I continue to work as a counsellor in a school.

When you're 20 and planning your work life you have lots of time. I don't have much time left, so I'm packing a lot in.

Helen Ryane
Vancouver, British Columbia

"When people asked me why I built a company that was only women, my response was always that I only hired the best people."

Helen Ryane began working in the late 1950s as a bank teller. After attending teacher's college, she earned a master's degree in education, and taught at Simon Fraser University. In the early 1970s, she became interested in consulting and incorporated her own management-consultant company in 1973. She is currently pursuing her interest in women and entrepreneurship.

I grew up on a farm outside a little town, Mossbank, Saskatchewan, where there didn't seem to be many opportunities for making money. We had as much as anyone else, which wasn't a lot, so I grew up feeling that if you were successful, you got out of Mossbank and out of Saskatchewan.

I finished high school in the late '50s. My mother thought I should get an education so I'd have something to fall back on in case my husband got sick. There didn't seem to be many options: teacher, nurse, secretary or housewife. I wanted to be an airline stewardess, but my Aunt Merle, who was a sort of role model—she worked in the post office in Moose Jaw and had an apartment of her own—said, "That's just a glorified waitress. You're better than that, Helen."

It's too bad we weren't freer to do whatever we wanted because being a stewardess might have been fun. It would certainly have been an eye-opener after growing up in Saskatchewan. But I felt that I had to do something worthy of my talents.

Since I didn't want to be a nurse, I went to the University of Saskatchewan. It was too much like high school so partly through the year I quit. I was the first in my family to attend university and I felt I was letting the side down, but I really wanted to be out in the world.

I went to work in a bank in Moose Jaw. I worked with another girl who, like me, had won awards in high school. We were tellers and it was clear we were earmarked to continue in that role. At one point this guy, Manley, arrived. He wasn't too quick, but he was clearly earmarked to be an accountant. He earned more than we did, even though we taught him to do his job and helped him discover his mistakes, which he made quite often. One woman had risen to junior loans' officer and she was considered quite a success. I thought, "Good God, this isn't for me. I'd better get a profession."

I thought teacher's college might be fun and, surprisingly, I loved it! Child-centred learning was just beginning and I developed an individualized programme for students. I got to travel across the country teaching people how to use it.

I was married, but my marriage wasn't working, so I left my husband, left Saskatchewan and went to Washington to get my master's degree. Then I taught in the teacher-education programme at Simon Fraser University. I really liked it there, too, because they appreciated innovation.

After awhile, I got tired of the university world. I liked Simon Fraser —it was a freewheeling kind of place—but I didn't want to be a professor and become part of the hierarchy. I could see these people acquired a hidebound approach to life.

While I was working on my master's degree I became interested in organizational behaviour—going into organizations and improving the quality of the workplace. At university, I'd gone out on jobs with one of the junior professors who did consulting, and I had a feel for it. I started doing workshops for people in business and the work gradually increased. I convinced another woman to join me, then another. My management consulting company was incorporated in 1973, and over the years it's evolved into a strong core group of women.

When I reached the point where I was successful as a management consultant, there were very few other women in the field. I thought that if I was successful other women could be, too, and I should bring them along. I hired women I liked with business backgrounds. I cared about the kind of people they were and they really appreciated the opportunity. I tried to bring a more co-operative atmosphere to the workplace, not only in the way we ran the company, but also in our consulting.

Hiring women worked well as a business strategy. The firm specializes in conflict resolution, negotiation, mediation skills, leadership training and team building. Most of our clients are men and they're far more likely to talk about their problems with a woman. They expect women to be listeners whereas they'd be more inclined to compete with a man. If people objected to an all-woman team, we won them over with sheer competence and humour.

I tried to bring a more "female" style to the company. For instance, during the 1981 recession, I didn't want to let anyone go, so we all took less.

Then we built the company on a broader base, which means we've weathered this recession just fine. We also constructed the company in a flexible way so that people could take time off to have children, to go on meditation retreats—whatever. We recognized the personal side of life and made a commitment to quality of life within the company structure.

Some people say I coddled the consultants, but I look at other companies, where people are burning out, and I think our approach makes sense. There's a pervasive feeling that if you get off the treadmill, you lose your points. But I strongly believe we must build organizations that are more responsive to people's needs. For many of the women I talk to, it's not even a matter of getting ahead. They know they can do that. The issue is, do they want to live their lives like this?

I should point out that we now have one man who works for us. We hired him because he's really good. He's about 42, seems to enjoy working with women, is definitely not sexist and very competent.

I just sold two-thirds of the company to one of my senior consultants because I now want to help other women become entrepreneurs. I think we can make strides in this area because women's track records in succeeding in small businesses are better than men's.

Looking back, I can see that growing up in Mossbank, Saskatchewan, has helped me in my career. I learned not to go overboard and to look at long-distance plans. You may have had a good crop this year, but who knows about next?

Anonymous
Toronto, Ontario

"You reach a point where you start to see the patterns. You continually get battered, but you get up and keep going until the next time somebody pulls the rug out from under you."

"Anonymous" graduated from university in 1968. Throughout the 1970s and 1980s, she worked as a consultant. In 1992, she took a position as a senior executive with a multinational corporation.

In the fall of 1971, when I was 24, my husband decided to go back to school. I had just started a job and discovered I was pregnant. I wanted to postpone telling my new employers until I had a good track record behind me, but my husband felt I was obligated to tell them immediately. In the end, I allowed his rational approach to win over my gut instinct. When the management committee met that week, I told them I was pregnant. They fired me—literally, on the spot. I remember one guy saying, "You're pregnant. Don't come back tomorrow."

I couldn't believe it. I asked the others if they agreed with him. They replied, "We have no obligation to you." I was absolutely stunned. Since human rights' legislation hadn't come in, I knew I had no legal recourse.

After that, I got really depressed. My husband was building his life, having a great time at university, and I was getting fatter and fatter. There were no other jobs in town, particularly for pregnant women, and we didn't have two cents to rub together. I felt rotten.

I didn't know what to do, so I joined the Y. I'd swim everyday, then I'd have a sauna. The other regulars were nine older women who got together to swim and socialize. Gradually they started talking to me and soon my visits to the sauna became therapy sessions. They gave me advice on childbearing, managing my husband, getting my networks in place—life skills' stuff. The sauna with these wonderful women became my haven. Years later when I saw the play and then the movie *Steaming*, it reminded me of this experience. I found my support network in the most unlikely place.

Instead of wallowing in self-pity, I used the remaining months of my pregnancy to organize a job after our child was born. I took a three-month leave, hired a retired nurse as a nanny and started working for an incompetent man who was an alcoholic. I needed the job to support the family. Over the next year, I worked and had a second child. I only took four weeks off to make sure I didn't lose my job.

I also figured out our financial-survival system. I took in two boarders. I cooked their meals and they paid our rent. Making it work meant that my days were pretty gruelling. In the second year, I'd get up at 5:00 and take the baby, who was too young for day care, to the baby-sitter. Then I'd take the older one to day care. I worked from 8:00 until 4:00 and after that put in an hour at the day-care centre looking after 20 under-two-year olds in exchange for free day care. Then I'd pick up the baby, cook the meals, do the laundry and whatever else needed to be done. Finally, I'd collapse.

My husband's life was different. He'd come home from school with friends who missed "home cooking." Then they'd all go back to study. It was the boarders who pitched in and became my support system. They liked the kids and they read to them and played with them before they went to bed.

It was the low point of my life. It wasn't a healthy situation, but it was survival.

During this time I remember an enumerator coming around for the election. She asked who the head of the household was and I said, "I am."

She said, "No, no, the head."

"But I am the head of the household," I protested. "I'm supporting my husband through law school."

"Ah," she said, "you have a husband. He's the head of the household." We got into a great debate, but I made no headway. He was the head of the household because he was male.

When my husband graduated, we moved to Toronto. I had given up my job and was on unemployment insurance while I looked for a new position. The kids were two and three, and I didn't have child care because we couldn't afford it. Our so-called extra money bought my husband's business suits because he needed to look good for the office. So when I visited the U.I. office, I always took the children—on public transit, since we didn't have a car.

I remember my first interview, vividly. I was taken into a room and asked to prove I was looking for a job. I'd taken all my correspondence and lists of the phone calls I'd made. But they wanted to know what companies had interviewed me and where I'd trundled around town to drop off my résumé. "How can I physically visit places to look for work with two children?" I asked. They were quite abusive. They tried to get me to admit that I wasn't really looking for work because I had young children, even though I was busy mailing out résumés and phoning. I was furious—my premiums had paid for this! "Believe me, I'm looking for work," I protested. "It's much easier than being at home with two small children."

I finally got a job as an administrator in a consulting firm. After awhile one of the senior people approached me and suggested I become a junior consultant. In this organization, internal promotions usually went smoothly. But the other senior people—all men, I might add—had me pegged in a hole. They declared that I needed the formal approval of a committee before I could be promoted.

Apparently, I was the first person wishing to transfer within the organization who had to endure that gruelling process. I rotated through the interview with eight members of a hiring committee. Some asked me incredibly insulting things like: how could a woman do the job, particularly a woman with kids? How would I fare as a single individual on a business trip? How could I relate to male clients and socialize over golf and beer with them?

I couldn't believe this could happen in a distinguished business environment. But by this time, I can tell you, I was getting a pretty strong steel core. I was mush until I was about 26, but after that, forget it.

I'm one of the fortunate people who can play the "game" and do well. But after working as a consultant for awhile, I could see great women who were being passed over for all kinds of reasons: they were too outspoken, they didn't have the image and so on. I realized that I was moving ahead because I was a safe token.

About a 1½ years after I became a consultant, one of my friends said to me, "You know you've changed. You should take a look at who you are. Do you want to be like them? Because if you stay, you will be." That was the wise advice I needed. I decided to move on. I didn't want to be moulded and shaped by the system, which I knew would happen.

Fortunately, this decision came at exactly the right point in my life. Soon after, my husband came home and announced, "We're going to be transferred. The company offered me a job abroad, and I told the president we'd be thrilled to go. Since you won't be working, you can co-ordinate all our social activities and...."

Half-way through this sentence, I stopped him. "You said I wouldn't be working?"

"Well sure, the wives who have gone over in the past haven't had time to work. You know, our marriage is a partnership. We discussed it and you'll be really busy socializing and doing all the right things."

"Who's we?" I asked.

"The president and I."

I was furious. Imagine, a third party being so presumptuous as to assume that I wouldn't work! I said, "If you don't have enough confidence to believe that I can make my own decisions about whether I'll work or not, then you can call the president up and tell him we're not going." I retreated into stony silence.

Deep down I knew I wanted to go, so I decided to move, settle the kids, get organized and show that I could work *and* do the socializing. In hindsight, this was significant. All spouses since my time have been offered the opportunity to work outside the home if they wished.

After we arrived in our new home, I got a job with the same consulting firm I had worked with in Toronto. The first year was great. Then they put me to work for a senior consultant who was having troubles. Once I refused to put my name on a significant piece of work because I didn't think the client was getting his money's worth. I felt so strongly that I walked into the president's office and said, "Either senior management confronts the issues, or I go." I left.

Once again, I was unemployed. I assessed my skills, interests and knowledge, and decided to open my own consulting business. I got a number of other women to work with me and we carved out a real niche for ourselves. I learned a lot about the globalization of business, in particular, and we were doing very well. But then I started to feel I didn't know enough so I enrolled in an MBA programme.

I loved it. In the evenings, when the kids came home from school, we'd study together. But after a year my husband rebelled. It was okay for me to be out between 9:00 and 5:00, but he wanted to come home to company and a home-cooked meal. He didn't want to come home and find his wife studying with his kids at the dining-room table.

My priority was to save our marriage. My husband may be right of Attila the Hun, but I really do love the guy. So if I can't straighten him out, I have to figure out a new strategy. I dropped out of business school and we threw ourselves into entertaining and socializing. In fact, we did it so well that the company asked us to go to another country and do it all over again.

When we were settled once again, I realized I wasn't terribly employable because I was moving around every three years. So I set up another consulting firm and ran it from my home. This meant if the kids got sick, the problem of baby-sitters was solved since good ones were very hard to find.

I got myself a partner, a really tough and determined woman. Together, we were successful, making money and providing good quality work. My goodness, it was easy. I liked being able to take risks. I liked the challenge of making a profit, of doing it our way, of drawing in different types of people to work with us. Again, the company was all female.

Every night at four our house went from office back to home. There's always been a battle about my business and my work. My husband's position is that my income is second-best. When we got married, the deal was that he'd be the major provider. He thought that was the contract and that it should never change, but we're still working on the revisions.

When we moved back to Toronto a few years ago, he said publicly that I had sacrificed for him so this could be my decade. And we started to turn our lifestyle around in many ways. The first year, as was my tradition, I spent my energies getting the kids settled in school and taking on small projects. For several years, I did volunteer work and ran a small management-consulting company, but eventually I realized that I really wanted to be in a corporate environment. So I researched the company I wanted to work for and went after them through consulting projects.

First, they hired me to do a small report which needed to be completed in three days. During that time, I lived at my computer because I knew this opportunity wouldn't come again. When they said they liked my work, I said, "I can do more."

Next, they gave me a global project to co-ordinate. I did the planning, orchestrating and budgeting, and during that four months, I demonstrated that I could run the project and was a committed team player. I used the project as an opportunity to understand the business and to determine where I could provide the most value-added to the company. When an opportunity came up, I was hired at a management level.

All large organizations are political and I was fortunate because I had a female mentor. I'm learning to make compromises that suit me and are consistent with my values. One of these is adapting to the corporate dress code. The women below a certain level dress one way and the women above dress another. There's a demeanour to being a successful woman. You're expected to wear classic clothes and heels. The colours need to be strong —no pastels. You can't wear jangling earrings or ostentatious jewellery. You need some makeup, but it shouldn't be loud, and your hair needs to be well cut. If you're management, no coloured nylons. The image is conservative

—capital C. It's a game, and if you don't play it, you hit the infamous glass ceiling.

I'd known it before, and I wonder now if that's why, unconsciously, I avoided business for so long. When I started, I dressed fairly informally, but once I decided that I wanted to accomplish something, I changed. The amount of energy one wastes thinking about clothes is amazing! But it makes a difference. When you go into a meeting, you can feel yourself being checked out and pegged in a box.

A tougher challenge has been adapting to new communication and presentation styles. For instance, corporate culture supports talking in bullets. It's structured and predictable, but that's what works. I find it too contrived and, in a way, too simplistic, but extremely challenging. I love what I'm doing right now.

Odd as it might seem, I can't help thinking that my marriage has played a role in my success. I've always been challenged and constantly pushed to the edge by my husband. He helped to make me who I am. I often wonder who I'd be today if I had been married to a compassionate, supportive, loving husband. I might just be a nurturing, loving, house-cleaning woman.

Joyce Myerson
Montreal, Quebec

"I don't define myself by this profession. I'm not Joyce the picture framer, although I say that on the telephone all the time. 'This is Joyce, your picture framer, calling. Your picture is ready.'"

Joyce Myerson earned a master's degree in Italian literature in the early 1970s. Originally intending to be a scholar, she also studied flute for many years and has been a support worker for mentally disabled people. For the past 10 years, she has operated a framing business with a partner. She is currently working on her second novel.

I've been a picture framer for about 10 years. I didn't set out to become a picture framer. I planned to be a scholar. I lived in Florence for a year when I was 12 and loved it so much that I studied Italian literature at McGill. I was in my Ph.D. programme when I quit. I was very young. I would have had my doctorate around the age of 22.

I left because of an obsessive professor. In graduate school, I worked from early in the morning until midnight. At two every afternoon, he'd meet me at the library and we'd work for two hours. He wanted me to write a particular thesis on music and literature. He was on top of every word I wrote, and I hated him for overtaking my life.

He was a tyrant who never encouraged me. His criticisms were devastating, although I had plenty of respect from the other professors in the department. Much of the work was oral, in the European tradition, and if I was delivering a paper, the entire staff came to listen. I felt they were waiting on my every word because they thought I'd say something original. But nothing was ever good enough for him.

He wanted to create a scholar, someone he had completely moulded. Once, in front of the whole department, he said I had a genius for capturing the essence of everything I read, but didn't have the academic background to develop it. He bemoaned the fact that I had a Canadian education rather than a European one. Although I never got the sense that he was in love with me, I think he was obsessed with his power over me. It was terrifying.

I'm angry because I wanted to be a teacher. I like educating people, opening their minds to things I care about. I did teach a bit, later, and I taught flute for years. At least I have that.

When I quit graduate school, I started to study music very seriously. I was playing eight hours a day and teaching around 20 hours a week. I enrolled in the music department at Concordia and it was wonderful. I was exposed to some great teachers. But I never played in an orchestra or anything. I never felt I was good enough.

My music phase lasted for eight years, until I was 30, when my mother died. During that time I also started writing and enrolled in a master's programme in creative writing at Concordia, earning my degree in 1986. While I was doing that I opened this picture-framing business with the woman who had been my piano accompanist. I had to earn a living since I had stopped teaching flute.

By that time I was married and had a baby so I used to take my son to work. We had a crib in the store, and when I went to school, my business partner took care of him. It was a nice arrangement.

We're very respected framers. We frame good works of art for collectors. I suppose in some ways you could say I learned a skill and I educate people. I teach them about ways to see and what the frame does.

Picture framing is pleasurable, but running a business isn't. I didn't choose to be a business person. It just happened. It doesn't matter what your business is, that's not what you do most of the time. Usually, you worry about business. I don't find it challenging because the ultimate goal is to earn money, which is ungratifying.

For a year, we also had an art gallery. I hated working for artists. They don't really see the framer as an ally and think you're taking advantage of them. All I did was work. At one point I couldn't take it any longer so I got a part-time job working with mentally ill people.

I found housing for people after they left a psychiatric ward or crisis centre, which meant I spent a lot of time interviewing and talking to very sick people—people who had been in and out of hospital, people who were on medication, schizophrenics, manic depressives. I liked it, but I think I intimidated many of my co-workers because most just had CEGEP (Collége d'Enseignement Général et Professionel) diplomas.

It was a relief to do that for a while. It was very good for me because I listened a lot, to many people. One of the main characters in the novel I'm working on is a schizophrenic, and I know that the material came from many hours of listening to a particular fellow.

I don't know how long I'm going to be a picture framer. I'm surprised

I lasted this long. I've completed the first draft of my second novel. I got my degree with the first novel, but I didn't make much of an effort to get it published because it was about Italy and not very North American. But I learned how to write with that book.

I'm thinking about translating from Italian to English. I'm also thinking about getting a Ph.D. Maybe I have my mother's tenacity. She wanted a degree very badly, and I want this Ph.D. I guess I want the respect that comes with it, although I don't want to be an academic.

I feel I work harder than my parents ever worked and they worked all their lives. When we started and the business was taking off it was much more comfortable. But things have changed. Now, you look for every sale and your suppliers are constantly phoning. I don't like to worry about paying bills. All that worrying wears me down.

Freedom is my ultimate goal. The problem with my life is that I don't have time to think and thinking is everything. I want to think, I have lots to think about. But I'm tired at the end of the day. There were periods when I didn't even read very much.

I'm poor, very poor. Well, that's also because I'm divorced. But being poor isn't important. It's being tied down that's so hard to take. I guess that's being in the traditional work environment.

I suppose for me the best thing about this business is that I tend to be very reclusive and the work doesn't allow that. If I'm selling a poster by Chagall, I have to tell the customer about Chagall. People tell me their life stories and I learn a lot about them. I'd probably communicate much less if I wasn't a picture framer.

Thinking is what I do and it's surprising how much time it burns up. When I was playing music eight hours a day, alone in my room, I used to say I needed to put in about five hours just to practise for two, because in between I was thinking. Writing is the same. It requires a lot of thinking time.

Thinking isn't traditional work for women. For centuries women were prohibited from thinking. I read a great book by an Italian writer, a woman, but I can't remember the title. It's about a 16th-century Sicilian woman who was taken by her father to watch a hanging when she was nine. From that point she never spoke, but she read and she wrote and was probably one of the great minds of the 16th century. It's a metaphor for being voiceless in a way.

I often think about all the voiceless people. You can imagine the number of 16th-and 17th-century women who were silent. They had so much thought in their heads that was never recognized.

Mairi Matheson
Calgary, Alberta

"A lthough I wasn't aware of a lot of prejudice, I was lonely because there weren't a lot of 'me's' out there."

Mairi Matheson began working as a dietitian in 1957. In 1971, she set up a partnership with a San Francisco firm to provide food services to large institutions throughout North America. She is an active volunteer and, at the time of this interview, was deputy chairman of the board of the Calgary General Hospital.

I was born in Vancouver 58 years ago and grew up in Ottawa. In those days, it was important for the girls in my group to be well educated so that if something unexpected happened, a married woman would have something to fall back on. A good education was also considered an asset in raising children, but one certainly wasn't educated with the idea that one would establish a career.

Once, when I was 16, I blurted out that I'd like to take political science because I was enamoured of my uncle who was a cabinet minister. There was a great guffaw, and a "My goodness, you can't be serious!" and that was the end of that. I was quite serious, but nobody was interested in what I thought.

I became a dietitian because my mother had been a nurse and she thought nursing was too hard. In her day, nurses did all the scrubbing and heavy work. My grandmother had been a dietitian in Scotland so that was to be my thing. I was very resentful, but in those days, one didn't challenge family decisions.

I attended Macdonald College at McGill University and obtained a bachelor of science degree with a home economics option in 1956. It was a strong science degree and I'm rather pleased I passed. I moved to Calgary to take my dietetic internships and after I finished, when I was 21, I got married and started working.

I was one of those '50s graduates who pretty much expected to get married, work for a few years, then stay home. My husband thrust the role of breadwinner upon me and, I guess, because of the kind of person I was, it didn't faze me. He decided to return to university to take his master's. I continued to work to bring money into the home. It was supposed to take him a year or two. Six years later he was still at school.

During that time I had three children with very little maternity leave. In my first job, I provided nutrition services in a Calgary hospital. Then we moved to Edmonton so my husband could attend graduate school at the University of Alberta, where I taught courses. My biggest concern in those days was getting the right child care. It was long before day care, but I did find some wonderful women who looked after my house and my children. One woman pretty well saw me through the whole time. She arrived at a 7:45 in the morning and left when I came home at 4:15.

Supporting three children, a nanny and a husband was a serious financial responsibility. One day I realized that my pay cheque was $274 a month—in the late 1950s that was fairly good—but I could charge $6 an hour as a freelancer. I also realized that by contracting out my time, I could dovetail working with things I wanted to do with my children. So I made my pitch to various hospital boards and got hired as a consulting dietitian.

I don't recall that my husband did any housework or cooking during this time. It was my responsibility to see that the house and child care were looked after because he was busy with his schoolwork. He was good with the children—he'd play with them and so on—but I didn't get the sense he was taking "the responsibility."

He finally got his MA in psychology and we moved back to Calgary. Shortly thereafter, in 1964, the marriage ended. I felt so guilty about building my career, particularly in a way that worked for both the children and myself, that I didn't ask for much in the way of support. Hindsight is 20-20, I guess, but I was more interested in carrying on and doing what needed to be done than in creating acrimony.

In those days, divorce was unacceptable so I was doubly stigmatized: a divorced career woman. I felt guilty for a long time because it was so inappropriate, but eventually I refocused on my priority, which was the children. I felt it was my responsibility to keep us all afloat.

My initial objective in working was to get my husband a graduate degree, then it became something I had to do for the children, but gradually I discovered that I enjoyed the challenge, the creativity and the excitement of a career. The downside was the stigma attached to being the sole breadwinner and a female. In my social group—the women who volunteered, curled, played tennis, bridge and so forth—that wasn't expected. At first I tried to participate, but I soon realized I couldn't meet my commitments.

I told myself that the children would benefit if I achieved my career objectives. My success would allow us to do fun things that we couldn't do otherwise. We'd go up to Banff for five days every spring to ski, and every summer the two boys went off to hockey school, among other things. The kids still remember some of those perks. When I travelled, I'd explain that I was going so we'd have the money to have fun together. I think we built a kind of a team spirit around my career.

Whenever I travelled, the nanny stayed over. I phoned at 7:00 every evening and the children could tell me whatever was on their mind.

I remained a single parent for about 14 years and was able to success-fully raise my three children and get them on their feet. Once that was done, I remarried—a widower with four children. To this day I wonder what was going on in my head since it meant doing that child-care stuff all over again. But his children have turned out all right, too.

I think women are amazing creatures, really. When they set about a task, they can juggle many different things to accomplish their objectives. I've worked all my life and often with very capable and powerful men, but I'd have to say that men don't have a similar ability. They're terribly focused on what they're doing to the exclusion of everything else, whereas women can focus not only on the job, but also on their families.

I incorporated my business in 1969, and from that point on I got very serious about contracts. I moved into the design and building of new facil-ities for hospitals, banks, industrial centres, jails—whatever was being built in Alberta. In those days, construction was booming and often the buildings needed some kind of nutrition service.

In 1971, I was very involved in the design for the food facilities at Calgary's Mount Royal College. We started to do kiosks, rathskellers, pizza parlours, pancake houses and so on, which was a radical departure from the student dining-room.

I was working with an architect, who brought in an educational consul-tant from Chicago, with a team of food-service experts from San Francisco. The chief consultant from the San Francisco group really liked my work, and when our initial meeting ended, he said, "I've told my people to carry on with these people, and you and I are going to Banff."

Everyone said, "By all means, take him to Banff." He was in his 70s, and quite a character. All the way out and back he negotiated: "Well, we're going to be working together. There's no question about that. Do you want to move to San Francisco?"

"I have no intention of moving to San Francisco," I said.

He was a typical American in the sense that he behaved as if you should just do whatever occurred to you. When he asked, "Why not?" I said it was because I had children and I wanted to raise them as Canadians. So he said, "Fine, I guess we'll just joint-venture."

We got some lawyers together and got the company set up properly and worked together for about 10 years. When I established the joint venture, my company consisted of a report writer, a designer, a nutrition consultant and an all-purpose office clerk, in addition to me. My new partner moved three people up from San Francisco, which created a fairly substantial operation, and we were very busy.

By that time, I had moved well beyond being a dietitian. I had seen the opportunity for business as a dietitian. Many people would say, "Where can you go with a home ec degree?" They don't realize that if you've got a business sense about you, you can get into all kinds of interesting career paths.

In 1976, I felt I needed to know more about business so I went to the Banff School of Management. I'd worked extensively with some very aggressive, clever and creative American businessmen and architects, but actually being in a 100 per cent male culture for six weeks, as I was at Banff, was a new experience.

When I registered for the programme, there were 75 registrants, two of whom were women. By the time I showed up, they had backed out and I was the only woman left. When I tell this story, women often say, "That's got to be the best." Actually, it was awful, because I didn't have anybody to chum around with, other than the guys. Also, the male culture is very different from the female culture in that men are very competitive and they never let that stop.

The men who go to the Banff School of Management are world-beaters, but it was interesting to see how they dealt with me. Because I was the only woman, they were worried that they'd be teased if they spent too much time talking to me. They elected me class president, which meant they could speak to me without being teased. I don't think they had any compunction about that, but I think it was strictly to serve the culture.

After six weeks at Banff, I couldn't wait to spend time with a group of women. I don't think I experienced discrimination working as a consultant—it's a very competitive field and it's pretty tough on the men as well. The only problem I'm really aware of is loneliness. I like men and I liked working with them, but I missed the company of women.

If I had my life to live over again, I think I'd like to follow my original inclination, which was political economy. But given my degree, and knowing what I know now, I'd take my MBA and probably a Ph.D. in business, or some sort of biological science. Basically, I'd spend far more time cre-dentialling myself.

I came out of university when I was 21, then got married and started having babies. Only then did I discover I was going to work for the rest of my life. Sometimes I wonder about my naivety because some of my choic-es weren't the smartest choices for me. But you do what you have to do.

Linda Marcott
White Rock, British Columbia

"**W**aitressing is like mothering in the sense that it requires many different skills: flexibility, a good memory, the ability to put on a good face and not appear grumpy no matter how bad you feel or how sore your feet are."

Linda Marcott was a student at Carleton University in the late 1960s. Throughout the 1970s she supported herself mainly by working as a waitress. The mother of two children, she has been working as an anti-poverty activist since 1990.

I'm in my early 40s and grew up in rural Ontario, outside of Ottawa, one of four children. After finishing Grade 13, I enrolled at Carleton University. My family was very poor and I was the first child to go to university from either side, so it was a fairly big deal.

My parents' marriage, which was very rocky, collapsed during my first year at Carleton. My parents decided to move to Calgary, away from my mom's lover, and my 16-year-old sister and I stayed behind. We were living in a rooming-house in Ottawa and trying to make ends meet, between my student loan and her low wages in a paper factory.

Not surprisingly, I found it difficult to keep my mind on my studies. After a year and a half, I couldn't handle the stress any more. One of my greatest regrets is not completing my degree since my marks were very good when I enrolled. Now I can see that having a degree would have changed my life.

I dropped out of Carleton, moved to Calgary with my sister and got a job busing in a restaurant. Then I moved up to waitressing which I did, off and on, for 14 years. Basically, it was hell. The job took a tremendous toll on my body. Sometimes when I got home, I couldn't feel my legs or my feet or my back. It was scary. I was young—I started when I was 19 and had my last waitressing job when I was about 33—so I was pretty fit.

The pay and the conditions were horrible. Some places insisted that I wash dishes, as well, and I also learned short-order cooking. The only good thing about the job was the tips. There was something almost illicit about those. It was thrilling to equate your performance with money. At the end of a good night, I took home 100 bucks.

The reality of waitressing meant moving from one job to another. If you didn't like a restaurant, there was always another job. In the '70s I didn't think twice about changing jobs because there were lots out there.

There was a lot of sexual harassment and figuring out how to avert that was an important part of the job. The employers and other male staff were often the perpetrators. Since there's a waiting period for U.I., you didn't want to get fired. Also, being fired looks bad, so if you were being harrassed you'd strategize around it: find a way to cajole the guy into not harassing you.

The customers often harassed us, as well. I've always thought I was a naturally shy person so it was very hard for me to deal with outrageous behaviour. I had to learn how to make a quick come back and keep it light. If a guy came on to me sexually, I had to say no in such a way as not to make an issue of it. It was very tricky and other waitresses taught me how.

There was a sisterhood among the waitresses which was the plus of the job. You'd talk about your kids and problems, with few barriers. One of the good things about waitressing was that the women stuck together.

The boss and the cook were power figures and you had to learn how to manipulate them. The cook could wreck your career if he—and they were all he's in those days—wasn't on your side. For instance, he could hold back making your food or he could not let you know it was ready and it would get cold. Either way, the customer would get a late or a cold meal and blame you.

Your objective was to keep the job long enough to put it on your résumé, so you could move up to nicer restaurants and get bigger tips. You'd make more money in better restaurants, but it didn't protect you in any other way. At one point, I took a course to be a dining-room waitress. I thought it was classier, a notch up from an ordinary restaurant. We learned how to make salads at the table and light things up for flambées. But basically, people treated you the same. If anything they were ruder.

In an ordinary restaurant you felt a commonality with the customers. You could joke with the regulars, even though there were always obnoxious drunks and people who tried to harass you. But in the pricier restaurants, the customers were snotty and treated you as a servant, not as a fellow worker.

I should add that it took me years to pay off my student loan on a waitressing salary. The theory is you get the degree and earn the money. But if you don't get the degree, that doesn't hold up.

I worked as a waitress in Calgary for about three years. Then I met my husband and we moved to Quebec. When I started looking for waitressing jobs in Quebec, I plummeted to the bottom of the scale. Since I had no

French, I could only get a job washing dishes.

For three years I worked in restaurants, took a secretarial course and did a bit of clerical work. Then I had one glorious year when I taught school: English as a Second Language. It was the only time I ever belonged to a union and was well paid with good benefits. My husband was working as a mechanic. After almost one year of teaching I got pregnant. It was a difficult pregnancy and I had to quit work.

I didn't think about working after my daughter was born. I wanted to stay home with her, although you'd have to be a middle class family to think about child care so it wasn't an option for us. Quite soon after that my husband lost his job and we moved to Calgary where my grandmother lived. We had a second daughter who was born with Down's Syndrome. Her birth was a horrendous experience. For about 1½ years I was in shock, and during that time my marriage broke up.

I've been a single parent since my children were babies; they're 18 and 16 now. I was on welfare most of the time they were growing up. Every time I tried to get a job outside the home, my kids brought me back. My daughter with Down's Syndrome needed me more, child care collapsed, or the job wasn't paying enough to make it worthwhile not to be on welfare.

I tried going to college but only managed to finish one course before my child care fell through. Both kids were in elementary school, and during the last three weeks of the course, they had to be on their own for an hour before I got home. That really scared me. I remember desperately phoning neighbours and getting them to check in.

I'm lucky that my Down's Syndrome child is doing very well. She's working at McDonald's, writing and reading at about a Grade 3 level. More than physical help, I need emotional support so I don't feel too isolated.

Throughout the '80s I volunteered quite a bit. I helped start a welfare-rights group in my area and was part of a group of low-income women who organized consciousness-raising workshops. Once my children were old enough, I was able to go back to work. Three years ago I got the job I'm working at now, anti-poverty activist.

For the first couple of years, I would have been financially better off on welfare, but I made a decision never to work in a job that doesn't involve social change. I have many skills and talents organizing people and I don't want to waste them.

5

~~~

Community
Services

~~~

Charity Grant
Toronto, Ontario

"In the mid-1950s, I tried to get hired by the immigration department, but they turned me down because they didn't want a woman. They told me this in no uncertain terms."

During the Second World War, Charity Grant worked with the Department of Munitions and Supplies. When the war ended, she went to Europe and worked with voluntary agencies, then as director of a refugee camp. After returning to Canada, she had a varied career as an administrator in Ontario's social-welfare system and as the dean of women at the University of Toronto's Whitney Hall.

During the war I worked in Ottawa with the Department of Munitions and Supplies doing statistical projections of rubber control. This was boring work, so when the war ended and they were hiring for reconstruction work in Europe, I decided to apply. I was promptly accepted, which startled me since I didn't think I was particularly well qualified.

Later, I discovered I was hired because I knew "Mike" Pearson, the former prime minister, who was the Canadian ambassador in Washington at the time. Although I didn't know it then, all the applications went through him. He told me later I got the job because I was the only person who hadn't exerted political influence to get a good recommendation. Well, that never entered my head!

We had this so-called training programme outside Washington, then we sat on a boat for a month waiting to get a convoy. There were 24 American psychiatric social workers and me, with my pass BA and no training in psychiatric social work.

Finally, we arrived in France where we were supposed to receive more training. I was sent to work with voluntary agencies, which I've always thought was somebody's idea of a joke because my name is Charity. We were shipped off to Versailles where we ate our meals in the Petit Trianon. It was all very lush.

There was one other woman who had been head of the South African Army Corps. I was told to show her around, and since there was nothing to do after supper, we went for a walk in the gardens. I didn't realize the gates were bolted at dusk. Consequently, we got locked in. I found this very funny because it was the middle of summer and nothing could happen. But my companion panicked. She was a woman of about 45 who, it turned out, had never been out at night without a male escort. Finally, we found a hole in the fence and I went through. Some American soldiers let us out and we got home. Meeting such a highly competent woman who was afraid to go out a night without a man was a revelation to me.

I didn't think I was very good at the voluntary-agencies work, so I applied and was sent to a German camp on the border of the Russian zone. It had a British supervisor and American staff—mainly ex-army people who wanted to stay because they had made alliances with German women. I was a very junior officer. Two days after I arrived, the entire American staff had a row with the British supervisor and flew home. When they couldn't find anybody to take over, I became acting director.

The people in the camp were Jews who had been sent home to Poland but were returning to Germany because of the pogroms. There were about 3,000 people and the camp life was dreadful. I was about 30 and I had never done anything like this before. It functioned, but in a totally disorganized fashion.

I was a real innocent. For instance, the Orthodox Jews lived in an auxiliary camp in the town. I had been taught that it was polite to shake hands with whomever you met, so when I visited, I shook hands with everyone. I didn't know that an Orthodox Jew doesn't shake hands with a woman. After meeting me, they all had to take ritual baths.

When the first Orthodox Jew died in the camp, the funeral required 30 yards of white linen. This was a very difficult proposition. We gave one of my staff some cartons of cigarettes and sent her out. When she came back with the linen, we didn't ask questions. It was a strange world. Many civilians were in the area because they were involved in shady activities like black marketing jewels across the Russian border.

Our camp was the nearest to military headquarters in Frankfurt so everybody but God came down to visit: generals, MPs (members of Parliament), senators, you name it. Needless to say, they all had suggestions about how things could be improved. One general was shocked that we didn't have separate toilets for men and women. He didn't understand that in Europe that doesn't happen. So we changed the toilets while he was there and, shortly after he left, changed them all back. These silly things made life difficult. After I'd been at the camp for six months, I was so exhausted, I quit and came home.

When I arrived back in Canada, I decided to help Jewish people who wanted to immigrate. I made speeches to any group that would listen about our duty to open up immigration. When it was opened up, I was hired to return to Europe to work with the immigration team.

That was a difficult job. Not only was I the only member of the team who spoke German—my mother believed strongly in the value of other languages so my sister and I had been sent to Vienna before the war to learn the language—I could also communicate in Yiddish with the immigrants. This irritated some of the older immigration officers since it meant they had to deal through me. But it was an experience that absolutely changed my life. I had never seen human misery like this.

In 1953, I went back to school to get a social-work degree so I'd be properly credentialed. I applied to the immigration department but couldn't get a job because I was female, although they never explained what I wouldn't be able to do. Finally, they asked me to reapply and I wrote back a rude letter saying I didn't intend to continue playing mouse to their cat. If they wanted me, they could appoint me. So that's what they did.

In 1964, I was offered the job of dean of women at Whitney Hall at the University of Toronto. I couldn't have been more surprised! My aunt had been the warden at Queen's Hall (at Queen's University, Kingston) and my mother had been the dean of women at McGill, so I guess it ran in the family.

I was there in 1968 when Hart House was opened up to women. A student who lived in Whitney Hall decided it was unfair that girls weren't allowed in Hart House. I agreed and I wrote to the university newspaper in support of integration. Then I went out on the protest. I also saw my uncle, Vincent Massey, the former Governor-General, since his family had funded Hart House. I told him about the protest and he said he didn't mind. Then I visited the warden of Hart House who said they wanted women because they needed the money. So it was all very simple.

Halfway through my time as dean of women, the university decided to amalgamate the residences and eliminate one of the deans. I became a kind of student advisor to look after non-residence matters. I did that until I finished paying for this house. Then I quit and retired.

Now, I keep busy doing things like Meals-on-Wheels and teaching arithmetic to people who are illiterate. I don't consider myself a pioneer. I would never be found on the bastions—I don't think. I will admit the time in Europe was extraordinary. It was pure chance that I knew "Mike" Pearson before he was very grand. Having political connections didn't hurt, I guess. And Uncle Vincent—people thought he was so grand. But he was just Uncle Vincent to me.

Jennifer Mercer,
St. John's, Newfoundland

"I had the support of the community, but not of the Department of Social Services, which is interesting, since unmarried
mothers are supposed to be their responsibility."

*After paying her way through university in the 1960s by working as a barmaid,
Jennifer Mercer became a social worker with the Newfoundland and Labrador
Department of Social Services. Five years ago, she took a job with the Newfoundland
Advisory Council on the Status of Women.*

In my longest-lasting job as a barmaid, I had to wear a vinyl loincloth. It's
very hard to feel any human dignity wearing a vinyl loincloth and sexual
harassment was a problem. People would hold on to my legs while I was
making change, often with a lit cigarette in their hands. I was terrified that
my panty hose would go up in flames.

After awhile, management decided we could wear clothes, but the manager would check us out before we started work—we called it "cleavage
count." He told me to get a push-up bra and, when I didn't, suggested I
wear something backless. My tips went up, as he said, but the men used to
put ice cubes on my back to see if my nipples would go erect, which indicated I wasn't wearing a bra.

One night, just as the club was closing, a successful local businessman
spat beer on my back. I picked up a glass of beer, and just as I arrived at his
table, the lights came on. "If you don't apologize and pay to have this dress
dry-cleaned, I'm going to throw this in your face," I said. He maintained it
was just a joke, but I pointed out that his customers wouldn't think it was
funny if he did it to them. The next day he apologized, but he asked who
put me up to it. I guess he couldn't imagine a barmaid standing up to him.

I was a university student, with a student loan, so if I had quit I wouldn't
have starved. But the other women who worked at the bar didn't have that
option and they resented me because I had things easy compared to them.
They often tried to cheat me, to ring up drinks on my key and so on. But
after I stood up to that man, they sort of liked me.

Work associated with drinking can be scary. Early in the evening, men
might be well behaved, but after a few drinks they'd become obnoxious. A

couple of times, around midnight, I was dispatched to a very rough bar across the street to get change. The first time I walked in wearing my loincloth, somebody was thrown out over my head. I never questioned whether my employers had the right to ask me to do these things.

When you work in a bar, the bartender has all the power, and if he isn't interested in helping you, you've got trouble. He can mix the drinks wrong, or give them to you late, and you'll be blamed. People would often run out on their tabs, in which case the waitress had to pay. Sometimes customers would run up a big tab and the next day, when they were sober, they'd return and complain that the waitress had doctored their tab. Again, we often had to pay because we didn't have as much credibility as the customers.

It was a horrible job. Most people don't even recognize you. They don't look at you, really. But that didn't stop them from trying to pull off your skirt and, of course, when we wore the loincloths, they'd try to untie them. I saw a side of people that I hadn't seen before.

I grew up in a small town in Labrador. It was near an American base, which meant there were a lot of rapes and, naturally, the servicemen were never charged because they were American. So it wasn't that I hadn't seen sexual injustice. I just wasn't aware of the seediness I experienced in that bar. The bartender used to ask if I "got any" last night. I used to reply, "If I work here long enough, I'll be so turned off sex, I'll become a nun."

When I graduated from university, I got a job as a social worker, based in rural locations, with the Newfoundland Department of Social Services. That job taught me that even social workers didn't understand the different realities of men and women.

At that time we didn't have special investigators so if someone phoned and said, "So and so is getting social assistance and she's got a boyfriend," we investigated. The first time I went out to discover if the woman was living with a man, I was told to count the toothbrushes and go through her closets and drawers looking for men's clothes.

So there I was, knocking on the door of some poor woman's house and I panicked. She was about my age and I could put myself in her position. Articles of men's clothing had been left at my place and I might have eight toothbrushes in various stages of use. So I just stood there and babbled. Then I returned to the office in tears.

I told my supervisor I just couldn't do it. "You can't get fathers to pay support for their kids. How can you expect some guy who is sleeping with a woman to support her children?" He told me not to worry, just to say in my case notes that I'd visited and didn't see any signs of a man.

Whenever I had to take a child from a family, I felt like one of the oppressors. I took a lot of children into care, and in virtually every case, I felt that the mother really was concerned about the child's welfare. The only reason she wasn't an adequate parent was that she didn't have the resources: financial, physical or emotional. The entire time I worked for social services, I didn't feel good about myself. I spent a lot of time trying to figure out ways around many of the policies.

One of my worst jobs was teaching parenting-effectiveness training. I remember being sent to show a film called *Your Child's Behaviour Is You*, which showed a women in a beautiful upper-middle-class home. The film narration went something like: "If your children won't clean up their room, it may be because it's too big a task, so you have to show them how to break it down." There was a decorated bedroom with a million toys and the mother was saying, "Why don't you pick up the balls and put them here?" I was visiting a woman who had eight children and needed parenting-effectiveness training because her children had been taken from her at one point. She had one bedroom, no toys and nowhere to put them even if they'd existed. I felt so ashamed that I couldn't meet her eyes. It was my job to show the film, but I felt so horrified I could barely stumble out of the house.

Single mothers are the highest case load on social assistance, and I found the community attitudes very hard to take. We'd get calls saying things like: "So and so had a baby and she's down at the club tonight. I think you should pull her out because she's spending our tax dollars." Or: "She just got pregnant to get on social assistance." Social assistance is so low that if a woman does get pregnant just to get it, she needs help more than judgement.

When I was 35, I became an unmarried mother myself. I was working for social services in a small community in Labrador and covering other small communities, which I visited either by small plane or Ski-Doo. I lived on top of a hill in a trailer, which also served as the office. That winter we lost our water supply and I had to pay $5 a bucket to have water carried up. Since everybody else lost their sewage, the whole community came up to my trailer to use the bathroom, and I was paying $5 a bucket to flush the toilet after them. So even without a small baby, things would have been quite hard.

Since I was breastfeeding, I had organized baby-sitters in the places I visited so I could take my son along with me. Travelling on small planes was difficult with the baby. I had to climb up and flip myself in like a seal. Once, I got stranded because of the weather. When I contacted the coastal boat, they said they wouldn't take women. "I'm not a woman, I'm the welfare officer," I declared. "And I have to get back to my office."

When the boat picked me up at low tide, it wasn't too tricky. But it was high tide when we arrived home, comparable to standing on the top of a two-storey building and looking down. Even though I'm terrified of heights, I had to climb down the side of the boat on a rope with my son in a Snuggly. I was afraid that if I wimped out, I'd never get on the boat again.

After I had my son, I was treated differently. It seemed like I had crossed a line. At one point our elected representative, the MHA (member of the House of Assembly) as we call them in Newfoundland, complained to my boss that I was flaunting my bastard and setting a bad example. So a note went into my personnel file suggesting I leave my son at home. The problem was, because the weather was so uncertain, I'd often get stranded for 10 days or so, and I wanted to have him with me.

The MHA contacted various leaders in the communities I visited and asked them how they felt about having an unmarried mother as a social worker. When he landed in the town where I lived, the people circled his plane in protest. He came up to the trailer and we had quite a set to. That, for me, was the final straw and I gave them my notice.

Not having a job to go to was scary because I didn't have a family or anyone to support me. In 1983, I moved to St. John's and did some contract work. Then the Department of Social Services offered me a job on Bell Island, which is about 20 minutes from St. John's by boat.

They wanted a social worker who would live on the island. It was a nice place, but being a single mother made the work-related travel very difficult. I'd find myself sitting at conferences worrying about my son instead of paying attention. Often I'd come to St. John's for a course and the boat wouldn't run, so I couldn't get home. I'd tell the baby-sitter to be prepared to sleep over, but I still found it frightening. One Christmas Eve I was out until 4 a.m. looking for children who were supposed to come into care and worrying that I wouldn't get home in time to be Santa Claus.

Just as my son was about to enter kindergarten, I got a full-time job with the Advisory Council on the Status of Women. The leeway and flex-time which didn't exist in social services made all the difference. I'm much more productive here because I'm not always worrying that something will happen to push me over the precipice.

By the time my son got to kindergarten, I had a new set of problems. Kindergarten isn't set up for working mothers. It's set up for Dick and Jane. In order to juggle the half-day programme, I had a fleet of people who picked up my son and took him to the baby-sitters—mostly male musicians and actors who had flexible schedules and were picking up other kids from school. The first time I went to see David's teacher, she said, "You're an unmarried mother, aren't you? I've noticed a different man brings David to school every day."

"Yes," I replied. "I don't have a car." It went right over my head. When I told my friends, they alerted me to what she was thinking and I was shocked. I haven't had sex since before my son was born because I've been too busy keeping all the balls in the air. I think this is true of many unmarried mothers. When I worked with social services, I discovered that many women who gave up their children for adoption never had sex again because the consequences were so extreme. That's something that's never discussed.

My son had trouble learning to read. When I first noticed the problem, the school denied it. Then they said, "Well, maybe things would improve if you weren't working and were able to spend more time with him." Getting him tested was a struggle, but finally they discovered he has a learning disability. I believe it took so long to identify the problem because the school assumed his reading troubles reflected his mother's unmarried status.

Once, his teacher asked if I'd ever thought of getting him a book. "What book?" I asked.

"Oh, any book."

I honestly feel that when I became an unmarried mother many people stopped seeing me as a professional. I think it was worse because I was 35. Many people thought I should have known better.

Most of the time I feel like somebody is rolling logs under my feet. It's a struggle to stay balanced. I get up at 6:00 and it takes me an hour to walk my son to school, then walk to work. My work is the most rewarding part of my day, both financially and emotionally. I get off at 5:00, walk over to pick up my son, and we're home by 6:00.

While supper is cooking I start to help him with his school work. We spend hours on his homework. Last year he won a medal for reading the most in his school. In Grade 3 he couldn't read at all, but now he can read at his grade level and I'm the one who taught him. I read all the books on learning disabilities because I realized he wouldn't get any help at school. By the time supper is cooked, homework is finished, the dishes and laundry are done and so on, it's time for bed.

All of this is incredible pressure, none of which is acknowledged. When you see a man out with a baby carriage, you think, "Isn't he wonderful?" But with a woman, the response is, "She's got some life, hasn't she? Nothing to do all day but be out walking around."

Margie Vigneault
Halifax, Nova Scotia

"When I went back to work, I went through a mother's anguish leaving her child."

Margie Vigneault began working as a child-care worker in 1967 at the Dalhousie Children's Centre, after graduating with a BA from Dalhousie University. She is now director of a non-profit day care in Halifax.

When I first started working at the children's centre, formal training didn't exist so I was trained on the job. I received a very good grounding from a woman with a phenomenal understanding of children. She could tell a story to 40 or 50 kids without the help of books or pictures—simply by using her voice.

A few years later, I met my husband and we moved to Montreal, where I worked in a Montessori nursery school which taught me to value games, music and drama. After we returned to Halifax, I got pregnant and stayed home for 1½ years with my son. Making ends meet on one salary was difficult, so I returned to work.

I got a job at a private day care, which meant I could bring my son to work with me. That was the only advantage. It was a terrible place. They had a poor ratio of teachers to children and practically no equipment. The sinks often didn't function, the food was awful and the attitude was poor. Some situations bordered on illegal and, at times, you had to shut your eyes to things like children being spanked.

Although I was horrified, I was able to function until the fall when we had to move inside and the lack of facilities became critical. I watched a co-worker, a very nice girl, change from being loving to shrill.

Meanwhile, my marriage wasn't working. When my husband and I separated, I got part-time work at the YMCA (Young Men's Christian Association), helping to get the early-childhood programme started. But I needed a full-time job since I had to support my child on my own. In 1972, I was hired as a preschool director for the Y.

I took that job with trepidation because I didn't think of myself as a director. Also, my son's day care was in a private home because no non-profit spaces were available. The care giver picked him up in a station wagon and dropped him off at night. He was 2½ and I went from knowing everything about his day to knowing nothing. That experience taught me that children don't tell you anything.

One day, a cousin, who lived down the street from my son's day care, phoned to tell me that fire engines were outside the house. I was alarmed and phoned. The woman's daughter said she couldn't even talk about what had happened. This made me even more panicked. The long and the short of it is that they had a crib death. It wasn't their fault, but it was upsetting and it left me constantly anxious.

It took about eight months, but I finally found a place in a non-profit day care. This was a cornerstone for me. Things improved 100 per cent. My son became much more lively and talkative and obviously enjoyed himself there.

In 1975, International Women's Year, the Y wanted to make a long-term contribution to benefit women. They started a women's centre and committed themselves to helping activist groups coalesce. I became the staff liaison to this woman's coalition, which meant becoming involved in different committees. Soon I was attending a ridiculous number of meetings. Sometimes I even had to go out of town to make presentations. Over time I started to become resentful. It was supposed to be all of the sisters, together, but in actual fact some of my sisters were unloading on me. I felt disgruntled and left in 1980.

At that point I became director of the North End Daycare, where I'm currently employed. I enjoy it, even though we had some bumpy times in the late 1980s around the issue of funding. It's a complicated story, but, basically, expected government funding didn't materialize and by 1989 we weren't able to settle our contract.

Things were moving towards a crisis and we began to organize meetings with other day cares. On March 8, which by happy accident was International Women's Day, all the day-care centres went out on strike. We met in the parade square in front of Halifax city hall, marched down to the legislature and filled both the gallery and the lobby, where one group of parents staged a scene for the media. They briefly left a group of toddlers alone and the television stations filmed the unsupervised children. It was unbelievably adorable—toddlers spilling their milk and juice all over the legislature floor, stepping their muffin crumbs into the carpet. I think that image stuck in the minds of everybody who watched the coverage and emphasized the value of quality child care.

I also found it personally satisfying that the cameras caught the premier trying to get out the back door. The gallery was packed with parents, children and students. The politicians, who had been ignoring the day-care issue, couldn't leave because the media were waiting to catch them. In speech after speech, the members of the opposition asked the government to recognize the need for day care. The noise of the strikers filtered in from outside, as did the horns of truckers who were tooting in support.

It was a great moment. The people were finally heard and the next day the minister announced a salary-enhancement grant. We got $23,000, which we used to raise salaries and pay off what we owed.

Barbara Martin
Fredericton, New Brunswick

"I see myself taking the skills I've learned in the workplace back to my own people."

Barbara Martin worked as a social worker on a reserve for several years beginning in the late 1970s, then returned to university and completed her degree in 1984. Since then she has worked as a cultural-liaison worker and employment counsellor for native people. She works for the Ministry of Employment and Immigration.

I started university in 1976, but left in 1978 because I was a single parent and had drug addictions that needed to be addressed. I knew I was heading for a rough time, so I took a trip out West with two friends. That's when I began my healing—as an individual and a native woman. We attended a ceremonial gathering and I fasted for four days and four nights. I don't quite know what I discovered, but I no longer needed my addictions.

At that point, I was 22 and my son was four. I returned to New Brunswick and found a job as a social-service worker on a reserve working with drug and alcohol abusers. A girl, with whom I became fast friends, got me involved in community development. We raised funds for the church, organized social events and so on, as volunteers. Even though I was quite naïve, we were able to make changes by strengthening women's involvement in the community and by building their self-esteem. We became "shit disturbers," although we didn't intend to be.

The power brokers within the native community perceive women as troublemakers. That has an impact on the work you can do. You work on the reserve only at the tolerance of the men in control, and there's no job security. You have to toe the line or you stand a real chance of losing your job. We tried to deal with unjust firings several times, but rarely was the band forced to rehire the women.

The band has the power and resources to isolate women and make their lives difficult. Sexual harassment is taken for granted because most of the chiefs and council are men. It has happened to others, but not to me—maybe because I had brothers who were cops.

I stayed on the reserve for several years, then decided to return to university in Fredericton with my son. I still don't know whether it was braver to leave, or to stay on the reserve as my friend did, trying to solve the problems there. In 1984, I graduated from St. Thomas University with a BA and a major in psychology.

When I left the reserve, I had a chip on my shoulder. I had a basic distrust of anyone white. I thought all white women were middle class. But once I became involved with what I called "white women's organizations," I learned not to paint them all with the same brush.

While I was at university, I joined the New Brunswick Native Indian Women's Organization and became involved with native women's issues. That's when I became identified as an agitator. We challenged the status quo and the native men perceived us as a threat. The chiefs resented Indian women trying to organize and change their lives.

In those days, I'd attend meetings and then realize that the issues under discussion were totally foreign to me. When the women talked about pay equity, I'd say it wasn't an issue for native women. Since we couldn't get jobs, our concern was surviving from one welfare cheque to another—not that we wanted to be on welfare, but we couldn't find employment. These meetings were often held in luxury hotels and were attended by well-dressed people, so I wore jeans as a statement. In some ways, I guess, I had a martyr complex.

When I became involved with the Native Women's Association of Canada, which is a national organization, I started travelling a lot. After graduation I only accepted short-term-work projects so I could remain flexible enough to travel. In other words, I did my paid work so I could work for free. I was lucky because I had good friends who helped with my son and the association provided a supplement for child care. But after a couple of years my son said, "Look, mom, I need a mother." At that point I realized he was more important than my work. So when my term was completed, I resigned from my position.

Although I didn't get paid, my volunteer work really helped my career. It raised my consciousness and gave me the opportunity to see the concerns of native women from many different perspectives. My career path also fell into the pattern of working with native people. I later worked as a cultural-liaison worker and an employment counsellor for native people.

When I took a position with the federal government, my stereotypes about white people were thrown out the window, once again. My supervisor was an outstanding mentor: fair, honest, flexible, an ideal boss. Sixteen months ago, I got the first of my jobs which wasn't in a special programme, which is where visible minority or native groups are usually tokenized.

I'm very consciously acquiring skills that will help my community when self-government becomes a reality and we'll have to devise alternatives to the band-council system. I know there will always be—in bureaucratese, which is another language I've learned—"interface" between community and government. That means people who are, essentially, translators will always be necessary to ensure that people understand each other's messages. The role involves translating not just Micmac into English, but the bureaucracy to native people.

I sometimes wonder how I survived. I think I was helped by the current renaissance among native people. I believe very strongly in spirituality and my own spirituality as a Micmac woman. I also believe that the Creator has put me on the world for a reason and this belief has affected my work.

Gene Errington
Vancouver, British Columbia

"I've always managed to integrate politics into work. That means
I've always been able to be committed to what I'm doing,
although it doesn't mean it's always been easy."

*Gene Errington began her career as a social worker and became an activist for
women's equality in the late 1960s. She is now working with the Attorney
General's Office in British Columbia.*

I became a social worker because I thought I could change things, but after
about five years I realized it just patched things up. So, like many social
workers, I left the profession. I returned to university to study sociology in
1967, just as the women's movement was hitting the campuses.

The University of British Columbia had the first women's programme
in Canada and, like a lot of women, once I became aware of feminist issues,
I never looked back. When the Royal Commission on the Status of Women
released its report in 1970, Vancouver Status of Women was formed to
implement some of the recommendations. Rosemary Brown became the
first ombudsman, and when she ran politically in 1972, I took over. It was
only a part-time job, but it was so absorbing I couldn't see the point in
sociology, although I forced myself to finish my degree so I wouldn't have
a blank year on my résumé.

I think it's fair to say that this experience changed my life. We were
working on Local Initiatives Project (LIP) grants, which the federal government was handing out by the dozens. Suddenly, everything seemed possible. We'd discover problems, and sincerely believed that once we took this
information to the government, things would change.

In those days feminism was novel, so we received a lot of media attention. We were very energetic and full of hope. We used to do things like
barging into restaurants where claims of sexual harassment had been made,
saying, "We're funded by the federal government and we demand...." We
had no right to do that, of course, other than a moral right, but it boosted
our self-confidence. We thought we were capable of anything and we
supported each other in this belief.

Virtually every one of us went on to do things we never imagined we'd do. One year, three women in our group ran for political office. Next it became trendy to get women on things like boards and committees, which we did. When I look at my résumé, I can't believe the number of boards I sat on.

I was appointed status of women co-ordinator for the provincial government, where I learned about the power of the bureaucracy. The bureaucrats determine where things will go and in many ways politicians are incidental—like in the British television show, "Yes, Minister." Basically, that experience taught me that our perceived opportunity to change things was more of an opportunity to learn how they worked.

Our political skills were honed by the climate of affluence. Unlike the American women's movement, we had substantial government funding. In some ways, though, the Americans might be stronger because they never received grants. Government puts its money into things and then co-opts them. Sure enough, over the years, we began to notice that as they changed the criteria for getting money, we changed our work to meet the criteria. In the process we became less and less radical.

But the first few years were very exciting. When we began, for instance, we had no idea that wife-battering existed. Women would ask us about family court, and we'd only learn they were being battered after talking with them. It was quite shocking to discover the extent of this violence. Although it gave us the sense we were pioneers, the intensity caused some women to burn out.

For awhile I worked in Ottawa for Status of Women, then I got a job with the B.C. region of the Canadian Union of Public Employees, where I stayed for eight years. The union was a male world, but it had a philosophy of fairness that could be used to bring women's issues forward. When I started, women were interested in tough issues like equal pay and sexual harassment, forming a women's committee and so on. But in an economic downturn, people entrench and they focus on keeping their jobs. The current economic reality makes it particularly important to be able to look back on that sense of freedom we used to have. Nobody was restricting us in any way, which I don't feel is true for women today.

Now I'm acting executive director of the newly formed community-justice branch of the attorney general. It's responsible for wife assault, victim-assistance programmes, legal aid and so on. This is a real challenge and will take everything I've learned to do it right.

One of my friends, who has always made a living at the grant-type women's movement, can't understand why people like me would work for

the government. This really surprises me. I've always believed we are trying to get our ideas institutionalized, whereas she feels institutions swal-
low them up. That's the dilemma: do you stay on the outside and remain
pure, or do you try to accomplish something by working from within?

I've spent a lot of time trying to understand how organizations work.
Whenever I've gone into a job, other women have said, "I'm really glad
you're here. Now something is going to happen." That's been a tremendous challenge, as well as a burden. Sometimes you can't achieve your goals
and that can be pretty draining.

Like many women of her generation, my mother married and stayed
at home, but I think she would have liked a job outside the home. She died
before I got involved in the women's movement, but I often wish I could
talk to her about it. I know it gave me something that I couldn't get from,
say, social work or teaching. It gave me a community of women and the
sense that together we were discovering something new.

Tracey Jones
Halifax, Nova Scotia

" I 'm 31 years old and having so much responsibility on the job can be scary when you're that young ."

Tracey Jones graduated from Dalhousie Library School in 1986, and has been running the North Branch Library in Halifax for the past four years.

I originally wanted to be a doctor so I did a science degree in preparation for medicine. But I wasn't that great at science. I had been working part time at North Branch Library, which is a very mentoring place, since I was 16 and the people there asked if I'd be interested in going to library school. To this day, I am the only indigenous black Nova Scotian who has graduated from Dalhousie Library School, although a few black immigrants have received degrees there.

Once I became a librarian, I loved it. I worked my way up from student to library assistant, and then to children's librarian. At that point, the branch head got sick and they asked me to fill in for him for a year. When he died, I got the job. I was only 27, so I moved pretty quickly.

I spent my first three years getting the branch in order. There was a lot of staff turnover and unhappiness because people were dealing with the death of a very powerful person. This is the first year they've been able to mention his name without crying.

As I said, I was a children's librarian before I became an administrator and probably the biggest drawback to this job is that my heart is in children's services. Black children's literature is my speciality. Leaving that to become an administrator—telling people what to do, directing work, doing budgets, dealing with renovations and so on—has taken a lot of the joy out of my work. As a branch head I still do things with children, but it's not the same as working with them on a daily basis.

I've never regretted becoming a librarian. This library is very community based. The kids play here and people gather around the entrance. I know everybody and I enjoy being able to shape what's happening in the neighbourhood. When we had the so-called rioting in 1991, I came into work at 8 a.m., and there were people waiting for me to open the doors so they could come into the auditorium and follow the events.

Because of our location, North Branch has had to address issues of race and race relations. We've had to look at how we reflect the community we serve—and at what we have on our shelves—do people really want poems by Shakespeare or do they want more contemporary black writers? Right now I'm looking at establishing a Vietnamese outreach position to serve the large Vietnamese community in the neighbourhood.

I'm so involved with my job that my five-year-old son often comes with me to community meetings. In that sense it's not hard to juggle a child and a career. He was raised to be very independent. When he was only five days old, he attended his first meeting and he's been coming with me ever since.

It's difficult when there's an administrative crunch and I have to be out of here by 4:30 to pick him up by 5:30 because that's when day care closes. I'm being pulled in different directions. There are times when I wish I only worked half days because I'd like to spend the other half with him. I miss being there, but I don't miss it enough to give up work or go to a job-sharing position. He's got enough support to know he's not being ignored, and if he felt he was, he'd let me know. We also have a large extended family so there's always somebody to take care of him.

I've had problems with people having to find their space around me because I'm very outspoken. They may have racist tendencies, I don't know. Just after I graduated, I went to work in a library where I was the only black person on staff, and things started getting tense. It's not overt racism, it's the Nova Scotia kind: quiet. My immediate supervisor was away, so I hauled everybody in for a meeting and said, "If you've got a problem with me, let's deal with it. I don't like the whispering, but I want to make it clear, I'm not going anywhere. You'll be the ones to leave." That cleared the air.

Because everybody else in a comparable position has 10 or 20 years on me, I have to be really cocky and willing to take chances. I get shaken up every once in awhile, then I go away, lick my wounds and come out fighting. It can be rough when the community places heavy demands on you and you can't always meet them.

I'm actually quite shy except when speaking about those things I feel strongly about. I get my confidence from my parents. We were raised to believe there was nothing we couldn't do. Not all of my siblings have gone to university, but we all feel very good about what we do.

As much as I love my work, I've been in this system for 15 years and I think it may be time to start looking at other options. If I had my druthers, in five years I'd be running a black resource centre—a strictly black programme dealing with anti-racism education.

Regina Ash
St. John's, Newfoundland

"**Y**ou can get all the credentials in the world and in the end it doesn't come down to what you've accomplished and what you can do, but your disability."

Shortly after graduating from Memorial University in 1989, Regina Ash entered the work force. She's currently a community-development officer in a transition centre for people with disabilities.

When I started working, I was almost 23 and still had very little work experience in the sense of taking home a pay cheque every two weeks. I think many women with disabilities find themselves in a similar situation. We tend to do a lot of volunteer work but not much paid work.

I'm totally blind and have been since birth, but I don't spend much time thinking about the hardships I overcame. Dealing with them was something I had to do. I have very loving and supportive parents, and I'm thankful they sent me away to school in Halifax, although it was difficult for them. I left when I was six and only came home at Christmas and in the summer.

I returned home to attend university in St. John's, but getting a post-secondary education was a big struggle because most of the textbooks weren't available in braille or on tape. I was usually six weeks to two months behind the other students.

My first job was in this transition centre which helps people with disabilities to learn living skills. I've worked here for four years, off and on, on various contracts, as funding became available. Making presentations to various committees and arranging workshops is a big part of what I do.

I still don't have a permanent position. I operate from grant to grant, on contract. I'd like something permanent, but given the realities of Newfoundland, I'm lucky to have anything at all.

There's no doubt I've experienced discrimination in interviews. I don't put my disability on my covering letter or in my résumé, but if you look at my résumé—the kinds of jobs I've had and the volunteer organizations I've been involved with—you could probably guess. If I get called in for an interview, I tell them I have a disability, and if I sense discomfort, I bring it up myself.

Once I applied for a job with a transition house for battered women, teaching literacy skills to children. The three female interviewers asked about my disability because they were worried I'd make the other women uncomfortable. They wanted to know how I'd deal with that.

I was surprised. They never looked at me as a person or considered whether I could do the job. Instead, they focused on the fear that I might make other people uncomfortable. That hurt more because it was women.

Often the interview comes down to: Can we accommodate this person's disability? I need two basic things to do my work. The first is a speech-synthesized computer with a regular keyboard which repeats what I'm putting on the screen. The second is reading material on tape or transcribed into braille. That's the biggest barrier. There's a reading machine that reads printed documents, but it won't read newspaper columns or handwriting, and it costs $9,000. What company, especially in the private sector, will pay $9,000 for a piece of equipment when they can hire somebody who has sight and doesn't need this expensive machine?

In my current position, I have a speech-synthesized computer and the night staff reads material onto tape for me when they don't have anything else to do. This often results in delays that make it difficult for me to get material when I need it. It's very difficult to convince people that my disability isn't a barrier. It doesn't matter that I'm a university graduate and that I've been able to absorb vast amounts of printed material. If you give me a 50-page document, I can't read it in that form. In some ways, being blind is like being illiterate.

Women with disabilities have problems in the workplace that extend beyond their jobs. We are, for instance, far more likely to be victims of violence than women without disabilities. That's why I pay someone to drive me back and forth to work. It's more expensive than the bus, but I don't feel comfortable with public transportation. Also, I don't walk by myself at night. Fortunately, I haven't experienced violence, but the fear is always there. You just don't acknowledge it because if you let it override you, you'd never do anything.

Physical accessibility is another concern. My biggest problem is elevators—it's hard to know what floor I'm at. Often there will be a braille number I can check on the door frame just as I step out, but this holds people up. If it's the wrong floor I have to get back in and hope I don't get squashed by the doors. In unfamiliar buildings, I don't know basic things like where the emergency exits are located.

The point is not equality, it's equity. Sometimes we need accommodation in order to be like everybody else.

I'm very involved in volunteer work. Not only do I enjoy it, I feel guilty if I don't do it. If you have a disability, you're expected to be out advocating because so many changes are necessary. But I've almost reached the point where I'm saying, no more. I need time for myself and my personal life.

Even though I enjoy my work, it's not my life. It brings in money and gives me a sense of independence, but I need other things. My parents are very important to me and they're getting older. I have two cats. I also have a boyfriend who is attending law school. This summer I'm spending time with him and working on that relationship.

Right now I'm going through a transition. I think I want to work, to earn money and to have financial security. But I don't think I want a career. You have to put your life on hold for a career and I don't want to do that.

I'm not sure where I'd like to be in five years. I guess like a lot of women I'd like to be married and have children. If I did that, I'm not sure I'd work outside the home apart from volunteering, because juggling all the roles would take too much energy. I don't think a woman can be all three things, wife, mother and worker, and still have something left for herself. Today, women are expected to do so much that many have lost knowing who they are.

6

Manufacturing, Construction and Engineering

Madeleine Parent
Montreal, Quebec

"Life is a constant struggle, especially for underprivileged women seeking justice, and I want to continue to be part of their struggle."

Since first becoming an activist while a student at McGill in the late 1930s, Madeleine Parent has had a long and distinguished career as a labour organizer and a champion of social justice.

While I was at McGill, I became involved in the Canadian Students' Assembly. We were fighting for government scholarships for students whose families couldn't afford to send them to university. At that time, higher education was a privilege that children from poor families were denied. We also had a battle to ensure that our platform included women, because it was often said that women shouldn't be educated since they would only get married.

Once the war started, there was a backlash against our work because it was thought we were taking money away from the war effort. Such strong opposition to students who were trying to help poor people made me think more than education was involved. My desire to get to the essence of this reaction led me in the direction of labour organizing.

I wanted to organize in factories where women were employed. One of my friends had a sister, Lea Roback, who was working for the International Ladies' Garment Workers Union. She took on male bureaucrats in the union who discriminated against the women members. In the garment industries, male employees were in the minority and companies could afford to pay them a little more at no great cost. They made their profit on the poorly paid work of the women who comprised about 76 per cent of their employees. Some unions struck deals with management and male workers at the expense of women.

On May 1, 1942, I started working at the War Labour Organizing Committee in Montreal, helping to recruit workers in the munitions industry. Some months after the campaign began, Kent Rowley, a young organizer, argued that we should seize the moment to organize the domestic industries where many women worked and their exploitation was well established. Some of the men were reluctant. They feared women might become a force in the unions and they didn't want their power threatened.

I got involved in the debate and joined Kent, working in the cotton mills, where generations of women had struggled against injustice. In those days children, sometimes as young as 10, worked in the mills. They supported women's efforts to organize because the women had always protected them from abuse by employers.

The first successful women's strike in Quebec occurred in 1937, when a few thousand ladies' garment workers struck the dressmaking shops in Montreal and won, in the face of virulent opposition by the Catholic church. When we were organizing in the 1940s, parish priests delivered sermons on women's place being in the home. Apparently, it was okay for women to work in factories, so long as they didn't stand up for their rights.

Equal pay for equal work was a priority and we won that in the 1946 strike of 6,000 cotton-mill workers. Seniority was another issue. Women understood that with seniority, they would not be fired or otherwise punished by a boss when they refused his sexual advances. Starting with the first cotton-mill workers meeting I attended in Valleyfield in 1942, I learned that sexual harassment was a serious problem. When a woman left work to have a child, she lost all rights to her job. If she hadn't given in to sexual harassment, her request to return to work was more likely to be rejected.

As a unionist, I was also challenged because of my sex. In the mid-1940s, I was the first woman elected to the executive of the Montreal Trades and Labour Council. Some men argued that I shouldn't be on the executive because a couple of the officers were drunk at the meetings and used bad language. I replied that that was their problem, not mine.

Very early on, I realized that if I was going to commit myself to a fight for social justice, I'd have to cut myself off from my background—not from my parents, but from my former convent friends and the milieu in which I'd been raised. There was so much to be done; it would have been too much to juggle all the contradictions between my middle-class background and the problems of less fortunate workers. So I chose to live a working-class life.

By 1945–46, Quebec Premier Duplessis and his friends were determined that gains made by organized working people during the war—particularly women—would be taken away. There were layoffs when the war ended and, in most cases, women had to go. Returning veterans were given the jobs that men had done before the war. And certain practices that had helped women working in war plants, such as day-care centres, were abandoned.

The government attack on unions was ferocious. Duplessis and his friends used strike-breakers, police, the courts and jail as weapons to break the will of the working people. Kent Rowley, whom I married in 1953, served a couple of jail sentences, and for nine years, beginning in 1946, I was under charges.

During the 1947 strike of Ayer's Woollen Mill workers in Lachute, Quebec, I was charged with "seditious conspiracy" and detained many times in jail. I was sentenced to two years, but was finally acquitted in another trial in 1955, as was Kent.

The dangers involved in union organizing in those times and the ongoing nature of the struggle for decent working conditions in the textile mills are two of the reasons why I didn't have children. Being in and out of court and jail for over nine years was not conducive to bringing a baby into the world. When that ordeal ended, I was almost 38 and had anaemia, which took over a year to cure. Also, if I had born a child while faced with jail under Duplessis, he would have used the situation to torture my parents. They didn't agree with my ideas, but they stood up to a lot of pressure from the premier on my behalf. If a baby had been involved, it would have been too much for them to take.

In 1983, when I was 65, I retired from my union position. I've become actively involved as a volunteer in the women's movement in support of aboriginal women and women of other minority groups. I also work with unions and with community-based organizations continuing the struggle for social justice.

Cathy Mulroy
Sudbury, Ontario

"I put up with sexual harassment because I didn't know I had a choice. Who would stand up for us? In those days, the union didn't know anything about this kind of stuff. They thought it was an acceptable way to treat women."

Cathy Mulroy started working at the International Nickel Company (INCO) in 1974 when she was 19. At the time of this interview, she was on workers' compensation.

One day I heard Prime Minister Trudeau on the radio, announcing INCO would be hiring women. The next morning I went down and got a job as an hourly rated production and maintenance worker. My feet were so small my workboots had to be custom-made.

I had a Grade 8 education and had worked at Canadian Tire as a clerk. I was married, with a three-year-old son. Money was the big motivation. At INCO I was earning much more than I would at any woman's job and the benefits were good. I have to admit, though, I didn't have a clue about what I was getting into.

My first job was in the anode. It was a terrible place: fire, furnaces, cranes and catwalks. Molten metal is poured into casting wheels that hold about 700 pounds each. It was dirty, dangerous work, and a woman who started a couple of years after me was killed. The bolts hadn't been properly screwed onto the bottom of the cage, and when she was hoisted up, it collapsed and she fell out. Her drill, which was huge, fell on top of her head and killed her instantly.

The social aspect was equally difficult. I started work with two other women and the men didn't want any of us to be there. Neither did their wives. When you went for a beer with the guys because you were trying to become one of the group, a wife was likely to call and ask your husband if he knew his wife was out with her spouse. My husband would answer, "Yes, lady, yours and 12 other men."

You had to prove yourself over and over again. When I first started, I was sweeping the floor. There's a wrist action that keeps the dust low, but no one trained us. The man on the furnace gave us a blast. When I challenged him, his response was that he was going to get his sister, who was a big woman, to "beat the shit out of me."

One boss on the midnight shift regularly ordered me to move a chain. When I moved it to where he wanted, he'd then say he changed his mind and tell me to put it back. I asked what the purpose of all this was, and he just said, "I'm the boss." The men complained that we were taking their jobs, and once a foreman tried to run me off the road.

At first the sexual harassment was terrible. For instance, they wrote on the wall: "Cathy is a cock-teaser." The first time I went into the lunch-room I couldn't eat because it was filthy and it stunk. I was experiencing nausea—I didn't know it, but I was pregnant—so I ate lunch on the railroad tracks with one of the guys. I got hauled in by the foreman who told me that if I valued my reputation, I wouldn't do things like that. The men used to tell us we were stupid, too, but after awhile it became the norm, part of the way we worked.

About a month after I started, I had an accident. I was working with molten copper moulds that weighed 700 pounds, and the hoist chain broke and hit me. They took me to the hospital, and when they did a blood test, they discovered I was pregnant.

I was told to discuss this with the union, but I didn't know what the union was. Somebody explained that's where those deductions on my pay-cheque were going. The union didn't know what to do with me because they'd never had a pregnant worker before. My pregnancy meant they couldn't take X-rays, so they didn't know how serious my injury was. Since they couldn't put me back to work, they decided to put me on compensation until I had the baby. I'd been hit in the stomach, among other places, so the pregnancy was difficult.

In 1978, we went on strike and that was when my husband and I separated. I was left with the kids, the expenses and I was making $36 a week strike pay. I needed to make money to survive so I approached a wholesaler and asked if I could sell meat. That got us through the 8½ months of the strike.

In many ways the strike was the best time of my life. It was my blossoming and I wouldn't change a thing. I had married at 16 and always had to answer to my husband, who used to make a point of telling me how stupid I was because I have a form of dyslexia. By the age of 23, I had left my teen years behind to become a woman. That experience helped me discover who I was. I learned I didn't have to answer to anybody.

About 10 years ago, I was stalked. I'm 99 per cent sure it was a boss from a different department, because it started after I turned him down and stopped when he was transferred to another city. He used to ask me out on dates and once sent flowers to my house, anonymously. A day or so after the flowers arrived, he asked me if I liked them. I told him I wouldn't accept gifts from him because he was married. He told me to come to his office.

I went to see him on my break and he tried to shut the door. I said, "Leave it open. You shouldn't send me flowers."

His response was, "Oh yeah, who's going to stop me?"

I suggested that his wife might like them, but he said I couldn't prove he'd sent them. "Maybe she knows your handwriting," I said, showing him the little card. He had it all planned. He said he'd claim I was after him, and she wouldn't believe me. I would have looked like a real idiot for reporting it, so I didn't.

For awhile he watched me from the catwalk when I was working in the cage, filling the moulds. It was an awful feeling because I was trapped and couldn't go anywhere. Another time, he followed me to a doctor's appointment and tried to give me some brass candle holders. I suggested we go into a restaurant to talk because it was full of people and I thought I might be able to reason with him. I told him I didn't want him calling, I didn't want his presents, and if he ever bothered me again, I'd tell his wife. He just sat there and said nothing because, of course, it was full of people.

That's when the obscene phone calls started. They were gross and some of the statements involved my present, second husband, whom I had just started dating. Only a few people knew I was seeing him, but this guy did because I told him as part of my technique for trying to get him off my back. One day, somebody filled up my driveway with industrial staples and I ended up with four flat tires. Not long after that, the man who I suspected was transferred and it all stopped. I heard through the grapevine that I wasn't the only woman he harassed.

In 1986, I had a serious injury and left the anode. I slipped on a mud-covered walkway and slid into some steel filters with hubs in the middle. Part of the hub caught my back and the other broke my rib.

That changed my life. I couldn't go on the hoist anymore, or do the jobs I used to do. I didn't want to quit totally because I was very involved in first-aid competitions. So I did a modified job until my team lost. After that, they put me on compensation.

I went back to work as a janitor, but I wasn't happy. Overall, I had liked working with the men. I had earned their respect during the strike because they could see I was a real go-getter. I missed their honesty and the sense of group solidarity. We'd have our fights and sometimes they'd still make references to the fact that I was a woman, but when you work with hard hats, you form a real bond. The risk taking is part of it. You're always listening. Much of the time the noises are all you have to go on—the furnace or the machines don't sound right—and having to be constantly in tune creates cohesion among the workers.

I'm the kind of person who wants to do a job the best I can. My boss said if INCO can use you in other ways, they will, but you'll have to go back to school. So I did. I took computers. I studied hard and aced it, but I didn't like it. I ended up teaching first aid and cardiopulmonary resuscitation, which I loved, but I ran into real problems with the men I worked with. They tried to sabotage me in different ways. They excluded me from meetings and wouldn't allow me to receive in-coming phone calls. Finally, they went to management and basically said, "She's trying too hard to change things. Get rid of her." And they did. They sent me home.

This time I'm not fighting by myself. They had no right to do what they did. I'm talking to everyone. I've written letters to the president. I've gone to the human-rights commission. After 20 years, we're still not people. We're only women.

Charlene Bahry
Vancouver, British Columbia

"The glass ceiling in that company is so low, you have to walk around bent over."

After working in drafting for several years, Charlene Bahry returned to school and, in 1987, graduated as a chemical engineer from the University of British Columbia. Since university, she's been laid off twice. At the time of this interview, she was actively seeking work as an engineer.

I went into drafting because my father was a builder and I enjoyed helping him with his work. I was very artistic, but I knew there was no money in art, so I got a diploma in architectural and structural drafting.

I started working as a draftsman in an engineering firm and did quite well. As my confidence developed, I began to think I could do much more. One day my boss asked about my long-term plans and I said I'd really like to go back to school, although I couldn't afford it because I had two young children. He talked to some board members and the firm agreed to pay my books and tuition. I thought a degree would create opportunities because there wasn't much decision-making power in drafting.

In 1983, I enrolled in chemical engineering at UBC. Chemical engineering is smaller than the other disciplines and we had the highest percentage of women—seven women and 65 men. I was about 10 years older than most of the other students and was there to learn, so I wasn't into the social stuff. Even so, I was quite disillusioned. University seemed like an extension of high school. Many people didn't seem to know why they were there. It was something their parents had suggested they do.

The climate was very hostile, as well. The engineering magazine was slanderous towards women, natives and homosexuals. Once I wore a red sweatshirt to school and was called a "commie." Another group of lab partners wouldn't let me get involved in an experiment and made me wash the glassware afterwards. Things like that were quite common.

Sexism also permeated the teaching. For instance, the professors tended to give examples referring to football fields or other dimensions they assumed the men would be familiar with. I had no idea of the size of a football field because I'd never seen one. It was often hard to grasp the concepts when the explanations were directed towards masculine areas of knowledge.

The extracurricular activities were male as well, and women's role was to stand on the sidelines and cheer the guys on. This really made me angry! Our student fees funded these activities which I never felt part of. Finally, I just wanted to acquire the necessary knowledge and get the hell out of there so I could work in the real world.

When I graduated in 1987, I got a job with the company that sponsored me. I believed it would be an improvement over university since the people were more mature—the average age was probably 50 plus. I also felt I'd be accepted on how well I did my work. But gradually, I realized my colleagues were just older versions of the engineering students.

I was accepted as a draftsman, but they seemed uncomfortable with me as an engineer. I had to keep pushing and asking for work. All the men were being sent on seminars and groomed for positions, but I wasn't. At first I thought it might be my imagination. I spoke to my boss who said I was too impatient. "If I were a man, you'd call me ambitious," I responded. He didn't appreciate that.

Some of the men recognized my work and treated me like an equal, but in their minds they differentiated me from other women. The message was, "You're not one of them, Charlene." If you're willing to play the game and make sexist remarks like they do, you can be one of the boys. To conform to their expectations, I'd have to live two separate lives, one at work and another after hours which they'd never see. I couldn't do that. I wanted to be treated as an equal, and as a woman.

Some were uncomfortable because they didn't know where I fit. I wasn't a wife or support staff, unlike the other women in the firm, most of whom were very young. I'd often advise the secretaries not to do certain things without realizing how strong an impact I was having. The men realized they couldn't call them "the little girl up front" any more.

Even though I love my work, it's very lonely. You don't meet many other female engineers so you tend to go for lunch and pair off with the secretaries and the receptionists. That's deadly. The men see you as a member of that subservient group and start giving you filing, copying and so on.

After two years, I was laid off. I heard through the grapevine that the fellow who let me go found me threatening—possibly because I was good at bringing business into the firm.

It took 18 months to find another job even though my letters of reference were very good. Again, I'm pretty sure it was because of my sex. Once, a male friend and I applied for the same job. He was interviewed after me and mentioned to the interviewer that the company hired women. The fellow smiled and said, "Oh, no. We just interview them so they can't say we're discriminating."

I found another job at an engineering firm, but I've recently been laid off. It was a systematic lay off. They were assigning my work to other people.

I feel I need a mentor, but there aren't any. The mentoring groups that exist serve new people coming into the profession. I know only one established female engineer, and she won't acknowledge there are problems because she feels she's in a good position and doesn't want to rock the boat. I, too, recognize I have to be concerned about how much I complain because it's a small world.

Every single day is a struggle for me in this profession. Sometimes I get very tired and wonder if I should continue. Occasionally, I think I'm going crazy, but every now and again I come across an article that parrots what I'm experiencing, so I know it isn't me.

I have two awards from the Association of Professional Engineers and good references. I keep wondering why I'm hitting this wall. I'm actively job-seeking and I'm thinking positively. I think I'll get a job more quickly this time because I've figured out how to do it, which is something they don't teach you in school. I joined a job club last year. They said my résumé and my covering letters were good and I interviewed well on the video. I get lots of interviews—I try to set up at least one a day.

The other women in my class at university have jobs, but most are working outside of engineering. One is a research scientist, another sells insurance. I'm unusual because I went into traditional engineering. But that's what I want to do.

For a while, I served on the executive of the British Columbia Association of Professional Engineers. Prior to the incident in Montreal, where women engineering students were killed, I was pressuring to establish a committee to deal with women's issues, such as sexual harassment. The association hummed and hawed and concluded that because women were such a small segment—about 3 per cent—we didn't merit a group. After Montreal, they couldn't ignore the problems any longer.

I know things will get better as the number of women engineers increases, but what about now, what about me? Given my experience, I wouldn't encourage women to enter the profession. I think we're back where other professions were 20 years ago.

Jean Holyk
Thunder Bay, Ontario

"I felt my work at Can Car was important. We believed we were part of the war effort and that gave us a sense of pride."

During the war, Jean Holyk worked at the Canada Car plant in Fort William, Ontario. Afterwards, she trained as a hairdresser, then left the work force to raise her family. In 1972, she retrained as a registered nursing assistant and retired in 1984.

In 1942 I worked in the inspection department of the war plant at Canada Car in Fort William. It was a pretty good job because I didn't experience the occupational hazards that some of the workers did—for instance, having their hair caught in machinery or working with noxious chemicals.

I was in my 20s and it was a tremendous opportunity. Before the war I worked shifts in a restaurant for $5 a week. They couldn't afford to pay staff for the whole day so you had to work the lunch shift, go home and return for dinner. Sometimes you even had to wash dishes. Those were the kinds of jobs that were available for girls like me.

My parents were immigrants from Ukraine and I can see now how the educational system discriminated against us. During the Depression, my dad could only find work three days a week. On the principal's advice, the girls who lived at the poverty level were streamlined into home economics. It was a tough sewing course and my mother thought I might make a living sewing for somebody. But it didn't work that way and, of course, there were no factories in Port Arthur with sewing jobs. So I went to work in a restaurant at a very low wage.

In a way the war was a positive experience. Even though I was brought up in a progressive atmosphere and consider myself a pacifist, I never would have been able to earn as much money under any other circumstances. We retrained for a couple of weeks, and I went from $5 a week at the restaurant to 78 cents an hour at Can Car. My father, who had been working for more than 20 years, was making less than that in the mill.

They needed women to work because the men had joined up. I enjoyed working with the other women and learning about their lives. In those days, a lot of girls got married because they couldn't continue living at home with their parents and they couldn't get jobs. They called it "love."

I joined the union—the aircraft local of the Canadian Auto Workers'—and that made me a great believer in their importance. When the war ended, I worked with the union and the Unemployment Insurance Commission, doing paperwork for the people who were laid off. I was told to make sure that everyone listed two occupations—a first choice and a second, which meant, in my case, for instance, that I could be forced to go back to working in a restaurant for far less money than I had been earning at Can Car. I advised people to list only one occupation and, after two weeks, was relieved of my duties.

Rather than returning to waitressing, I took a hairdressing course with the money I had saved. I soon realized that hairdressing wasn't for me. It's a substanceless job. I think women pay too much attention to how they look rather than developing skills and intelligence.

I didn't have to worry about hairdressing for too long because I got married and had four children, which put me out of the labour force. I didn't want a lot of material things—just a livelihood—but even to achieve that my husband, who was a barber, had to drive a taxi part time in the evenings. There was no possibility of my working because there was no day care. Once my youngest child was in high school, I got a part-time job in an office.

In 1972, I decided to retrain again. I took a course to be a nurses' aid and went to work in a hospital. I was 52 when I started and I stayed for 12 years, until I retired. It was very interesting and it provided a better livelihood than office work, although there was continual bargaining and we were always short-staffed. I worked with handicapped children, which was very rewarding.

Even though I don't have an education, I've never stopped learning. I belong to political and cultural organizations. My volunteer work has allowed me to grow, but when my husband was very ill, I couldn't get out as much as I wanted. I worked all day and cared for him in the evenings.

I've had an interesting life, but I wish I had been able to study something like psychology. When I worked with the children, I realized how much it interested me.

Anonymous
Ottawa, Ontario

"If I differentiate myself from any of my male colleagues, it's usually in my approach to identifying and solving problems. I'm more open and less likely to pre-select solutions because I'm a better listener. I also see solutions in terms of implementation, which always brings people to bear. In other words, I'm a lot more holistic than the men I work with."

"Anonymous" is a 40-year-old engineer and a senior executive in the telecommunications industry.

I have a master's degree in engineering. I started in natural sciences, primarily out of a love of nature, and shifted orientation towards the end of my undergraduate degree, which meant I had to work double time to make up courses. My family on both sides were engineers, and my mother, who was very strong in math, wanted to be an engineer but was told that it wasn't appropriate for a woman. I think I originally discounted engineering for the reasons most women do. It's too hard, or it's not appropriate and engineers aren't very nice as a group.

I was attracted to the engineering programme at Stanford University because it didn't fit the stereotypes. They wanted generalists and emphasized the role of engineers as change agents since they believed that technical knowledge was the basis for orchestrating broader social change.

In most ways I enjoyed my time at Stanford. In 1978, after I graduated, I took a job with a consulting firm in Ottawa. That was a difficult transition: California versus Canada, West Coast versus East. The one thing that saved me were the people with whom I worked. They were all men, but they acted as my mentors and helped me to understand, among other things, that Canada is a more formal, structured and hierarchical environment than California.

For my first couple of years, I did contract work which was a great opportunity because I worked with various firms. One, in particular, had some high-profile and politically charged projects that were very ill-defined. They were trying to apply scientific methods to political decisions and I was having difficulty—not only with applying the models, but also with understanding the value of the process. I was pretty green and, in fairness, didn't figure things out fast enough for their satisfaction. So in a very short time I was out.

When you're young and you're struggling to find your place, being fired is very traumatic—particularly when you don't really understand why it happened. I was 23 and didn't have the skills to sort it out. Other people helped me to understand that I shouldn't shoulder all the blame, that the environment and the situation were responsible, too. But at the time, that was hard to grasp.

On the positive side, that experience helped me to understand that I have a predisposition to team work and need a supportive milieu, which didn't exist in that company. Now I've learned to trust my instincts and avoid environments where my sensibilities are out of place.

Anyway, I got a job with an oil company in Calgary, working in energy utilization. Over time, I moved from the technical side of things into managing technology. I worked in the field for a couple of years, as a technical supervisor, directing the process control, automation and instrumentation folks. It was tremendous experience, but I started to feel very alone. I was the only woman and pretty much the senior individual.

Around this time, computers were being introduced on a broad scale so there were many changes which I didn't feel were being made as effectively as they might. The problem wasn't in the technology, it was in the management of the technology. Although I didn't feel qualified to comment, I figured there must be a better way.

After three years in the field, I was also feeling the need to get back into the mainstream. I took a leave of absence and enrolled at the Harvard Business School. That was another tough transition. I'd been out of school for years and was pretty established. I pulled up my roots and went off to be a student with people who were quite a bit younger and, perhaps, a little more current than me.

Harvard certainly thrust me back into the mainstream. Like Stanford, it was very up to date—for instance, at least 25 per cent of the class was female. These places are training and developing the leaders of tomorrow, so they're very attuned to diversity and how to manage change.

At Harvard, they undo you and rebuild you, which is a pretty humiliating process. You think you've achieved things, but everybody else is at the top of their world, too, and 10 per cent of the class is going to fail. Suddenly, you're not as smart as you thought you were.

As a senior executive, one of my challenges is to provide the right insights.

Harvard helped to reinforce my perception that those insights have a strong human component—in fact, a stronger human component than most managers believe. So in that sense it reinforced my values and beliefs as a female.

After I left Harvard, I returned to Canada and moved into the computer-information technology field. Three years ago, I went into telecommunications, and I'm currently vice-president of strategic planning for a fairly large company. Our business environment is changing rapidly and I think my sensibilities as a woman make my job easier. I don't express that publicly, but I believe it strongly.

The challenges I face are, perhaps, more complex in the field of telecommunications than in any other setting I've been in. How do I apply a more holistic approach to this world, which has become functionalized and routinized over time? Although it's an opportune time to introduce new models, they're really struggling. It's not easier for me as a woman, it's just more comfortable because I'm less threatened by uncertainty.

I sometimes wonder if I'm being taken seriously and if I have the attention of our management team. I can't tell how well they're listening to me. In fairness, I don't know how much of that is being a woman, and how much it reflects their model of looking at the world, which is so narrow. I do know that to be heard you have to communicate in their terms, deal with their issues and present yourself in a manner that's consistent with their views. I think they're struggling with me as much as I am with them, because I'm introducing a different way of thinking.

I often walk into situations where I don't feel confident and I generally rely on my curiosity and interpersonal skills to help me make transitions. I think I got a lot of my confidence from being physically strong. I've always been athletic and I used guys as benchmarks for activities such as sport. It wasn't competition so much as a standard of performance I was trying to achieve.

I love to work with people and help them, so I've coached quite a bit and find that very satisfying. I think there's a strong correlation between the visioning and self-discipline of high performance sport and the business world. The discipline required to build a team, to keep your eye on the ball, to have a vision and execute it, parallels what's required to be successful in business.

I know I've been very, very privileged in terms of being able to self-select. Somebody said I'm heat-seeking—I tend to go after challenges. I'm not afraid to work and I get pleasure and enjoyment in accomplishment.

But I think I find working with people to achieve a common goal the most satisfying aspect of my career. That's probably what keeps me in corporate life.

Still, there's another, more introspective side to me and I have to keep my finger on that pulse or I lose my balance. I've come very close to losing it, twice—when I was fired and in another high-pressure situation. I won't let that happen again. I won't jeopardize my health or my happiness. It's not worth it.

I think women have a better basis for balance because they have to juggle so much. If I had a family, I don't think I would have gotten so out of whack. I couldn't have. I'd be divorced before I reached my physical limit which is probably what happened to me.

I haven't juggled a career and family, but I have sisters who do. When you have kids, they come first. The last two weekends I've skipped out of work early and asked for time off to help my sister whose kids, were sick. They're not my kids, but I'd die for them and they're more important than any job.

Many people have told me that I'll never have children if I keep working this hard, which I'm sort of waking up to. I'm not happy about that. I'm 40 and I think that birthday was a turning-point. Although I may be ready for another transition, I have a lifestyle that would make that difficult.

I've been told I send signals that I'm not interested in settling down. I put a lot into the job and I'm comfortable enough with myself that I don't have to seek people out, although I do have many wonderful friends. Often, I rejuvenate and get my energy back by not being social. The problem with that is if you don't seek people out, they won't seek you out.

I think I learned something extremely important from my mom. She had five kids, all of whom had different capabilities and interests. She figured out how to channel our energy so we wouldn't compete against each other. She's one of the most exceptional people I've known and is still a constant source of knowledge. Even though she never worked professionally, she's a wonderful contributor, so I'm not really worried about losing my title and position. Her whole point is that it doesn't really matter what you do. What matters more is how you do it.

So far in my work I've been able to enjoy the journey, although sometimes less so. It's very easy to get caught up in this world if you don't have a fairly good grounding in what's important for you. I don't think I'll fall prey to that, which I attribute to my female sensibility. It gives me a sense of who I am as a person, which my male colleagues often don't have.

Palma Polzi
Montreal, Quebec

"Speaking of women's liberation, I was born liberated."

Trained as a dressmaker in Italy, Palma Polzi got her first job in Canada in 1954. After staying home to raise her family, she worked at a day care, but when this closed in the mid-1980s, she lost her job. Now she's considering a job in retail.

When I first came to Montreal from Italy, I didn't speak any English or French, and a family friend took my mother and me door to door along Notre Dame looking for work. Finally, a restaurant offered me a job washing dishes. In Italy, my mother had a woman to wash clothes and do the heavy work, so it was awful to be told that I had to wash dishes. I said I'd die first and started to cry. My mother was embarrassed because her friend had found me work and I wouldn't do it.

My mother was a dressmaker and so was I. When I came here, it was natural to look for the same trade. I was told dressmakers in Canada made a lot of money, but I didn't realize they work differently. In Italy you start one dress and you finish it. In Canada, it's piece-work.

In 1954 my brother found me a job on St. Lawrence Boulevard where all the factories were located. The first day they sat me down in front of a pile of coats with a needle and a thimble and told me to work as fast as I could. I worked very hard. At one point a young man approached me and said, in broken Italian, "You Italian? Me.... *Parlare Italiana?*" So I said yes and he let out a long chain of bad Italian swear words. I was shocked.

It was November, and it was beginning to get very cold. I used to leave very early in the morning when it was dark, and it was dark again when I came home. For a long time I didn't even know what road I took.

I worked like a dog. I didn't have any friends. I tried to do the best I could and I made 40 cents an hour. After the coat factory, I went to work in a factory that made children's clothes and there I became friends with a few young Italian women. We had a tough woman supervisor who was very mean to us. She didn't want us to talk among ourselves, so we used to sing.

There were many young girls like me. The owner of the factory, or the big boss, pushed us to work harder and harder. I used to come home with a big headache every day. I worked from 8:00 to 5:00 with one hour for lunch and I ate at the machine. We didn't have any breaks. We couldn't even go to the bathroom.

We were expected to work very quickly. The more experienced workers were paid by the piece, so the more they worked, the more money they made. But since I was paid by the hour, I had to be fast because they wanted to save time. They would try to get me to finish by 4:00 so they could send me home with an hour's less pay.

After I finished work, I'd come home and do housework: rinse the clothes, wash the dishes and so on. If I wanted anything new to wear, I had to sew my own clothes. Once my brother rented a machine and I had to sew all the curtains for the house. That was normal. Because I was a girl, my parents were very strict. I loved to read, but I had to hide my books and read in the bathroom. My grandmother used to say that my father should never see me with idle hands.

I used to get very upset with my mother. If we were sitting at the table and my brothers asked for a glass of water, my mother would tell me to get it for them. "Why?" I'd ask. "I am younger, I am smaller." And my mother would say, "Because they are men." I recognized things like that at an early age.

When I arrived in Canada, at the age of 16, my parents thought I was too old to go to school. In Italy, I had loved school and had done well. But in Canada, because I was a woman, any money that was available for school was for my brothers, not for me, so I didn't learn any English.

I got married when I was 17 and my husband wanted me to stay home and keep house for him. I had my first child at 19, so for 18 years I only worked a few hours here and there, mostly seasonal work sewing for a boutique.

We spoke only Italian in the house until my oldest daughter was six. The school gave a medal to the brightest children, and one day the principal called and said, "Mrs. Polzi, your children would have a medal but their English is terrible. Why don't you turn on the radio and speak English to them?" So all of a sudden I made sure everything in my house was English. We had a little black-and-white television set and I started watching soap operas. That's how I learned English, because nobody told me I could take a course. Going from work to marriage at a very young age was tough because my husband is a typical Italian man. You're the little woman. You stay home, look pretty, cook good, keep the house and the children nice, and I do the real work. That was fine up to a certain point, and then it wasn't.

I mean how much cleaning can a woman do?

After my daughters got married, I met a friend who was working at the day-care centre at our church. I told her I was bored and wanted to go back to work. She suggested I apply for a job at the day-care centre. I said, "Children, me? No." She suggested I give it a try, so I said I would. She offered me pretty good money.

My first day, I had 26 two-year-olds. It was the first day for one little boy, as well, who was crying for his mummy. I was looking at him wishing I could cry, too. It was terrible. My head was pounding. I didn't know what to do with these children. I felt I couldn't hug them all.

But my friend encouraged me, and I met a kindergarten teacher from Italy, whose daughter was at the day care. She started giving me advice, and little by little, I began to enjoy the children.

At the day care, the parents were all working people, often one-parent families. It really broke my heart. The mothers would tell me not to call them, even if their child was sick, because there was nothing they could do. At that point my mother instinct took over. I acted like a mother, not a teacher, and that's what worked best for me.

By then I could read English and write a little. When I started reading, it took me a long time to read a book—I'd stay on the same page, trying to figure it out. But, gradually, I learned. I read books and developed my own programme. Then I took courses, at college. My English is terrible, but the teacher was very nice and I made progress. If I had taken three more courses, I would have had my equivalency certificate. But after I'd been there for 10 years, they closed the day care because the church needed the space.

I would have liked to pursue child care as a career, even though it was hard work. But I can't work in a day care because I don't have my certificate, which is required today. I might like to work in a boutique or a gift shop. That would be suitable for someone my age. I'd like to do something to get out of the house. I have a colourful family life, but my work life is pretty boring.

Kate Braid
Vancouver, British Columbia

"I was very naïve. Lots of guys I knew were going north and making buckets of money. I didn't know this was something women didn't do."

Kate Braid graduated from Mount Alison University in the late sixties with a BA and a secretarial certificate. She worked at a variety of "traditional" jobs, until 1975, when she was hired for her first "non-traditional" job in a sawmill. Since then she has worked mainly as a carpenter. She is also an educator, a broadcaster and, in 1991, published her first book of poems, Covering Rough Ground.

I graduated from Mount Alison University with a BA and a secretarial certificate, but I was a terrible secretary. I only had one secretarial job and they asked me to leave because I kept making disastrous mistakes.

After that, I remember my mother asking me what I wanted to do. This seemed very novel to me—working at what you wanted to do. I thought you had to pick from secretary, nurse or teacher. When I thought about it, I decided I'd really like to become a writer. My mother said, "Well, do it."

By great good fortune, in 1969, I got a job as assistant editor of an in-house publication. I was apologizing all over the place because I had no experience, but they said they liked to train people from scratch. It was quite wonderful. I left—this is embarrassing—because I started having an affair with one of the guys in the office. I was only 20 at the time and I didn't know any better. When they fired me, it didn't strike me as odd. Now I look back and think, why didn't they talk to us and ask which one was going to go?

So I left Montreal and came west to Vancouver. I went through a series of jobs that seemed to be appropriate for a woman: child-care worker, teacher's aid, youth-related things funded by LIP (Local Initiatives Programs) grants. But I kept having trouble with the structures. For instance, in the schools they didn't want me to wear long skirts. This was in the early 1970s when short skirts were fashionable. But I didn't like short skirts, so I left. I began to feel very lost.

Since I didn't know what to do, I decided to go back to school to get my MA, which meant I needed to earn money fast to pay my tuition. In those days, lots of guys were going north to make money, so I thought I'd give it a try. By a wonderful coincidence I met a woman who also wanted to work in the North. She had taught up there and she knew the culture. We looked for jobs in pulp mills, plywood mills, anything. We got as far as the fish cannery in Prince Rupert, but when they didn't have any work, we started back to Vancouver. Then we ran into someone who told us CN (Canadian National) was hiring people to lay tracks in Hazelton. This was the first definite opening we had heard of, so we went roaring up.

When we got there, the foreman was coming out of the office. He looked at us and laughed, "What are you girls doing here? Looking for work?"

When we said yes, his face changed. He said he wouldn't hire women because the work was too heavy. We replied that like the guys who probably found it heavy at first, we'd get used to it. Then he told us that we'd get blisters on our pretty hands. We said we didn't mind, we'd wear gloves. He said we'd be in the bush and we said that was okay. Finally, he said, "I'll think about it. Come back after work and I'll meet you in the bar."

We gave him a good hour in the bar, in the hope that the more beer he drank, the more agreeable he'd become, but he said no anyway. At that point we pulled out what we thought was our real heavy gun. We said, "This is illegal. CN has an affirmative-action policy. There's been a legal case and you have to hire women." He challenged us to file a complaint and finished by saying, "I'm not going into the bush with two women and 35 raging guys who are isolated for three weeks at a time. When they start drinking, I'll be spending every night in front of your door with a shotgun."

Later, I was thankful we didn't get the job. But at the time we were highly righteous. We were also very worried because this had seemed our one chance to find employment.

We started hitchhiking back and got a ride with a woman who said she was going to Fort St. James, where there was lots of work and they hired women. So we went to Fort St. James and started in the sawmill that day.

I worked there for the summer and fell absolutely in love with physical labour. It wasn't until years later that I realized my boss at the sawmill was way ahead of his time. In those days, nobody was hiring women to work in the mills. But this guy had clued in—his work force was half female. He told us he loved hiring women, and if he had his way, he'd only hire women because they worked harder, were never drunk or late, and if the machinery broke down, they grabbed a broom and started cleaning up. The other absolutely hilarious thing was that the women did all the heavy physical work. The men had the machine jobs and pushed the buttons.

Working in that mill was a revelation. I had never done physical work before. The boss put a hard hat on my head with Mickey Mouse ears, and stood my friend and me in front of a planer chain. That's where the lumber goes to be piled by hand. We jammed the chain a couple of times, but the people were quite nice. So I didn't feel like I was under a lot of pressure. I just felt like I had to survive physically.

On the first day, we started work at 10:00 and finished at 5:00. By 4:50, I was so tired I thought I was going to throw up. I wouldn't have made 30 seconds past the hour. That night I was in agony, my calves were so sore. This went on for about a week, then I started to feel incredibly good. My body began to tighten and I became trim and strong.

The mill was so noisy that you couldn't speak, so I got into the pure physicalness of the work and its rhythms, competing with myself to see how many pieces I could pile at one time. I was proud of how smoothly I could work.

It was a great experience. The whole crew was terrific. The lumber piler was a phenomenal worker who laced her tea with rye. She introduced me to a whole subculture of Northern women who are very outspoken, as tough as nails and very aware of their lack of privilege as women. The experience was a revelation to a protected city kid.

It was hard to find housing up there and we didn't want to spend any money, so we ended up living in an old cabin that somebody had dragged out of the bush. It was nothing but a frame and a roof: no doors, no windows—there wasn't even any tar paper on the walls so you could look through the cracks. We bought pots, a Coleman stove and lamp, and slept in sleeping bags. We carried our water from a stream down the road. We lived like that for about four months. I felt incredibly healthy and good, like everything was right in my world. I'd never felt that way in my work before—maybe even in my life.

At the end of the summer they asked me to stay on. I was giving the offer serious consideration, but one side of this so-called house was open to the weather and it started getting very cold in August. So I decided to leave.

I went back to Simon Fraser and did another semester before I realized that I didn't want to be an academic. So I dropped out and went to the Gulf Islands. By this time I was really getting worried because I was 30 years old and still didn't know what I was going to do when I grew up.

I started applying for all the jobs I could think of: barmaid, waitress, clerical worker and so on. But there were no "women's" jobs. One night,

I was telling someone that I'd have to leave the island because I couldn't find any work. He had just quit work as a carpenter, building the community centre, and he suggested I apply for his job. I thought he must be joking. All I'd ever built in my life was a flower box, and that was pretty rickety.

A couple of other guys said they'd lend me some tools. They also told me to lie about my experience, to say that I'd built other things. That was very useful information. So a couple of days later I showed up with all this borrowed gear and told the foreman that I had built houses up North. When he hired me, my life changed. I adored construction.

I was obviously not used to a construction site. I couldn't walk in the big boots without tripping, but I was hired as a labourer, which was perfect. As a labourer you get to watch what's going on, to learn how to handle and carry materials, to understand tools and vocabulary. When the job was over, one of the guys hired me as a helper and I worked with him for a year. He showed me all his books and stuff and talked me into doing an apprenticeship to become a qualified tradesperson.

About this time, I moved back to Vancouver to finish my MA. I had never heard of another woman doing the kind of work I was doing, and I was beginning to feel split. I'd go to parties and the guys would be talking about tools and the women would be talking about relationships, and it was like I was expected to choose sides. And I couldn't. So I decided to finish my degree and do my thesis on non-traditional work. Simon Fraser agreed and I travelled around the province talking to other women who were doing traditionally male jobs. That experience helped me to feel sane again.

Eventually, I became a journeyed carpenter. Having the skills to build things and to use tools made me feel very capable. And when it went right, I loved the camaraderie of being on a crew. It was also nice to work with people without having to talk to them. You never had to be nice, which is required with so-called women's jobs. You just had to hit the nail.

I also loved the money. When I started non-union construction work, I was already earning more than I had ever earned at a woman's job. But in 1981, when I joined the carpenters' union, my pay cheque went from $7 to $14 an hour. I couldn't believe I was worth that much. But I could see by looking around that I was working at least as hard as anyone else. That one pay cheque made me realize the scam that's going on with women. Why didn't they tell us how much fun this was and how much it paid?

Lots of guys hated the work, though, and they had trouble with the fact that I loved it. I remember the first time I built fly forms. These are prefabricated molds for pouring the concrete floors in high-rise buildings. The forms were aluminum, and as the crane lifted them, the sun glinted off them. I said to the guy beside me, "It's like an eagle," and he looked at me like I was crazy. But to me it was beautiful.

Working as a carpenter, I didn't have a lot of overtly hostile treatment. A lot of what happens is more like the ton of feathers. It's not the first guy or even the 10th or the 100th who says, "I've got to see you pick up a sheet of drywall." It's the 1000th time you hear it that you just want to pack it in. One of the reasons I eventually quit construction was that I became tired of proving myself. After 15 years I got fed up with having to show one more guy that I can carry a 2 × 10.

The construction culture is very different from women's culture, and when you walk in, it hits you in the face. Even the nicest men are part of it. They may not wish you ill, but they have a different value system, speak a different language, learn in a different way, and you never really fit.

After I left carpentry, I taught at the British Columbia Institute of Technology. Now I'm director of the Labour Programme at Simon Fraser University where I act as a liaison between the B.C. trade unions and the university, organizing labour education.

This job combines my skills and experience and I enjoy it very much. But recently I've recognized that I also need to do more creative work. I've started to do some broadcasting, and in 1991, I published a book of poems, *Covering Rough Ground*, which was very well received. Now my problem is too much of a good thing. I have a good full-time job and I would also love to be a full-time writer and broadcaster. It's gone from: what am I going to do with my life? to how am I going to do all the things I want?

7

Law,
Finance and
Architecture

Nancy Morrison
Vancouver, British Columbia

"When I began working, the myth was that women wouldn't support other women. You bought into those myths because you didn't know any better."

Nancy Morrison grew up in Yorkton, Saskatchewan, and attended Osgoode Law School in Toronto in the late 1950s. After serving nine years as a judge on the British Columbia bench, she now practises law in Vancouver.

I was lucky. I had no brothers and I had a father who said, "Anyone can have sons. It takes special luck to have daughters." He had two. He gave me the message that I was one of the greatest people of all time and this really influenced my self-esteem.

So law school came as quite a shock. Thirty-six years ago, when I entered, law was impossible for a female. I remember my first day vividly. A thin fellow in third year sauntered up and said, "You must be one of the girls in first year."

I thought, isn't this nice. I didn't know anyone in Toronto and I was thrilled someone had noticed me.

"I hope you realize what you've done," he said.

"What?" I was puzzled.

"Well, by enrolling in law school, you've lost your femininity. Girls have no business being in law school."

Before I could absorb the full impact of what he'd said, he asked if I'd seen Annette. Annette was hard to miss. She was a beautiful girl who looked like Marilyn Monroe and was wearing a pink angora sweater with a matching skirt. She had flunked first year and was back.

"Well, she's lost her femininity, too," he declared.

I remember going back to this grungy little room I'd rented from a woman whose son kept coming on to me and thinking, maybe I should get some more frills on my blouses. Although I liked tailored blouses, I was suddenly wondering if they might be too masculine. In those days, nylons had seams and I began obsessively checking the backs of my legs to make sure I didn't look dishevelled. I'd always worn Chanel No. 5 perfume, but I began to bathe in the stuff, hoping it would help.

It took me about 15 years to get over this. It wasn't until I came across "femininity" in the dictionary and found it defined as "pertaining to the female genitalia" that I was able to laugh.

While I was in law school, I came back to Saskatchewan for the summers. I loved going to the country dances with the engineers and the local guys on the survey crews. But I'd learned not to say I went to law school because I knew they'd drop me like a live cobra. So whenever anybody asked where I went to school, I said I was in nursing, which always got a positive reaction. "I bet you give great back rubs," they'd comment, and I always assured them that I did.

For awhile, after I became a lawyer, I continued to pretend I was something else, a more nurturing, non-threatening professional. But eventually I stopped because I realized I wasn't interested in men who couldn't handle my being a lawyer.

I don't want to be misleading, I've had some wonderful times. There's no question, though, that in the early '60s, when I started to practise, women lawyers had to try harder. There were so many eyes on you, you didn't dare cut any slack for yourself. So few women practised that when you entered a courtroom, people sucked in their breath.

In those days, property was the big issue. I can't tell you how many women came into my office who were 45 to 50 years of age and had done all the right things. They were well groomed, had kept their figures and raised four wonderful children only to discover that their husbands were taking off with their 24-year-old secretaries. These women had never worked outside the home and had no property in their name, so they got virtually nothing when they divorced. Without doubt, they would not be supported in the manner in which they had lived. The most they'd be awarded was enough to get by on.

When I spoke to women's groups, this was the major concern. Even so, when I recently reread the Report of the Royal Commission on the Status of Women, I was surprised. It was published in 1970 and was a revolutionary document for its time, but it focused entirely on income and property rights. There was nothing on physical or sexual assault, harassment, child abuse—the issues that dominate today. It's astonishing that nobody came forward in the late '60s with those stories. I guess there was no point talking about these issues when you had nowhere to go, no access to property, jobs or income.

In 1968, I sought the Liberal nomination in Yorkton-Melville. That experience taught me how much women support other women, contrary to traditional wisdom. I was travelling to farms where the people were primarily Ukrainian or Russian and didn't speak much English. The women couldn't talk with me, but they'd each grab my arm, with a wonderful grip, and give me a loaf of home-made bread or a jar of jam. Then they'd stand there and nod, with tears coming down their faces. I knew within days of starting to work for the nomination that the women in Yorkton were my sole support. It was the men who torpedoed me.

The men viewed me as a possible career politician and they parachuted a man into the riding. I lost the nomination. The women who had been working on my campaign were outraged. They all quit: every single woman. They said, if a woman candidate isn't good enough for you, you don't need our help either.

I was such a team player, I didn't want to upset the guys. So I said I'd talk to the women because I knew that if they left, the men wouldn't be able to run the election. Women were—and still are—the machinery of grassroots politics. I even offered to be campaign manager for the male candidate, but they wouldn't let me. By the way, he lost even though the City of Yorkton went Liberal in the Trudeau sweep.

In the late '60s and early '70s, a wonderful thing happened to women. We became aware of the great joy of each other's company. I never again envied the guys going off doing whatever they did together. In fact, I always felt sorry for them.

About that time, some of my women friends started getting together on a regular basis. Because these monthly gatherings were held in a restaurant in Vancouver's Gastown, they became known as the "Gastown Dinners." The initial group of four or five quickly grew to 40 or 50 women, the maximum the room held. At some point, someone started taking names at the door. Then cards. Then it became networking—"This is what I can do for you"—and the joy of getting together purely for the pleasure of each other's company died. To this day, I can't stand the word networking.

In 1972, I was appointed to the bench even though I wasn't seeking to be a judge. I'd known judges all my life because my dad was a lawyer, and I felt sorry for them. I recognized that they were lonely. When they came to Yorkton, they couldn't come over for dinner since my dad was on the cases.

I was far too active in politics and having too much fun to aspire to the bench. I had so many good friends in the bar and I knew I'd be cutting myself off from them. Any good judge feels that way, but very few single women are appointed at the age of 35. I had to distance myself from a lot of good friends because the lawyers who appeared before me couldn't be guests at my house.

Being a judge is enormously prestigious, but whenever I travelled, I never used my title. Once, checking into a conference, I ran into a lawyer I knew. He said, "I'll bet you got a great room because you're a judge." When I told him I never used the title, he didn't believe me. So he whipped around and looked at my reservation card. When he discovered I was telling the truth, he wanted to know why.

"Because I know how they treat judges," I said. "I'm still interested in how they treat single women."

I had two conditions when I was asked to go on the bench: I said I wouldn't gown and I'd continue to give speeches on the social conditions of women and other minorities. Many people thought that unless I gowned I wouldn't be able to keep control in the courtroom. I believed that if I needed a piece of black fabric to keep control, I had no business being a judge. I'm convinced you control a courtroom through courtesy and respect for those who appear before you. I never gowned and it was never a problem. I had nine wonderful years as a judge.

Elizabetta Bigsby
Montreal, Quebec

"It never occurred to me that women have to behave in a certain way or have to fulfil certain roles. I believe this attitude has an impact, not only on how you behave, but, most importantly, on how other people perceive you."

Elizabetta Bigsby graduated in economics from the University of Genoa, Italy, in the early 1970s. She joined the Royal Bank's Economics Department in 1977 and is currently senior vice-president, Residential Mortgages and Retail Banking.

I'm Italian. I'm in Canada totally by chance because I met my husband, who is Canadian, when he was working in Italy. As with most things that have happened to me, there was no design.

I think as I go along I become more and more convinced that I really am who I am because of how I grew up. I have one sister and we happened to grow up in a family where there was no perception that there were differences between men's and women's roles.

When I went to university, I started in mathematics and then got terribly bored so I went into law and got even more bored. I ended up someplace in between—at least in the Italian university structure—in economics. I finished in 1973 and, after working in two different places, found a job at the Canadian consulate promoting Canadian forest products, of which I know absolutely nothing. The salary was astronomical—three times as much as I was making in my previous job—since they were paying Canadian rates. That's where I met my husband, who was the junior consul. Two years later we got married.

Then my husband was posted in Algeria and neither of us was very keen to go there. Also, I didn't want to spend my life being a diplomat's wife, so he resigned and we ended up in Montreal. When we got settled, I applied to approximately 12 companies with an economics department. The Royal Bank phoned me back first and that's how I ended up here.

I was very lucky because you can't choose the people you work for and my boss was a most objective, open-minded individual. Over time he provided me with challenging work. He was the opposite of many bosses, who often use subordinates to do the work and then take credit for it. He also provided many opportunities for exposure to senior management, which allowed me to be known by people who might not have known me otherwise. So nine years later, when I had gone as far as I could in that department and asked for a change, the bank was very supportive.

I moved into line banking. A line banker takes care of a company's financial requirements. It's fascinating because you get to know the clients. There's also a negotiating aspect in which, naturally, you want to protect the bank and the other person wants to achieve their objectives. You try to arrive somewhere in between—remaining quite friendly on both sides. It's a rare type of role and I quite like it.

Fourteen months after that, in a rather miraculous fashion, I was appointed vice-president of international trade for the Quebec region. This supposedly made sense because I'd been an international economist for many years. But it didn't make much sense because all of a sudden I had a 90-person department to manage. Also, although I know quite a lot about international trade, in principle, I knew absolutely nothing about international-trade instruments. A letter of credit is an excessively scary document, with zillions of strange conditions that only people who have spent years unbundling this kind of stuff know. You say, "Sign here, it's a million and a half," and hope the thing is right.

When I was named to the trade centre, my husband and I went out to dinner to celebrate. We had a lovely evening with a bottle of champagne. Then I went to bed and woke up at 4:00 a.m. wondering, oh my God, what am I going to do now? I kept waking up for quite some time.

I enjoyed the work because it was absolutely fascinating, but managing 90 people was totally different from anything I had ever done. In my opinion you do that by helping them to participate in as much of the decision-making process as you possibly can, so they can shape their own environment.

Then there was the issue of women because women do have humungous problems in the work force. Often the structure reflected the belief that women were supposed to remain in junior positions, while some men were supposed to be promoted clearly because they were men.

Paternalistic concepts were another concern. Once we were going to make a presentation at 8:30 in the morning and a senior manager said, "We'll ask Joe to attend the meeting because Georgette has to take her kid to work and she can't be in early." So I said, "No, no, let's ask Georgette, and if she has a problem, we'll see what we can do." Of course, Georgette was perfectly capable of finding a solution for the kid and she attended the meeting. But this preconceived idea, "I'm not going to ask her because she can't do it," is very dangerous since it's intended as friendly and courteous. It's a lot easier to fight an enemy you recognize, than to fight an enemy who thinks he's your friend.

I was in international trade for four very interesting years. It was one of these rare occasions in which, I think, one got to go from A to B despite the fact that going from A to B ended up taking longer than I thought. Last July, I moved to another job in the same geographical district. Then I was moved to vice-president, marketing, for the Quebec district, which turned out to be interesting and in some sense easy, because it's a conceptual job. I have no trouble laying out a plan and figuring out what the premises should be if we want to reach a certain solution. It was quite peaceful, relative to the trade centre, where I was managing so many people.

Now I'm being moved again to senior vice-president, private banking. The bank is structured into essentially two divisions: the corporate division which looks after companies, and the retail division which looks after individuals and, naturally, is much bigger. I've never been in retail and I don't know the players or the products so it will be another fascinating exercise. But after the trade centre nothing will scare me in my work environment because I think, as one grows, one learns how to put things into perspective and not to be overwhelmed.

One thing I have always done is to make sure that women don't miss any opportunities whenever they arise. I recognize that often women are afraid to take opportunities because they've had a history of being beaten on the head. So I've insisted that the opportunities exist long enough to allow them to accept.

Every time an appointment is made, women are considered. I'm sure for many years, certainly in other institutions, nominations were made on the basis of Joe Blow is the perfect candidate and there's nobody else.

I've been at many meetings where I'm the only woman, and I've always made a point of ensuring that the unfounded stereotypical comment that inevitably goes around the table is corrected. I don't do this pedantically because I don't think that helps, so I try, wherever possible, to stop it with a joke.

I think many men are now at the level of stopping these types of remarks, which I don't think was the case five years ago. In many cases, they have wives who are professionals so they've experienced the problems through them. And, if they have daughters, they are concerned about their careers.

One thing that really helps women in the workplace is their ability to listen. If you negotiate with a client and you listen, the client will tell you, directly or indirectly, absolutely everything you need to know. Even so, it's amazing how many men won't listen, which will help women's careers.

I have never personally experienced discrimination. I've experienced bad manners or what I ascribe to bad manners—for instance, someone not saying hello because I'm a woman and, therefore, probably a junior. I feel you should say hello to everyone when you walk into a room, so I correct that. I always stop the person and say, "We haven't met. I'm Elizabetta Bigsby," and watch them respond.

My husband is very supportive. That, again, is luck. I could have married the kind of man who wanted to keep me in my place and it might have been totally different. Canada is not a difficult country to move to, but there are traditions and behaviours that are very Canadian—definitely not Italian. He's been very helpful in explaining situations that to me seem very odd. I certainly wouldn't have integrated into Canadian society without his help.

He and I discuss things and give each other advice. It's very helpful to have an unbiased sounding board. Every company has its culture and politics, and an intelligent external person can help you to find solutions you may have overlooked because you're looking at things from inside. Also, when one is anxious, it's nice to have someone who listens to your worries, then says, "Are you through? This won't kill you." My husband was particularly supportive when I was getting up at 4:00 a.m.

We don't have children and that, again, is very fortunate because for some reason I have always been adverse to having children. If I had met somebody who cared very much about having children, we might have had a family and that would have changed our lives. Children have an effect on a woman's career. I think they should have an effect on both parents' careers, but I don't think they do, although that, too, is changing.

Two fellows in my current department are very involved with raising their children and it's the first time I've seen that. They'll say they've leaving early or coming in late because they have to take Julie to the doctor or whatever.

Women will get there, eventually, but I think a numbers game is beginning to play a role. The rate of progress is accelerating. In the summer of 1988, I was the fourth woman vice-president. Now we have at least 20. So it took maybe 12 years to have four, and it took five years to go from four to 20. It's not miraculously quick, but it's an improvement. And the more women there are, the faster the process will become because the assumptions and habits will break down.

Mary Eberts
Toronto, Ontario

"I've always gotten a lot of pleasure from work and it's always been an important part of my existence. I think my approach to work is that it is a dignified thing to do and, most of the time, I bring a fair amount of zest to it."

Mary Eberts graduated from the University of Western Ontario Law School in 1971, then did her master of laws at Harvard University. She was called to the bar in 1974, and began teaching at the University of Toronto Law School that year. In 1980, she left the university to practise law and has become one of Canada's most highly esteemed lawyers in the area of equality rights and constitutional affairs.

I've been working without a break since the end of Grade 13, which means through scholarships and jobs I've been self-supporting since I turned 17. I'm quite proud of this, although I'm not happy I had to do it.

When I was in Grade 13, my father, who had been a recovered alcoholic, became an active alcoholic for awhile. He lost his job and my mother had to go back to work. As a result, I had to get all of the available cash prizes to cover the costs of university. I worked hard, stood first and was able to put together quite a large portfolio of scholarship money. But it was difficult, especially given the turmoil in my family.

I finished my BA at the University of Western Ontario and was intending to do a master's in English. Since I'd always been interested in politics, I was working on the 1968 election. At the same time I was also coping with being a very low-income person and was trying to get premium assistance for my medical insurance. There was so much red tape that I said to myself, "Gee, an ordinary person almost has to be a lawyer to cope with life." Then I thought, what a great idea!

The lawyer and federal cabinet minister, Judy LaMarsh, was one of my heroines. I combined this idea of red tape with my admiration for her and applied to law school at Western two days before the deadline.

When I went to law school, there were eight women in a class of 140, so it was an unusual choice. It's unlikely I would have gone if I hadn't quit university for a year and experienced the poverty that went along with the jobs I could get: waitress, a clerk in a library, a library clerk at a newspaper.

I also experienced the frustration of taking orders from people who had credentials, but who weren't as smart as I was.

At Western there was a certain amount of hostility and resentment towards the women law students, and we were somewhat taken aback at how frankly our fellow students expressed this. I roomed with two other women and the guys told us they couldn't condone our being in law school because we weren't bad looking and we were marriageable. That meant we were unfairly taking places from men who would have families to support. On the other hand, they said they could understand why so and so would be there—they were so homely they'd never get married and would have to support themselves. This was stated in a very serious way.

I also learned from a man I later dated that, in first year, the guys had a contest to guess our bra sizes. A prize was given to the guy who could supply proof thereof from his exploratory exploits. My informant told me this without realizing how offensive it was.

I was very active at law school. I was editor of the newspaper and had a pretty high profile. In second year, a good friend who was president of the student's law society encouraged me to run for president. For the longest time I was the only candidate. Then, at the last minute, they convinced some guy to run against me because they didn't think the law school should be represented by a woman president and I lost the election.

So there was fairly dramatic evidence that things were not very rosy, but in day-to-day classroom activity, we didn't have, or we didn't notice, the kinds of abuse that women students often report in law school today. I don't think there were enough of us to elicit that.

If I remember correctly, in second year I stood second in my class. As a matter of form, the law firms wrote asking students to interview with them. My letters were addressed to Mr. Eberts. When I visited firms in the summer of 1970, I got questions like, "What would you do if you had a family?" This was from a guy with the classic family photograph on his window sill, who was interviewing me at 7:30 in the evening. I said, "Well, I suppose I'd do just about what you do. I'd be working at 7:30 some evenings and my kids would be on my windowsill." I didn't get a job offer from that firm.

To make a long story short, instead of articling, I decided to go to Harvard Law School to do a master of laws degree. About six of us who graduated from the law school at Western went to graduate school in various places. I was the only woman and the only one who didn't get an offer to return to Western as a first-year professor, although I was applying for teaching jobs at various places and, pro forma, sent my application to Western. I never even received a response. I had interviews at Dalhousie (Halifax, N.S.), the University of British Columbia and Osgoode (Toronto, Ontario). The first two places offered me jobs, but I didn't get an offer from Osgoode. They told me I was too young.

I turned down the jobs at UBC and Dalhousie because my mother developed cancer. Since I'm an only child and my dad had no other family support, I decided to take a job in Ontario.

My interest lay in constitutional jurisdiction over communications—that's what I did my thesis on at Harvard—so I articled at the Canadian Radio-Television Commission (CRTC) for a year. While I was there, I was seconded to McCarthy & McCarthy, a law firm in Toronto, to work with Peter Grant, a communications lawyer who was developing regulations for the commission. We worked at U of T, where he taught, and through that connection I was offered the opportunity to teach a course in Women and the Law at the law school. As the dean put it, obstreperous women students were demanding the course, and they had no one to teach it.

That sounded good to me. It was 1972 and I didn't know much about women and the law, but my custom was that if someone offered me a job, I'd take it because I was a job junkie. I also knew I needed to support myself through the bar-admissions course. First, I had to meet with the women students and pass muster, which I did. Then, I had to develop the course.

The senior staff person at the CRTC, Monique Copal, had been secretary to the Royal Commission of the Status of Women and she helped me. She also passed me along to two or three other women in Ottawa who had been instrumental in women's issues, and it was thanks to their combined help that I could develop the course and get it approved.

Only in retrospect did I realize the hurdles I had to jump through to get a job. No guy would have had to be politically vetted by the students. No guy would have had to invent the course and get it approved. That one experience set the tone for the rest of my working life. When I look back at my 20 years as a lawyer, I see that it's been a continual experience of making my place in the world, just as I made that course. I have never been able to simply walk into a job involving my avocation: working for equality and women. I have always had to create my own space.

Until I went to U of T, my experience in the legal profession had been quite positive, although I didn't realize that until years later. Throughout my undergraduate and legal education, I had the happy experience of being mentored. In high school I was the sort of kid who really liked my teachers.

I hung out with them and received a lot of validation from them which I didn't get at home. I was always a pleasure to teach. I read widely, was very clever, tried hard and always got good grades. In fact, I was a little Goody Two-Shoes. So my teachers always helped me a lot and I related well to them.

By the time I got to university, I had learned the ropes of how to get mentored. When I had to make the transition into my working life as a professor, that came to an end. I was orphaned and it was very traumatic, although at the time I didn't understand why.

My years of teaching at U of T were pretty miserable because I couldn't get mentors in public law, the area where I wanted to work. Lots of projects and research work were floating around, but I was never a part of those teams because my mentoring opportunities lay in the area they thought suitable for a woman: family law.

Although my credentials were in constitutional law, administrative law, civil liberties and regulated industries, they wanted me in family law. My only background in family law was one summer in law school when I worked for a professor doing his family-law casebook. They asked me to teach family law and then to organize a conference on the child in the courts, which I did. The handwriting was on the wall. This was where the dean wanted me to flourish. Family law was going to be mine. The problem was, it wasn't what I wanted.

I was also assigned to every committee going because they wanted a female representative and I was the only woman on the faculty. As a result, the students constantly came to talk about their problems. Years later, when they started doing status of women reports on university life, it was interesting to learn that it was the women faculty, usually young and untenured, who had to do the emotional work of the faculty. Of course, you never got any credit for doing that and it distracted from your classes, as well as your scholarly responsibilities.

Long afterwards, I realized I had spent those years berating myself for not being good enough to attract opportunities, when that wasn't the issue. The real problem was that I was marginalized, isolated and not supported—a very common experience for women in academic life in those days.

I would have gone quite nutty if it weren't for my great support networks, which existed in several places. One was among the students. When you sit and listen to people's problems, day in and day out, you get something back from the experience. Some of my friends today were my students then. A few professors, some of whom were men, were also supportive and

I met many women through the larger women's network.

Finally, I decided to leave the law school. But I had recently given birth to my daughter, and since I was the first person on campus to take advantage of the 18-week paid maternity leave I'd helped to negotiate, I felt I had to return or people would be prejudiced against women. So I taught out the next year, then resigned, but had to teach an additional year because the school needed a year's notice.

I was at the law school for six years and I've since made my peace with them. I now teach two courses there and it's much better. The dean is very supportive, there are nine women faculty and I have some good relationships with faculty members.

I like to have closure on things. When I have a problem, I may walk away from it in the short run, but I always like to return to see if I can get something back on track. So I'm pleased to have closed the circle with the law school.

In general, though, the theme of being a feminist has dogged my days. A woman who espouses the gender-neutral agenda or allows herself to suppress the odd bit of the women's agenda so that she's no different from the men, and maybe even fits their purposes, will likely flourish. But an out-and-out feminist and advocate of social change is a lightening rod for attracting disapproval.

That happened to me at U of T. For instance, if they wanted an opinion on some area of law in which I had done a lot of work, they'd ask some guy who wasn't as knowledgeable because they said I wasn't really an expert. I was an advocate. So when I started looking for something to get me out of the university, I took this seriously and became an advocate.

In 1980, I got a job with a large Toronto law firm, Tory, Tory, and became a barrister. By that time my husband was a partner in a large law firm, we already had one child and soon had two more in quick succession. It wasn't easy for me to say at 5:00 in the evening, "Oh sure, I'll stay until 11:00, no problem." And this, among other things, became a problem.

I felt the pressure both ways. My husband wanted me to be his consort and he thought I should be the main overseer of the children, which meant I'd encounter difficulties at home if I were too dedicated to my career. But lawyers on the rise weren't supposed to give their families priority. So right from the outset, I was in an awful bind.

In addition, reasonably early in my life at Tory's, they realized I was a feminist because I was asked to do the Fraser Committee on Pornography and Prostitution. Since it was reduced-rate work, I asked the firm's permission to accept the position. They saw me devoting huge amounts of time to a feminist issue that didn't pay well.

I also wasn't in the loop for the best briefs. Almost as a fluke, I wound up with a brief that absorbed enormous amounts of time and was very lucrative. I was working for a person who, I think, was not seen as a premium client. He was an unusual guy, a very flamboyant meat packer who had grown rich in property speculation. His work turned into a high-quality brief and, as a result, I was made a partner at the end of my third year.

My mentor during this period, ironically, was my husband, who gave me my single most important piece of advice: "They'll tell you at the beginning that you don't have to worry about developing your own files. They'll say they have lots of work for you so you should just do the work you're given," he said. "Then when it's time to be made a partner, you'll be judged on the basis of how well you developed your own files—how well you broke the rules."

So when this big case for the meat packer finished, I set about developing my own practice. About that time the Charter of Rights and Freedoms was coming into effect and I began to work in that area. I was one of the women who founded the Women's Legal Education and Action Fund (LEAF). I always did a fair amount of pro bono work and I give Tory's credit for letting me do that. It was advantageous for them because they got a lot of prestige out of it but, even so, many firms wouldn't have done it. Through this work I got the professional development opportunities that passed me by because I wasn't the protégée of a great man.

I had been to the Supreme Court of Canada once as a junior with a senior man, but for many years all my other attendances were on human rights or charter briefs, all of which came to me directly. It was a good combination. There was tremendous intellectual capital within the firm, which I could access when I needed it.

Although I was developing a reputation in the courts as someone who was very good, I never excelled at catching on as a Tory's lawyer. It was a compromise existence, but it seemed a reasonable trade-off. Tory's was a good base for me, there were people I liked and the general ethos of the firm was supportive of the kind of work I liked to do. In this sense Tory's was unusual for a big "Bay Street" firm, and their in-kind contributions of legal expertise had a lot to do with getting LEAF's casework off the ground. I was prepared to handle the negatives because there were many positives. Then the balance shifted and the price became too high.

Towards the end of my tenure I found I was running aground on the conflicts system. The firm was starting to find more and more conflicts between the work I wanted to do and the work they already had, and I was always the loser. This came to a head with the Native Women's Association of Canada (NWAC).

With my assistance, the NWAC brought an application for an injunction to stop the referendum. The firm took the position that it didn't matter the NWAC was on the no side. The problem was, the association was trying to prevent the vote from being taken. It was seen as an undesirable brief and I was given the choice between finding the NWAC other counsel or taking a leave. I took the leave and that was very unsettling. Afterwards, it wasn't possible to return to the compromise I'd been willing to make before, although I made some stabs at it. I don't think it was possible on either side.

I left Tory's early in 1994, after 14 years, and since then I've been practising on my own. It's a good move, I think, and some of the things I feared haven't happened. I don't feel isolated because I'm in a small practice. In fact, I feel much more a part of the world than I did when I was inside a large organization since the world is now on my doorstep. I recognize, though, that I'm well established in the profession. Younger people would have a real struggle.

Basically, I'm quite happy with where I am. I have a very interesting practice. I think I'm useful to people. I crave a lot of intellectual challenge in my work and I get it.

There is one thing I'd change, though. While I tell myself that I'm a very accomplished person and that I have a lot to be proud of, I actually don't have a lot of confidence. I think that's an aspect of being female. Women are cursed with that sense that we're not good enough. It starts from our earliest days. You can never do enough to overcome the feeling that you've been born second class. You can only change your mind about it. It's an act of will.

Sometimes I'm successful exercising that act of will. Other times I'm so overwhelmed by my context and my society that I just can't do it. I have to push to keep myself going. Now, I see myself as a very privileged woman and I say, "If this happens to me, it happens everywhere." I don't know what to do except to keep on going. And, thank God for other women.

Pat Cooper
Calgary, Alberta

"After 20-plus years in the work force, I can see quite clearly that I'm nowhere near the levels of responsibility and power that I would have reached if I'd been a male in the same business."

Pat Cooper graduated from university in 1971 and gradually moved into mortgage administration. Towards the end of the 1980s, she became a real-estate appraiser. Currently she works for the City of Calgary.

I grew up in Lethbridge, went to university in Calgary and, in 1971, started working in the mortgage department of a major insurance company. With a BA in sociology and English, I had no desire to do this kind of work, but in those days, if you were a woman who couldn't type, you started out as a clerk.

I was fortunate to have a department manager who recognized my ability. He pushed me and tested the limits of what I could do which, of course, made it interesting. I started processing mortgage payments and, as I progressed, became more involved in the actual management of properties and, finally, moved into doing mortgage deals, inspecting properties, dealing with developers and underwriting.

After I had been there about six years, the assistant manager's job became available. My manager wanted me to have the position, but head office in Toronto was against it. One day I was sitting in his office while he argued with them on the phone. He said things like, "If you don't make this woman assistant manager then she and I will sue for discrimination." We both knew the only reason Toronto was hesitating was because of my sex. Finally, they gave in, but only because my manager really fought for me. As far as I know, I became the first woman to hold the assistant manager position in a regional office of that company in Canada. He was an unusual man in this business. I talked to him a few years after I'd left the company and he told me about doing a similar thing for another woman. He said he didn't know how many times he'd have to put his career on the line just to get a deserved promotion for a woman.

I really believe that if I were a man, I would have eventually advanced to the manager's job. I was repeatedly told, "It's wonderful you've been made assistant manager, but that's it."

I could have gone to the Human Rights Commission, but Calgary is a relatively small community and I planned to stay here. Ten or 15 years ago, if you sued your employer, you'd expect to be blacklisted.

Once I was promoted, I seldom had problems with clients. I remember one developer, who told me he didn't think I could do the job because I was a woman. About six months later he said, "I take it back."

Also, people would say things like, "When I discovered that my appointment at the mortgage company was with a girl, I almost cancelled."

One of the problems at that company, which has dogged me throughout my career, is that until very recently I never worked anywhere with a woman directly above me in the chain of command. That meant I've never had anyone who could be a mentor and it's been quite lonely.

Having a mentor would have helped in the simplest ways—having someone to discuss my problems with or to provide advice on dressing or how to behave in tricky situations. For instance, I used to go out with the guys for drinks after work because I felt if you didn't, you weren't one of the movers and shakers. After awhile it became apparent I wasn't anyway, because I had experiences that would likely be described as sexual harassment today. Unwelcome advances were made, but always in situations that I was stupid to get into. They took place after work, and alcohol was involved, but with no role model, I didn't know what was right.

I left that company because I thought I could make more money elsewhere. I applied for a number of jobs and I know there were at least two I didn't get because I was female. One was through a personnel agent, who admitted that was the reason. I dealt directly with a local mortgage manager on the second, and he confessed that his head office wouldn't approve my hiring because I was female, even though I was his first choice.

The mortgage field was more male dominated then, I think, because the prevailing wisdom was that women couldn't understand bricks and mortar. I was beginning to realize I wasn't getting jobs because I was a woman, but I was still enough of a fighter and an idealist to think, oh well, there are always idiot companies out there, I can still get where I want to go. Only within the past few years have I begun to recognize the seriousness of each of those missed opportunities. When you're 10 years into a career, not getting a promotion or a new job has repercussions for the rest of your work life because you're not moving forward as quickly as you should.

After I left the insurance company, I worked for a developer for two years, then I got a job with a trust company as the mortgage-administration manager. In 1988, that company was sold and I became the victim of reorganization. However, I was able to talk myself into a job at another trust company. When I first applied for the position, an acquaintance said I wouldn't get the job because he'd been told by the fellow doing the hiring that a woman couldn't handle the work. That spurred me on and I took the offensive in the interview. This tactic worked, and in the end, I got the job. But that was only five years ago, so in some circles things haven't changed very much.

As it turned out, that company was having growing pains and I wasn't happy there. Fortunately, an appraiser I knew suggested I get into that field. I hadn't thought about becoming an appraiser, but I'd taken many of the necessary courses since I thought they'd benefit my mortgage work.

One of the reasons I switched to appraising is that I felt I was as intelligent and well connected as most of the men who were above me in the mortgage business. Since Calgary is such a small market, I know most of the people who run offices. It made me think, I'm just as smart as him. And had I been able to progress in the normal manner, I wouldn't be reporting to him.

I worked as a fee appraiser for four years. Basically, I appraised buildings for clients and prepared a detailed report justifying the appraisal. I quite liked it, but I was let go at my last place of employment for no good business reason. I'd been doing what I understood to be extremely good work and was bringing in lots of clients. They called it a lay off due to a lack of business. Legitimately there wasn't enough business to go around, although I was supporting myself in terms of the volume I was bringing in.

There were four people in the office and I was the one chosen to downsize. I was the only woman. Interestingly, the only other person they'd ever let go was also a woman. One of the two partners in the firm didn't like me, and I always suspected it was because he didn't like women who knew what they were talking about. But that's a hard one to prove.

Seven weeks ago, I joined the City of Calgary Assessment Department. I'm doing business assessments for tax purposes. Since the city is an equal-opportunity employer, and it seems to be serious about its commitment, I'm reasonably confident that I can use my skills and contacts in an environment where it may be an advantage to be female. I've promised myself that either I'd never work for anything other than a very large organization with checks and balances and pay-equity policies or I'd be my own boss.

I married but never had children. I'm 43 and I recently remember saying I couldn't imagine they're no longer hiring me because I might stay home with my kids. I know other women still run into that problem. Not long ago, one of my male co-workers was grumbling about a lawyer who is planning to stay home for a year or two with her baby. His position was that she shouldn't have been allowed to go to law school.

I'm good at keeping in touch with people. I'm in two different networking groups, one of which involves women in real estate. This compensates for the absence of women in my workplace. The group also provides support. The last company I worked for had a reception a couple of weeks after I lost my job. I had invited five female clients and three returned their tickets. They said they wouldn't go if that was how they treated women employees. Support like that makes you feel wonderful.

Over the years, I've noticed a real change in solidarity among women. When I was working as a fee appraiser, I felt female clients pushed as much business towards me as they could. I don't know what would have happened if I had done bad work, but I think women are becoming a little more aware and possibly even militant because so many of us have experienced discrimination.

I've probably been well paid compared to other working women, although my earnings are not that far off from those of a teacher or a nurse. And they're certainly nowhere near what the men I started out with in this business are making. When I was making $50,000 they were making $200,000, and they weren't a comparable amount smarter than me.

One piece of advice I'd give to young women if they're really interested in commercial real estate is to keep educating themselves. Taking the appraisal courses improved my career choices, and keeping appraisal open as an alternative path actually saved my bacon a couple of times. Appraisal is more concrete than mortgage work because you're providing data, not your opinion, so you're not as vulnerable.

It's hard to believe I've been in this business more than 20 years. When I took the job in the mortgage company, it was my intention to pay the bills until I could find something better. If I knew then what I know now, I would have tried much harder to find a different job.

Last Christmas I went to a party where I was, once again, the only woman. I wouldn't have believed it. After all these years I thought I'd be fighting a different battle.

Janet Lee
Vancouver, British Columbia

"I believed a career would be my ticket to freedom."

Janet Lee studied to be as an architect in the early 1960s. In the 1980s, she returned to school and trained as a ceramic artist. She now divides her time between art and investing in real estate.

I'm 56 and I remember thinking about work when I was growing up in Hong Kong. People would say, "When you get older, you'll marry and you'll follow your husband for the rest of your life." But already, at that young age, I knew that wasn't what I wanted to do, because it wouldn't allow me to be myself and have the freedom I had as a child.

As I grew older, I decided to imitate my brother and get an education. In the early 1960s, I trained as an architect in England. At that time, it was pretty difficult to be a female in that field and some of the women tried to compensate by acting tough. I wanted to follow their example, but couldn't, probably because of my upbringing.

Even though I did very well in my studies, I was waiting for someone to direct me. I think my reaction was very cultural. I feel I'm a product of 10,000 years of Chinese tradition that says females are not supposed to talk or have opinions. We're supposed to receive, which is quite devastating. It means we shouldn't go out in the world and do things. I've struggled to break through this conditioning.

I wanted to be independent, to work and earn a living, but I couldn't escape the idea that my place was at home. I married halfway through my architectural training. I thought my husband would let me have a career and even offer to help in the house, but it didn't happen that way. I felt very guilty about wanting a career and my studies suffered.

My husband went on to graduate school while I had children, as well as several miscarriages, and engaged in part-time study and part-time work. Finally, when I was pregnant with my second child, 8½ years after the first, I gave up work altogether. My husband didn't think we should have baby-sitters, and I didn't think I deserved a nanny or household help. I felt it was my responsibility to keep the house in order, make my husband happy and raise our children properly.

It was heartbreaking. Looking back, I can see many reasons why I failed. I wasn't culturally assimilated enough to take on responsible roles in the architectural profession, and I was so torn between work and home that I couldn't manage either situation. Essentially, I hadn't developed enough self-centredness. I couldn't allow myself the imagination necessary to change my predicament through creative problem solving.

I stayed home for several years and it was a bad time in my life. I became very depressed. In 1974, we came to Canada. Five years later, our marriage ended. My husband was very Chinese and I had always been told I was too Westernized. It was bewildering because I worked hard in my marriage and couldn't understand why I failed.

For a long time, I wasn't sure what it meant to be a woman and that bothered me greatly. Although the divorce shook me up, it also helped me to discard beliefs and attitudes I had accepted without understanding. Eventually, I realized I needed to use my brain and to express myself.

About this time, I became very interested in the human-potential movement. I attended workshops and took courses to find out about myself and the world around me. Later, I enrolled at the Emily Carr College of Art and Design and graduated from their four-year course in fine arts with a major in ceramics. Between my second and third year, I left school for three years to invest in real estate with assets I had inherited from my father.

My investments made me feel financially safe. Once I reached that point, I began to divide work into two categories: one that made a living and the other that gave me pleasure.

Over time I changed my idea of work and work ethics. Before, I was a very good girl: I worked to be safe, to secure a position. Now, I work more for satisfaction, which is what my art gives me. I also like to initiate and create which is very much against my upbringing. There's a part of me that needs to achieve, to prove myself, to be satisfied that I've been having some adventures. That's what I'm searching for now... not to be safe.

In business, I play it safe, but in art my world opens to adventure. And since I operate so differently in these two fields, I find it difficult to do both at the same time. This is why I took time off my studies to invest, and while studying, didn't do business at all.

Due to health problems, I've given up ceramics for awhile, but I plan to resume work this fall. In the meantime, I'm deriving a lot of pleasure from learning to sing. Work has become what I do well and what I like to do. It's part of my lifestyle.

Anonymous
Toronto, Ontario

"I've been told that people from visible minorities are often underemployed and this certainly reflects my experience."

"Anonymous" graduated from university in 1969 and began working in customer service for a large Canadian corporation. Eight years later, she moved into sales and in 1980 left to have a baby. She is currently teaching French in a Toronto school.

I started working for a major Canadian corporation in 1969. Even though I had an honours BA in French, I was hired for an entry-level job as a service representative.

I was the only black woman working as a service rep, and in the six years I held the position, I consistently received excellent performance reviews. But during this time, many other less qualified people—all of whom were white—were promoted while I was passed over. A number of my colleagues became very upset at how I was being treated. Eventually, they instigated a complaint of racial discrimination with the Human Rights Commission and testified on my behalf. Three months later, I was promoted to a management position. At that point, the Human Rights Commission sent me a letter congratulating me on settling my complaint.

The problem is, the discrimination didn't end. It just took another form. I was never accepted by the rest of the management team. They didn't include me in meetings and didn't provide me with the information I needed to do my job. I felt this was unfair to my staff. My outsider status meant I couldn't give them the information they needed to do their jobs. So I returned to my position as a service rep.

That experience taught me that there was no place for a black woman in management. Sales seemed the obvious move. Again, many other employees in the group had been approached about moving into sales, but I had never been asked. During a two-year period I had to keep pushing, reminding them that I wanted a sales job. Finally, I found a sympathetic woman in personnel who helped me make the move.

I spent three years working as a sales rep. For two of those years I was the division's top performer, one of the top four performers in our area and a member of the Director's Club. In fact, my performance appraisals said

I was the model other sales reps should follow.

Even though my performance was top notch, I began to get the feeling that my supervisor resented me. For instance, he would make snide remarks about the fact that I drove a Mercedes. Then, in 1979, when I achieved the highest sales results of my group, he gave the bonus for top performance to a man because I, he said, "didn't need the money." It's true, I didn't—my husband had a successful business and we were quite affluent—but that had nothing to do with my job performance. Years later, when I started reading research on racial discrimination, I concluded that my success and the fact that I had a prosperous husband who happened to be white must have bothered him. I think he thought I was a black woman who didn't know her place.

In 1980, I became pregnant. The company allowed new mothers a year's leave of absence and during this time they held your job for you. I decided to take advantage of this opportunity. But while I was at home with my son, I became so attached to him that I didn't want to go back to work immediately. So I wrote to the company and extended my leave for an additional year.

At the end of the second year, I notified the company that I was ready to return to work. Instead of offering me a job, my supervisor advised me to apply at the employment office. I went down and filled out an application but, still, nothing happened.

My former colleagues, who knew I wanted to come back to work, were surprised that I hadn't been contacted because the company was actively hiring at that time. It took quite a while but, finally, after much toing and froing, I was sent for an interview in sales. The reason for the long delay, according to the company, was that they hadn't been able to find my telephone number.

The interview was very strange. The interviewing team consisted of my old boss and a newly promoted manager who had worked as a sales rep with me. Both these men treated me as though they had never laid eyes on me before. I thought the interview would take about 15 minutes—after all, I had worked there for 11 years and they knew me well. Instead, it went on for two hours. Their questions suggested that I was a complete stranger, and after the interview, I left with an ominous feeling.

When I arrived home, the employment office called and told me that I didn't get the job. I couldn't think of any reason why I wouldn't have been hired for that position. In the 11 years I worked for them, not only did I have excellent performance reviews, I had perfect attendance and punctuality—no days away from work and I was never late.

I thought I was the kind of employee any company would want to hire back. Instead, they belittled me. I couldn't see any explanation for their bizarre behaviour other than racial discrimination. I decided that I wouldn't let them deprive me of my job and called the Human Rights Commission.

After examining the evidence, the commission agreed to hear my case. Discrimination on the basis of gender as well as race was a major component of the argument my lawyer prepared. After all, if I had been a man, I wouldn't have left my niche in the company, and my leave of absence gave them the opportunity to practise racial discrimination. My lawyer thought that age discrimination may have been an issue as well, since there were no other new sales reps in my age bracket.

Almost immediately, it became clear that the company intended to stonewall the proceedings. They had lots of money and they could keep this case going forever, if necessary, figuring I'd get tired and drop it. That was their basic strategy and it worked.

The case at the Human Rights Commission went on for so long I didn't know what was being appealed and why. After 7½ years of proceedings, the commission wrote and said they would close the file. My mother had just died and I was getting divorced. I had too much on my plate to be able to deal with it any more.

In the end, it also became clear that the commission wasn't as thorough as it should have been in compiling the evidence. For instance, there was nothing in the file about my first complaint, which would have helped to establish a history of discrimination on the company's part.

Throughout the proceedings, I continued job hunting. It took me four years to find another job. It was very demoralizing and I began to wonder if I had been blacklisted.

I still think that women who are victims of discrimination should fight, although my experience made me wonder about the justice system. I had an excellent case, an outstanding lawyer, lots of resources and, yet, I couldn't win. If this is what happens in the system, how does anyone get justice?

JoAnn Lowell
Yellowknife, Northwest Territories

" I often think about those women in the bank. I'll bet they're still there, 20 years later, doing the same jobs, for the same pay, looking after their homes and being completely unrecognized for what they do."

JoAnn Lowell has been self-supporting since 1973, when she was 16. In 1976, she got a job as a bank teller and was gradually promoted to the position of currency trader. In 1982, she left banking and ended up in architecture. Since the birth of her daughter in 1990, she has been working as a home-based consultant.

I'm 37 and grew up in Calgary. I got my first job when I was 14, packing hospital supplies for a medical packaging company. I was terrified because we were packaging things like heroin, so there were very tight controls which gave me the sense that employers had absolute power over workers.

When I was 16, I left home and became self-sufficient. I put myself through high school working with "mentally-retarded" children, as they were then called, and in an automotive shop at night.

In those days I looked for jobs that were traditionally male, either outdoors or shipper-receiver-type things. I remember applying for one job and not being able to get past the secretary. "But you're a woman," she said. "You can't apply." I think I wanted "male" jobs because they fit my personality. I had always been a tomboy, and when it came to work in the home—there were seven children in my family—I wanted to work outdoors with my dad. I finally decided to apply for a "female" job, as a bank teller, with a real sense of resignation.

At first, I was gung-ho because I wanted to get into management and have a career. I repeatedly asked to be admitted into the training programme and was constantly put off. Meanwhile, any 18-year-old guy who walked through the door and applied to be a teller was shunted into management training. The moment he signed on, he received a third more salary than I did, and in six months, after I'd trained him, he became a junior manager with power over me.

All the tellers were female. Some had 30 years' experience and they knew more than the managers, but no one complained because most had children and lived close to the branch so they could be home with their kids at lunch and after school.

I'd been bugging my manager about the unfairness of it all and, in 1977, I finally confronted him. "Aren't you getting married this September?" he asked. When I said yes, he said, "The next programme begins in September and it's not available for married women." Supposedly, this was because managers were subject to transfers. Not only was my first husband a mechanic whose skills were portable, I was the family's main breadwinner.

At that point I began to grumble. I took great delight in cutting out articles about bank tellers unionizing and posting them on the bulletin board in the staff room. Suddenly, management started having lovey-dovey meetings with staff and I got a job at the new international banking centre.

I quickly moved into foreign exchange and became a trader on foreign-exchange money markets. I was wheeling and dealing multimillion dollar amounts and eventually reached a management position where I was responsible for as much as a billion dollars a day. It was amazing to get a taste of the larger word of power as traditionally defined.

Around this time, I started to feel something wasn't right. On the surface I had everything I wanted: a glorious house, 2.5 cars, a husband, prestige and excess money to spend. But something wasn't connecting.

For two years, I struggled with the sense that I was living an illusion. I began to realize this was somebody else's definition of success, not mine.

Luckily, a woman who was one notch higher on the ladder wrote a scathing 10-page personnel review of me. I was quite hurt, but within 24 hours was ready with a rebuttal. I demanded a meeting with management. I asked if they knew the report was being written. When they said yes, I asked if they knew there was a personality clash between its author and me. They said they did, and I asked why they didn't have somebody else write the review. They said they thought she might learn something through the process.

Until then, I believed management was on my side, so this was a serious blow. Now, I'm grateful for that experience because that's what it took to get me out of the bank.

I had poured my heart and soul into that job and, when I left, after six years, there was no gold watch. The women who had been my friends took me out for a nice dinner, but that was it. I think I imagined there would be some kind of glory, some kind of acknowledgement like: "You've given your heart and soul to this profession and thanks." But it wasn't forthcoming.

In 1982, at the age of 25, I left everything, including my marriage. I felt I had gone into banking because it was an area that hired females. Now, since I was making a change, I decided to approach work in a more thoughtful way.

At the time, Manpower, as it was called, had a programme directed at women. They offered aptitude and interest tests, followed up with counselling, and in my results, architect, designer, urban planner came up repeatedly.

To make a long story short, I got my diploma in architectural design and drafting, then decided I wasn't satisfied with being somebody's drafts-person, so I applied to university schools of architecture and ended up in Halifax.

That was the beginning of an incredible blooming, even though I soon realized that architecture was extremely patriarchal. For instance, we didn't learn about a single woman architect, so I managed to organize a course on women architects. That was interesting because I learned that women architects of any stature worked differently from the men. Many of their projects were based on social models of community—with communal house-keeping, child care and so on.

I started to apply this knowledge to my projects. Perhaps not surpris-ingly, it received a lot of criticism from my professors.

In my first year, I met some women who were organizing to get a maternity hospital in Halifax and, as a result, my thesis project became a birth centre. Most people spend six months on a thesis. I spent years immersing myself in birthing. I moved to Holland, where about half the children are born at home, and this provided a model I could study. I worked in architectural offices during the day, and at night I was on call with mid-wives, going off to births.

I wanted to design a prototype for a building that had never existed. I didn't feel I could look for models within the patriarchal vision of what space and building meant. I interviewed 400 women from Europe and Canada about their birth experiences and concluded that home was the ultimate birth environment for the majority of normal women. Not only was it familiar, it was their own territory.

After all these years of research, I almost wanted to do a drawing of a frame house and say, "There's my conclusion." However, I felt that would diminish my chances of getting a degree. I also recognized that home birth is a goal we're nowhere near achieving in this culture, so there's a need for bridging institutions such as free-standing birth centres.

I designed a birth centre for a Toronto group and then came up to the eastern Arctic to do some design workshops around a birth centre for the North. I work in a participatory way, which is almost unheard of in architecture. To my mind, it's common sense. You move from people's experience into the design. You don't go in with your own ideas.

For my master's thesis, I presented two birth centres in front of 200 men—and about 20 women. My presentation was partially a critique of architecture and how it's defined. I had a huge 16-foot circle, with a fetus in the middle. When I presented this, the head of the graduate committee —a man who had previously said to me, "I don't give a fuck about birthing or what you're working on. What's important is that you learn to be a good student in this institution"—stopped me a third of the way through and said, "Thank you. We have visiting dignitaries who have to catch planes and we have to stop."

I was shocked. I had spent five years on this project and he just stopped me. "Ten minutes, your time is up." Other people with projects as complex as mine had been given as much as an hour to present their conclusions.

None of the professors would give me a critique and tell me what was wrong. When I talked to the professor who had stopped my presentation, he told me, "You're not getting out of this institution until you learn to conform." The bottom line was a power struggle. I was supposed to look and behave like everybody else.

That was the end of chapter one of my work life, which revolved around an external definition of success, and the transformation period of my schooling. The second chapter is about me creating my own work, by the old adage, necessity is the mother of invention.

It began five or six years ago, when I was pregnant with my daughter. When I became a mother, I remembered those women in the bank who slid into a position because it was part time or close to home or the hours were good. That ends up becoming the work scenario while you're parenting, not because you choose it, but because it's the only thing available that works.

When I began working in the North, I started with a contract position in human-resource planning for the health department. It wasn't my field, but I talked myself into it, because they were looking at making the work force more user-friendly for women. In the midst of the project I got pregnant.

I started to negotiate my maternity leave and they played hardball. The most they would agree to was three months off without pay. I was committed to breast-feeding and being a hands-on, skin-to-skin mother, so I tried to negotiate bringing my baby to work or working from home. They said no to all my suggestions. I couldn't believe the hypocrisy. I was working on a project that explored barriers to women re-entering the work force and I was running head-on into them myself.

I found it impossible to predict that at exactly three months of age my daughter would be ready to leave me, so I left the job and swam around in thesisland for a while. I finally got my master's degree. Ultimately I accepted that sometimes you have to do what is required while trying to maintain as much integrity as possible. I didn't want to say to myself 20 years down the road, "Gosh, my life would be so different, if only I had that."

I had my daughter at home and brought a midwife in from Vancouver. When she came, we had a couple of public evenings, after which she suggested I become a childbirth consultant. I had all this information, why didn't I share it with other women?

Now I have a home business. I'm writing, doing research and selling ergonomic products, as well as being a childbirth consultant and workshop facilitator. I'm less an architect, but I do some design and graphics. I'm also a political activist.

After three years I've found that one of the advantages of this lifestyle is having my daughter in my life. But there are disadvantages, too. It's isolating, there are no benefits and I can't really leave my work because there's no clear designation between work and home. If, for instance, I'm having a serious discussion on the phone and my daughter happens to be screaming in the background, this can be hard on my sense of professionalism.

When the 1991 Census came out, I discovered that I'm not officially counted. My employment comes in spurts of paid work, and when that's not there, I do unpaid work. One of the questions was "How many hours of paid employment did you have last week?" In that particular week I had spent about 100 hours working on a non-profit project without pay. If you answered the question with a figure that was less than such and such, they didn't want you to answer questions 20 to 40, which meant they were completely missing out on people like me who do paid work in spurts. I filled in the section anyway, but I plastered the Census form with sticky notes criticizing the questions.

I ended up writing an editorial on the subject for a magazine, saying, basically, that information is power and when you don't have information about a significant part of your population those people end up being marginalized. I was one of a group of women who went to Statistics Canada and lobbied the head people because they don't ask the right questions to discover more about people's lives. Recently, they've started to consider adding questions about unpaid work.

Speaking philosophically, I've encountered many stones in the path of my work life, but when I stumbled, I discovered they were jewels because they moved me into new areas. Sometimes, though, I feel sad because I imagine other women who stumbled but got stuck.

8

~~~

Natural Resources and Transportation

~~~

Mickey Beagle
New Westminster, British
Columbia

"They used to say women got paid less than men because we worked for pin money. But for many women, a job was an absolute necessity. If a couple both worked in the fishing industry, the family needed two wages to survive because the work was seasonal."

Mickey Beagle, who was born in 1906, began working in the fishing industry in 1949. In the early 1950s, she became involved in the United Fishermen and Allied Workers' Union and worked full time for the union from 1955 to 1971, when she retired.

In 1942, I was married with a young daughter and working as a welder in a shipyard in California. The shipyard is the only place I've ever worked where the women earned as much as the men. My daughter was about eight when I started working there and child care was a problem. After school, she went to a neighbour's house. Often my husband and I worked shifts at different times so she wouldn't be alone. It was hard. People had to depend on neighbours, parents, whomever, to take care of their children.

After the war, our family returned to British Columbia to care for my aging parents. When the war ended, they stopped building steel ships so there wasn't much work for welders. I took a job in a wood-veneer plant and joined the International Woodworkers of America. My union involvement taught me that workers had to unite to achieve anything, but I left that union because of political infighting.

Things were tough because my husband, a longshoreman, wasn't getting much work so I asked my brother, who worked at one of the outpost canneries, if they ever hired women. He said they did, and in 1949 I got a job washing fish in a plant on the Skene River.

In a couple of years, I was working as a filetter. Most of the filletters were women, and although it's a highly skilled job, we were paid less than any guy who walked in off the street and swept the floor.

In those days, there was job, as well as wage, discrimination. If a job was posted specifically for a man and a woman applied, she never got it. Because men's jobs paid more, they couldn't see why women should have them. The native people were treated very badly, as well. In a couple of canneries up north, the washrooms were identified native and white, not men and women. We kept raising the issue but the company never did anything.

Just as an aside, when my daughter was going to university, she worked in the cannery during the summers to pay for her tuition. They still had separate washrooms for natives and whites, so one day she and another young woman decided this had gone on long enough. They were still in their teens, but they took a hammer and knocked the signs down. Those signs never went up again.

As women, we were very aware of being discriminated against. We were continuously fighting for equal pay and child care—all those things that women should have. We finally received equal pay in the canneries, but not in the fresh-fish and cold-storage department. Child care is still an issue, and not only for fish workers. You know it's a myth that women just started fighting for their rights a few years ago. It was going on long before I started, too.

Sexual harassment was also a concern, particularly when there were male bosses and female employees. I remember one incident when I was a salmon inspector. A big-shot manager came over and put his hand under my breast. I knew how important he was, but I had no intention of putting up with that.

"What the hell are you doing?" I asked.

"Do you know who I am?" he responded.

I was furious. "I don't give a goddamn who you are, I don't put up with that kind of stuff."

I knew he wouldn't fire me because I was a good worker and there weren't many people who had the knowledge to be salmon inspectors. But some of the women tolerated it because they thought they'd lose their jobs. It was seasonal work so you tried to earn all you could in the short time available. Even so, most of the women were pretty good at taking care of themselves and looking out for each other by sharing information about what men to watch out for.

In the early 1950s I became a shop steward with the union. I didn't really want the job, but somebody had to do it. You needed to have a lot of guts and I was pretty feisty when I had to be. I worked at several plants: in Prince Rupert, New Westminster and Steveston. Subsequently, I was elected to the general executive board of the United Fishermen and Allied Workers'

Union. When they asked me if I'd run for vice-president, I said yes and was elected. In 1955 I applied for full-time work with the union and was selected for the job of organizer. I stayed until 1971, when I retired. I'm 86 now.

So many things happen, just by chance. People ask me, "What made you want to be a union organizer?" I say, "I didn't. It never entered my head." You get into something, you work at it conscientiously and it just happens.

Whenever I think about what I did in the fishing industry, I'm reminded of how much struggle it involved. But I always believed very strongly in equality because of my father's influence. He was a trade-union man, and he'd also been in the old socialist movement. When we were kids he used to say, "My dear, you're a woman and places for women are very limited. But women should be able to do anything they feel they want to do." So I always knew I should be equal.

I'd also like to say that my late husband, Mervin Beagle, an active union member, was very supportive and proud of my union activity. I think women need unity at home to realize full equality in the workplace.

Ida Gatien
Sudbury, Ontario

"Imagine, going from $14 a day and being a driver to sewing caps!"**

After delivering milk by horse and wagon during the war, Ida Gatien left the work force to raise her family.

I was born in Denmark and came to Canada in 1928, when I was four years old. I left school in Grade 7. My brothers didn't go much farther, because there wasn't any money. In those days, young people had to go out to work to help their families.

While I was growing up, my family managed a farm in Fort William. at one point, we had 60 cows, which my mother, sister and I milked by hand because the guys were working in the field. In the evenings, our arms ached.

Once the war started, small dairies couldn't get equipment like tires so a number of people formed a co-operative. My parents went to work there, and since all the guys were away at war, I got a job in the cooler around 1942.

There were 12 glass bottles in a case and I stacked the cases 12 high. I wasn't tall, but I was strong because I'd done so much physical labour on the farm. I could handle the heavy lifting. I got $7 a day and worked seven days a week. That was good money for a girl. The girls in the stores only made a couple of dollars a day.

Then I noticed that the guys who were driving a horse and wagon were making much more. When I asked for a raise, the boss told me I could only earn more if I went to work on a milk wagon. I found one and doubled my salary overnight. I also had to join the Teamsters' Union. I was the first girl in that local and I remember thinking, "How can I go to a meeting with all those men?" but the rest of drivers were older because, of course, the young guys were all away at the war, and they were pretty nice to me.

Since I'd grown up on a farm, I knew how to drive a horse. We had to harness our own horses in the morning and load our own wagons. We also collected the money, which people left in the empty bottles. You couldn't do that today. The horse knew the route and he walked along from house to house while I ran in with the milk.

One of the things I liked about the job was that I started early and finished by about 10:00, so I had the rest of the day to myself. In the summer, I drove a two-ton truck down to Loon Lake filled with ice cream and milk. I'd leave about 4:00 in the morning, get back about 8:00, then do my regular route in Port Arthur.

It was a good job for me. Although I didn't have enough education to work in a store, I was good with figures. I also liked the fact that you didn't have to get dressed up. I delivered for about two years, then the war ended, the guys came back and that was that—the girls were out.

When I was laid off, I applied for unemployment insurance. They offered me a low-paid job sewing caps, which I refused to take, so I got cut off. Basically, I never went back to the work force.

While I was working at the dairy, I took a night course in sewing. After I got married, I became a seamstress in my house. The first Christmas I was married, I made 30 or 40 sashes for the Fort William Male Choir. I got 50 cents a piece, which gave me the money to buy my husband a Christmas present. Another year, I made about 15 formals for girls who were graduating from the collegiate. I got $5 a piece, which worked out to about 50 cents an hour.

My first child—I had seven—was born within the first year we were married. Once I had a husband and a child to look after I didn't think about working any more, although I've always kept busy. Right now, I'm making needlepoint Christmas stockings for my grandchildren.

Linda McNaughton
Halifax, Nova Scotia

"I'm glad I worked in the wilderness. It was an experience I wouldn't give up for anything."

Linda McNaughton worked as a hairdresser in the late 1960s. She left the work force in 1971 to care for her young children, and in 1977 began to work for an oil-exploration company in Alberta. In 1984, she moved back to Halifax and took a job in the packing room of a large mail-order company.

I grew up in Halifax, left school in Grade 11 and trained as a hairdresser. I worked at a salon for about four years and hated it. Then I got married, had two children and, basically, stayed out of the work force for eight years.

In 1977, I was divorced. I received only $40 a month support from my husband, which hardly kept the kids in breakfast cereal. I recognized I needed to further my education so I took my Grade 12 English, but a week before I finished, my brother, who worked for an oil-exploration company in Alberta, suggested I come out West.

I'd never been away from home before. When I got married, I lived next door to my parents. I was terrified, but I got on a plane and arrived in Calgary. I didn't know a soul. I had forty dollars in my pocket and, it turned out, my brother was in California. The people he shared a house with were very nice. They picked me up at the airport and took me home.

The next morning one of his friends drove me to the company where my brother worked. I didn't tell them who my brother was because I wanted to do this on my own. I was very proud of myself when I got hired.

The job involved laying cable where no roads existed. The cables weigh thousands of pounds, and when I started, I weighed roughly 110. I was so small they called me "Munchkin." On my first job, I stood on the back of the truck and lifted the cables over the side to run in a straight line. The cables attach to each other every 15 metres, and part of my job involved picking the cable up and sliding pins into it to hold it together. It was very difficult work.

Another job involved drilling holes every 50 metres and laying a charge. I learned to use dynamite for blasting and carried it in my truck. I didn't have any formal training, but it wasn't that dangerous. I knew it was men's work, but it was good money and I needed to support my children. It wasn't a lot per hour—sometimes only $5.50 or $5.60—but you worked 12 hours a day, seven days a week, for 90 days, three months at a time. In the end, you made good money because you worked the hours.

While I was away, my mother took care of the children in Halifax and I sent my pay cheque home. We used to get hot-shot money—the company put us up in a hotel and paid us $17 a day for expenses. I ate on $7—lots of peanut butter sandwiches—and saved the $10 to call my kids. I phoned home every day and sometimes at night, if I got really lonely. Being away from my children was the most difficult part of the job.

On most of the crews, there were about 10 women and 50 men, although at one point I was the only woman. You had no access to stores—or even to bathrooms. There were also no trees so the best you could hope for was a little slope in the ground to hide you when necessary.

Despite these unusual conditions, sexual harassment wasn't a problem. These men were good to me. When I came into the room, they'd stop using bad language, and if someone swore, they'd say, "Oops, sorry." I'm not a drinker, but if we did go into a tavern, which often was the only entertainment available, nobody bothered me.

I started work out West in 1979, and in 1981 I began dating my second husband who worked for the same company. He was my boss for a year before we dated, and in 1982 we married, after he came home and met the children. Two years later we went on our own as oil consultants. We commuted back and forth to Halifax, and we'd fly my mother and the children up for the summers, which meant I was never away from the children for any extended period of time.

Although the work was hard, it was rewarding. I loved the peacefulness of the barren landscape in the middle of nowhere. Once I came across a herd of wild horses, and another time my husband and I encountered a black widow spider. It was in a hole, covered with a cobweb, but we could see the orange-coloured hourglass on its back.

We'd go out at 7:00 in the morning and come back late at night. It was like heaven. The peacefulness is still sort of in me. It becomes part of your life, and when you're away from it, you really miss it. I've never spoken to anybody who did this line of work who felt differently.

We had a flourishing little business as oil consultants. My husband was making $350 a day and I was making a $150 a day. When you're working seven days a week that's a lot of money even though we had big expenses. But, in 1984, things took a bad turn. My husband lost everything in the stock market. We had to declare bankruptcy and move back to Halifax.

Of course the work situation in Halifax was worse than in Alberta, but my husband managed to get on with a survey crew. In 1988, I started working in the packing room of a large mail-order operation. I had to have a job because we needed the money, but this work was even harder than the work out West. I had to lift huge plastic containers about the size of a table, fill them with mail I'd sorted, then push them to a conveyor belt.

The fellows were supposed to move the tubs to the conveyor belt, but most of the time the women did that job. I'm not into women's lib, but the guys were usually standing around talking or complaining that the tubs were too heavy, so we lifted them. They were earning quite a bit more than us, too. My wage was $8.94 an hour when I left, and I believe the men were earning in the vicinity of $13.

We sorted the mail for the entire Maritimes and there was a lot of pressure. I went through about 100 tubs a day, each containing about 400 pieces. If one went to the wrong place, I'd get criticized.

I also got filthy. Sometimes, when I finished work, I'd be embarrassed to get on the bus to go home. I felt everybody was looking at me because I had dirt, literally, in the pores of my arms. In Alberta I could walk up to a cap wire after setting off a charge and have it blow in my face and I never got dirtier than I got sorting mail. My hands would crack and bleed, and when I got home I'd notice that my heels cracked, too, from standing on the concrete floors.

Once I got hit in the face with a box that came over the top of my chute. I've still got a mark on my nose where it hit me. At the time I thought I'd broken my nose because it was all swollen up and bleeding, but the bosses were more upset that I went home early. That was what we had to put up with. We were paid well—$8.94 is pretty good for labourers—but we weren't treated well.

The morale was always low and we never got a "thank you." At Christmas, the managers got together and came through in the morning to shake our hands. We used to say they came early, before our hands got too dirty. Even though it was terrible, I needed the work. I'm not trained for anything, so it was a job and that's what I miss now.

The mail-sorting operation eventually moved to Ontario and I've been out of work for the past two years. I've been trying to get some training, but I haven't had any luck. When I started receiving unemployment insurance, I was told I couldn't take a course because while you're training you weren't available to work, which U.I.C. (Unemployment Insurance Commission) demands. So I waited. The week my unemployment ran out, I thought I'd get some training. I called my officer who informed me they had changed the legislation. Now you can only apply for training while you're on unemployment, but they didn't notify anybody of this change!

I applied to the library to take a beginners' computer course and I'm trying to get a job at the company I worked for in the phone-order room. I have a very good reputation as a worker. I'm hoping I'll be able to get back on, because I really miss having a job.

Elizabeth Wieban
Thunder Bay, Ontario

"When I was flying full time, I eventually got to the point where I didn't even think of myself as a female."

Elizabeth Wieban graduated from the University of Western Ontario with a degree in business and economics in 1965. She received her commercial pilot's license when she was 19 and has had a long career in aviation, which was often interrupted by family responsibilities, including the births of her four children. In 1982, she began teaching the Women in Trades and Technology Course at Confederation College, where she currently trains commercial pilots.

I grew up around planes because my father ran an airline out of Fort William. I learned to fly when I was 16, went solo at 17 and got my commercial licence when I was 19. I think my father was a great influence. Not only did he drag my sister and me around with him on airplanes, he made certain we had the same opportunities as our brothers.

There was a strong work ethic in our family and I think the girls benefitted from this more than the boys. My parents owned a lodge and the girls did "male" jobs as well as the conventional female work. As a result, the boys didn't learn as much about cooking as we learned about airplanes.

Even then I sensed that other people had attitudes that differed from ours. Once my father was supposed to teach and he sent me, instead. I got out of bed at 5:00 to do the lesson and the man refused to fly with me because I was a woman.

I didn't intend to marry or have a family so, since my grades were good, I went to the University of Western Ontario to study business and economics. It seemed like the nearest thing to flying that might allow me to make a living. Western was a tremendous culture shock. The only things the other students seemed to be interested in were how they looked and dressed and what sorority they belonged to. I value the education I received, but nothing else.

In 1965, I graduated with a degree in business and economics and went into aircraft sales and flight instructing. A friend and I took courses for our mining licences and were all set to stake claims. Then, within a couple of months, I fell madly in love and married an exploration geologist from South Africa.

That changed my plans, dramatically. We immediately moved to a particularly backward part of Australia. My licences weren't accepted there so I retrained and got hired to open a flight-training and aircraft-sales outlet in the outback. The day I went down to pick up the planes, I discovered I was pregnant. My medical for my licence became invalid and I immediately lost my job.

The irony is that before we left Canada, I went to the doctor and got supplied with two years' of birth control pills so I wouldn't get pregnant. To make a long story short, four years later, I returned to North America with three kids—even though I was taking the pill faithfully. I ended up having four children, and if I had it all to do over again, I'd have five or six. I took to motherhood like a duck to water, although I would never have done it consciously.

In Australia, between pregnancies, I did some charter work. I remember landing at a place on the west coast where a guy refused to refuel my plane because he didn't believe a woman should be flying. I gassed up myself, but since I had a paying passenger, it was particularly humiliating.

When we got back to Canada, I requalified for my Canadian licences and got a job as a flight instructor. Within a month, my husband was transferred to the United States. That meant I couldn't fly again. Not only did I need a work permit, I had to redo all my licences. I plugged away and got my American commercial-pilot's license, but I could only do odd flying jobs since I didn't have my green card. To get a green card I needed a chest X-ray, but my doctor wouldn't authorize it because when I went for the medical, they discovered I was pregnant.

I did a bit of flying while I was pregnant. "I'm not sure what the regulations are, but pull your belly in, keep your mouth shut and keep on doing what you're doing," the doctor told me. I flew in a DC-3 for about five months with another captain, and once my stomach started to expand, I had to make sure I didn't meet him in the aisle. I was flying at 16,000 feet with an oxygen mask, which I probably shouldn't have done. But things worked out. I had a healthy baby and eventually got my green card.

By 1979–80, I was finally ready for full-time employment. I went for an interview, but the owner of the airline wouldn't hire me. He said he wasn't prepared to risk his financial security testing the public's willingness to fly with a woman. The captain went to bat for me. He said I could do the job and promised to keep me out of sight. They used to refer to me as "George" so the passengers wouldn't know the pilot was actually Elizabeth.

That's the story of any progress I've made in aviation. There has always been some man who came along and said, "She can do it. Give her a chance." When I started flying there were no laws to back me up. They'd admit they weren't hiring you because you were a woman and there was nothing you could do.

Within a month of starting that job both my parents became ill. I had to return to Thunder Bay, and when my father died, I had to help sort things out. That took a year, and by that time, my flying job was gone.

My mother owned and operated a lodge at Pays Plat on the north shore of Lake Superior. Since we had bookings, I decided I'd take it over. I hired a pilot to do the bush flying, and when he didn't show up, I thought, "To hell with this, I'll do it myself." So I called my husband and asked if he'd manage the lodge. He left a very good position to come north. We bought the business from my mother and ran it for eight years.

Most of my bush flying was done after my four children were born. Until my husband arrived at Pays Plat, I had a young woman to look after the kids, but I didn't consider her too reliable. So I took my son on all my flights. He sat on a passenger's knee on the way out, and on the return trip, I stuck his car seat on the seat and strapped him in. Taking him along wasn't something I wanted to do. It was something I had to do because I was concerned about his safety.

Once my husband arrived, the situation improved. He ran the business and was the primary parent. Most of my flights were short and I could see the kids in between. We had a woman who did the housekeeping, and my husband and I did the cooking.

I find this part of our lives interesting from the perspective of gender roles. It reversed my parents' roles where my father did the flying and my mother looked after the land operation. It also inverted the existing pattern of our marriage. Even though it was unlike me, I had done the traditional stuff for 10 years. I grew up in a family where I was encouraged to be nontraditional, married a British South African who was very traditional and accommodated myself to his life. Then I became even more non-traditional than my upbringing.

As a woman in a non-traditional field, you're a new animal. The reactions vary, from people who think you shouldn't be there, to people who think you should be, but have no idea of how to cope with you. For instance, one customer I had at Pays Plat was French and terrified of flying. He wouldn't fly with anyone but me. He'd come out when it was rough and bumpy and the plane was bobbing all over, terrified to board. Even so, he always made a point of holding the door open for me. Once we arrived, he'd jump off the plane, kiss the ground three times and then rush over and hold the door open while I climbed out.

Unfortunately, not all discomfort is as benevolent as this. I've been flying as captain when an inebriated passenger reached around from behind me and put his hands on my breasts. I've also had my earphones on and overheard male passengers discussing the merits of going to bed with me.

While we were at Pays Plat, I remember working on the engine of my plane and thinking, I'll probably get grease on my face and my hair will look awful. How can a woman look like this? I always felt that I had to be neat and look good. And then, one day, I said to myself, "This isn't working. I'm not going to be a woman any longer. I'm going to be a person." So if I wanted to be dirty, or wear my workboots, I did.

Some people were shocked. A couple of the customers told my husband that it must be terrible to be married to a woman like me. Society is pretty strict about keeping those barriers in place, so you pay the price. But later, after we'd left Pays Plat, one woman told me she'd never met anyone who was so comfortable in their skin. She said she could see me one day in workboots and another all dressed up and I was equally at ease. That's because I stopped worrying about what it meant to be a woman.

In 1982, I was approached and asked if I'd be interested in starting a programme for women in trades and technology at Confederation College. I was the first woman in the trades building at the college and I brought 16 female students with me. One day, when I was teaching a shop class, I was standing at the photocopier in my workboots and shop coat. A guy passed and commented, "Well, we finally got a woman, but she sure doesn't look like a woman." "Well, if you wanted one who looked like a woman, you shouldn't have hired a lady bush pilot," I replied and kept right on going.

The Women in Trades and Technology course is a powerful course. We teach the terminology, as well as the practical stuff like wiring. I used to say to myself, "Every woman should go through this before she goes out in the world. Then she'd be truly equal."

Teaching the course also taught me an enormous amount about where it's really at for women. I had battled some of the problems head on, but I hadn't recognized they happened because I was a woman. It helped to give me a sense of myself and what people can—and can't—do to you.

Also, I had never worked with women before. I was the only female in my class at university, and wherever I went, to fly or to work, I was the sole woman. I got tremendous satisfaction from seeing these women learn to do non-traditional things like welding. We had our ups and downs, but it was a period of great personal growth for me, as well as for the other women.

After I left, I went into the college aviation programme. That dusted me off from wearing workboots and a cap to where I am now, training commercial pilots for Confederation College. I instructed when I was 19 and said I'd never do it again, but now I find it very rewarding. I'm considered to be a good teacher and I think a lot of that comes from raising four children. I have a better understanding of individual differences. I would never have known that without raising a family because I was a high achiever and I thought everybody was like me.

When I think about what I've done, the image of my dad comes up repeatedly. He pointed me in the direction I took. When I was trying to figure out what I should do and how to do it, I looked to male role models simply because there were no women ahead of me. I could figure out what I liked or disliked about how particular men conducted themselves, but how I could fit that into being female was another matter.

I've encountered a lot of impediments because I have a family. I didn't get to do many of the things I thought I would, but I have no regrets. I'm 50 years old. I've done many things and I've enjoyed myself.

Pam Fleming,
Vancouver, British Columbia

"I've never been interested in reiterating the middle class life-style that I came from. Now, even if I wanted it I couldn't get it."

Pam Fleming, who started working part time in 1972, when she was 14, got her first job as a wilderness maintenance and construction worker in 1975. In 1988, she began working for a non-profit organization devoted to fighting poverty.

I'm 35 years old and I started in the paid work force when I was 14—slinging hamburgers, working in a children's zoo, that kind of thing. Although I'm now working for a non-profit organization, which requires word-processing and people skills, for many years I refused to do traditional women's work. From 1975 to 1983, I worked with Parks Canada and the Alberta Department of Parks and Recreation building hiking trails and doing maintenance in the big parks.

I started working in the parks as a university student when they introduced affirmative-action programmes for women. We actually had an all-woman crew. We got lots of skills training and on-the-job experience with climbing and back-country work.

Entering the labour force at the end of the 1970s, I wasn't necessarily a women's liberationist, but I'd had my consciousness pricked, especially around issues of poverty and violence. I could see the undervaluing of women's traditional work and I didn't want to be paid that way. In retrospect, I also think that at some level I bought into the idea that women's work was dull, which I found to be true.

At the parks, I was doing work that was exciting: flying around in helicopters, building bridges and so on. The work requires a variety of skills—engineering, construction, carpentry and wildlife management, to name just a few. Sometimes we lived in tents above the snow line. All these demands meant that we also had to be able-bodied, and I found it exhilarating to use my body in ways that were intense and integrated.

The training programme also prepared us for some of the full-time jobs like warden and maintenance naturalist. Most of the women went for the management positions, but I was more interested in doing the hands-on work. There's something about wearing a uniform and being associated with the power of management that's never attracted me. I always wanted to be a worker. Often, the lower you were in the park hierarchy, the more control you had over your work. You also didn't have to be accountable to the public because without a uniform, you were less visible.

After that initial all-woman crew, the other crew members were mostly men, as were the crew bosses, although the commitment to affirmative action continued. The bosses agreed it was nice to have women on the crew, and that men and women complimented each others' diversity and skills. It wasn't necessarily that there was a skill variance between the men and women, but sometimes the differential in body size made it an advantage to have women. Because we're smaller and lighter it's often easier for us to reach difficult places, among other things.

Sexual harassment was always implicit, although we rarely called the guys on it. I had a crew boss in Lake Louise who was a dirty old man. He used to pick me up and spank me, and people would laugh and say, "Oh, that's just John." He also used to spy on the women. Sometimes, we would be working in the bush by ourselves and we'd take our shirts off. Since we were out in the middle of nowhere, it seemed okay. John would show up at totally inappropriate times, but there didn't seem to be much point to launching a complaint.

Working in the parks is like being a hockey player. Twenty-five is old. Your disposability is structured in, so you don't really leave, you're just sort of flushed out. As that gradually dawned on me, I started to value my body in a different way. I realized that as much as I was using my body, I was also exploiting it. The pressure was constant to be ultra performing to prove yourself to the guys. We internalized the "high-baller" label. It took me awhile to see how exploitive that was.

I had offers to do outdoor work for private companies, but in 1983, I made a conscious decision not to do this kind of work any longer. After I left the parks, I did a lot of things, including a fair bit of travel. Once I tried to work in a hospital doing food-assembly work; this was so awful I've blocked the experience out of my mind. I don't want to remember the rote work and how it felt to wear that little blue uniform. In those days, there were lots of jobs so if you quit one, you could easily get another.

Because I've never had children, I've been able to work for relatively low wages. I thought that not having children would buy me some options like disposable income, but I was wrong. As a sole-income support person without a heterosexual relationship I have no mission in society and I feel highly marginalized because there's no niche for women like me.

After almost 20 years in the work force, I've never had a full-time salary, probably because I tried so hard to avoid traditional women's work. The work I'm doing now is kind of linear, and unlike my park work, it makes me feel split from my body. On the positive side, I'm working with an organization, Stop Legislated Poverty, that's committed to social change and that gives me a stronger sense of doing something worthwhile than using my body ever did. I'd like to do some writing and spend some time finding my creative voice. But if you work at a job without much disposable income, you can't take time off to write.

Vicky Hammond
St. John's, Newfoundland

"I like work that's intense and all consuming and then goes away. When I come ashore I have a big hunk of money and time."

Since graduating from high school in the early 1970s, Vicky Hammond has had a variety of jobs. She worked in a health-food store, made furniture, delivered mail, toured with a theatre group and was a bartender. In 1989, she was hired as a fisheries observer.

I'm a fisheries observer, which means I go out on fishing boats, usually alone, to observe, record and report. Observers don't have enforcement powers, but our presence helps to keep everybody fishing legally. We also sample the fish, so the work has a biological component. And because we're often on foreign boats, some of which are very high-tech, we're asked to observe the technology.

I got the job through an advertisement. I used to be a bartender and many of my customers were fisheries observers, so they urged me to apply. I'd been planning to open a specialty seafood business with another woman, making things like smoked salmon. We did a short course on seafood processing, which included sampling. Although the business didn't pan out, the training was useful for this job.

In the past, they looked for inshore fishermen or people with biological training to be fisheries observers. Now, I think, they look for a certain personality type: people who can work alone and are pretty diplomatic. When you're on the ships, you don't want to aggravate the crew. You have to be sociable but self-sufficient, because on many boats no one speaks English. You also have to be able to deal with paperwork and math.

I had no particular training for the job. I graduated from high school in St. John's and went to work in a health-food store. Then my son was born, and his father and I made furniture. We did that for years and made a living, although it was hard. After that I worked in the post office as a letter carrier and then in a touring theatre group. I did acting, writing, costumes, stage managing, whatever was on the go.

Aside from assorted gigs in theatre, my main job before observing was bartending. I was a good bartender and I liked it. I put a lot of energy into the job, but seeing my friends drunk all the time was a problem. My boyfriend often drank in my bar and, after awhile, dealing with him became tiresome. The hours were also stressful. I usually got home at 5 a.m., exhausted, slept until noon, got up, did errands and went back to work again.

On the positive side, being a bartender paid fairly well—at least it did for me, because I worked in a busy bar and made good tips. It was also an incredible training ground. Still, the idea of tending bar for 40 years didn't appeal to me. I like variety, excitement and adventure.

In that sense, being on the boats suits me. You don't know where you're going, who the other people are or what you might encounter in the way of weather, or anything else. There's no drinking, no partying, no phones, and there's lots of time to read and reflect. I love being at sea. I sleep better and I find it fascinating—the fish, the weather, the water. I'm an observer by nature. I watch and think about things.

One bonus about being at sea is not having a boss. I like working with other people, but in my own fashion. They tell me what they want and I decide how to get it. The hardest thing is the arithmetic and the paperwork.

Although I'm sometimes away for as long as 3½ months, the norm is 30 to 40 days. When I first started, about 4½ years ago, I worked about 150 days a year, but when things were at their peak, the norm was 200. I've been working less and less—now 60 days a year is a luxury. Because of the problems with the fishery, there isn't enough work for all of us, so if things don't change, they'll be major layoffs. My seniority puts me right on the cusp.

We're paid per day and laid off when we're ashore, but U.I. (Unemployment Insurance) treats us very well because the government wants us. Some of us do a bit of work on shore, but it's difficult because you can't commit to anything. If you want to keep the job, you have to be available when they call, and that's becoming a problem because I get offered interesting work catering for film crews or other cooking jobs, which I'd love to do. On the other hand, I want to hang onto observing because it suits me so well.

The company has had good luck using women as observers, possibly because the job requires diplomacy. Although they're willing to hire us, they don't get too many applicants, probably because many women are dubious about being at sea with a bunch of men, or their significant others can't handle the idea. Sailors have a bad reputation, which in my experience is totally unfounded.

Although I've experienced some discrimination, I've also found that being a woman can work to my advantage. For example, women observers almost always get private accommodation, whereas men have to share with the crew. The amount of paperwork makes sharing a real hardship for the men, as well as for us. Sometimes the fish they want us to watch have diurnal cycles so we have to observe them at night, which is difficult if you're sharing a cabin. On the other hand, women probably don't get some trips because not all boats have private accommodation. We can insist, but we don't because we know it creates hardships.

A few skippers—men from traditional cultures—have problems with women, but they know better than to express these directly. I have to be very careful with those guys and it's tedious. They won't help women observers the way they'll help men. Sometimes the crew members are difficult, probably in response to concerns raised by their wives and girlfriends, although it's hard to imagine a less romantic situation.

It's a perk to get on a Canadian boat; it's like being out to sea with a bunch of big brothers from around the bay. And, obviously, communication is much easier when we all speak the same language. I can ask detailed questions and get answers I readily understand.

Even so, I really like the Russians. The Canadians go to sea for short periods—10 days out is the general routine—whereas the Russians go for six to eight months at a time. They're more sailors than fishermen, if you get my meaning. Also, there are women on the Russian boats. They're working-class people with lively intellectual lives. They read and stay up all night, drinking tea and arguing about religion and politics, or whatever. They're like Newfoundlanders, but there's something added—for instance, you get a girl who scrubs floors for a living and reads poetry.

Observers can't really work past 50 because of the physical demands, and I'm almost 40. Right now my biggest option for new work is cooking and catering in film and theatre. I'm a good cook, but it's not something I really want to do—it's something people are willing to hire me to do. I'm more interested in art development, but I also like working outdoors. If I get laid off in the spring I'll probably look for work up north, which is something I've always wanted to do. I'm qualified to supervise a small fish plant.

I've entertained a lot of lofty ambitions, but I don't always have the discipline to achieve them. I like writing, and one day I may get the nerve to do something about that. I'd also like to make short films. On a day-to-day basis, I associate with the arts community in St. John's. There are a lot of similarities between people who do that kind of work and those who go to sea. Security isn't the issue.

Judi Vinni
Thunder Bay, Ontario

" I don't know why I keep ending up in places where they tell me, 'Oh, you're not a boy? Well, then, you shouldn't be doing this.'"

Judi Vinni trained as an athletic therapist and graduated from Sheridan College in Oakville, Ontario, in 1981. She began working as a heavy-equipment operator in 1983.

I got my first non-traditional job—as a skitter operator—when I was 22. A skitter is a piece of heavy equipment that prepares land so they can plant trees. it's hard physical work, and if something goes wrong, you have to walk half a mile out through the bush. But I had never felt such power, so physically strong and in control.

I worked 12-hour shifts day and night. I loved being out in the bush, and on my days off, I stayed there. The problem is, I was the only woman in a camp with a bunch of men and I was a real oddity. They brought a separate trailer out for me, and the rule was that I was not allowed to go near the men's trailer when I was off work because of potential problems.

The sexual innuendos were constant and I was always under a spotlight. For instance, if I got a flat tire the guys would stand around watching to see how I'd cope. On the other hand, if a guy got a flat, they'd pitch in and help.

Being female in this position was such a source of constant pressure that in the end I left the job. I had never quit anything before and it was very demoralizing. I felt like a failure.

I decided to go to heavy-equipment school at Quetico Centre. Heavy-equipment jobs are hard to get—you usually get hired because you know someone—and I thought taking the course would open doors for me. But the same problems I had experienced in the bush surfaced again. At the school, the men lived in a beautiful residence and studied together. I had to live in a house, half a mile down the road. I wasn't allowed to go into the residence because, I was told, the wives of the men who were training had complained about having women students around.

Once again, everything came back to my sexuality. I thought my treatment was very unfair. I just wanted to do what the men did.

In the end, my heavy-equipment training didn't pave the way for employment opportunities. The only job I could get was as a labourer at a mine west of Thunder Bay. There were 300 men and me, and I was on guard every moment. Finally, I was offered the chance to operate a scoop tram. My father has been a miner all his life and he begged me not to do it. By that time I had met my husband-to-be, so I decided to leave.

I moved back to Thunder Bay and got a job with the North Western Ontario Women's Health Network. I had trained as an athletic therapist and could develop workshops. I had never worked with women before and now I was part of a collective. It was the first time I had felt such support. I'd walk in and they'd say, "Your dress is beautiful" or, "You look down today." Being able to relax about my femaleness was quite overwhelming. It was also exciting to discover the joys of working with women because working with men, I'd always been ready for anything.

In 1986, I started to teach in the Women in Trades and Technology programme at Confederation College. Again, being the lone woman was very difficult. The male instructors make good money, and are supposedly professionals, but many of them are as bad as, if not worse than, the men I encountered in the bush.

For instance, in January, after I'd been there about three years, the new calendars were posted and someone complained about the images of women. Even though I'd had nothing to do with the complaint, the guys showed their fists to me when I passed them in the hall.

It took me awhile to realize that when men start telling dirty jokes in the coffee room, it's time to walk out. It's no use trying to raise their consciousness because they just aren't going to stop telling the jokes.

When I was pregnant I remember picking up a bag of screws and hearing a guy say, "Oh, she's already been screwed." Another time, I was having coffee with the secretary and she asked if I was going to breast-feed my baby. When I said, "Of course," one fellow piped up, "Well I can hardly wait to see that." I was so offended, my body quivered. How could something so natural as feeding a child become so demeaningly sexual?

When I moved back to Thunder Bay, my husband and I set up a transmission repair shop. In the beginning, I washed parts at night. Now I help to run the business.

We're doing quite well, but the automotive industry in this area is very traditional and the sexism is constant. When I answer the phone, men say things like, "That's all I want to do, talk to a woman," and hang up. And when I come in to fix my own car, the guys who work here gather around to watch. They want to do it for me, and it's reached the point where I often just let them.

At the shop, we make a point of treating men and women the same way. This has turned out to be good for business because many women have commented on how comfortable we make them feel. Some of this is due to me, but I also happened to marry a guy who has the same attitude.

I have one child who's 1½ years old and I've decided I'm going to have some more babies. We're building a house and I've made a decision not to go back to the college in the fall. I plan to work at a sawmill in the mornings, sawing wood and piling lumber, because I need to do physical work to feel fit and happy with myself. I'm also planning to work with an artist friend doing woodworking.

All my life I've questioned my interest in non-traditional work, but as more women get involved, the situation is improving. Eventually, society will have to accept that we're regular women who just happen to be heavy equipment operators, electricians or stationary engineers.

Candace Crossan
Saltspring, British Columbia

**" I 'm big for a flight attendant. I'm also curvaceous and volup-
tuous and, in certain situations, the pilots have taken outrageous liberties."**

*Candace Crossan graduated from high school in 1973 and became a flight atten-
dant the following year. In 1991 she became part owner of a store selling clothes
for size-plus women, which she operates while continuing her airline work.*

I've been a flight attendant since 1974. I was 19 when I started and it was
my first job. I decided to become a flight attendant for no very good reason. I'd been accepted at university, but wasn't ready to go. I had a taste
for travel and, like many people, thought it would be great to get paid for
seeing the world.

There's tremendous discrimination in flight attending. Last year I
came off what they call the incharge list. I bid down to be a flight attendant
so I could get better flights and go overseas. No one laid a hand on me
when I was incharge, but as a flight attendant, all of a sudden I was free
game. I'm still reeling from the shock. I'm not talking about the traditional slap, pinch and tickle. Big, sturdy guys just grabbing and fondling—
anything is fair game.

My outrage was totally dismissed. The response was, "We're only having fun." But when I was in a power position as an incharge, nothing inappropriate ever happened.

Many of the senior male flight attendants were recruited from major
hotels in Europe, and their attitudes towards women are archaic. I remember one guy who kept following me around the aircraft, grabbing me.
Finally, I said, with a wonderful smile on my face, "If you don't stop touch-
ing me I'm going to knee you in the nuts." Most of the other women choose
to go along with it. So most of the time, I'm out there by myself, which I
don't like.

The passengers can be a problem, too. Last year, I had an Australian
chap in business class who slapped me on the tush as he came into the plane.
I wanted to call the police, but the male incharge wouldn't support me.

Once I was crawling around on the floor, looking for something that

had dropped, and a male passenger said, "While you're on your knees...."
He literally said that! His wife was sitting in front of him with their two
teenage kids. It was very obvious that he wanted a blow job. I was outraged.
"I hope you don't mean what I think you mean," I retorted. He just smirked.

I went to the incharge, and instead of supporting me, she was ready to
apologize for my anger. "Oh my dear, with what goes on in the cockpit, we
don't have time to worry about things like this," she said.

When I put on my uniform I get hungry, I get tired and I get amnesia.
Although I enjoy the job, when I put on the wings there's clearly a dichotomy between myself and the role I'm playing. I'm sure this happens to other
women, too, because when we get together the stories flow.

Trying to be that perfect person in uniform is always an issue. The
boarding uniform is a little-girl uniform and I've got a woman's figure. The
other flight attendants call me "Boom Boom" because I'm, you know, busty.
I come down the aisle, boom, boom, boom, boom.

Eating is a big issue with flight attendants. All they talk about is the
food they don't, can't and won't eat. First class often has a great surplus of
food. On long flights, there's nothing else to do but eat and we're not supposed to. In 1990, I decided I wasn't going to be a size 12 any more, and
I went to a size 16. People started asking me if I was OK, because being
fat means you're not OK.

They call this job the golden handcuffs because it's so hard to leave.
Most of my colleagues were nurses or teachers when they started, but they
haven't kept up their skills, so they worry, "What am I going to do if something happens to the airline?" Often you feel trapped.

I'm a lesbian so I certainly don't fit the stereotype of a flight attendant.
I don't know of too many lesbians in the job. There are a few, I've heard
from the boys, but they're not interested in being visible. I have no idea
why it's such a big secret for women, because it isn't for male flight attendants. In a sense you'd think the profession would be even more supportive
since the majority of flight attendants are female. But it's not an industry
that lends itself to rabid feminists. If you showed any signs of that, the
pressure to leave would be tremendous, because the job revolves around
serving—mostly men.

In 1991, the airline offered intermittent leaves of absence so I decided
to pare down to one flight a month, which would give me time to think of
an alternative career. One day, a friend of a friend phoned me out of the
blue and said, "I have an idea for a business, do you want to be partners?"

"What's the business?" I asked. She told me it sold clothes for plus-size women on consignment, then she said, "It happens to be for sale. Would you like to see it?"

"It has to be before I leave on the 4:21 to Bangkok!" I replied. We went, we saw and we bought, within a few hours. On a whim. Then she turned to me and asked, "Do you have any money?" It was sweet actually. We're very good business partners and she takes care of things when I'm flying.

The business was an immediate success, much to my chagrin, since I wasn't ready for it. But it's been a fabulous learning experience and it's wonderful to provide a product to people who really need it.

My involvement in the business originated as a fashion issue. Women's figures and how they relate to their clothes and their images is a big concern, and I feel very strongly that the economic and emotional support for larger women doesn't come from the fashion industry. Thirty-nine per cent of North America's female population is size-plus. If you're a large size 14, which is really quite medium, you have to pay a great deal for clothes and you have very little selection, especially in Canada. I'm appalled at what is out there. I wanted to target a market I believed in.

I'm a size 14-plus myself. You can imagine being a big flight attendant and buying clothes all over the world. I had an entire store in my cupboard so I recycled a lot of my own things. Then I flew to Hong Kong and bought a lot of samples. We opened with very little ado and right away the people flocked in. It's thrilling to hear people say, "A store for me!" And they don't have to pay through the nose.

Shortly after we opened, I hired a full-time alterationist because large women, even more than small ones, have figures that are interesting shapes. A little nip and a tuck, here and there, makes a world of difference with used clothes.

I've always liked fashion. I wear make-up and high heels and I love to get gussied up. And, of course, because I'm a lesbian this is perceived as a dichotomy. I've been criticized for that in the lesbian community. In fact, once I was dating a wonderful woman who wore Nikes and some friends of hers invited her for dinner. When she asked if I could come, they said, "Oh, she's the one who wears lipstick and high heels. She's not welcome." My friend said, "I'm not coming if she's not coming."

When she told me this, it really got me fired up. I thought, one day I'm going to have the power to dress lesbians. They want to look good. So what started as a fashion statement quickly became a political statement.

We opened in July 1991 and in March 1992 we had our first fashion show. The models were all lesbians, large, beautiful women and the community was invited. We sold out. It was so successful, we decided to have another show the following September and it was stupendous, too.

I decided that I wanted older women, younger women, soup to nuts, and the show just took on its own life. We got a wonderful Harley-Davidson with a sidecar and a woman who is 78 modelled denims in the Harley. She wanted to be a motorcycle mama! The models had a ball!

I'm not worried about the store making money and expanding. The integrity and loyalty of our customers has been exciting. I've also enjoyed being committed to something. The recycling aspect alone is thrilling. Our motto is: "If we could get into each other's closets, we'd never buy retail again." There's a lot of stuff out there, but trying to get people to part with their things takes great tact. It's an art form, in itself, as I'm finding out.

I really believe that fashion is fun and I worry that we've lost this. In the move to liberate ourselves from sex roles, we've thrown the baby out with the bath water. The F-word isn't feminism, it's fun. Fun with clothes, with shopping, with adorning the body. Nothing is more empowering than feeling good about your body.

9

Public
Administration
and Defence

Willa Walker
St. Andrews, New Brunswick

"It was soon established that we would be a regular part of the RCAF, not a separate women's entity. Unlike the army and the navy, I had men reporting to me."

Willa Walker was born in Montreal in 1913. She celebrated her 21st birthday in Japan, while working as postmistress on the Empress of Britain. *When war broke out, she joined the Royal Canadian Airforce (RCAF) and, in 1943, became head of the RCAF's Women's Division. That year, she also became the first member of the Women's Division to receive the rank of wing commander.*

I had a wonderful time on the *Empress of Britain*. Every member of the crew was gunning for me because they'd never had a female postmistress before. I worked very hard to prove myself. I wanted to make a career of it, but my father insisted I return to Montreal.

After travelling around the world and earning my living, I couldn't go back to being a debutante, so I got a job with William Notman, the photographer, as a kind of receptionist. I was determined to go back to China, but my father felt it was too dangerous. One day, sitting at breakfast, I picked up the (Montreal) *Gazette* and read that Sir Herbert Marler, a family acquaintance, had been posted to Washington as head of the Canadian legation. "I wonder if Lady Marler would want a secretary in Washington?" I mused.

"I'm so fed up with you wanting to go places and do things. Why in God's name don't you send her a cable and apply for the job?" my father snorted.

I did just that and received a cable in reply that terrified me. "Delighted. Will interview you in August in Montreal." I got the job and had two exciting years in Washington, 1937–39, during the abdication and leading up to the war. The position involved a lot of socializing, and when I found myself reading the social columns to see if I'd been mentioned, I decided it was time to return to Montreal.

My father was an honorary aide to Lord Tweedsmuir, the Governor-General. They had these ridiculous events where you had to be presented and curtsy. One of the Governor-General's aides was a very good-looking man in a Black Watch kilt and full-dress uniform. That summer we were married.

It was one of those extraordinary things—love at first sight. Three days after we returned from our honeymoon, war was declared. David joined his regiment in Scotland, the Black Watch, and my father got me passage on an American ship from New York, so I could join him.

I was with David from September 1939 until May 1940. Then he went to France with the British expedition and the entire highland division was captured. He was listed as missing in action for three months. We finally got the message that he had been captured, but that he was alive and well.

My family was anxious to have me return to Canada, particularly since I was pregnant. In November 1940, our baby, Patrick, was born in Montreal, and 2½ months later he died suddenly in his pram of crib death.

After Patrick died, I had a pretty hard time. I was living with my parents and didn't have anything to do so I got involved with a volunteer group that raised money to buy Spitfires for the war. Then I decided to start the Canadian Prisoners of War Association. Under the Geneva Convention a family could send one clothing parcel and one of food every two months. We tried to make sure the prisoners were getting what they needed.

I should mention that David tried to escape many times and was decorated at the end of the war for these attempts. I'm very proud that I was able to help by sending him a map in one of my parcels. I had the RCMP put the map in the soles of a pair of black shoes. I also sent him some skates, which he made into blades that could be used to cut the barbed wires.

When they started recruiting for the air force, a friend telephoned and asked if I was going to join up. I said I didn't think I could because my only relevant skill was typing, although I could also ride a bicycle, which I thought might qualify me to be a messenger. Anyway, I was persuaded to enlist.

I was one of the first 150 women from across Canada who joined the RCAF. We were given a basic seven-week training course by the most splendid WAC officers from England. Since we were a regular part of the RCAF, our women officers would be members of the officers' mess. We'd have separate barracks, but we'd work with the men, eat with them and share their rec halls.

At our first breakfast, awful old male air-force cooks doled out baked beans from a garbage can. Then we got our uniforms and were drilled up and down the parade square. In seven weeks some of us were made officers and some NCOs (non-commissioned officers). It sounds conceited, but I came out as the top recruit.

There were ten commands in Canada. I got Ontario and was based in

Toronto. But I was also responsible for getting all 10 stations ready for the arrival of women. I had to visit each station with a medical officer and the person we called "works and bricks"—the officer who was in charge of building barracks.

When I started my visits, the men didn't think I should eat in the officers' mess because I was a woman. I didn't think this was right—particularly since more women officers would be arriving in a few weeks. So I told my staff that I planned to teach the men a lesson. I instructed my driver to park my car right outside each officers' mess, and ate my lunch in the car, even though it was 10 below zero.

I followed my plan for three stations with no results. Meanwhile, my male friends were so upset by the image of me sitting pathetically in the car, freezing and talking to my driver while I ate lunch, that they spread the word. By the fourth station, I was allowed into the officers' mess, and when all our women officers arrived, they were allowed in, too. I think this is a lesson for women's lib. If you play it carefully, you can get your own way.

I also discovered that at one station an officer had put barbed wire all around the women's barracks, I assume to protect them from the men. I said this was ridiculous and eventually the barbed wire came down.

Of course, there were a few incidents of rape and harassment, but I think they were isolated. The world was pretty tame in those days, and everyone was determined that nothing would happen to the girls who, in most cases, knew nothing about sex. Also, the women had their own women officers so they always had someone to go to. We never sent them anywhere without a woman officer. Young women today don't necessarily have that option.

Kay Walker (no relation) was the first woman to head the women's air force, and when she was sent to run the women of the RCAF in England in 1943, I took over her position in Ottawa. That was a great experience! I loved watching those young women grow and develop. They arrived in civilian clothes to be outfitted in their uniforms, then they'd go on to their trades training. We started with six trades and 150 women. By the end of the war, we had 17,000 airwomen and 55 or 60 trades. These young women were working as photographers, telegraph operators, teleprinters, meteorologists and so on. It was extraordinary.

At one point, our uniform was redesigned to make it smarter. Eaton's said they would run a picture of the airwomen wearing the new uniform to encourage other women to join up. Yousuf Karsh was the photographer. He came out to the base and inspected 500 women on parade. "Willa," he said, "there's not one who has what it takes to be a model." Eaton's eventually used a professional.

At my husband's request, I asked Karsh if he would take a photograph of me, as David wanted a picture of me to put over his bunk. When he received it, he wrote that it was a "handsome likeness," but he had trouble relating this person in a military uniform, wearing the three bars of a wing commander, to the wife he had left behind. Worse still, once his fellow POWs (prisoners of war) saw it, they immediately christened me the air vice-marshall and "How's the air vice-marshall doing?" became the running joke. So Karsh took another picture of me wearing a tweed jacket and smiling, and David liked it very much.

I had gone to headquarters in 1943 and I left in 1944 when our troops reached the Rhine. There was talk that the war would end by Christmas and I wanted to be in the UK when David was released. This was the only time I ever used women's tears to get what I wanted. Although I'd signed up for the duration of the war and the period of demobilization, I went to Air Vice-Marshall Sully, who was an awful old stuffy stick, and I burst into tears.

"You've simply got to let me go," I cried. "I've got to be back in the UK when my husband is released." Sully was just marvellous. He arranged for me to be retired in England, which meant I could go over in uniform on a troop ship. I sailed from Halifax with seven nursing sisters and 1,000 men.

As I was going up the gangway, a Royal Canadian naval officer who was standing on the dock called out, "Hi, Willa, I'll see you on board. I've got a couple of barrels of oysters set aside."

I didn't remember ever seeing him before, but the oysters turned out to be a great boon. We were only fed twice a day, at 8:00 in the morning and 8:00 at night, so we got pretty hungry in between. We used to go to the purser's office, with a couple of other male officers, and the purser would provide brown bread and butter. I consumed four or five dozen oysters at a time, everyday.

When we arrived in London, I was still in my uniform. One day, I was walking along the street and I saw the oyster man coming along with two other navel officers. They had obviously been celebrating. I said, "Hello, George." He looked at me and said, "And who in the hell are you?"

Well, at least I enjoyed the oysters, I thought.

Before I was retired, I had a marvellous interview at Buckingham Palace with Queen Elizabeth, who is now the Queen Mother. I waited in a little sitting room with a blazing fire, and by the time she arrived I was boiling hot. I also had to curtsy, which was difficult in my uniform. I spent about an hour with her and she wanted to know all about David and her nephew, who was also a prisoner of war. By that time, we were allowed to wear silk stockings with our uniforms—we had started off with grey lisle—and at the end of the interview she asked if we could get nylons in Canada. My heart sank when I realized I should have brought her some nylon stockings.

After David and I were reunited, he arrived home one day and asked if I wanted to go to India as he'd been offered a position in the vice-regal household. I was a terrible cook and hated cooking so I asked if going to India meant we could have a cook. When he said definitely, I said let's go.

I never returned to the work force after the war. Our second son, Giles, was born in January 1946, then we had three more boys. Wouldn't you know after being in charge of 17,000 women I'd have five sons?

Margaret Littlewood
Edmonton, Alberta

"I would have loved to work on the airlines, but I was born at the wrong time."

Margaret Littlewood had her first flying lesson in 1938. She taught flying at a Toronto school until 1942, then moved to Edmonton where she taught at an Air Service School for 14 months. After the war, she went to work for the federal government and retired in 1980, after 35 years of service.

I had my first airplane ride in 1938 with the Gillies' Flying Services. The Gillies had an only child, Marian, and they were friends of my family. She never bothered with flying, but her father wanted to advertise the school so he asked her to get her licence for publicity purposes. She agreed, but only if she wasn't the only girl at the school. Since the family knew me, he suggested I learn, too.

Today, when I read of girls who had three part-time jobs, and so on, to pay for their flying lessons, I feel guilty. It was handed to me on a platter. I didn't have to pay a cent for my training, until after the war when I got my airline-transport licence.

In 1938, I shared Marian's lack of interest in flying, but I soon learned the basics. Mr. Gillies publicized our training and got write-ups and pictures in the newspaper. Then he suggested we get our commercial licences. During the day, I was working at Eaton's in the mail-order department as a parcel girl, making $12.50 a week. It was a long trip to Barker Field after work.

Once we got our commercial licence, Marian and I flew passengers on weekends. We gave them five- and 10-minute rides over the city. Over a period of about three years, Mr. Gillies acquired quite a few aircraft, but his real love was fishing. He got the bright idea that Marian and I should run the school, so he could get away to Lake Simcoe to fish with his friends.

Marian worked in the office during the week. When it wasn't busy, she could put in flying time. I was still working at Eaton's so she got her instructor's licence before me. Once she started to teach, I left Eaton's and went to work in the office, which meant I had more opportunity to chart my solo time. Finally, we got a girl to look after the office and I went to Trenton and finished my instructor's licence.

It's kind of a strange story, but it all worked out. Marian and I ran the school, we had a girl in the office and Marian's father got away on his boat.

The job didn't lack excitement. I remember at least one forced landing in a little Cub 50 flying back from London. Jimmy, a commercial student, was in control. Ten miles west of Malton we heard the most awful bang. Then another one. I looked around and I just can't describe the look on Jimmy's face. He took his hands and feet off the controls and said, "Marg, it's all yours. " I managed to land safely in a farmer's field.

We had one part-time male instructor, Stan, an awfully nice chap who stayed with us until the war broke out. All the instructors had their own students and if a person started out with one, they'd stay with him or her so long as they were satisfied. Sometimes, though, people would react to the idea of a female instructor. "You mean a girl's going to teach me? I'd rather have a man." We could understand. We were a novelty, so we didn't take offence.

Of course the war was building and we sensed it would have an impact on us. Sometime in 1941, the government closed down civilian flying for gas rationing. Marian and I were devastated. We'd worked so hard on getting our licences. We decided to close the school in November of 1942, and at that point, one of my students suggested I write to the Air Service Schools.

Ten of these training schools were scattered across Canada. I wrote to all of them and, of course, I didn't expect to be well received because I was a woman. I heard from nine, and in short they said, "Thanks, but no thanks. We don't have time." Between the lines was the message "particularly for a girl." But they were polite.

That left only one more school to hear from: Edmonton. The great Wop May, a famous bush pilot, was head of that one. He didn't bother writing. That's the way Wop was. He phoned and said, "How soon can you be out here? I'm losing one of my instructors."

I was 27 and that's how I became the first woman Link Trainer instructor. I immediately wrote to Stan, our part-time instructor, who was already in Edmonton. Like many of the boys who had commercial licences, Stan headed for the training schools when the war broke out because they didn't want to be drafted into the army and waste their flying skills.

We arranged that I'd arrive in Edmonton by train on February 1, 1943. Stan met me, and Wop May wrote a nice little note. That was quite an honour. I have it my scrapbook. He said, "Miss Littlewood, I understand you're arriving at the CPR station, uptown. Stan says he'll meet the Train, but in case he doesn't, I'll meet the train myself."

When I arrived at the school, I met Mr. May and then saw the Link Trainer room. There was a big, black-and-white sign on the door: No Unauthorized Admittance. Suddenly, I had the horrible feeling that I'd be caught out for bluffing. I'd never even seen a Link Trainer, but I'd said I thought I could master it because of my experience in the air.

As a ground-training device for pilots, a Link Trainer does pretty much everything an airplane will do. You can spin it and get the same effect, but it's on a pedestal and never leaves the room. When I first saw the two Link Trainers at the school, I thought, "What darling little airplanes!"

It was the best job I ever had. I only worked four hours a day, I guess because they figured the radio signals were hard on you. I never called Mr. May by his first name and he never called me Margaret. I was always "Skinny" or "Slim." I was so busy that there wasn't enough time to eat and my weight dropped dramatically. One student after another wanted to join the air force.

Some of these young boys would arrive for training with such big smiles and happy faces you could just, like a mother, hug them. There was one likable 19-year-old kid who loved to fly, but was a little daredevil. I gave him the elementary work and we were working on radio-range problems—I'd send him out in the rain and lose him, so he had to figure out how to get back in. After I finished, I showed him his errors and I asked if he had any questions. He looked at me and said, "How come you aren't married?" He wasn't listening at all, the little monkey. Of course, that floored me.

I enjoyed teaching Hollick Kenyon. He's a great name. He was Admiral Bird's navigator on his expedition to the South Pole. And Grant McConachie and Vic Fox, who were legendary bush pilots. The first time I met Vic, he had a bushy beard and was wearing a Siwash sweater. I thought, he's such an experienced pilot, he'll never listen to me." But eventually, Vic would phone up and say "Is Marg on duty? I want to book with her." My greatest satisfaction was knowing that if these boys got lost in bad weather, my training might save their lives.

I taught 140 pilots and I can only recall one who seemed to resent the fact that I was a woman. I just got the feeling that he didn't like taking instructions from a girl. When you feel that, you don't want to force a person, so I told the other three instructors that when so-and-so came in they should do their best to take him because I felt he'd rather have a man.

Stan told me that when I was hired, it was circulated around the station that a lady Link instructor was coming. One day, a bunch of the guys were in the canteen having coffee and one said "Why did we have to get the first woman?"

"Yeah, and I'll bet she's some old dame with a hatchet face!" said another.

Then a third said, "I bet she wears size 12 shoes!" That really cracked me up. I thought it was just great. I put myself in their place. Why *did* they have to get the first woman?

After I'd been there for about 14 months, the government closed the Air Service schools because the war was progressing favourably. I thought, "What am I going to do now?" Through Wop's connections, I learned they were getting six new Link Trainers in Montreal. One chap told me to get down there quickly because there was a vacancy as a secretary in the office. The idea was that I'd be there when the trainers were installed, prepared to work.

I moved to Montreal and rented a room. My job was typing and filing in the crew-assignments office and, wouldn't you know, shortly after I started, the war went so well they cancelled the trainers. What a letdown! Since I didn't care for Montreal, I came back to Edmonton.

I wrote a few letters to Canadian Pacific airlines and Trans Canada, as Air Canada was known in those days, but I knew they'd never hire a woman. Now, the women pilots are doing fine, and I'm happy for them, but in those days, forget it. So I got a job with the post office, doing shorthand and all the usual stuff. I needed the job because I had no one to take care of me.

After about 12 years, I got tired of people asking why I wasn't with an airline. It embarrassed me so I got a job as secretary to the superintendent of airports for the western region. At least it was in the government division that controlled flying. I stayed with the federal government for 35 years. I retired in 1980, from Environment Canada, a bit early because my boss felt I should have credit for the 14 months I worked as a Link trainer since it was similar to the air force and the boys were getting benefits for that.

Even though I knew I'd never get hired by an airline, I got my public-transport licence, which qualified me to be an airline captain, in 1953. I wanted to do it for the sense of accomplishment. It would have been different if I'd married and had a family, but I had nothing to hold me back.

I do regret not having the chance to fly commercially. That's definitely what I wanted, but it was hopeless. How I envy the girls now. I gave up because I could see I wasn't going to get anywhere. I thought I might as well settle down to doing office work. Thank goodness Mom and Dad made me take a full three-year commercial course.

Madeleine Delaney-LeBlanc
Fredericton, New Brunswick

"I had thought about rejoining the work force and had read so much about it that I was ready to go. I can't say that I felt guilty. But I remember many people—friends, relatives, neighbours—trying to lay the guilt on me."

Madeleine Delaney-LeBlanc graduated from nursing in the early 1960s. She nursed briefly, got married, had two children and worked at home for seven years. In 1971, she returned to the work force as a television host in Moncton. She then worked in public relations; and in 1978 was appointed founding chairperson of the New Brunswick Advisory Council on the Status of Women, a position she held until 1985. In 1988 she became CEO and chair of the New Brunswick Occupational Health and Safety Commission.

I grew up in the Magdalen Islands in the Gulf of St. Lawrence, which is part of Quebec, and came to New Brunswick at the age of 18 to study nursing. I didn't nurse very long. I worked for a year, got married, worked another six months and got pregnant. Then I worked at home for seven years, during which time I had another child.

I wanted to go back to the work force, but not to nursing because of the problems nurses still have as women in a women's profession. And since, in those days, you didn't seek a job that was totally different from what you had trained for, I wasn't actively looking. I also wanted another child, but was having difficulty getting pregnant.

All of which is to explain why I became involved with volunteer work, first with the Acadian Society, then with women's issues. I had been following the marital-property act in Quebec, and someone called and asked if we should make a presentation to the Royal Commission. This was in 1968 when the activities of the commission had stirred up a lot of interest in women's issues, and I said yes, but I wasn't sure what we should say, so I started calling employers in town asking them about their policies—did they hire women, and so on? I ended up being in charge of the women-working-outside-the-home section of the brief, even though I was a woman working at home.

I got a fair bit of profile from these efforts which helped me to land a job as a researcher in radio and television. At the same time, I discovered I was pregnant. I took six weeks off when my daughter was born and, when I returned to work, was offered a position as a TV host in Moncton. It was 1971, the beginning of French-language TV production in the Atlantic region, and it was an interesting time to be a woman working in the media. You didn't ask any questions that were particular to women, but because of my volunteer work, I was known as a woman's advocate, which made my journalistic role a little complicated.

In those days, women's groups were actively trying to get women into the news, but this was difficult when you were on the inside. You're supposed to be objective and neutral. I worked with an editor who would, systematically, throw press releases that came from women's groups in the garbage.

It's interesting to compare being a minority, French-speaking Acadian person in New Brunswick to being a woman. I remember talking to the manager of the television station and telling him that, if necessary, I could perhaps be neutral on the language issue as well as the nationalism issue, but I didn't think I could make an abstraction of the fact that I'm a woman.

For the seven years I worked at home, I was a supermom. I did everything, but I felt very much like a parasite because I wasn't bringing any money in. So when I went back to my journalism work, I more or less felt that I had to make everyone forget I was working. At first everything continued as it had been before, plus I worked an eight-hour day. I did this even while I was pregnant and having morning sickness.

I soon realized that I had to establish priorities. The first thing I set aside was the sewing. My oldest daughter was six at the time. She never used to say, "Mommy, will you buy me this?" It was: "Mommy, can you make me one like this?" I bought her first dress the first Christmas I went back to work. That was the easier part. The more difficult part was feeling guilty because I thought I might be too absorbed in my work. On one occasion when I was away doing research, I realized my thoughts had never drifted to the kids. What kind of mother was I?

That was really the pioneer time and some women would say things like, "Yes, but what does your husband think about your working?" I felt that a lot of women didn't totally disapprove, but they found it odd. I guess they didn't feel they could do it themselves. While women asked me a lot of questions, men always had plenty of digs and putdowns.

I didn't mind people disagreeing with my ideas or what I said. It was the personal things that hurt. A lot of people felt the need to dismiss me as a man-hater. So the stories would go around that my husband and I were divorcing or having affairs. Well, we've been married 30 years. Also, it was felt that travelling for a job was okay for a man but not for a woman.

I worked in television for five years, then left primarily because of the women's situation. The director of programming wouldn't put up with a woman who had her own mind and was her own person. It was a painful experience, but I simply wouldn't take what he was offering me.

After that I worked as a public-relations officer at CN, another place where women were in clerical jobs and the men had all the well-paying positions. That was my first experience working mostly in English and I felt very isolated. Then I was appointed founding chairperson of the New Brunswick Advisory Council on the Status of Women. That was the most exciting appointment I've had. At that time—1978–1985—everything had to be done from scratch, and, of course, the council was often criticized. We became pretty high-profile right across Canada.

A lot of women would say, "You're doing a good job, but I wouldn't want to be in your shoes, not with all the criticism and so on." I used to answer, "Look, this is the best job I've ever had. I used to do this on my own, at my own expense. Now I'm doing it full time and being well paid for it. Why wouldn't I be happy?"

In 1985 I became director of public affairs for a Crown corporation. The dynamics there were quite incredible. I had the feeling that I was hired because I was a French-speaking woman. Before they hired me, I had eight interviews, one of which lasted three hours with a board of eight people. I told them not to hire me unless they intended to do something for women and to increase the amount of service in French. But they didn't do anything and I stayed a little less than two years.

When I left the council, I thought I would never have another job I enjoyed as much, but the one I have now qualifies. I chair the New Brunswick Occupational Health and Safety Commission and I'm the CEO. Until very recently, occupational health and safety was a male domain, and I understand they've had some pretty rowdy sessions, including a fist fight. When I arrived, they told me I might have a hard time because they didn't vote. They operated on consensus. I told them I was very familiar with that because the women's movement operates on consensus. I don't think that was the parallel they expected.

I also came with a reputation as a feminist. A lot of people only knew me through the comments in the press and I had to make them know me for who I was. So it's been a very interesting relationship. Now there are three women directors. Five years ago that would have been unthinkable. I'm told by people who were in the boardroom before that the behaviour has changed. It would be a cliché to say that the presence of women has tamed people down. I think it's more style than sex. The women have the style—non-confrontational and upfront—to bring the needed effect.

Early on, I got really peeved with one of the guys who had done something to upset the staff. So I came into the boardroom and, in front of everyone, told him he had no business telling staff these things. My explanation was short and to the point.

The next day one of my staff said, "By the way, I want to commend you on how you handled him yesterday."

"I'm not sure," I said. "I think I was a little too strong."

"No. You're the third chairperson I've worked with, and out of the three you're the one with balls."

I told him that on the face of it, his comment was pretty sexist. But considering the context, I had to take it as a compliment.

My children are 29, 27 and 22. They are all well adjusted: my oldest daughter is a journalist, my son is a Rhodes Scholar and my youngest daughter has just graduated in education and landed a permanent contract. I think my working outside the home has really helped them. Even when I was at home I thought the biggest service I could render was to encourage them to become autonomous. I did it from the perspective that they were doing it for themselves, not for me. And that helped me to work things through.

Paula Andrews
Canmore, Alberta

"I've taken every time management course going and they don't make any difference. You just can't find time for it all."

After graduating from university, Paula Andrews began working as a social worker in 1969. She stayed home with her family in the early 1970s, then became involved in local politics after moving to Canmore, Alberta. In addition to social work, she owned a property-management company, a real-estate firm and, in 1983, was elected mayor of Canmore, a position she held until 1992.

I graduated from university in 1969, with a BA in English and psychology, and got my first job as a social worker at a community centre in Toronto. I did well and was made a department head after six months, over two of my male colleagues who also applied for the job.

I worked there for about two years, until my husband got a job as a supervisor of a wilderness park in the middle of nowhere. Sudbury, which was 180 miles return-trip, was the closest city. My job at the community centre was better than my husband's new job, but in those days, you automatically followed your husband.

We lived in the park and our son was born there. Because of the isolation, the lifestyle was unfamiliar to me and there wasn't much for me to do. I did some writing for a newsletter and made up Secret-Word puzzles which I sold to publications. But after a couple of years, I'd had enough and basically said, "Either I leave or we leave."

Alberta's Kananaskis country was just being developed, so we moved to Canmore, population 1,700, again for my husband's job. Since I was pregnant with my daughter, I didn't look for work, but I was soon volunteering because the town had absolutely no services for families.

Day care was the start of my community involvement. People had tried to get day care before, but I knew we had to show some grass-roots support to be successful. We took 100 people who were committed to using the service to a council meeting. In those days, 100 people could get you elected, so day care was a go.

In 1978, I was hired as the assistant director of preventive social services for the Banff-Canmore corridor. Since the Landlord-Tenant Act was part of my responsibility, I went to Edmonton for a training session on the act. It was one of my first experiences of the male-oriented Alberta culture. I was amazed at how many men suggested we have an affair, even though they knew I was married. I had never been hit up like that in Ontario. It was very blatant and continued throughout my career.

Not long after I got the job, they split the social-service areas and I became director for our region. After a couple of years, my husband and I started a small property-management company, which grew so fast I decided to leave social services and run the company, myself.

There were many young families, like ourselves, in Canmore who felt their needs weren't being met. Canmore had been a coal-mining town and the mentality was, if you had a family you should stay home. But the cost of living was so high that most families couldn't survive on a single income. They persuaded me to run for council and, in 1980, I got elected by the skin of my teeth. The mean age of the other council members, including the only other woman, was about 60, and I was in my early 30s.

It was quite a learning experience. All the younger people could see the need for change, but the older people couldn't. The town wasn't even efficiently operated. I wanted to get a computer, but one gentleman, who often slept through meetings, suggested we "sharpen the pencils," instead. The tax notices didn't go out until fall, which meant we were running on borrowed money nine months of the year. Since I'd run a small business, I knew how things could be improved.

Although Canmore still had a small-town attitude—if somebody's dog barked, you called the mayor—it was growing rapidly. After three years on council, I was so frustrated I decided not to run again. But so many people pressured me that after much soul-searching, I agreed to take a shot at becoming mayor. I told myself being mayor would be different because I'd be in charge.

When I ran for mayor, two other women ran against me. A substantial number of people—I suspect men—spoiled their ballots rather than vote for a female. The other two candidates were old Canmore, including one who had been on council forever. She campaigned on not increasing the mayor's salary. I said it had to increase because I knew how much time sitting on council involved.

In fact, I was so busy with my council work that I was paying people more money than I was making to run my property-management company. So when a man I knew asked if I'd go into partnership and purchase a real-estate business, I decided to go for it. In 1983, I got my real-estate licence, we bought the company and I was elected mayor. Soon after, I sold the property-management venture.

When I became mayor, the Calgary Olympics were on stream and Canmore was making a pitch for the nordic events. Once they decided to build the cross-country and biathlon in Canmore, I applied and was appointed to the Olympic Organizing Committe board of directors. I had no idea how much time the Olympics would involve. It was another full-time job, on top of being mayor, having two kids and running a real-estate company.

But when you're a woman, you expect to do it all. My husband wanted me to work, but I'm not sure he wanted me to do as much as I did. Sometimes he helped out at home and he said all the right things, like, "It's your turn for a challenge," since we'd moved around for his career. But I think he resented it. Obviously he did because we separated in 1984, not long after I became mayor. It was a good thing we waited. I might have lost the election if I'd been divorced!

Canmore was one of the fastest-growing towns in Canada, so I was dealing with problems of rapid growth, as well as the fact that the mines had closed and the direction of the town had changed. I also felt a great deal of pressure to do the family things. The kids were nine and seven when my husband and I separated. I had total custody, which was a big responsibility, but my husband didn't even try for joint custody. Of course, I felt guilty. I think a woman feels more guilt, especially after a divorce.

If you have a career, children and a household, it's impossible to balance it all. That means you become an expert in crisis management. If the crisis is with the family, that's where your energy goes, and if it's with work, it goes there.

Men would never put in the hours women do, I don't think. You feel guilty if you're not working, or doing something around the house or for the kids because you always want to be the best mom. Something has to give and it's that you stop doing things for yourself.

I trained myself to manage with less sleep and cut back on my personal relationships. Other than for business, I didn't socialize much. The Olympics involved a lot of entertaining, and on top of everything else, that was exhausting.

In politics, you work a lot of nights. I wanted to be there for my kids' sports events and so on, but often I couldn't. When my son was rushed in for surgery for an incarcerated bowel, I was in Ottawa. I was phoned and was immediately on the plane, but by the time I reached the hospital the operation was over. I felt sick because I wasn't with him.

Meanwhile, I had to run the town which, among other things, involved a lot of reading. When you're at the top levels of government bureaucracy, you're inundated with paper. I used to read until one or two o'clock in the morning trying to keep up on things like water and sewage studies.

I think there were times the kids enjoyed my political involvement because of the places we went and the things we could do. But there's a public side to the job that often made them uncomfortable. For instance, they hated going downtown with me because people would stop me to complain. It was a big deal when I was elected mayor since I was the youngest mayor in Alberta and I was a woman. One interview really embarrassed my kids because it revealed my age. They didn't want everybody to know I was so ancient. I was still in my 30s.

Anyway, there I was, a single parent, a mayor, and up to my neck in the Olympics. During the last year, I worked 18 hours a day, seven days a week. It was absolutely insane.

The Olympics were the ultimate volunteer effort because we chose not to pay top volunteers. That meant I was really pushing it financially. I didn't get the town to increase the mayor's salary to $24,000 until 1987, and only then because they realized I had no time for my business. My partner was great, and if I hadn't owned the business, I wouldn't have been able to manage financially. I lived on the profits from my share and squeaked by for a couple of years.

I was lucky because the town manager never had a problem with the fact that I was a woman and his boss. In fact, I had worked for him when I was a social worker so it was a real turnaround. Actually, all my top executives were men. This really irritated a feminist friend of mine who said it meant I wasn't a feminist. I agree. I'm an equalist. I've never looked at hiring a woman for a position if a man had better qualifications or did better in the interview.

I'm a common-sense, to-the-point kind of person, but it's tough to be a mayor in a place like Canmore. Some people don't want another tree taken down or another house built and others want a workable economy. Balancing these competing needs was very stressful and I was always making enemies.

By my last term, the town had changed and the negativity really got me down. There were so many extremists that the job wasn't satisfying. I used to look forward to council meetings because I enjoy making decisions and getting things done, but during my last three years, I started to dread them. There were always shouting matches, and in addition to the pressure groups, it was an all-male council, some of whom had trouble with the fact that I was a woman.

Even so, as a result of my experience in politics, I've concluded that women make better politicians than men because we're more empathetic and used to sharing. Women are accustomed to running families and finding compromises at the family level. That takes a lot of skill and I think this skill makes us better at politics. We're used to finding the answers that work for everybody, not just for ourselves.

I served three terms as mayor, then decided to run provincially. Probably the biggest mistake I made was not running for the legislature four years earlier, when I was asked and my chances would have been much better. But it was a bad time in my life. It was just after the Olympics and I was totally burned out. Also, my father was ill.

Running provincially was a great experience because it was a different ball game. But it was probably the biggest disappointment in my political life because, obviously, I didn't want to lose, although losing was an education in itself. Provincial politics were much dirtier than the municipal level. For instance, a rumour that I was gay was spread which damaged me in certain ridings.

The year I resigned as mayor, I sold my real-estate company. Obviously, I thought I was going to win a seat in the legislature, but I'm 45 and I think you reach a point, your menopause point, where you need a career change.

At that point, my mom was very ill so it was easy to slow down. I started writing a column for a few weeklies and took care of her. I guess it was a healing period for me, too. For 12 years I had run seven days a week, 18 hours a day, and I needed a break.

For about a year, I've been involved with a gentleman who travels a lot. That's been nice because I often travel with him and fax my columns to the paper. Now, I'm having trouble deciding what to do. I'm looking at buying a few weeklies with someone and possibly starting an Alberta-based magazine that focuses on positive, human-interest-type stories. I'm also considering a town-manager-type position, but since men still dominate the politics in small towns in Alberta, I'm struggling with that choice.

I think I'm at a crossroads. I'm not sure where this relationship is going and I sometimes think I'd like to have a job that didn't require too much thought. For 12 years every moment of my life was scheduled. Now, I have lots of time to think and I find it hard to focus.

Mary Gordon
Sudbury, Ontario

"**M**y life has been tied to the economic demands of raising kids. I've almost had to pay to work because I bring home so little and need to have the right clothes and the right car for work."

Mary Gordon began working in broadcasting in the late 1960s. After having two children and doing a variety of mainly media-related jobs, she became publisher of the Nipigon newspaper in the late 1970s. From 1982 to 1988, she worked for the CBC (Canadian Broadcasting Corporation) in Sudbury, then left to take a position with the Ontario government.

I'm 47 and I've worked since I was 21, so my 26 years of experience has bridged the women's movement. When I had my first baby, in 1968, I had to quit work because maternity leave didn't exist. I suppose I could have used my three weeks' holiday and then gone back to work—some women did.

Although I went to university on bursaries and scholarships, I dropped out before graduation. When I hit the work force I discovered I didn't have any skills, so I got a job as a continuity writer for a radio station outside Vancouver. The other writer was a male and he got paid twice as much as me because he had a family.

When my son was born, I was unemployed for four months. At that point, my husband and I were separating so when a job became available at a television station in northern British Columbia, I accepted it. I was getting $50 a week and I was a single parent. I found a really good woman to care for my son, but because I earned so little I was struggling financially. A family of do-gooders in the community took an interest in me and offered to care for my little boy while I was at work. Since it meant so much in financial terms, I moved him from the wonderful baby-sitter.

One day, when I came home early, I discovered that the man looking after my son had spanked him. He said the baby needed to be taught that he should take a nap. My son was alone in a dark room and crying to break your heart. He was about a year old and the imprint of the hand was still on his bum.

That created another right turn in my life. I quit work and returned to my husband. I got pregnant again and was out of the work force for more than a year. After my second son was born, my marriage broke up for good and I came east to Ontario.

For awhile, I worked for a department store as an advertising manager. This didn't suit me at all, so I went back into media, eventually becoming publisher of a paper in Nipigon, a small town on the north shore of Lake Superior. That was probably my best work experience, because I was left alone to do it. I had to take the newspaper over and make it into something that was creative and useful for a community of 2,500 people. I breathed, ate and slept the paper.

At that time, I was raising my two kids as a single parent, which is probably easier than being married. If I hadn't been on my own, I wouldn't have been able to take that job. My husband wouldn't have been able to move to Nipigon since all the male jobs are either in the bush or at the mill. All the important community jobs—postmistress, the government clerks and so on—are held by women.

That job taught me most of what I know about work—about being independent and sticking to your guns. As the publisher of a paper, the people in the community gave me power I didn't know I had. I was 32 when I went there and certainly not as confident as I am now.

On the day before the paper went to the printer, I worked all night to get it to bed. It was printed in Thunder Bay and the only way I could get it down there, unless I drove it myself, was to wait for the bus, which arrived at 6:50 in the morning. Since the bus station wasn't open, I used to sit in my car and listen to "Fresh Air" on CBC. I became very familiar with the programme and eventually became a contributor.

The downside to the job was that it didn't pay very well. Also, my kids are of a mixed race and they suffered socially in a small town. But the big thing was money. We were poor, although my kids didn't think so, which I think is a real coup for me. I started to string for CBC just to have grocery money.

After five years in Nipigon, I decided I needed to earn a decent wage. Maybe I was just getting older, but pensions, sick leave and so on—all the things I now take for granted—became very important. So in 1982, I went to work for the northeastern network of CBC, based in Sudbury.

I did various programme-consultant and production jobs, and then was convinced to go into management. It was a step up, but it was a mistake for me. The job didn't involve any interviewing, cutting tape or developing stories—all the things I'm really good at. I was wasting away so when CBC began to cut back, I quit and moved over to government.

I started as an information officer and gradually moved into public consultation. If people can be shown the dignity and respect to run their own affairs, then I'm in the perfect place because I'm interested in empowering them.

Thank God, I have friends. My friends are a very important part of my life. For years, all my friends were women in the work force because we had something to share. Our generation saw ourselves as the new wave of women, making our way in careers. It was wonderful to have that support, but there was a negative side to that working-women clique in that we became a kind of league of our own. We even wore pin stripes—mind you, with slender skirts and high heels. We had a certain amount of contempt for women who were satisfied with staying at home pleasing a husband. We didn't feel they had the same values as we did because we were higher up in the male power structure.

It took me a long time to realize that if my work at home with my kids had been valued, we wouldn't have been in that élitist mode. But because it wasn't, men flattered us for being successful. "You must be really something, you're so busy," they'd say. I accepted that as being exemplary, because I didn't realize I was buying into the male package.

I also think my kids suffered because my work with them wasn't valued. It took me years to realize that I joined the men in putting down women who stayed at home because my need for some kind of control and daddy love was so strong. When I finally understood that, it was scary.

Now that I work with government, I'm a beneficiary of employment equity. I've seen a lot of change over the years, but I still feel I work much harder than most of my male colleagues. Employers love me. I have never minded working 16 to 18 hours a day because I've always felt I was getting an education on the job. I still don't know whether it's my strength or whether I'm really good at denial—denying the reality that I should be fighting harder for my rights.

Currently, I'm on the negotiating team in native affairs. We've just concluded a three-week intensive public consultation on a claim which is heart-rending. When it's two o'clock in the morning and the kit has to be photocopied for the next workshop, I'm the one who's doing it. I earn lots of money and have good benefits, but I'm not sure they'd ever give me the deputy minister's job because I work so hard at the actual hands-on stuff.

When opportunities for climbing the corporate ladder come up, I tend to shy away from them. People are clamouring to have me work with them and my dilemma is, should I accept these offers of work or should I try to rise in the hierarchy? It seems to me I've had this debate every day of my working life, but I always end up just doing the work.

If I have a role model for getting my hands dirty and working until I can't stand up any longer, it's my mother. My parents married in 1943 and my father died in 1954. At that point, my mother had five children and was pregnant with her sixth. She hadn't nursed in 12 years and she had to go back to work in a French hospital that was virtually all nuns. She had a tough life, and she went from being very conservative to becoming quite radical in her old age.

Carol Loughrey
Fredericton, New Brunswick

"**When I came to government, I was shocked to find that I was considered a left-wing feminist. I had kids, a husband, a happy marriage. I didn't see myself as a trailblazer. I saw myself as very balanced.**"

Carol Loughrey graduated from the University of New Brunswick with a bachelor of business administration degree in 1970 and received her chartered accountant's degree two years later. She worked as an accountant until 1974, when she left the work force to have children. In 1977, she took a part-time teaching position at the University of New Brunswick and eventually became the assistant dean of the Faculty of Administration. Eleven years later, she accepted the position of comptroller of the Province of New Brunswick. In 1994, she became the first woman chair of the Board of Governors of the Canadian Institute of Chartered Accountants in its 90-year history.

I'm a chartered accountant by profession. I graduated from university with a business degree and went into the articling programme in 1970. I received my CA in 1972.

To the best of my knowledge, when I became a CA. I was the first woman in the province to obtain this designation by examination. The graduating class was very small, about eight, I think, and we were allowed to invite our spouses and certain guests. They asked the graduates to stand up and introduce their wives and guests. They thought it was a big joke when I introduced my husband. There were gifts for the spouses: silver charm bracelets. My husband got an empty box.

In those days, I felt very resentful towards the accounting profession. I think it started in university. I remember one professor telling me that women had no place in business and he'd do everything he could to make life miserable for me. In my first year, 1966, I had an English professor who made the five women business students leave the class and take English with the physical-education class because he used language that wasn't suitable for ladies. Incredibly, I went! But I was 18 and very naïve.

Once I got out into the work place, the issue was that women accountants were very new and the firms were afraid we wouldn't be accepted by the clients. I was the only female student in the firm and, surprisingly, I never had any problem with the clients. If anything, I was more successful than the men because the senior accounting staff in our clients' firms were usually older women. The young whippersnappers would come in and be very condescending to these women, who would get even by deliberately impeding their work. I probably showed the women the respect they deserved and, as a result, they accepted me.

Two years after I became a CA—it was July—I went to my partner and said, "Ron and I have decided to have a family. We thought that if I got pregnant now, I could have the baby in May and work until the end of the tax season in April."

I thought he was going to fall off his chair laughing. But my eldest daughter was born June 1 and I worked to the end of the tax season. I was so huge they volunteered to cut out a piece of my desk to make room for me.

I had planned to go back to work in September, but when the time came, I cried for three days. My husband said, "This is crazy. If you don't want to go back to work, you don't have to." I'm not sure he expected me to stay home for three years.

I wanted to be with my children when they were little, but I found staying home very difficult. I have all kinds of admiration for women who can maintain their sense of self-esteem while working as housewives. I feel that people treated me as if I didn't have a brain.

I still say that if I hadn't gone back to work, I'd be one of those women who stay inside the house with the drapes drawn. It got so bad that when we were invited to a party where I knew I wouldn't know many of the people, I pretended I was sick. My whole sense of who I was was totally destroyed.

I remember lying in bed one night and thinking, "Is this all there is?" I couldn't see myself moving back into public practice with two young children. It's too demanding. I know lots of women are doing it now, but in those days there were no role models. The next day, I got a call from the university.

When the university offered me a part-time teaching job, seven hours a week, it was the answer to my prayers. I would actually get to talk to adults who had to listen, three mornings a week. The peace, the quiet, a little office—it seemed fabulous. And it paid $6,000 a year.

When my teaching evaluations came back, they were very good, so they offered me a full-time position. It was nine hours a week and paid $16,000. I thought, wow! They didn't explain that there was lots of administrative work and committees.

I went in at about 7 a.m. My husband looked after getting the girls off to school and I'd be home for them at 2:30. I never took lunch or coffee breaks, and if I had more work, I'd take it home to finish.

I couldn't have asked for anything better. The department worked around me. I never had to teach after the kids got home, but of course I'd take the 8:30 a.m. classes, which everyone else hated. It was a terrific compromise. I was doing something I enjoyed, and although the money wasn't comparable to what I would have made in public practice, I could balance my home life. I also did my master's degree at the same time.

It was a wonderful opportunity and I credit the person who hired me. He had been my accounting professor when I was an undergraduate and he'd been incredibly supportive of me. People like him are wonderful to have in your life. He used to give me a hard time about women's issues, but I got to the point where it rolled off my back.

I was at the University of New Brunswick for 11 years, and by the time I left, I was an assistant dean responsible for the graduate programme in business. I think I was the first woman outside the School of Nursing to have a deanship. My dean wasn't aware of that until I was leaving and the president told him. I thought that was a compliment, because being a woman obviously didn't have anything to do with my promotion.

When I started working at the university, there were no other women in my area. By the time I left, half the accounting faculty was women. When the accounting firms came to recruit, they used to say, "Don't you have any good men? There are far more good women coming from UNB than from any other university from which we recruit." If that doesn't tell you that having women in positions of authority isn't important, I don't know what does. The role modelling and mentoring is critical.

Mentoring is what I missed most when I worked in an accounting firm. There was just me and the secretaries. I had a mauve polyester pantsuit that I wore to work. I want to crawl under the table in embarrassment when I think about it. But there was nobody to tell me what was appropriate. My mother was a stay-at-home mom and I had only two female professors, one in English, the other in math, who certainly didn't think about being role models for young women.

Men had this wonderful uniform: the suit. I bought John T. Malloy's *Dress for Success for Women* and I used it as a bible because I had absolutely no idea what I should be wearing. When I taught at the university, I made an effort to be a role model by showing the students how they would have to dress in the work place. On teaching days, I always made sure I wore business-type attire.

I understood the dynamics of clothes and what your clothes say and I didn't want that to be a handicap when I went to talk to somebody. I wanted to be taken seriously and your clothes do send that message. I was a missionary to the point of probably being a bit pedantic about it all.

Now I'm rebelling against it. I never would have worn slacks to work six months ago. I guess I've reached the point where people know who I am, and unless I'm going into a very different situation, where somebody hasn't met me before and I want to impress them, I don't think too much about my clothes.

One day, I got a call out of the blue from Frank McKenna, the premier. He asked if I'd be interested in a deputy-minister's position. I had no political background and had never met the premier, but I'd been president of my professional association the year before and I was very visible as a woman in an organization that was only 10 per cent female.

I came to government in the position of comptroller of the province, on a leave of absence from the university, and decided to stay. I've been here for five years and enjoy it very much.

When I first arrived, I had a bit of a problem because women had just started moving up. The men had never had to compete against women before, and suddenly I was hearing things like, "Oh, to get anywhere here you have to be a woman."

I made a point of addressing the issue. I sat down and listed all the people who had been promoted after I came, and it was something like seven men and three women. The reaction was along the lines of "Don't confuse me with the facts. The only people who get promoted here are women."

The perception that I favour women over men is troubling. I can't afford to do that. I don't have to do it. I only have to choose the best person. But, I guess, because historically women have not been in positions of authority in this office, the change has been very dramatic.

When I came to government, some of the men tried baiting me because I'd been identified as a feminist, but it didn't work because I'd had so much experience with this behaviour while I was at the university. They couldn't figure out why they couldn't get me going, and one guy actually asked me why I wasn't rising to the bait. But I had learned not to get angry about it.

Women in my generation—it may not be the same for younger women —walk along a kind of knife edge. If we're going to make changes from within, we have to stay on that knife edge. We can't be the person banging on the door. It's important that someone does that, but people like me have to maintain credibility with the people who make decisions.

But doing that and still making change for women means walking a very fine line. If you fall over, you're perceived as a fanatic, and I suspect some people here perceive me that way. But if you lean too far in the other direction, you buy into the male definition of things and you don't make changes. Whenever you go into an organization, the line can be in a totally different place and you have to find where the line is and be sensitive to the people around you.

Most of the men I know aren't the enemy. They'd like to think of themselves as fair and rational, as liberated. But if you approach them in a confrontational way, they'll become defensive and resist. Instead, you have to present your ideas in a non-threatening way.

Because I've always worked with men, my style of doing things is what studies define as "masculine." That's the role model I had. I tend to go from A to B, because that's what I know. I don't talk about things in a circular way, which has been described as a "feminine" approach. I taught Girl Guides for five years and I think I intimidated some of those women. When I came here it was the same thing. The men and women I was working with weren't accustomed to women who had that methodology. I didn't fulfil their image.

So I recognized that I had to be more aware of how people were reacting to me. I suddenly found myself doing stereotypical things, like: "Well, I think...." or "I might be crazy, but...." I was trying not to be intimidating, but now I feel that I've got to stop doing it. It just isn't me.

In 10 years, when I'm 55, I plan to retire. I expect to be financially secure at that point. My pension plan will kick in and my kids will be through their costly period. I want to give more back to the community. I'm a good organizer and manager, and a lot of non-profit organizations are desperately in need of those skills. There's so much to be done and I'd like to be part of it.

Sylvia Hamilton
Halifax, Nova Scotia

"**O**ver the years, I learned from my family and especially from my mother, how to handle racist or sexist situations."

Sylvia Hamilton, daughter of the late Marie Hamilton, graduated from Acadia University in 1972. She worked with the Company of Young Canadians (CYC) in Ottawa for 2½ years. In 1981 she went to work with the Department of the Secretary of State, where she stayed for more than 10 years. She left her position as acting regional director to devote herself to writing, making films and community work.

The summer I graduated from high school, I worked with a community-development project in a rigidly segregated area of rural Nova Scotia, near Cape Breton. I was 17 and the job introduced me to many things, not the least of which was how some white people dealt with the black community.

Even though my co-workers were white, the local people isolated us. I remember shopping for groceries and seeing the shock on their faces when we entered the store. It seemed they had never seen black and white people interacting as social equals.

It was the late '60s, when social-development work was in its infancy. We were working on a project sponsored by the provincial government, called "Head Start," which was primarily aimed at black communities throughout the province. As summer workers, we helped the kids learn skills, such as colours, numbers, arts and crafts. I found it interesting because it allowed me to use my learning in a new context. I had experienced racism as a child when our segregated school closed and we entered the neighbouring white school, so I understood their experience.

The next year, I decided to work in the city to help pay my university expenses. I began job hunting in Halifax and soon discovered that business establishments didn't hire black people. Our money was fine, but we weren't. I believed that I had capabilities and people should judge me according to these, not according to my colour.

I went to one department store and got the usual response that I needed experience. I asked how I was expected to I get experience if I couldn't get a job? At that point, I had 12 years of school plus a year of university. It hurt to be rejected because I knew many of the cashiers and sales clerks hadn't finished high school. I also knew the company was hiring.

I persevered and, finally, got hired as a sales clerk. It didn't take me long to discover that the wages of the other clerks were low, but mine were lower. It also became clear that some customers were shocked to see me. They didn't know quite what to do, other than to stare, which happened all the time and reflected where white people in Nova Scotia expected black people to be. If I had arrived at the back door to clean their house, there wouldn't have been a problem.

Gradually, the regular customers realized that if I was the only clerk on the cash, they'd have to deal with me. My employers recognized that I was competent, and if something needed to be done, I could usually do it. So after a few weeks, I asked for a raise. My co-workers couldn't believe my boldness, but I think my assertiveness made a difference and I got what I asked for. Unlike my co-workers, I had nothing to lose. If the company wanted to fire me, it wasn't the end of the road because I was going back to university. But I saw how the other women were exploited. They never complained because they could be fired in a minute.

I worked at that store a summer and a half and also at Christmas, while I studied English and sociology at Acadia University. I graduated in 1972 and started my professional career, so to speak, as a teacher in a non-traditional, alternative school for kids who had dropped out of high school. It was the first school of its kind in Nova Scotia. I spent a lot of time teaching reading and basic arithmetic to the younger students, many of whom were dealing with problems like poverty, drug abuse, racism and homelessness.

The school received some funding from the Company of Young Canadians for the volunteer teachers like myself, and through this connection, I was invited to apply for a job as the assistant director of communications for the CYC in Ottawa. To my surprise, I was hired and within a short time moved to Ottawa. Thinking back, I realize the position was a heavy responsibility for someone so young—I was only 21. But at the time, I rarely thought about my age. My family was very supportive and encouraging, as were my colleagues.

It was an invaluable experience and I still draw on the knowledge I gained from that job. Issues of gender—and race—constantly cropped up. For instance, people would come in and ask to speak to someone in charge. When I arrived at the reception desk, they'd say, "No, I want to speak to someone in charge." I'd say, "Well, that's me." One person seemed to find my presence such an affront that he left.

I tried not to take incidents like this to heart because my mother always taught us that if someone had difficulties with race, it was their problem, not ours. I was not to take responsibility for their ignorance.

The job involved a great deal of travel and I took many early morning flights where most of the passengers were white businessmen. I'd have my briefcase and files, and they'd have theirs. There was an unspoken but clearly felt question, Who are you and what are you doing here? At times, it bothered me, especially because I was alone and realized just how alone I was. I'd look around and see no one who was the same colour and very few people who were the same gender or age. Because I also looked young and I'm small, it was a triple whammy: young, female and black in the early '70s, holding a position of responsibility.

I stayed with CYC for about 2½ years and then decided it was time to move on. By the time I left, my work had developed to such a point that they had to hire two people—both happened to be male—to replace me. I spent a long winter and a short spring in Labrador, examining the potential social impact of offshore oil development on the coastal communities. Some of the government officials had very sketchy knowledge of Labrador and its people. I encountered attitudes at the bureaucratic level that made me feel sad. The relationship between the Newfoundland government and the people of Labrador seemed very colonial. More than once I heard phrases that echoed: "What those people need is…." It reminded me of the attitudes I'd encountered towards the black community when I'd worked in social development in Nova Scotia.

Then, I moved back to Halifax and volunteered with several community organizations while I looked for paid work. Even though I wasn't paid, I still considered it my work. Between 1975 and 1980, I had a series of jobs, and during this time I studied broadcasting. I remember one situation where I was the only woman and the men received all kinds of breaks that didn't apply to me. The discrimination was clearly based on gender, and that came out in one argument I had over salary. Although they told me constantly how well I was doing, they wouldn't pay me what the men were earning because I wasn't male—they said it was because men had families to support and I didn't.

I had to decide if it was worth staying in a situation where I was being exploited. The work habits of most of the males were horrendous—they took long lunch-hours and when they came back, the smell of alcohol preceded them. The sexual innuendos were constant, so much so that once I told them to go somewhere else when they were telling dirty jokes. They also had Playboy-magazine-type material on the walls—I think because they wanted to get a rise out of me. One day I got so mad I ripped it down and put it in the garbage. Nobody said a word although they knew I'd done it.

Finally, I decided to leave not only because they wouldn't pay me appropriately, but also because the climate they created diminished my ability to be successful.

When you're black, you constantly have to deal with how people treat you. You can spend all your time reacting and taking stress onto yourself, or you can find ways to force people to deal with their problems. I realized it was important for me to know how to use my energy and my anger. I had to decide which incidents, social as well as work, shouldn't pass.

For instance, a male colleague once told me about sexist jokes which were told at a meeting where no women were present. I asked him if he challenged the teller and he said no, which made me quite angry. When I said he should have signalled that he didn't appreciate the jokes, he became more cautious about what he told me. I wondered why he told me this story and what he expected me to do or say. Did he want me to congratulate him for identifying sexism when he encountered it?

In 1981, I went to work for the federal government in the Department of the Secretary of State and stayed for more than 10 years. I began as a programme officer and became assistant regional director and then the acting regional director. This wasn't part of any "career plan." I took the job because the work was interesting. It involved community development and supporting those groups involved in social change. It was also a new challenge. I wanted to see if I could take my knowledge in community development and somehow use it to benefit both community groups and the bureaucracy.

While I was at Sec State, I kept up some of my volunteer work and also my research and writing on the social and cultural history of black Nova Scotians. This led me into film work. I'd done some video work with a women's collective as well as some hosting and producing on cable television in its infancy in the 1970s. When I became involved with a group of women who were interested in making films, I thought I might try my hand at it. But after 10 years with the federal government, I was, once again, running up against what people expected of me. I was typecast as a bureaucrat. People didn't think I should do anything creative. My refusal, or perhaps inability, to conform to people's expectations is why I have always shunned labels.

My first film, *Black Mother, Black Daughter*, was put together by an all-woman crew—a first for the National Film Board in the Atlantic area. Male technical people were involved as mentors and advisors, but the goal was to give women the opportunity to do the work.

The film was a breakthrough on another level, as well. I wanted to look at the amazing amount of work, both paid and unpaid, a number of women did individually and collectively to sustain the black community. I felt compelled to have this story told because it wasn't recognized or even valued.

Many black women were forced to do domestic work because nothing else was available. Many were treated badly by their employers—confined to eat in the kitchen or offered food or old clothing as payment. It took an incredible amount of courage and sense of self to go into those work situations and to come away feeling valued. We wanted that sensibility to come through in the film.

I can see quite clearly that my attitudes about work were influenced by what I saw when I was growing up. I never thought I wouldn't work because work is what women in my community did. And I remember older women, including my mother, saying whatever work you do, do it well and with dignity.

10

Entrepreneurs

Amy Friend
St. Bruno, Quebec

"You have to be very sure of yourself when you're dealing with banks. You must be absolutely unafraid, particularly when you're in trouble. You don't take the first 'no' for an answer—you must learn to treat 'no' as a request for more information."

Amy Friend graduated from university in 1958 and worked at home until her youngest child enrolled in school. In 1979, she began working with her husband and is, today, executive vice-president of their company, ATS Aerospace.

When I graduated from university, I was still on the traditional path. In those days, you got your BSc, then you got your "MRS." I was married immediately after graduation and stayed home until my youngest child went off to school. Then I eased into a career in a low-risk way by opening a retail natural-food business with another woman. It was an easy fit since my university degree was in home economics.

We operated a shop-by-phone business out of our garage. It required almost no capital. After six months we moved into a small commercial space. We also got into selling the flavourings, extracts and so on for making wine and beer at home, which had been our hobby.

When I started the business, my youngest child—we have three—was six. There was no support then and those were pretty busy years. I remember how long the days were and how hard we worked.

After we'd been in business for about three years, the company that imported the extracts for making liqueurs was offered for sale. We had to dig deep to find the necessary capital between the two families, but we bought it and sold the retail business, which was less profitable.

At that point, I retired for a year. My partner, who had been widowed, needed the income and I needed a rest. But in 1979, the company my husband worked for went bankrupt and we had no income. We had seen this coming and incorporated a company which enabled my husband, who's in aerospace, to become a consultant. At that point, he said, "Amy, you'd better learn how to type." I went to night school and achieved 14 words a minute, with tremendous accuracy. I've picked up since then.

I started typing our technical proposals, which I found supremely interesting. Bill is technically gifted, but if you can't communicate with your reader, you'll lose their attention. I wanted the proposals to be understandable to someone who didn't necessarily have a technical background. Not only did we turn out some very good proposals, we won almost every contract we bid on.

Somewhere along the way Bill said, "Amy, you'd better learn to keep books." That was my next night course. At this point we were working as a team out of our house, which we did for three years. In those days, the closest we came to high tech was two telephones, one for business and one for home. I was a jack of all trades. I did bookkeeping, typing, invoicing, answering the phone, laying linoleum, plastering, sanding, painting and so on. It's the ideal way to learn a business, from the bottom up.

In 1984, we decided to diversify and took our first commercial space. I still wasn't feeling empowered. I'd never worked in an office, so it was easy to think everybody else was competent and I wasn't good enough to dry the coffee cups. When they finally dragged me kicking and screaming into the office, I discovered I could type faster and more accurately than the other girls, and I was better organized.

At that point, we had only one big client. We knew this was extremely risky, so we diversified into air-traffic-control simulation—it's in the field of virtual reality—and since then we've averaged growth of 55 per cent a year, although some years have been much better than others.

We've had some hard times, especially in the beginning, because of the lack of resources. But I soon learned that, even with my minimal knowledge of finance, I could go toe to toe with the bank and usually get what I wanted.

Until recently, when we hired a vice-president, finance, I did most of the front-person banking. At one point, we left a major Canadian bank, which shall remain nameless. Not only were they being unresponsive, they were obstructing, for their own internal reasons. They didn't want to take any risk at all. They would have been happy if we had a term deposit to match our line of credit. You can't operate that way. So I went to another major Canadian bank and got a line of credit that was 12 times bigger, and we were able to grow again. We've just done the same thing all over again.

There's so much to learn about banks. When we first got started I thought banks were like soap. You know, what difference does it make if you use Oxydol or Cheer? But banks have their individual cultures and they go through cycles. Their corporate culture can change completely, depending on what's happening internally.

There were times when I knew the bank was pretty close to pulling the plug on us. I guess in these situations you're whistling in the dark a bit, but I've always found that even though you may have some difficulties in the short term, if you take a positive long-term view, it affects people around you and lifts their spirits.

One project I really enjoyed was building our head office. It's a beautiful building, very high tech and very much us. It was my project. I got the financing and worked with the architect and the builder, and things went quite smoothly.

I think Bill and I are a good team. We work closely together and we're best friends. I think our optimism made a significant difference to our success. It kept our original bank involved long enough to enable us to improve our position and get a better arrangement with another institution.

The personal approach, and the relationships with the people I work with, are very important. We started out as a family and we've tried to keep it that way. We hired our first employee in 1984 and now have a staff of 120. We play together and we work together.

They're a prize-winning group. We won the Prix D'Excellence for business in Canada. American Express and *Profit* magazine designated our company one of the 50 fastest growing in Canada. We brought home the 75th anniversary prize from the National Research Council for our product development. I don't mean it to sound like a bragging session, but we're very proud of our people.

All of this stuff about flat management and getting rid of the layers of authority now has a name: total-quality management. But it's what we've been doing all along and I think that has to do with my being a woman with common sense. I'm kind of friendly, like a wet pup. I like people to be happy, and if they're not happy, I try to make them happy. I know I have to watch that I don't get too carried away. After all, we are in business and a balance has to be struck. But looking at the bottom line, a lot of time and, therefore, money is spent in business dealing with hurt feelings and trying to regulate squabbles. Worrying about people's well-being makes good economic sense.

My husband is the president and I'm the executive vice-president, which is not to say that the vice-presidents in any way take direction from me, because they're experts in their own right. But in the event Bill is away, I'm the person who has to say yes or no. And, of course, he and I are still the major shareholders.

Only on rare occasions is working with my husband a problem. I mean everybody's human. It's very important to keep it professional because a row of any kind is disruptive and upsets the office. So obviously we've never had a row, but if I perceive he's feeling pressured or worried, I'll give him a little more space that day.

It may be because of our company culture, but the men here treat the women with respect. I see no evidence of chauvinism. Occasionally, when someone new comes in, I feel that I have to prove myself all over again. Sometimes people will assume that I'm only here because I'm the boss's wife.

I guess if anybody asked me for advice, I'd say don't be afraid to dream big. If it doesn't go according to plan, just go back at it again. But don't change your dream. They call it a vision now. Spending half a day with your peers to define your company's vision is very interesting. It's incredibly difficult to come up with two sentences. But if you have your vision and hang onto it, it almost becomes a self-fulfilling prophesy.

Our business is very exciting and it's hard to quit. We've been saying we'd take it easier when we got the company properly capitalized, but that's just happened and I don't see any slow-down. When you enjoy what you're doing, you just keep doing it and getting better, little by little.

I've been very fortunate in that Bill has encouraged me to be myself and he doesn't feel threatened by my success. Growing up in a farm family has also helped me in my career. Farm women tend to be strong, because they have to be. As Bill says, I come from a long line of uppity broads.

When I met Bill, I had an inferiority complex that would choke a horse, and he supported and encouraged me for a long time. He used to say, "Of course you can. Go ahead do it, go for it." I think it's a great privilege to have someone who helps you to be brave, because so many times in business, the difference between making a success of something and not making a success of something is just getting up every morning and being brave. You may not know how you'll get through it, but you know you will if you give it your very best shot.

At the risk of sounding too much like a missionary, that's the way it works for me. Don't quit and don't be afraid to shoot high. And choose some good people along the way.

Mary Sutherland
Toronto, Ontario

"My business partner and I realized we'd have to be the main providers for our families."

Mary Sutherland immigrated to Montreal from England in the late 1960s with her husband. After working at home, she moved to Toronto with her family in 1972 and opened Lovecraft, a sex shop.

Twenty-odd years ago, my husband became very ill and it became my responsibility to support the family. My primary interest was in alternative education, so I took a trip to London to see an exhibition of equipment for children's learning disabilities, with a view towards discovering if I could turn it into a business. I soon realized that I didn't have the resources. Since we had recently emigrated from England, we had no connections in Canada and no access to capital. I also had no one to mentor me.

I had worked for a time in England with my husband. He was in advertising and film making, and I was a kind of gofer while I was having babies. I didn't have any profession as such, but I always had lots of interests.

About that time there was an article in *Time* magazine about a sex shop in London. I visited the store and could see that it required very little inventory. I was pretty sure that there was nothing like it in Canada, so I decided to give it a try. I was under a great deal of pressure to make something happen as we had about $7,000 between us and the breadline.

We were living in Montreal and the War Measures Act had just been enforced. Although I was sympathetic to the Quebec nationalists, I knew I wasn't a francophone. One night I was listening to a fascinating programme on CBC Radio about the Stop-the-Spadina-Expressway movement. It seemed that lots of interesting things were happening in Toronto, so we loaded all our possessions into a van and came here.

I had just read Jane Jacobs' book, *The Death and Life of American Cities*. She'd probably die if she knew this. I've never met her—but I used her book to find my location for Lovecraft. She wrote about what makes streets happen, and at that point Yorkville was a magnet for all kinds of people. I rented the store on Yorkville Avenue and started to find products. I knew it was on the edge of what was legal so I consulted some lawyers, but even they didn't know how the law might respond. I took the risk and opened in 1972 with my partner, who had also moved from Montreal.

The store I saw in London was very clinical and that was how we opened. Even our sign was Spartan. We used Times-Roman typeface, like the Bank of Nova Scotia. We were anxious to create an image of respectability.

The business really took off, and even though there are huge over-heads, we've been successful. We're now running three stores, although the recession has affected us.

People came in for all kinds of reasons: to pursue jokes, to solve their problems; a few hearty souls even admitted that they were trying to see if they could add some pleasure to the sex act in Toronto. We hadn't thought about the kinds of problems people would bring to the store and some-times they were disturbing. Some people had focused everything on sexuality and you could see their whole lives were out of kilter.

Over the years we found that many people treated the place as a kind of adult joke store. I have some conflict about this. There's a vulgarity about it I can't stand. I'm more interested in the healthier aspects of sexuality.

For instance, one of my concerns is the sexual rights of people who have been disabled. We had ramp access put in at the back of the building to facil-itate their use of the store. I try to get some satisfaction from helping them, but much of the rest of what we sell doesn't fill any function except to triv-ialize sex. I'm not terribly happy with how my business has gone. It's my fault and I take full responsibility. I left it alone and viewed it as an income producer. Lots of what the store represents is an anachronism.

For the most part our customers are just ordinary people looking for something to spice up their love life. But we do get our share of things like obscene phone calls and men coming in to size up the nice young women who work here. The thing that upsets us most are the men who come in looking for magical potions, such as Spanish Fly, that they can sneak into an unsuspecting woman's drink, transforming her into a raging nympho-maniac. That fantasy angers me a lot.

I think a lot of the women who work here share my conflict, and we talk about it, but they also like the job because it's a nice place to work. I have always had absolutely wonderful young women and I think they like working here because they feel supported from the top down. It's always been very important to me to create a team spirit and a non-hierarchical environment. It's a woman's way of working.

In the past they worked here part time while they were at school and moved on after they completed university. Now, in this tough economic climate, there's no place for them to go and many are staying on. It's heart-breaking, really. They should be able to do more.

We carry a selection of good books of interest to women and I'd really like to expand that section. Books like *The Courage to Heal* for women survivors of incest, and *Our Bodies, Ourselves*, which gives women the kind of information they need to ask the right questions when they see the doctor. We used to have parties in places like Timmins and Kenora, where women wouldn't have access to that kind of information, and we put *Our Bodies, Ourselves* in the kits. I felt good about that. I can't carry the full range of books available in a feminist bookstore or one devoted to therapy, but I think it's important to have a representative selection of books that empower women, to help them have some more control over their lives.

I've thought about opening a small store for women that would be much more focused on a feminist approach to sex, on sensuality rather than on penises and vaginas. Not that that's not important, but we need to broaden our approach to sex—to think more of an ecology of sex—and the store doesn't reflect that. The iconography of sexuality as it functions in the marketplace is very male.

The idea that women should own their own sexuality and have a right to have their needs met—that's the kind of perspective I'd like to see. As a business it would have to be scaled down since you'd be going ahead of the marketplace. But at this stage in my life, I want to do something else.

I'm 57 years old and I'm in the process of changing my life. Fortunately, women live long enough these days to do that. I've been interested in psychology for many years and started to do a degree when I lived in Montreal, but had to give it up for financial reasons. Recently I decided to go back to school and formalize some of the psychological training I've acquired over the years by belonging to the Jung society and attending various conferences and so on.

I'm currently interested in feminist psychology and I'm finally doing my undergraduate degree. When I finish that, I'll do a master's. My goal is to become a psychotherapist with a feminist approach, since many traditional models of psychology have pathologized women. I'm enjoying my studies, but it's a struggle because I'm used to having discretionary reading time.

My grandmother was a suffragette who worked to establish birth-control clinics with Marie Stokes, the British birth-control pioneer. So there's a continuity in my feminist direction, although it may not be immediately evident.

Pat Andrew
St. John's, Newfoundland

"I was willing to work so hard because I wanted the lifestyle I had when I was married."

Pat Andrew finished school in the late 1950s, trained as a hairdresser and opened her own business, which she sold when she married. After her marriage ended, in 1976, she held a variety of jobs including bank teller and travelling salesperson. She currently owns a hairdressing salon and a bed and breakfast overlooking the harbour in St. John's.

I finished school when I was 16 and then took a hairdressing course. The following year, my father lent me the money to open my own business in St. John's. The business did very well.

Then I got married, and after my two children were born, I sold the shop, although I continued to do hairstyling in my own home. In 1976, I left my marriage because I was afraid of my husband. My divorce was granted on grounds of extreme mental and physical cruelty, but since family-law reform hadn't come into effect, I didn't get a cent. I had bought the house, I made more money than my husband and the judge gave it to him!

When I walked out the door, I had to rebuild the previous 16 years. Working was the only way I could do it. No one would give me credit because I was a single woman, even though I was the one who struggled throughout the marriage to pay the bills. I had to get someone to take a loan out in their name, which I co-signed, so I could buy a car and furniture for my apartment. I paid it off in two months because I didn't want to be beholden to anyone.

To get ahead, I had three jobs. I worked as a bank teller during the day, cut hair in my apartment until 9:00 or 10:00 at night and sold vacuum cleaners door to door on Saturdays. I made most of my money on Saturdays. I used to fill up my trunk with vacuum cleaners and come back with an empty car. I think a woman is better at selling vacuums than a man because she's more familiar with the machines. Even so, the company I worked for had never had a woman salesperson before.

Then I became the first woman to travel the island selling hardware products for 3M. Being on the road was horrible. I'd eat in my car and go to my room at night. When I walked into a store, they'd say, "You must be the salesman." I'd say, "No, I'm the saleswoman."

I increased their sales substantially by selling all their leftover stock. I'd go into the warehouse to see what was available, then I'd find someone to buy it. No one had bothered to do that before. I don't know if I could do that now, but in those days I was desperate to make money.

Even though I was doing well financially at this job, I wanted to work for myself. I was also travelling a lot and felt guilty for leaving my young son. I had had a couple of close calls on icy winter roads, which made me nervous.

I went into beauty supplies, then, in 1979. When I came across a beauty shop that wasn't doing well, I approached the owner and bought it. That got me back into hairdressing. At one point I owned three shops. Now, I'm down to one and leaning out of it.

I still employ seven girls, but I've done my term in office and I'm ready to pursue something different. The operators work on commission and I have all the headaches—problems with the plumbing, the lease, things like that. One thing I've noticed through this work is that women don't support other women. If a woman customer tells a male stylist how she wants her hair done and he says it will look horrible, she'll take his advice. But if I or one of the other female stylists offers the same advice, the customer will never come back.

Seven years ago, when my second marriage broke up, I bought a house with a wonderful view of the harbour. I intended to turn it into a bed and breakfast. Now I have four guest rooms.

I can work at night and in the early morning; then I have a free day to do what I want. I make all my own bread, muffins and jams. Until recently, I did all the chores myself, but now I have a girl to help. I love my house. I love working on it and puttering around.

I get up at 6:30 a.m. to serve breakfast at 8:00. In the evenings, I spend time talking to the guests. I have to sell myself, and they want to know about places to go and where to eat. I like people, which is important in this line of work.

I like everything to be clean and wholesome and fresh, the way I want things to be for myself. I love decorating and I take a lot of pride in doing it myself. I also do a lot of the painting and repairs. I've almost always worked from my home and I think you have to like your home a lot to do that. I guess I plan to do it until I get my pension.

I think running a bed and breakfast reflects the mothering instinct.

Most women who stay say things like: "I'd love to do something like this." But I've never heard a man make that statement. Perhaps this kind of work fits women better because women put more emphasis on the finer things and a woman's day never ends. She's still working while the couch potato is flipping the remote.

I never wanted to depend on a man. I always said I'd make it on my own and I have. My brother thought I was crazy to come up here, but now, every chance he gets, he's got someone coming up to look at the place.

Mary Black
Toronto, Ontario

"I'll do everything in my power to promote women. If you have women who are anxious to make things happen, you can't hold them back."

Mary Black began working as a draftsman in 1958. In the early 1960s, when her two daughters were born, she worked at home intermittently. In 1965, she returned to drafting and, in 1969, became graphics co-ordinater at an educational publishing house. She entered the printing industry in 1975 and now owns and operates her own film-separation company, Colour Technologies.

I was brought into the printing industry in 1975 as a token woman. I had trained as a draftsman and was working as a graphics co-ordinator at a publishing company. The company that did our film work knew me, and one day the president invited me out to lunch. "It's time we had a woman in sales," he said. "One of our competitors has hired one and she's not doing too badly, so we thought we'd ask you."

Two weeks later, I was working as a salesperson on straight commission. They gave me two weeks of training and told me to go to work. "I've never sold before," I said. " Perhaps I could go along with the sales manager for awhile?"

"Oh, no. You know publishing," was their reply.

I didn't have a clue. I drove around the city, taking down the names of companies that did billboards or might do catalogues—anything that involved colour work—and started making cold calls.

My first two years were pure hell. Management was trying to be progressive—they wanted to do the right thing and hire a woman—but they didn't tell me that nobody else in the company wanted me. The men resented a female. They put me through all kinds of hassles and deliberately delayed my work. I was told that I shouldn't be in this business—literally told that I should be in the bedroom or the kitchen instead.

One day, after I'd been there for a couple of months, I went out to the parking lot to get in my car. My license was LZY 895 and someone had taken a black pen and put a great big A between the L and the Z to make the word LAZY. I was devastated. I drove away in tears.

When I pulled into my driveway, my daughters, who were 12 and 13, were in the kitchen starting dinner. I think it was the first time they had ever seen me cry. I rushed into the kitchen, grabbed a cloth and wiped the letter off. When I came back in, I told them the story. I don't have to wonder why they're feminists today.

The next day someone put the A back on. I came home and washed it off again. The third day it was back. When I got home, the girls asked if I was going to wash it off and I said I wasn't. I decided if someone was so anxious to have that message on my car, it could stay there.

I remember those three days as one of my most skin-toughening times in the industry. Initially, the experience was devastating. Then, I accepted that life in this business wouldn't be easy, so I might as well get on with it.

Another funny thing happened. Although I had never thought of myself as a man-killer, I suddenly had all kinds of men wanting to go out with me. It took me a long time to figure it out, then all of a sudden, it hit me: I was a woman in a prominent position and the only way they could bring me down was by getting me into bed. It was almost a contest to see who would be successful. How silly that they think getting you into bed will put you on an equal footing. They never consider the statement it makes about them.

After I'd been there for 2½ years, I had another character-building experience. At that point I was outselling three of the six salesmen, all of whom had been there longer than me. They used to give the new accounts to one poor guy who wasn't doing very well. I kept hoping they'd give me an account that I didn't have to develop myself, but that never happened.

Then the sales manager left to start his own company. He and the president decided who would get the accounts he was leaving behind. They called me in first and gave me two accounts. I thought I'd died and gone to heaven, but when I checked the records to see how much the accounts would be worth, I discovered they'd both been dead for over a year.

I was devastated. By that point I had learned never to let them see me cry, which meant I was often off by myself, repressing tears and thinking, I've got to get out of here. The truth is, though, I had left a $16,500-a-year job in publishing and 2½ years later I was making $35,000. Not realizing my value to the industry and not knowing I could go somewhere else, I used to tell myself that I'd more than doubled my salary and I'd just have to accept the downsides of the job.

During the day, I kept overhearing the guys talking about the big accounts they'd just been handed. I knew some of these fellows wouldn't be able to make them work, and at the end of the day I walked into this office, the very office we're sitting in today, and said to the president, "I want you to know that I know what happened today."

"What do you mean?" he asked.

I said, "You've just split up $1-million-worth of accounts among the six salesmen."

"But, Mary, we gave you two accounts."

"Yes, you did, and they've both been dead for over a year."

He started to get flustered. "I'm not here to complain," I said. "I'm here to tell you that I plan to revive those two accounts, and within the next two years, I'm going to be outselling the three salespeople I am currently not outselling. I just wanted you to know that." I turned around and walked out.

And that's what I did. I became their top salesperson 2½ years later. Then I left and went to another company.

I left because I was going to be offered a partnership, although the man who hired me insisted on paying me on a commission basis. It takes awhile for business to move with you, but by the third month, I was doing $1-million a year. At that point the owner of the company decided that no woman should be making more than anyone else in the shop and he stopped paying my commissions. It was unbelievably stupid since he was making money from the work I was bringing in, but he couldn't cope with the amount of money I was earning. That ended the partnership.

For the next few years, I moved around a bit. Then I decided the time had come to go into business for myself. So I sold my house, bought a scanner, rented some space and brought someone in as a shareholder who had the technical knowledge to run the machine.

I'm the only woman in Canada who owns a business in the trade end of our industry, and I don't know of any in the United States. We do colour separations, which must be done before the work goes to the printer. I started off with five employees, eight years ago. Now I employ 35 people.

When I started, I didn't have a clue about what I was getting into. I really believed I could just run around selling, which is what I'm good at, and that everything else would happen. But suddenly I had to clean the washrooms, do the billing, baby-sit the people in the office, listen to their problems—the list was endless. In addition to getting the work and making sure it was done properly, I also had to learn how to run a company, which is what I've been doing for the past seven years. It's been very exciting, but if I'd known what I was getting into, I don't know if I ever would have done it.

I've always had a tremendous amount of energy and now that I'm living on my own—my daughters are grown up and I ended a long-term relationship a couple of years ago—I also have time. I work out every morning and arrive at the office between 7:30 and 9 a.m. I often stay until 10:30 or 11:00 at night, if I'm not at functions or meetings.

On Friday nights, I go up to the country and spend the weekend hibernating. In this business it's constant people, so I long for the other extreme. I often see a friend for lunch on Saturdays. Otherwise I read, walk or do nothing and it's wonderful.

I don't have much of a social life these days, but I really feel I'm in a building mode with the company. Maybe because I'm a woman, I like to work in teams, so at least once a month we have a staff meeting to allow people to express their concerns. About six months ago, I told them that it was great that we had survived the recession, but that from now on it was time to fly with the eagles. In response, the staff gave me a sterling-silver eagle for my birthday.

That was one of the few times as a business owner that I really felt appreciated. Usually, you don't. People are constantly wanting things—more pay, more time off, different positions and so on. You always feel you're never giving them enough.

Three and a half years ago I almost lost the company. I had to learn very quickly how to be a better manager and to keep my eye on the bottom line. That was probably one of the best things that ever happened. I learned and put the controls in place that enabled us to survive through a very tough time. If it hadn't happened then, it would have happened during the recession and I would have lost the business.

Half my staff, including the technical people, are women. The top five women graduates from Ryerson are always sent to me because the school knows I'll do my best to promote women and often other companies won't. I try to do a lot of mentoring, to make sure they learn to stand up for themselves and don't put themselves down. That's especially important in this industry.

As far as I'm concerned, one of these very bright young women is worth two bright men because she's going to try that much harder to make it work. I have great men, too, and I'm glad I do. Some have been with me for a long time and they're wonderful.

My mother was a very determined woman and I think I got my determination from her. I was driven to make things better for my daughters, too. Now one daughter is my top salesperson. My second daughter learned the technical end of the industry here and she's gone to work for another company. Maybe they'll both take over the business one day. One thing I've been able to do is to give them extremely high-earning power.

I moved to this location after we outgrew our first space. I take a great deal of pleasure in the symbolism of this office because it was the president's office in the first company that hired me. After he folded his business, I drove by, for over a year, looking at the For Rent signs, thinking there would be some sort of justice in moving back into the building.

When I finally called, the male real-estate agent treated me like I was looney. Sometimes there are great advantages to being a woman. Whenever you deal with a man who looks at you like you're not capable, you know you'll come out on top. He kept telling me how peculiar the space was. Although I knew that it suited me to a T, I agreed it wouldn't be easy. I played the role—I never told him I'd worked here for seven years. As a result, they ended up renting me the place for what it cost to keep it empty.

One of the things I consciously did was to set about making myself visible in the industry and it's really paid off. I joined the Canadian Printing Industries' Association (CPIA) so I'd get to know all the printers. Now I'm about to become president. Since I'm a woman, it wasn't hard to make myself stand out, but I also made sure they knew I was capable.

I still encounter discrimination, very often from younger men, but I react differently now. I think my attitudes have changed over the years. Early on, I was vulnerable. I got my back up and reacted in ways that probably made things worse. Now I take a more reasoned approach.

The other day I met a young man at a supply company I deal with. Somebody introduced us and we shook hands and he gave me one of those limp handshakes, where they sort of hold your hand in a strange position. I didn't even think, but to me that's a degrading way for a man to shake hands with a woman, especially in business. So I looked at him and said, "Excuse me, do you mind if we try that again?" After he gave me a good firm handshake I said, "That's much better, thank you," then we went on to something else.

About a week later, I met him and he shook hands with me properly. "I just want you to know, Mary, I'm a fast learner," he said. Those little things make you realize you've achieved something. This man will now treat women with respect when he shakes hands with them.

Last year, we had a CPIA meeting to introduce the new board members. Someone brought a man over to meet me, and before they'd even started to introduce me, he turned and walked away. He was extremely rude. The person who was introducing him realized what had happened, so he grabbed him by the arm and said, "I really think you should meet Mary. She's the first vice-president and she'll be president next year." When he realized I might be somebody important, his whole attitude changed.

I was very polite to him, but he's sat on the board for the past year and I won't have anything to do with him. He slowly recognized the respect I get from my peers and he's tried very hard to become part of the inner circle. It may be awful to say, but I'm just giving him the same treatment he intended to give me. He was very stupid.

People say to me, "Look at what you've accomplished." I don't see it that way. I see what I still have to do. From that perspective, I've still got a long way to go. I've got a goal for this company. In five years the whole city will know that we're the number-one film house. I think we are now, but I want everyone to acknowledge that.

Grace Skavinski
Yellowknife, Northwest
Territories

"I work so hard because it give me a great deal of satisfaction. Money is quite immaterial to me. If I've got it, I spend it."

Grace Skavinski began working as a registered nursing assistant in 1965. The following year, she moved to Yellowknife and worked in the hotel business for 18 years, beginning as a coffee-shop waitress. In 1984, she opened her own business, Our Place, a restaurant and lounge.

I grew up on a small farm in Manitoba and left when I was 17 to take a licensed practical-nursing course in Winnipeg. After graduating, I worked for a year and then came to Yellowknife in 1966. A friend wanted me to move here because her husband was expecting a transfer. I said I'd go ahead and get settled, but they never made it because his promotion didn't come through.

The papers in the South portrayed the North as a place that was crying for nurses, but by the time I arrived, the matrons at the hospital were fed up with young girls. Once they were trained, they'd run off with rich prospectors. The matron who interviewed me asked how long I'd been in town, and when I said two hours, she told me to come back in six months.

I checked in at the Yellowknife Inn, planning to stay the night and carry on to Norman Wells or Inuvik. The lady who worked at the counter stopped me on my way to the coffee-shop and asked if I was looking for a job. I said I was, but it hadn't panned out. She gave me a job in the coffee-shop and I started the next day.

So there I was at 18 working as a waitress. Other than the money, being a waitress isn't exactly the most rewarding job. I had only worked as a nurse and I could see that people treated waitresses differently. Nobody gave a damn who I was because I wasn't going to be there next week. Within a year, though, they were my best friends and it was heaven.

After working in the coffee-shop for three years, they promoted me to the front desk. I didn't want to leave the coffee-shop because I felt so secure. I had my own group of people and they were wonderful. I knew that if I left that area, I wouldn't have the same contact with them—and I didn't. When they were walking through the lobby they said, "Hi, Grace," and that was the extent of it.

At first, I lived in staff housing provided by the hotel. That was very interesting because everybody was different. There were 18 of us, and you couldn't put two of us in the same pod. We had the RCMP visit us many times, for being rowdy, but we were just having a good time.

I worked at the inn for a total of 18 years and loved every minute of it. I worked on the front desk for two or three years, then was promoted to front-office manager. I was the dining-room manager, and for a couple of years I worked in the tavern until I got promoted to the accounting office. I was the manager's secretary for awhile, and I finished by being the food-and-beverage manager.

In the course of all these promotions, I was learning about the hospitality business. I even washed my share of dishes, cleaned rooms and made beds, although it was never on my job description. But if someone didn't show up, you had to do their job.

Anyway, after 18 years, I thought about starting my own place. The inn had a pleasant dining-room, but it didn't have crystal and the nice things that people should have. That's where I thought there was a need.

I opened Our Place, a cocktail lounge and restaurant, in 1984. I have a silent partner, but I'm the major shareholder. The money to get started came from savings I'd accumulated while working at the Yellowknife Inn. Don't forget, I grew up on a farm where there was no such thing as an allowance or a place to spend money, so I didn't really know how to do it.

In Winnipeg I lived from hand to mouth, because the wages of a practical nurse weren't great. So when I came up here and got free housing, free food, free everything, my pay cheques were... mine! I had nothing better to do with them than put them in the bank. And that's exactly what I did.

Once the bank account starts, there's no end to it. I wasn't depositing thousands of dollars on a monthly basis, but $200 here and $500 there, plus interest, after 18 years, certainly gives you a nice sum of money.

When I decided to go into business, every businessman in Yellowknife told me it would take four or five months to get my loan approved. I went to my own little banker I'd been dealing with for 18 years. He told me he had more faith in me than anyone else in town as far as the restaurant business went, but because it was a substantial sum of money, he had to get head-office approval. Head office didn't have one question for him and the loan took 10 days to go through.

The work started immediately. Building the restaurant cost $580,000. The walls are oak and the oak, itself, cost just short of $200,000. The wing and club chairs were a lot more expensive than run-of-the-mill stuff, but that's what we needed to create the atmosphere I wanted. I decorated it with a friend who's an interior decorator in Calgary.

After we opened, we were packed solid for three years. The bank gave us three years to pay off our mortgage—they wouldn't give us a 10-year loan—so I literally worked 24 hours a day for the first three years. The payments were so high that I didn't collect a pay cheque during that time. I ate and drank at the restaurant and never went anywhere. I'd never owned anything in my life and my life savings had gone into my share, so I couldn't sleep until I had it paid off.

When the three years were up, we bought up all the Dom Perignon in town and had a big mortgage-burning party for about 100 of our best customers.

From then on, it was pretty smooth sailing, although 1992 was a tough year, because of the recession. But as long as you don't have the banker knocking on the door, you can buy your food and pay your rent and your staff. You just have to work twice as hard.

It's a difficult business, and a very time-consuming one. The hours are long and staff is always a challenge, although I've been lucky in that regard. We work with a skeleton staff. There are only three full-timers and two part-timers and, of course, two kitchen staff.

That means that we really run at lunch and there's a lot of pressure, but it's senseless to have five people taking home $30 each in gratuities when two people can take home $70 or $75 for the two hours of work. Consequently, the staff stay a long time. I run like an idiot with them and I don't take my share. We pool the gratuities and they get to take the money home. It's certainly not a secret to keeping good staff, but few company presidents would serve a meal at lunch-time.

I do all the necessary extra stuff. I've never had a cleaner or a janitor. Everybody laughs at me because I'm too fussy. I'd never have anybody vacuum for me or oil the walls because commercial cleaners are commercial cleaners. It takes me an extra three hours a day, but it's worth it because I don't have to fight with anybody. I know that if there's dust on a ledge, it's my problem.

I go in at 7:30 every morning and I work until the lunch rush is over and things are cleaned up. I leave it turnkey for the night shift. At 3:30 I go home, have a little nap and start washing tablecloths and napkins for the next day.

Everything is cloth. I don't know if I'm more conscious of this kind of thing because I'm a woman—I'm sure it has a bit to do with it—but as the money became available, I made improvements. When we opened, we had paper napkins. We brought in cloth napkins four years ago. That's a lot of extra work and I don't charge an extra penny for it. I'm just giving my customers something better.

Over the years, we've put $150 prisms in the windows, added velvet cushions and Waterford crystal. We've gotten bigger and better every year. We have the same customers, and naturally they see these improvements.

Washing and pressing 300 napkins keeps me busy until 10:00 at night. Then I watch a little TV and always have a late dinner. I get to sleep at about 1:00 in the morning. I do the exact same thing six days of the week. On the seventh I do all the bookkeeping. I order the food and liquor, pay the bills, do the payroll and make the deposits.

Prior to owning Our Place, I had a very short-lived marriage. I got married in... let's see, I can't even remember... it was probably in the late '70s, and I was married for a year. I'm just too much of a career person. There isn't one man in this world who would be happy with me when I'm working because I'm too involved. I guess I look after the bare necessities of the relationship, like making sure the laundry is done, there's food on the table and the house is clean. But I don't take the time to build on a relationship the way a person should.

I've never had children, and after my marriage ended, I never tried to have a serious relationship because that experience taught me it just doesn't work. I did have a six-year relationship with a man who also owned a restaurant. That relationship functioned in the sense that he had just as little time as me to worry about whether or not he got that peck on the cheek when he came home.

I'm a high-energy person, so seven days a week doesn't bother me. When I get off on a Friday night at 11:00, I think nothing of going to a party and I can do that every night of the week. I drink a bottle of wine a day, and I have for the last 20 years. No more, no less. And I quite enjoy life, even if I put in many an hour working.

I'm 47, and in January it will be 30 years since I came to Yellowknife. One of the benefits of my success is that I've been able to be extremely good to my family financially. Nobody is lacking—my mother, my sister and my two brothers.

At my age a person should be starting to relax and I'm about to start. I think I'll sell the business in about four years. All that matters to me is my nest egg for retirement, which I have. Nobody is going to be looking after me. I'm going to be looking after myself.

I've never regretted leaving nursing. It was wonderful, but since that day I've always taken a little step up. I shouldn't say that. I laugh when I talk to the customers because on a busy Friday night I'm usually the one bartending, washing glasses and cleaning ashtrays. People laugh at me and say, "Grace, are you still washing dishes?" I reply, "This is the only place I've ever worked that hasn't given me a promotion."

Frances Wright
Calgary, Alberta

"You only go through life once, so you might as well try to make a difference."

Frances Wright graduated from university in the late '60s and went to work on Parliament Hill as a secretary. She had a variety of careers throughout the 1970s, including stockbroker, television host and political candidate. In 1980, she opened the first Ports International store in Calgary and was running six stores by 1990, when she sold them. She is currently working as a consultant.

My career path isn't exactly typical. I graduated in the late '60s with a BA in psychology. The first question was always: "Do you type?" and since I did, I got slotted into a variety of different jobs, which, in retrospect, were absolutely fascinating.

When I finished university, I left Calgary and moved to Ottawa and got a job on Parliament Hill, as an assistant to a secretary for a member of Parliament. After 18 months I decided I could be a special assistant. I applied to a number of ministers, but was turned down by everyone because they said they were concerned about travelling with a young woman.

At that point I decided to take a journalism degree, and enrolled at Carleton. I completed all my course work, but didn't write my thesis because I had a serious car accident and moved back to Calgary.

I was 26 and even though I didn't have any background in money and finance, a friend suggested that, since I was good at meeting people, I should become a stockbroker. Although I liked the access to information that came with the job and the variety of people who came to invest, I don't think I was a good stockbroker. I became too involved with my clients. I was rapidly going broke because, if they lost money on a deal, I'd personally make it up.

I also didn't appreciate the accounting side of the business. I saw the job more as that of a treasurer—taking people's money and making it grow. But you have to be a lot more savvy. You need a cynical approach to the data you're given, and you have to be able to figure out other ways to get at the information. At that point, I didn't have the skill or the confidence.

This was in the early '70s, and in those days stockbrokering was a largely male, ya-hoo, cowboy kind of business so it was difficult to be a woman. Also, I was politically identified as a Liberal and people would constantly say derogatory things about Trudeau and the federal party. Being a sort of ornery person I'd ask, "Don't you think that by the law of averages they might have made just one right decision for Alberta?" "No, absolutely not," was the consistent response.

On the day that John Turner, who was then finance minister, brought down his budget disallowing provincial royalties as a tax expense, everybody exploded. This was going to provoke the separation of Alberta from Canada! I was working in a three-tower building and, in the course of walking to the third tower for lunch, was stopped four or five times by men. They did things like throw me against the wall, grab my arms, shake their fists in my face and say, "That god-damn Trudeau. He's screwing up everything." By the time I got to my lunch, about 20 minutes later, I decided, what the hell. If I have to take this abuse anyway, I might as well be a candidate.

In 1972, I had been a campaign manager for a woman candidate and felt it was very important for women to run for office. I talked to a few people and they said, "Sure. Nobody else wants to do it." So in 1974, I ran as a Liberal in Calgary Centre. Of course, I didn't win, but it was a phenomenal experience.

The only serious drawback was when the Calgary chair refused to sign my papers because I was thought to be too radical, probably because in those days Calgary wasn't very conscious of the necessity for equity. The idea that women stayed home was very much a part of the culture. Fortunately, because of my Ottawa experience, I knew Pierre Trudeau and some of the people in his office so I got them to fix the problem.

I ended up doing the best of all the Liberals in Calgary and the second best in the province. After I lost, I went back to school and finished my journalism degree. Then I did a number of short-term jobs, including a TV show which ran for about 1½ years on local television. It focused on key decision makers and how their decisions affect the general public.

At one point, I became campaign manager for a man who was running for mayor. We won and I expected to be hired as an assistant, but the commissioners at City Hall weren't keen to have somebody who was as strong and outspoken as I was and they dissuaded him from hiring me.

Then I ran in the 1979 election and lost ingloriously. I don't have any regrets because I enjoyed the exposure to issues. You had to know about everything, from immigration to interest rates to seniors. In politics you meet the best of people and the worst of people, but they are what they are and it's absolutely fascinating.

I never expected to marry, although I always thought I'd have children. In 1980, I became campaign manager for a Liberal candidate running in the federal election, which is where I met my husband. He had just arrived in Calgary from Ottawa and thought working on a political campaign would be an interesting way to meet people. He was wonderful. Whenever I had a difficult project, I'd ask Richard to do it and he always did it better than I expected.

About that time a male friend said to me, "I think you should look at having your own business. Take a look at the Ports International label." I'm no shopper. I think if you've got time you should use it to write a letter of protest, organize something, take a course or whatever. Don't go shopping! But I went to see the clothes in The Bay, anyway. I thought they were nice, basic clothes, well made, but they were quite a price.

Even so, I screwed up my courage to call Toronto and I talked to the man who ran the company. He very quickly took charge of the conversation. "Do you have a fashion background?" he asked.

"No."

"Do you have money?"

"No."

"Do you have a merchandising background?"

"No."

"Do you have any retailing experience?"

"No."

We talked for 1½ hours and he asked me about different things such as community involvement, and what I knew about the Ports line. In retrospect, I realize I knew relatively little. I should have known a lot more before I phoned. Finally, he asked me to come to Toronto the following week.

Since I didn't have any money, I went to my dear mother and asked her to buy me a plane ticket for my birthday. I spent a day meeting with the man who had interviewed me on the phone, and when we were finished, he told me I'd passed on certain qualifications, but I had to raise X amount of dollars. He also told me to get some retail experience.

It took me quite a while to get a job in women's wear—nobody wanted to hire me for a $4-an-hour sales position—but I found it quite fascinating. One day, after I'd been working for about three months, I got a phone call saying that Ports wanted to open a store in September 1980, so I'd better get my money together.

At that time the banks were quite liberal in lending money, so between my silent partner, the chap who had suggested the idea, my husband and myself, we were able to raise the necessary money. We opened one Ports store and closed with six.

I was the initial operating person and I ran the stores. When we decided to open a men's store, I brought my husband in. Having both male and female staff was interesting because it highlighted some differences between the sexes. Every time the men had a performance review they'd say, "How much more money am I getting?" When I gave raises to several women who were doing an excellent job, they said, "You don't have to do that."

It was also interesting to observe the difference between male and female customers. Bob doesn't phone up Stan and say, "Hey, let's go shopping Saturday afternoon. I want to try on two or three things." They come in under duress—either dragged in by a female or because they need a new suit since their current one is threadbare. As a result, they expect you to be intuitive about their needs. It's up to you to ask them things like, "Do you also need shirts? Ties?"

I also enjoyed studying the husbands who came in with their wives. Often, you were able to observe the dynamics of a relationship. In one instance the husband sat in the chair and said abusive things like, "Nothing will suit her. What can you do when you've got a pig?" I was so upset I kicked him out of the store.

I realize I might have jeopardized my business, but there are certain issues I feel strongly about and I believe that if you don't speak out, things get lost. I think that's probably why I've continued to be a small-business person. I wouldn't be a particularly good company person.

I don't know where my sense of wanting to make a difference comes from. Maybe I'm ornery. As a child I was extremely shy, and if a teacher asked me to speak, I'd die a thousand deaths. I think it happened step by step—reading books like *The Second Sex* by Simone de Beauvoir opened my eyes. It reinforced the sense that my instincts were right and that other women were having thoughts similar to mine.

Working closely with my husband was wonderful because we're very complementary. Unfortunately, our areas of responsibility broke down into traditional male-female divisions. He was better with the financial side of things, how the numbers crunched, and perhaps with planning. I was better with the people issues and with coming up with new ideas of how to do things.

Sure, there was conflict—it wasn't always smooth sailing, but we tried not to bring our fights into work, although I must say that sometimes proved harder than it would seem. But by and large it was wonderful because I could trust him totally. I'd dearly love to work with him again.

We sold the stores in 1990. Ports sold out to a company that didn't value any of the things Ports valued so we were sort of forced out. But it had a silver lining because the economy crashed and we would probably have had to close stores anyway.

Running the stores was my most satisfying work experience because we were building something from nothing, and by industry standards we were the top of the heap. It wasn't just a little job. It had many different facets and it just seemed to go step by step. Also, Ports was a very good company to work with. We were lucky to have a climate in Calgary that was tremendously buoyant. We had a fabulous product and, of course, there was a pent-up demand. We also had phenomenal staff, most of whom stayed with us for years.

A year after we sold the stores, Lawrence Decore, the Alberta Liberal leader, was doing very well in the polls and he suggested I get involved provincially. "I won't run again," I said. "I've had my two cracks, and it was wonderful but I'm not interested anymore."

He kept at me and finally I agreed if he'd commit to ensuring that at least 25 per cent of the candidates were women and that they'd receive extra support from the party.

So for two years, from 1991–93, my husband basically supported me while I travelled around the province, encouraging women to run and helping them, as well as men, with their candidacies. I ran in Banff and lost. Three strikes up, three strikes down.

Now I'm consulting, which is fascinating. I'm currently working on a project that involves interviewing about 50 companies in Calgary, across Canada and a few in the States, which are known to be outstanding in terms of how they treat their employees. I'm about halfway through my interviews and I'm very encouraged by what I see.

As much as I always thought I'd have children, I haven't been able to and that makes me sad. On the positive side, I think that not having children has allowed my husband and I to be more involved with community things and to be a little more outrageous because we don't have to worry about remarks reflecting back on our family. Some of my volunteering, such as my involvement with AIDS, which is fringe in terms of Calgary, might provoke a backlash.

If I had my life to live over again, I'd be much more specifically directed at university. I wouldn't take a BA. I'd probably take a bachelor of commerce. I think getting some kind of financial background is very important, because it influences just about everything you do in life. I'd also be much more directed in terms of the type of jobs I pursued after I graduated, instead of letting things happen, because here I am at 46 and I'm not quite sure what I am in professional terms. If I had to fill out a passport application, I don't know what I'd put for occupation, and that's causing me considerable distress.

11

~~~

Sports,
Entertainment
and
Communications

Mildred Marion McAuley
Edmonton, Alberta

"None of us was aware that we were making history. We were just doing what we wanted to do and what we loved to do and getting paid for it. That was the big thing—getting paid."

"Millie" McAuley, who was born in Regina in 1924, became a professional base-ball player in 1943. She played third base for the Rockford Peaches in the All-American Girls, Professional Baseball League for two years, then quit to get married, although she continued to play amateur ball until 1951. In 1960, when her youngest son was four, she took a government job and worked as a typist and then as an administrator for 27 years.

At a very young age, I became fascinated by balls: sponge balls, tennis balls, beach balls, you name it. My family hated this interest because I was always bouncing balls around the house. I grew up in Regina and in those days the city had lots of fields, so when I was about 10, I started to play baseball with the boys.

I'm from a family of five girls and five boys. None of my sisters played ball. I played catcher on a girls' team at school from the time I was in Grade 4, but we weren't allowed to play with the boys. When we won the championship in Grade 8, I was hit by a bat and got a tooth knocked out. My mother was annoyed and got angry with me for being a tomboy.

In 1939, when I was 15, I started to play organized ball for the Army-Navy Bombers, a company-sponsored team. Kappy Kaplan, the coach, put me on third base and I've played third base ever since. In 1943, I got my chance to turn pro, which was really exciting. When the war started, the male professional baseball players joined up, and someone suggested the idea of starting a girls' professional league as a substitute.

People who had been following our league contacted two other women and myself. When they told us about a professional league that paid $85 a week, we couldn't believe it. Woweee! Getting paid to do something you love. We knew we couldn't miss the chance. So we signed a contract and went to Wrigley Field in Chicago to try out. Initially, my mother didn't like the idea because she was afraid I'd get into trouble, but she was reassured when she learned we'd be well chaperoned. In the end, Mom was very happy I went, and I am, too.

I was 18 years old when I left home. One hundred and twenty girls arrived in Chicago for try-outs. They planned to pick 60 of us for four teams so we knew we had to work. I was worried. I didn't know if I'd make it, but Johnny Gottselig, from Regina, was helping to run the camp and he coached me.

We were all quite nervous. In the morning the teams were posted on the board, just as in the movie *A League of Their Own*. My only disappointment was that the other two girls who had played ball in Regina ended up on another club. We'd been playing together for so long, it was hard to be separated. In the end, I was thrilled I made the Rockford Peaches, but I felt badly for the 60 girls who were cut.

Our uniform consisted of a skirt over shorts. The fans liked that. It was feminine. In the early part of our training, we were sent to a charm school run by the famous Helena Rubenstein. We were taught how to wear our hair, how to do our eyebrows and so on. We also learned good manners and how to be ladylike—how to sit, walk and cross our legs. I remember the instructor telling us, "Always cross your legs with one knee over the other so you can see the full leg." When it was my turn, she told me I should wear my hair up, behind my ears, because I had nice ears.

I think some of the girls probably took it all in, but it's difficult to wear make-up playing ball because you're perspiring. Also, you can't play ball with long nails. We enjoyed these lessons in beauty and charm, but I don't think we took them too seriously.

We weren't allowed to wear slacks in public, as it wasn't considered ladylike, but we were permitted to wear them at the homes where we roomed. We were boarded in private houses, and to my knowledge, most of the girls stayed at wonderful places. We travelled around on a bus and sang and talked to pass the time.

For awhile, I roomed with a girl who never heard from her family even though she was from Chicago, which was only 90 miles from Rockford. I was getting letters from all over the place and she finally confided in me. "Mill," she said, "would you like to come and meet my family? We'll take the bus to Chicago. You're the only person I'll show where I came from."

Her home was in a very rough part of town. Her family were immigrants and very uncouth. The language was terrible, just awful. When we left, she said, "Now you know why I don't want to go back home." It was clear she escaped her family and became independent through playing ball.

It gave her the opportunity to decide that she didn't want that kind of life. We still keep in touch and she's doing well. Eventually, she got married and, like me, she has two boys. She's still living in Rockford.

Some of the other girls on the team worked in factories on assembly lines, and some worked on farms. Many of them just wanted to get away from home. They were a part of that era, they wanted to do something different. I think that's good. That's progress. Then the men started to come back from the war and some of the girls got married and didn't continue to play ball. Once that happened, the calibre of the league started to drop because it was harder to get top-notch players.

I played for two years. I was very successful and I enjoyed it, but when I was offered a contract to go back for a third year, in 1945, I turned it down because I got married. My husband wanted me to continue playing and I often wish I had because Rockford won the championship that year. But you can't have the best of two worlds.

I guess our league did make history. I think we were the first group of women to really get out on our own and to travel as a team. We changed roommates every trip so we all got to know each other. We were very honest with one another. As I said, some of the girls were from very adverse family situations, but playing professional ball was very good for their self-esteem.

I think it's good for anyone to get away from home and see how other people live. When you're thrown in amongst 120 girls, you're going to learn something. You're certainly going to learn to get along with people because you have to play as a group. On the ball club you're all for one and one for all. I'd just hate working by myself, because I need to feel that I'm part of something other than Millie.

Our professional league wouldn't have happened if it hadn't been for the war. But at the time we didn't see it in that light. We knew there was a war, but somehow it was blocked from our minds. I often think we were in a state of denial. We didn't realize the seriousness of the situation. We were just playing ball.

There were some parts to *A League of Their Own* that weren't right. We never did meet Mr. Wrigley, the founder of the league, and the manager never came into our dressing room. My coach, Eddie Stumpf, wasn't a drunk, either. He was true blue. He used to tell us to go to church and pray for base hits. At times I was embarrassed watching the movie because in reality the girls didn't swear like that. We all smoked, though. I'd say nine out of 10 girls smoked and I think they still do. Back in those days, who knew it was bad for you?

One thing that did disturb me about the league—and they suggested this in the movie—was the way they treated blacks. We should have had a few black girls in the club. They were good enough. I was friends with some black girls who played organized ball for their company in Rockford and I felt badly. I used to say, "She's a better ball player than I am" and I'd just about get my neck in a sling, because that's how it was.

As I said, we did wear those little skirts. Later, the women ball players started wearing pants, and some of the girls—I'm not criticizing them—but they somehow got the idea that they could compete with the men. I think they were making a big mistake; women may be able to field like the men, but you can't beat a male pitcher. We should play ball like women, because when a woman steps over that line, she becomes too masculine, too authoritative, and I don't think that's what we want. We want our place in the world, as women. And men can keep their place as men.

I often wonder what would have happened if we hadn't had the opportunity to play professional baseball. I have four sisters, and we've talked about the fact that they didn't have the chance to get away. My sisters got married young. I didn't want to get married young or have a bunch of kids at a young age. I wanted children when I wanted them.

I played organized ball in Edmonton for seven years after I got married. I hung up my uniform when we won the Dominion Championship in 1951. I was still playing third base. And when I was finished playing ball I had my family. That's the way I wanted it. I think I learned that through getting away on my own.

In 1960, I took a refresher course at school and went to work for the government for 27 years. I loved it. I started out in a typing pool and ended up in administration. I retired five years ago when I was 66 and I miss it.

When I first went to work I hated leaving my sons, who were nine and four. I felt so guilty that I went to the minister who said, "Mill, if anything happened to your husband, you'd have to work. So as long as you get home and tuck them into bed, it's not going to hurt them." I don't regret working, because I became independent and looked after myself. It's a good thing, because my husband died last year and I'm on my own.

I loved playing ball. I hope there will be another league one day because we had a lot of fun in ours. We also made some money from the movie and from selling our All-American logo, and we're using the money to help former players who need financial assistance, as well as to promote women's baseball. We're trying to organize another league so that women can get back into a league of their own.

I went down to the Baseball Hall of Fame in Cooperstown, New York, for the opening of the display on women's baseball. It was great. Then, last August, we had our 50th anniversary. Quite a few of the girls have died, but those of us who were able to attend the anniversary had a wonderful time. Dottie Collins, our secretary, was on TSN (The Sports Network) not long ago and she talked about not realizing how much the league meant until we saw one another again. It doesn't matter whether or not you were a star then. Now you can share your memories and reflect on things that happened and it's great.

Doris Anderson
Toronto, Ontario

"I was very idealistic and thought it would be wonderful to be a writer because you could change things through writing."

Doris Anderson graduated from the University of Alberta with a BA in 1945. After a number of jobs in advertising and promotion she was hired for a staff position at Chatelaine. *She became editor of the magazine in 1960, a position she held until 1978. She has written two novels and* The Unfinished Revolution, *a book on the status of women in 12 countries. An activist on behalf of women for many years, she was recently awarded the Order of Ontario.*

I was a product of the Depression, so I started to work at 18. I wanted to go to university, but teaching was what was offered to me. In those days, that seemed like a good profession for a woman. I took one year's training and then taught for two years in country schools in Alberta. I saved enough money to pay my parents back for my training and to attend university.

I wanted to work in journalism, so as soon as I got my degree, I left the West and came to Toronto. By that time, the war had ended and people were afraid there weren't going to be enough jobs for the returning veterans. Women were being fired everywhere. I was aware that this was why I wasn't being hired, but, at the time, I thought it was okay.

I sent letters everywhere. Although there were lots of jobs, they didn't want women and they didn't even pretend you were going to get hired for anything, except, perhaps, some sort of service job. I was interviewed at *Maclean's*, for a copy-editor's position, and was told that I'd never get out of the copy department because I was female. I was so depressed at the thought of shifting commas around and checking whether rivers ran north or south for the rest of my life, I turned the job down. Everybody thought I was mad, but I knew I wouldn't be able to stand that job. I was never even particularly good at spelling.

I kept being offered secretarial jobs and research jobs for men who were really quite mediocre writers. I tried advertising copywriting and radio scriptwriting, took university courses at night and started writing short stories. I finally got so frustrated, I went to England for a year, where I continued to write short stories and had a wonderful time. I came back because I was getting involved with an Englishman and I knew I didn't want to spend the rest of my life in England.

While I was there I managed to sell a short story to *Chatelaine* and that got my foot in the door. In 1951, the magazine hired me to do advertising promotion. After six years of frustrating jobs, this was my first break. I didn't have a big budget and the approach to promotion was quite amateurish. I did things like trying to persuade Eaton's and Simpson's to put in window displays tying-in with something in the magazine.

I was quite successful at promotion, but it didn't interest me. Meanwhile, the editorial people were working extremely hard. I kept offering to help, and within six months I got a job on the editorial staff. Six years later I was the editor.

I often tell young people that all you really need is one decent break. Mine was getting in at *Chatelaine*.

The staff at *Chatelaine* was mostly women, but soon after I arrived, they brought in John Clare, as editor, to work with Jerry Anglin, the managing editor. I didn't think either one of them was really happy about working on a woman's magazine, but they were good to me because they had both worked on *Maclean's* and they had a very professional approach to writing. They certainly gave me a lot of excellent coaching on editing, writing and the construction of an article.

But I didn't become editor without a battle. I was getting married about the time John Clare was told he had to leave for health reasons. They were going to make Jerry Anglin, who was now editing another publication, editor of *Chatelaine*. Although I liked him enormously, I believed I could do a much better job and said I'd quit if the position wasn't offered to me. Floyd Chalmers, the president, was shocked that I might want to continue working. "But you're getting married," he said. "You'll be busy as a hostess and mother!" They made me editor, but they didn't give me the title until after I had my first baby and returned to work.

I got pregnant pretty quickly because I was in my mid-30s and couldn't wait much longer. When I became pregnant, the rule was that you had to quit at five or six months. They decided to give me six weeks off. I was to stay at home four weeks before the baby was born, and two weeks after. Since I wasn't doing anything at home, the staff were running back and forth in taxis with layouts and manuscripts. It was ridiculous. There are legendary stories of my correcting proofs on the way to the delivery room. It wasn't quite like that, but it was close. The day after I had the baby, people were coming to the hospital with work.

I stayed home for my two weeks and went back to work. When I got pregnant again, I just kept on working. One day, Chalmers came down to my office. I was very pregnant and he looked everywhere but at me. "When are you going home?" he finally asked. "I'm not telling you," I said. "It will be the day after I have the baby." I agreed to come in to work late and leave late so I wouldn't be obvious. I also told them I'd like to spend more time with the baby after it was born, and they finally agreed to that. By the time my third son was born, there were pregnant women all over the company.

Of course, organizing children and a career was as difficult then as it is now, for women. I paid top dollar and I got a good, reliable woman who stayed with me until the youngest child was in school, but it still wasn't easy. For instance, I sent them all to nursery school and the housekeeper didn't drive. That meant they had to be driven there in the morning by me and collected at noon. I couldn't drop everything and go running off to pick them up, every day so I'd send a taxi to take them home. Although I always used the same taxi driver, other women were very critical.

I also had to shop around for nursery schools. Two of my sons didn't like the first school so it had to be changed. None of these problems fell on my husband. The family was the woman's responsibility and most men did even less than they do now. My husband wasn't very pleased when I became editor of *Chatelaine*. He liked the idea of me having an interesting job, but he didn't like the idea of being married to the editor of a magazine. Periodically, he'd lay guilt trips on me and complain that I wasn't laying his clothes out, or arranging dinner parties for his clients.

Another problem with being a woman editor was that I was underpaid. Once, the editor at *Maclean's* called me up and asked what I was earning. I told him, and he told me he was earning substantially more. He announced that he was getting fired, since *Maclean's* wasn't making any money and *Chatelaine* was. I went to the head of the magazine division and told him I wanted a raise, which I immediately got. That kind of stinginess really irritated me. Here I was, running a magazine with a bigger circulation, that was earning more money, and I was being paid less.

Even so, I loved my job. I saw the magazine as a wonderful vehicle for changing things. I think I was a feminist years before I knew what the term meant, and I guess that was part of the reason I took so long to get married. I wanted children, but I didn't think marriage was a great institution for women.

I thought there needed to be lots of changes and I still do. I wanted much less discrimination in the workplace than I had experienced and I wanted women to have access to many different kinds of jobs. I was also very concerned about social issues. When you look back, the restrictions on women were incredible. You couldn't get divorced if your partner refused to co-operate or, if you wanted an abortion, you had to go to backstreet abortionists. We ran one of the first articles in North America on abortion, and we certainly ran the first article on child battering, which was an issue nobody acknowledged. Of course, we were criticized for dealing with such "controversial" topics.

But, in the end, it paid off. When I took the magazine over, I discovered that the women I wanted as readers boasted that they never read *Chatelaine*. These were women who had graduated from university and were mostly at home looking after children. They were bright, lively women and, I thought, pretty frustrated. Often they would back me into a corner at a party and lecture me about having a job and being away from my kids.

That was my generation of women and I felt they were being incredibly underused. Also, there was this ridiculous myth that if you really worked at it, you could produce perfect children, which, as any parent knows, is impossible. Women were held responsible if anything went wrong with their kids, their marriage or their husband. Even if the man was a Don Juan and cheating on them, it was their fault!

I thought all those things had to be changed. All we did, really, was write about them in a fairly progressive—but careful —way so we didn't alienate mainstream readers. We just kept bringing them along and it was a wonderful thing to do.

I found it very stimulating, but after about 20 years, I didn't want to do it any more. Once the women's movement took off in the '70s, a mainstream magazine like *Chatelaine* became less exciting because the smaller magazines were much more radical. I was ready to do something else.

I wanted to be editor of *Maclean's*. Even though I had a track record of success and *Maclean's* was floundering, Maclean-Hunter was not prepared to give me the job. They also wouldn't consider making me publisher of *Chatelaine*. They made a male editor of *Maclean's* publisher, but not me. I left because I was so frustrated.

I think I helped other women because, after I left, they moved into some of those jobs in the company. The people from Maclean-Hunter are still wonderful to me when I meet them. They thought they'd done all kinds of extraordinary things like putting me on the board and changing the rules about pregnancy—and they had—but they wouldn't give me the jobs I really wanted.

Lisa Hobbs Birnie
Bowen Island, British
Columbia

"Although it created stress, I liked breaking rigid stereotypes. So did my male editors: they'd assigned me to the stories in the first place."

Lisa Hobbs Birnie began working as a journalist in 1949 in her native Australia. In 1954, she immigrated to the United States. She worked for a number of papers there, and, in the late 1960s became Vietnam correspondent for the San Francisco Chronicle. *In 1969, she immigrated to Canada, where her work has appeared in many publications. She has written seven books, is the winner of a National Magazine Award and is a contributing editor to* Saturday Night.

I was always conscious of women's secondary status—I left my native Australia at 20 because women seemed to have a fairer "go" abroad—but at that age it didn't dawn on me that women's status was a worldwide political, as well as cultural, question. Often in the 1960s when I covered Rotary or Kiwanis Clubs as a reporter in San Francisco, I'd be asked who I was and told to leave the room: "Women aren't allowed." I'd say if they wanted coverage, they'd have to let me stay. Because doing this required toughness, I was considered aggressive, but the question would never have arisen with a male reporter.

Later, I had a column in a metropolitan daily, travelled widely and felt pretty lucky. Many men would have wanted to do what I did. Some of this sense of luck came from the awareness that I'd escaped the stifling fate of most women, so this took the edge off discrimination whenever I encountered it.

All this while, my brother, who's no more talented than I am, was sailing ahead. He became the managing editor then head of a newspaper chain. The reality was that I was allowed to exercise my talents within an acceptable invisible periphery, but there was no glass ceiling to limit what he could do. I remember being invited to have dinner with him at the National Press Club in Washington, D.C., in 1970. Even though I had been a war correspondent in Vietnam, Cambodia and Laos, I wasn't allowed to eat there because I was a woman.

By then it was clear to me that the history of power was the history of double standards. So I wrote my fourth book, *Love and Liberation*, which was published in 1970 by McGraw-Hill in New York. I wrote it without reading any feminist literature, except perhaps *The Second Sex* and *The Feminine Mystique*. Feminism was just beginning and many of the general concepts were still being formulated. I wasn't an academic: everything in that book was based on my own knowledge. It was a very personal statement. The only thing I regret is that at that time I had no understanding of, and was very ignorant about, lesbianism.

When the book was published in Canada, a senior executive of McGraw-Hill came to Vancouver and invited me for lunch at the Bayshore. He was in his 40s. I can't remember his name—I wish I could: I'd write it on every lamppost. When we sat down to eat, he opened the conversation with: "I brought a copy of your book to read on the plane, but after three pages, dumped it in the toilet." That's exactly what he said. It had taken me a year to write and a lifetime of experience, but this nerd, who controlled the promotion and distribution budget at McGraw-Hill had the power to kill it. The book was translated into Dutch and did extremely well in Holland, but in Canada it didn't go anywhere.

Sharon Fraser
Halifax, Nova Scotia

"It was an accident that I didn't go back to nursing, but when I think what hard work it is and how unappreciated nurses are, I wonder how I didn't notice."

After 10 years as a nurse, Sharon Fraser left the profession in 1974 for a career in journalism. In 1975, she became editor of the Miramichi Leader, *a weekly newspaper in New Brunswick, and in the mid-'80s, following a stint with the Canadian Broadcasting Corporation, was made editor of the* Atlantic Fisherman. *She currently works as a freelance writer and broadcaster.*

When I was growing up in Chatham, New Brunswick, in the 1950s your career choices were nurse, teacher or secretary. I wanted to go to Toronto to train as a radio announcer—I must have read about Ryerson College somewhere—even though there was only one woman's voice on local radio. Irene did a programme called "Good Morning, Mrs. Housewife," which consisted of recipes, how to get the stain out of your tablecloth and so on. My mother and I enjoyed the programme and we always listened. When I graduated from high school, the commentary beside my picture read, "Looking forward to a career as a radio announcer."

Of course, my mother wouldn't let me go to Toronto because I was too young, so I spent a year at Mount Alison University. I was completely unstimulated and, in 1960, enrolled in nursing school in Montreal.

I nursed in Montreal until the mid 1970s, then I became a journalist, almost by accident. I was living with a man who was a writer and we used to travel a lot. Since he had the flexibility to work anywhere, we decided to spend the summer in New Brunswick living on a boat. In those days, there were lots of jobs so you could quit and return to the same job at a later date.

The weekly newspaper in Chatham had just been sold to a new publisher, and he'd heard about me since I'd grown up there. I was known to be outspoken and opinionated, a person who wrote letters to the editor and so on. One day, totally out of the blue, he called and asked if I'd like to write a weekly column about anything that interested me. Of course, I jumped at the chance. My first column took a position against nuclear power. The column was instantly popular in the sense that it was very much read and responded to.

After a few weeks the publisher asked if I'd come on staff as a reporter. Obviously, I had no training, but for some reason, I knew how to be a journalist, possibly because I'd read lots of newspapers and listened to current affairs. I had the antennae. I knew how to get a story, I knew who to call.

Within about a year I was made editor of the newspaper, the *Miramichi Leader*. I stayed for five years and, from the beginning, was thought to be controversial.

I soon discovered that if one or two stories on women's issues appeared in an issue I'd almost always get calls from people saying something like, "This is a home-town paper and you're trying to turn it into a feminist rag." The publisher would also get calls complaining about me. He'd tell me to be careful since there was no point in alienating the readers.

The publisher has become quite a feminist, which I take a lot of credit for, but I did have one angry-making experience. My staff consisted of about four reporters, all of whom were women, and a photographer who was male. Women employees are very common in community newspapers because the papers pay so little. However, my employer knew of a fellow who needed a job and he decided to hire him as the managing editor. I'd be his boss.

We interviewed this guy and I didn't like him. I told the publisher, but he still felt we needed a man. I couldn't imagine why, but he said a man could go places I couldn't. When I asked him where, he said many news stories were generated at so-and-so's poker party on Friday night in the back of his store. I said those weren't the kind of stories I wanted to do and that I'd get better stories from the Women's Institute meetings. But he hired him anyway—I guess to go to the poker games.

Although I was editor-in-chief, for the first time he wouldn't tell me what we were paying a staff member. The paper had two offices, and one day, when I was driving from one to the other, the office manager asked me to take the payroll cheques. On route I pulled my car over and opened this guy's envelope. Of course, he was making about $2,000 a year more than me. And I was his boss! This was the late '70s, and when I confronted my employer, he said, "Well, he has a wife and three children."

Despite my poor pay, the *Leader* won both regional and national awards in its category, and I went from there to the CBC in Fredericton, doing public relations and contract work in current affairs. There I was, many years later, finally working as a radio announcer.

When I went to the CBC, my feminist consciousness was becoming more analytical and I was gaining a real understanding of how the world worked. Not surprisingly, I had more problems within the CBC than with the listeners, who were very supportive. We had regular story meetings and I'd arrive with ideas, only to be laughed out of the room.

For example, I worked on a current affairs programme. One morning when I went to the bank, my teller informed me that all the tellers had just been told that their jobs were being cut from full to half time, which meant they were losing all their benefits, as well. I was horrified, but when I raised the matter at our story meeting, I got stifled yawns around the room. "What's the story?" people asked. I suggested that if this had happened to male foresters at the Department of Natural Resources, they'd see the story. The bank didn't qualify because it involved women.

In the early '80s I was caught by the recession and was out of work. I tried everything, but even though I was quite well known as a journalist, nobody had any work. I was so desperate I called the hospitals to see if there were any nursing jobs, but there were 18-month waiting lists just to take a refresher course.

However, as in so many cases, when you need a job and get one, it's because of who you know, not your qualifications. A friend, who's a newspaper publisher in Prince Edward Island, started a new newspaper to cover the commercial-fishing industry of the Atlantic provinces, and he hired me as the founding editor. I went to P.E.I. and began a newspaper that became the *Atlantic Fisherman*. To this day it remains my favourite job.

I loved the fishing industry. I loved covering it and I loved the people. It's very fractious, political, complex and endlessly fascinating.

People expected I'd have problems with the fishing industry because I'm a woman, but I didn't. I had problems with my employers, as I often do. I don't think I'm a good employee because I'm a kind of I-know-best person. But I never had problems with the fishermen or the people who work in the industry.

I think my ideology helped. I believe some people are in power and some people aren't. This is true whether you're talking about a man and woman in a marriage, or employers and workers in a factory. The fishing industry has three segments: government, big business and the independent people who make up the inshore fishery and the fish plants. Right from the start, my writing revealed that I cared about the people.

There was another element to my acceptance. Many fishermen who own and work on the small boats had fished from the age of eight or nine.

They know the industry like the back of their hands, although they never went to school and often don't know how to read. So it was the women in the family, the wives and daughters, who kept in touch with me. They wrote the letters to the editor, made the phone calls and, I think, very often communicated what I was writing about to the men.

Fishing had never been seen this way before: as a small family business, in which each person has certain responsibilities. People always thought it was the men who fished and the women who raised the children. Women certainly did that, but they did many other things, such as interpreting government regulations and keeping the books.

I think these small family-run businesses accepted me. I could walk onto any wharf in Atlantic Canada and start to talk to people. I'd say, "Hello, I'm...." and they'd immediately respond, "I know who you are. You're Sharon Fraser," because they recognized my picture. And they were anxious to talk to me.

Before my time the government had defined the industry issues with the help of their big-business buddies. But once I came along, the people who caught the fish and worked in the plants were defining the issues. By the time I left *Atlantic Fisherman*, I could phone Ottawa and ask to speak to the minister of fisheries and oceans, and they'd get him out of the House of Commons because they knew if they didn't, I'd write something damaging. I was very cheeky and chippy and I felt very powerful.

I loved that job and I want to do it again. I'm not through with the fishing industry, but who knows in what capacity I'll return. I left the paper because my employers were so cheap. I was invited to speak at an international conference in Maine. It was a great honour and my employers agreed that I should go. My speech was prepared, but about two days before I was supposed to leave, they said they wouldn't give me the money. I walked out, slammed the door and came back long enough to put my letter of resignation on the desk.

It would have been too humiliating to call the University of Maine and tell them I wasn't coming because my employers wouldn't pay. So I phoned a writer from St. Andrews who contributed to the paper and asked him to deliver my speech. Isn't that a sad story?

I was so angry, I quit without having another job, but I was offered the editorship of *Atlantic Insight*, a general-interest magazine. That brought me to Halifax in 1986 and into a job that paid more than I had ever earned, although I later discovered I was making $4,000 less than the male I'd replaced, and he was only acting editor. The magazine had been in financial difficulties for years, and by the time it went under, I had left.

Since then I've been doing freelance writing and teaching at various universities in the Halifax area. I also do a fair bit of speaking and I'm often invited to be a media analyst.

I've always been a very political journalist. When I started, I did things like covering the exhibition and so on, but I still had the chance to delve into what was going on in the community. I don't want to sound too noble, but I'm a journalist because I want to change the world and nowadays I do stories with that in mind. I work mostly for the alternative media now, because I reject the myth of objectivity. People ask me about telling the other side and I always say, "This is the other side."

Looking back, I realize that one of the things I hated most about nursing was working shifts and weekends, but as a journalist I worked them all. I think journalists put up with the poor pay and working conditions because it's so much fun.

Vicki Gabereau
Vancouver, British Columbia

"My motivation is to learn and I've found the perfect livelihood."

In the late 1960s and throughout the 1970s, Vicki Gabereau worked at many different jobs, including taxi driver, clown and waitress. She finally came to national attention in the summer of 1980 when she guest-hosted "Morningside" on CBC radio. From 1981 to 1985, she hosted the weeknight entertainment series, "Variety Tonight," and in 1988 became host of her own weekday afternoon show, "Gabereau." The winner of two ACTRA (Association of Canadian Radio-Television Artists) awards for best host-interviewer, she published her first book, This Won't Hurt A Bit, *in 1987.*

I got my first job when I was 11. Somehow I managed to con the guy at Woolworth's into letting me clean the birdcages. Then I used to work at the dry cleaners pulling men's pockets out, cleaning out the lint. I made about 50 cents a day and thought I was quite rich. I quit school before I finished Grade 12, which is something I've always regretted. Then I had a variety of ridiculous jobs because I couldn't figure out how to get back in the stream. How could I admit I hadn't finished Grade 12? I wouldn't go back to school, which was incredibly stupid.

I got married. I was 21 years old when I had my first child and 23 when I had the second. Then, my husband and I moved to Toronto and I got a job answering the phones at a radio station in Brampton. Brampton is about 30 miles from Toronto, which is a bit of a commute when you don't have a car, but the job was in a radio station, which is where I wanted to be. I did other odd jobs, like door-to-door market research when it was so cold my glasses cracked. That was a fruitless experience because English wasn't the mother tongue of many of the residents, and they didn't know what to say about cake mix.

In 1970, I became a taxi driver when my husband's union went on strike and he couldn't work. In those days, it was unusual for a woman to drive a cab and even then you couldn't drive at night. My mother was completely hysterical. She said, "Driving a cab is a reckless act. You have two young children, you can't put yourself in jeopardy."

"Well, guys do," I replied.

Her response was, "You're not a guy. You're vulnerable. Don't tell your grandmother." So I had to promise I wouldn't.

The thing was, I had to have a job that was flexible because I had kids. I also had to have cash at the end of the day because my husband's union was on strike. He made enough to pay the rent, and by driving a cab I never had to hit on my parents.

Driving a cab wasn't too bad. I had a couple of minor "incidents," but only one bad experience, which happened when I was on crutches due to an injured leg. A man who was quite disabled got into my cab and told me to take him downtown to get his pay cheque. When we reached the building, I, on my crutches, climbed the three flights of stairs with him to a leather-wear shop. By the sounds of things I could tell he was being fired. Tears were streaming down his face when he came out and told me to take him to the liquor store. He gave me $5 to buy five bottles of a particular sherry. When I placed the order, the clerk said, "Madam, I hope you're not planning to drink this stuff because I've seen what it does to paint."

The sherry was in a screw top and my fare immediately drank half a bottle before telling me to take him home. When we arrived at his house, he asked me to help him carry his two shopping bags into the house. The man was disabled, how could I say no? But when we get through the door, all of a sudden he turned into superman. He locked the door. He was still a physical mess, but his brain was working overtime.

"Give me my money or I'm calling the cops," I demanded. Actually, I had decided it was more important to get out of there than to get paid. I had the same Francis-of-Assisi aluminum door in my house so I knew how it worked. I got it unlocked and escaped from the house, but the driveway was hard to manoeuvre, particularly with crutches. All the while he was leaning out a window shouting at me and the neighbours were peering. I took my cab back to the company and said, "You keep this taxi. I'm never working again."

I wasn't terrified but I was horrified. I couldn't believe I had been stupid enough to allow myself to get into that situation. And I had. I'd walked right into it. I decided my mamma was right.

Later, I worked as a waitress, mostly at the Brunswick Tavern. I wasn't a very good waitress. Every time the entertainment started, I'd go crazy and watch the performers instead of working.

Then I went to acting school. It was an improv school taught by Lorne Michaels. I wasn't very good at improvisations, although lots of the students were. Dan Ackroyd, for instance, was so good he made everyone else look like idiots.

Even though I was a terrible actress, I liked it. I was quite a hambone and I knew I wanted to perform in some way. But I certainly wasn't going to go back to finish high school. I was scared that I'd fail. I still won't go. It's terrible and I'm ashamed of myself.

In 1974, I ran for mayor of Toronto. I had joined a clown troupe called Puck's, although I didn't know a thing about being a clown. There were four of us, and since we had no gigs, we decided that one of us should run for mayor. I got to do it as Rosie Sunrise and ran against David Crombie. It gave me a certain degree of notoriety. I was married to a man who was working for the CTV Public Affairs Program, "W-5", and he never said a word. What a darling!

One night I was in a bar with my clown friends and we met a man who did an open-line show on my old radio station in Brampton. "You're that thing that ran for mayor," he said. "I wish you'd come on and explain yourself."

"You bet! And I know exactly how to get there. I used to work there."

After the show, I asked the host if they needed a summer replacement. "As a matter of fact, I'm going away for two weeks," he said. "I'll ask Harry." I knew Harry, too. I think they let me have the job because I knew someone they wanted to sell the radio station to.

I filled in for two weeks. It was pretty simple. I knew Jack Webster and I used to watch him at work when I was a kid. So I knew how it was done. I didn't have much information, but I had a newspaper. All you do is read the newspaper and say, "What do you think about this?" It's just amazing—everybody phones. And once in awhile you have a guest. When the next guy took a holiday, I had a job.

One regular caller said he thought I should be working for CBC, so he called somebody and got me an interview with "Morningside." The woman who interviewed me said, "I'm going to audition you for a host. But I will never hire you in a million years. You're green and you have no life experience. I'll probably hire Harry Brown and I want a woman with him." Harry had interviewed me when I was running for mayor and I loved him. I would have loved the job, but I didn't get it.

I did get hired as a researcher. About six months later the producer said, "I think you'll have to go on the air." I started doing the odd bit with the co-hosts, but I was so nervous, I wasn't wildly successful. I had a problem with the CBC which took me about five years to get over. I was intimidated because I didn't finish high school. We live in a society that requires a certain level of education to get certain jobs. I'd never get a job at the CBC today—not even as a researcher.

After "Morningside," I got a job at TVO (TV Ontario) producing a show about the changing roles of women. I worked at TVO for two years and every time I got paid they asked for my credentials. I never gave them a thing and they never knew I hadn't finished high school.

I went to Edmonton for awhile, then came to Vancouver. "Gabereau" is a perfect job for me because it changes every hour. I'm driven by curiosity. I read the encyclopedia for amusement when I get into bed at night. I can sit in my closet and get a free education. My greatest reward is having all this fascinating material handed to me on a plate.

I think I really pay attention to the material because I'm terrified of being caught out. My loyalty is to the story and people who've taken time to come and talk about things. I'm desperate to make it not only the best interview it can be, but one that makes me feel sated. There are some interviews that never quite get in the groove, but when they do, it's like an engine that starts to go and I never have to look at my notes.

I love it when it works. If I knew what I know now—that I can concentrate intensely to the exclusion of all else—if I could have learned to do that when I was younger, I could have gone to university and got a proper education. It's taken me a long time to realize it, but this job has taught me how to organize my mind. It isn't anything I couldn't have known before, but I wouldn't allow myself to know it. To tell you the truth, I couldn't think of anything else I could do. I'm very lucky.

Peggy Holmes
Edmonton, Alberta

"I believe in changes. I don't think we should just keep on in the world."

Peggy Holmes, who was 97 at the time of this interview, began her broadcasting career in the late 1960s, when she was 70. She published her first book It Could Have Been Worse, *in 1980.*

I married when I was 19 and came to live on a ranch in Alberta, as an English war-bride from the First World War. I remember being absolutely lost. Worse still, the Canadian people didn't like war brides. They felt we were taking their boys away and they were pretty nasty. When the Second World War ended, I thought, "They're not going to treat women like that again," so I worked with the Red Cross meeting the trains when the girls came through Edmonton.

I had three daughters, which I hardly like to mention because they were breech cases and they all died at birth. Then, 10 years to the day that the last baby died, my son, who's now 55, was born.

After the Second World War ended, I started public speaking and became quite well-known. I never thought about what I was going to say until the night before my speech, although I always had something to say about any subject.

I wanted to take a creative-writing course, but I was terrified of the teacher, Elsie Park Gowan. She was a brilliant and powerful person and, in comparison, I felt like a worm. One day, I saw her tramping through the snow on the way to her class. I pulled up in my little Austin and asked if she wanted a ride.

"No," she said, "I like to walk in the snow."

I recognized the brush-off, but I carried on. "You teach the writing class, don't you?" I asked. " Could I come to your classes?"

"What's stopping you?" she replied.

I don't know why I wasn't intimidated, because I was very sensitive and easily hurt, but if I'd been downed by this domineering lady stomping though the snow, I wouldn't be what I am today. I went to her class, and once she discovered I could write, she became one of my best friends and promoters.

Elsie was very anxious that we write in plain language and in a style that everybody could enjoy. I remember one lady who wrote that she'd purchased a blouse, and Elsie corrected her immediately. "No, you didn't," she declared. "You bought it." She also wanted us to write about what we knew, so I wrote 19 episodes about my life on the homestead.

I had them typed and showed them to her. After she'd read them, she banged the manuscript down on the desk and demanded, "Do something with these!" I didn't know whether she wanted me to burn them, or what.

Instead, I decided to take them to the CBC. My husband, who was nearly blind, came with me, carrying his white cane. As we were leaving, he turned to me and said, "I think if we had a little dog and a tin can we'd have it made."

If you'd seen us that day. I was 70 and Harry was 80, but he was very tall and elegant. In those days, I thought you just walked into places, so I didn't bother making an appointment. When we arrived, the first thing the receptionist said was, "Do you have you an appointment?"

I think she was so intrigued with us that she asked to see the manuscript. She gave it to a producer, who read it immediately and asked if she could send it to Toronto. Toronto's response was, "Get a hold of that person." I arrived at just the right time. It was the late 1960s and they were tired of doing broadcasts on hippies and wanted things from seniors, instead.

That was the start of my 15-year career in broadcasting. I guess I was a late bloomer. People asked if I was frightened of the mike. "No, should I be?" I asked. " What could that little thing do to me?" It never dawned on me that I was reaching millions of people. In fact, I think I got on so well because I never gave it a thought.

The things I did were mostly topical. I'd take life today and comment. It was all off the cuff. I don't remember going to a library because I couldn't be bothered to research. Whatever came, came. The night before I might say, "Oh, please God, give me the words," you know, something like that. I had a faith—of sorts.

The mind always interested me. I read a book on psychocybernetics, which really gave me an insight into things by helping me to realize there's another dimension. I can see more about life that way than by going to church. I never got anywhere listening to a minister.

I didn't push psychocybernetics in my broadcasts because I thought people would say, "She's a nut." I think it would go over better now, but at that time they would have thought I was a bit of a crank. Possibly I was.

I was in my '70s when I started writing books. *It Could Have Been Worse* was published in 1980. *Out Of The Ashes* was my next book and *Never A Dull Moment*, published in 1984, sold out completely. Of course, my books were so popular because in writing them I followed Elsie's advice. They weren't just for highly educated people. They were for everybody. Many people wrote to tell me I was writing about their life, too.

Writing wasn't difficult for me. When I left England my mother and father were still there and, of course, we corresponded. We didn't have long-distance telephones in those days. I think the loss of letter writing has prevented a lot of people from becoming writers.

I never went out to work. I wrote my things from home. If I were doing it today, most likely I would have developed a career and collected a salary, but I wasn't conscious of wanting to do that. I was happy. I was a positive person, although I don't believe in being positive altogether, because you could be positively wrong.

When I started broadcasting, I joined ACTRA, the performers alliance. Years later, they phoned me and asked, "Could you do with $3,500?"

By that time, I'd retired. "Have you robbed a bank?" I asked.

"No, but we've discovered that the CBC underpaid you for 15 years and we've caught up with them. We can get you $3,500 now, or if we dig deeper, we can get you much more."

"I'll take the money now," I said, so they got the CBC to cough it up. Once I got paid, I thought I better spend it before they took it back. A friend was travelling to England and I went with her. I was 88. We had a lot of fun and I spent every cent.

Ulli Steltzer
Vancouver, British Columbia

"In all the work I've done, art for art's sake has never been my motivation. I'm a documentary photographer trying to show what's going on in the world."

Ulli Steltzer was born in Germany in 1923. After immigrating to the United States in 1953, she became interested in photography. Throughout the 1960s she documented the experience of poor people living in both urban and rural areas, and in 1986, she began to photograph the natives of the southwestern United States. Since moving to British Columbia in 1972, she has published several books of photographs, including, Indian Artists at Work *(1976),* Inuit: The North in Transition *(1982), and* Eagle Transforming: The Art of Robert Davidson *(1994).*

I grew up in Germany and, during the war, had to go underground because my father was Jewish. Once the war was over, I went home, studied music, married, had two children and divorced. When I came to the United States in 1953, with my kids, I was able to get a job teaching music in a private school in Massachusetts. It was not a good experience. The arts were treated with little respect and I left after a year.

As a house-mother, I had supervised a student who had a darkroom and I became interested in photography. I moved to New York where I learned how to print, then I went to Princeton and got a newspaper job. By incredible luck, I was able to buy a small photography studio and started doing portraits.

Slowly, I worked my way into America, if you can call Princeton America. It was a very élitist society with a black ghetto. Eventually, I photographed many of Princeton's distinguished residents' including Robert Oppenheimer, the nuclear physicist, Leopold Stokowski, the conductor, and Martin Buber, the theologian, among others. I also found my way into the black ghetto and did work for them.

Gradually, I started to branch out from portraits. I photographed the migrant workers for the New Jersey Department of Labour and Industry, and, because they worked under such terrible conditions, I became curious about their home situation. So I took my Volkswagen and went south to explore.

On my birthday, I went into a bar in Tuskalusa where there were lots of local businessmen. When I brought out my photographs, they became very upset. I quickly realized it was a stupid thing to do, so I went back to my room and locked the door. They followed me and pounded on my door, but I didn't open it. I figured they'd have to leave to go to work in the morning, which was true.

At 9 a.m., I got into my little red Volkswagen and started off with the police right behind me. Obviously, the local men had informed on me. That was in Alabama. Once I got over the Mississippi border, there were no more police.

Princeton University has the photographs I did in the South. A lot of my work focuses on discrimination, likely because having been discriminated against by the Nazis, I developed a great sensitivity to injustice. In 1968, I went to the Southwest to photograph on the Indian reserves and, in 1972, came to British Columbia and started doing the same sort of thing. I discovered stores with beautiful baskets and masks, and when I asked who did them, the clerks would say, "The little man" or "The little woman" brings them. Nobody had a name.

I decided to do a book on native artists. The university wasn't much help because at that time they believed Indian art was all in the past. The only known artists were Robert Davidson, who was very young, and Bill Reid, who had carved some poles and was working at the university. I went to Bill and asked him for help. He directed me to Doreen Jensen, who was an Indian artist herself and in touch with many artists.

I interviewed artists and photographed them. At the time, my appreciation of Indian art was not what it should have been. But you learn as you go along.

I did one book after another: one on the coast, another on the potlatch, one on the Inuit, one on an interesting health programme in Guatemala and so on. I've travelled in the North as well as the South and I've always travelled alone. But wherever I've gone, people have protected me. In the North I was often asked whether I was the new teacher or nurse because those were the only white women who visited these remote communities. Or they wanted to know where my husband was. But it didn't take long to get beyond that. These are natural questions because white women don't travel alone up there. So you explain.

Only once was I discriminated against in the Arctic and that was by another woman who felt it was wrong for a woman to go hunting with the men in the winter. But the men were very eager to take me because they wanted to show me what they do, and most women were very helpful. They gave me the right clothes to make sure that I was properly dressed.

You can go hunting with two or three Inuit and sleep in the same tent without worrying. They give you the place of the woman which is at the side, and you're respected. There's never any problem.

I've always enjoyed what I did, sometimes to the point of feeling guilty. Not every situation I photograph is a happy one, and yet I enjoy being there. I wouldn't want to go to any of the places I visited as a tourist because you can't contribute other than with money. Once I paid a young Inuk $90 to cover my food, accommodation and transportation for a week. The next week when I wanted to give him more, he said, "Why would you do that? I still have money." It's a very different attitude.

When you take photographs, at least you can send pictures back and I always do. The people give more than you can possibly give in return: hospitality, friendship, knowledge, their understanding of life. It is so rich you can never fully repay.

I think all the people I've photographed have enjoyed my books. They say they do. It's a nice way of living because you move around and meet people. And while you're at it, you hope you can make a little bit of difference. Not much—none of us does—but a little.

Line Gagnon
Yellowknife, Northwest
Territories

"I like my job because it allows me to succeed at work, but it also allows me to have a life and to travel. It's easy to lose sight of that and to start measuring success by titles and the power we hold over others, which is very scary."

Line Gagnon, who was 30 at the time of this interview, was born in Edmundston, New Brunswick, and grew up there. After studying communications and political science at university, she moved to Yellowknife in the late 1980s to work at a community newspaper. She now manages a bookstore.

My first language is French, but I attended school with English students and grew up bilingual even though no English was spoken in our house. It took me awhile to figure out what I wanted to study at university, but in 1985, when I was 21, I finally ended up in communications with a minor in political science.

During the summer I worked with a provincial women's network, as a researcher. I got the job because of the way I wrote, which was a big boost for my self-esteem since I wanted to write. Although I liked the work, I felt the woman who was in charge preferred the English-speaking women.

I was very close to my grandmother, and when she died, I decided to go to Europe to get away from everything. So, after one year of my new programme in communications, I quit university, moved to Ottawa and got a job as a hostess in a Swiss Chalet to earn money for my trip. After I returned, I enrolled at the University of Quebec in Montreal, where I studied political science. At the end of my second year, I applied for, and was offered, a job at the *La Quillon*, the French newspaper in Yellowknife. I expected to stay for a year.

Approximately 700 French people live in Yellowknife—more are scattered around the Territories. There were only two of us working on the paper. I wrote, did paste-up, advertising—everything, which often happens with a non-profit organization. A lot of volunteer work is involved when you work for minority groups. You can't cash in all your hours because they can't afford to pay you.

I was a reporter for a year and a half and really enjoyed it. I met a wide variety of French-speaking people and learned about politics in the Territories. I quit because of internal politics, which were killing me. I had nothing left in myself and I lost interest in my job. In the beginning, I wrote quite well and, by the end, I couldn't write at all. I'd just sit in front of the computer.

After I quit, I took the summer off and did nothing. It was a beautiful summer: 30 degrees all the time. I met Danny, who's now my partner, and we went fishing and hung out.

I took a number of contract jobs before ending up in a part-time job at a bookstore. After I'd been there for about two weeks, the manager didn't show up one morning. I told the owner I'd do the job while she looked for somebody.

For the first two weeks I worked 12-hour days, which was awful, so when the owner offered me the job, I thought, she's crazy. I don't want to be doing this. But the following week, I had a 40-hour week and it seemed OK.

I took the job because I was offered good money and lots of time off. I've never worked for more than nine months out of the year, which is ideal. I like travelling, and I get my job back when I return. The owner is a very human person and easy to talk to. I haven't had a good boss like that before. She's very empowering.

I love working with books. I'm a fanatical reader, so I'm in my element. It's neat to know all these authors and to know who writes about what.

I worked for eight months, then I left for Guatemala and Honduras for three months and came back to my job and a house, which the owner gave me to live in as a promotion. That was a great perk because it's very expensive to live in Yellowknife. I was living in a shack in Old Town before, and after I got this house, I got pregnant.

Living is a lot easier now that I have running water, although I was one of the lucky ones because my shack had water delivery twice a week in the winter. The lines here run above ground and they freeze up. I lived in that shack for three years. Getting dressed in the morning was a challenge. I heated water on the stove to wash myself and went to friends for showers. You get used to the lifestyle. The honey bucket is the worst thing. That's your toilet. The city picks them up.

I'd work all day, come home and chop wood. My only source of heat was a wood stove which lasted 12 hours. I'd stoke it up before I went to bed, and in the morning it was just a bit cold. I could stay out until 8:00, and when I came home, there would be coals, so I wouldn't have to start it all over again. Within an hour, it was comfortable.

Since everyone else is living like that you're not alone. It's a neat way of life, although it's disappearing. I loved living in my shack. I got connected to the earth. I learned how to chop wood, how to use a chain saw, and became self-sufficient, which was very important. It was a good learning-experience, as was living alone. I started drawing, writing and painting—which I hadn't done in years.

I just turned 30, which has raised questions about the meaning of success. I realized that success has nothing to do with my job, my partner or my child. It has to do with me and how I feel about myself.

Betty Baxter
Vancouver, British Columbia

" I have a huge sense of social justice and responsibility to help create change. I think that comes from my own experiences of a painful work-place. I'm interested in making a workplace where anybody can be valued."

Betty Baxter is a 42-year-old consultant who ran for the New Democratic Party (NDP) against Kim Campbell in the 1993 federal election. She is a former captain and coach of Canada's national women's volleyball team.

From the beginning, I was very clear about not wanting to be a teacher, a nurse or a secretary. The only thing I really wanted to be was an athlete. It wasn't that I saw a career in it. I remember watching the 1958 Olympic Games in Mexico and being overwhelmed by the pomp and ceremony. The degree to which people celebrated achievement and the sense of power that came from being your personal best inspired me to pour myself into sport.

I grew up in Brooks, a small town in southern Alberta. From an early age, I was reaffirmed as strong and capable in sport. I recognized that my athletic ability attracted attention from my family and friends. I could throw the ball the farthest, run the fastest and tackle the big boys playing after-supper football.

In my Grade 1 class, a little boy used to bring a butcher knife to school and scare people. One of my earliest school memories is being strong enough to grab him from behind to prevent him from hurting anybody. So from age six, the knowledge that I was strong and capable of taking action was part of my sense of self. I also have a brother who's seven years older than I am, and by the time I was 10, he was the high-school basketball star. That gave me a sense of sport as a source of status and power.

I was a basketball star throughout junior and senior high, but because volleyball had a better development programme I was channelled into that, which brought me to Vancouver. Although it was evident there wasn't really a career in sport, I didn't care.

By the time I reached university, I was moving into élite sport and doing heavy, heavy training. I wasn't really conscious of discrimination until I reached those levels. In the weight room men would say things like, "Why is a woman trying to lift 400 pounds? You should be in the lighter section." In comparison, the stuff in high school was very subtle: the boys' games always followed the girls' so we could watch the boys instead of preparing ourselves.

In my second year of university I had a chance to try out for basketball, but by that time I was pretty hooked on volleyball. On reflection, I think volleyball is appealing because it's a bit like chess. All sports at a high level are mental games, but volleyball perhaps more so. It's a strategic sport in which you're always thinking, "If I do this, you'll do that," so that you're several steps ahead of your opponent.

I made the national team in 1972, when I was 20, and by 1974 I had a career as an athlete at the international level. I played international sport until I was 28—the Montreal Olympics, world championships in the Soviet Union and so on. I loved it, absolutely loved it!

With hindsight, though, I can see that some of the tragedies in my life have involved being caught in a sport system that makes fairly arbitrary decisions about people's lives. I think this happens to both sexes, but there's less support for their impact on women. The expectation is that women will eventually do something else. I was an exception because I continued to work in sport even though I was shunted aside and out of it several times.

The first time came at the end of a winning streak when I was 26. I had been captain of the women's national volleyball team in the 1976 Olympics. I'd also been an all-star in the 1978 World Championships. I was one of the more senior members of the team and, along with four others, was cut while we were flying home from the Soviet Union. The team was going to be located in Toronto rather than Vancouver, and we were told it was time to start with a new group. Until then, I believed I was going to the next Olympics.

Who knows why that happened. That particular coach just said, "We don't want them," and cut the top four people. But then he quit, the new coach didn't work out and opportunity knocked.

So within two years of being thrown off the program as an athlete, I was asked to coach the national women's volleyball team. At that point, I had just finished a graduate degree in the psychology of sport and had started an apprenticeship coaching at the University of Ottawa. This team had come second in the Canadian championships.

I was the first Canadian to coach the national team and, at that point, the only woman in the world coaching a national team. Suddenly there was a huge spotlight on me.

I was 28 and that was my first full-time job. I coached for about 2½ years, then I was fired, with no cause, because of rumours or beliefs that I was lesbian. It was 1982 and the association felt quite justified in firing me on the basis of my sexual preference, although they never committed it to writing. At that point sexual orientation was only included in the human rights legislation in Quebec, so I had no legal recourse.

I was devastated. Although performing at a high level had been an integral part of my life, I didn't go into a gym for three years. Sport had been my life and I walked away from it.

One of the great ironies of my life is the situation in which I was fired. I left one meeting, where we were founding an advocacy association for women in sport, to attend another, where the firing took place. Then I returned to the original meeting to found the Canadian Association for the Advancement of Women in Sport. It was one of those beautiful moments.

After the firing, I finished a contract I was working on for Sport Canada and came back to the West Coast to try and put my life back together. I wanted it to be more well rounded, less focused on a single aspect. I had done my undergraduate degree in Vancouver and had a social community here. In spite of being fired for sexual preference, I had very few lesbian friends in Ottawa and didn't have a strong support system because I'd spent all my time working.

When I was fired, I was "out" to a few friends, but not in public by any means. I felt I had to make a clear decision. I'd gone through a year of agony, basically being rumoured about and slandered, and I "came out" as part of that process. I had just lost a job that was the best in my field. I was the top in the country and the only woman doing the job in the world. I needed to tell people what had happened.

When I came out to my parents, we were sitting at the kitchen table in Brooks. I was trying to find a gentle way to tell them I was lesbian and that I'd been fired because of it. I was couching my words when my mother reached across the table, took my hand and said, "I thought you'd been a lesbian for a long time." She used the word.

My father is one of those men who eats dinner and goes to read the paper. He never stays in the kitchen and certainly never does the dishes, but at that point he got up and started doing the dishes. He couldn't leave the room even though he didn't know how to stay at the table. My parents were very supportive, but I think it took them several years before they really grasped what it meant.

At that point, I had to decide what I was going to do for a career. I had a master's degree in sport psychology and my only work experience was in sport, but I didn't want to get too involved in the sports world, which was probably a wise decision. Although attitudes are changing, homophobia is still a big barrier to women in sports. I've coached at the club level in Vancouver and femininity in the gym is still an issue. It doesn't matter how bulging your leg muscles or arms are, the pressure is to wear perfect earrings and a necklace and eye make-up so you're seen as feminine.

After I left sport, I got a job as a technical writer with a sports association, adapting manuals for athletes with disabilities. Then I moved to writing all kinds of manuals on a contract basis. From there I began to work in adult education. After awhile I realized I was much better at running my own show than working for a large organization, so about four years ago, I started my own company with a couple of other women.

The focus of our company was on preparing educational materials, which we believed would constitute about 60 per cent of our business. The other 40 per cent would come from workshops. But as the company evolved, our emphasis shifted. We decided to work more on equity issues like sexual orientation, discrimination and sexual harassment, and since then the work has taken off. It's June and I'm booked into next February.

I'm happy because, in fact, I get to coach in the workplace almost every day. I think my understanding of team games helps with the work. When you understand sophisticated team games in the strategic sense—how you can manipulate people as chess pieces—you also understand large organizational concepts. I'm not afraid to take on huge strategic-planning projects because I understand how the pieces interconnect, and much of that comes from volleyball. I know how to get six people to participate in a co-ordinated plan to move a ball, which is a kind of thinking that fits well with basic kinds of management.

It's been full circle, but I think that may be the way the world works. You refuse to be, or can't be, exactly who people would like you to be. But as more diverse and open workplaces are created, the person who didn't fit becomes the expert on not fitting.

I believe that gays and lesbians who can be visible should be as visible as possible. Since I've already been fired, that shadow is no longer hanging over me. I don't come out for every client, but I assume that people know because I've been a public figure.

My work led me into politics. I guess I developed a profile from being out as a lesbian and trying to create change for the gay community. I ran for the New Democratic Party in the last federal election in Vancouver Centre, against Kim Campbell. Obviously, it was a high-profile riding with national attention. I ran quite deliberately as a lesbian.

I'd say the media treated me reasonably well, as an individual, though I don't think they treat the New Democratic Party particularly well, in general. And it took almost 10 months for them to be able to write my name without writing "lesbian candidate" alongside it, which was rather discouraging. But by the time of the actual campaign, it was clear three strong women were running and they became quite focused on who we were as candidates. I suspect, though, if I were to jump into the public spotlight again, for whatever reason, it would be "the lesbian candidate" anew.

By and large running for political office was a positive experience. I learned a tremendous amount about my community, myself and my party, as well as about a wide range of issues. But the personal sacrifice was huge.

I was a candidate for about 18 months, officially, which meant about 24 months of preparation and planning. When it was over, we had a $32,000 debt, which we managed to drop to $20,000. Elections Canada doesn't care who the party is, it's the candidate who has to pay the bills, so my commitment to the riding has to continue since my name is on the loan. Luckily, I have a good relationship with my bank. But it means I'll have about four years of something absolutely central in my life that doesn't have a product, a finished point.

People often ask me whether I'd run for political office again, and I don't know. I won't consider it until I'm out of debt because I don't want to put that financial pressure on myself. I'd also have to think very carefully about being fair to the people I work with since it's so time consuming. I guess the biggest question would be whether I believe it's possible to make change inside the political system.

I ran because I believe we can do better as a society and I have skills that can help to achieve that. But I'm not sure if our system actually enables anybody to make change or if it only enables you to be part of the circle that continues to reinforce existing imbalances. That's my dilemma.

I'm 42 and it's easy for me to say that in X years, I'll be Y. The truth is, I don't quite know where I'll end up. It gives me tremendous gratification to run my own business, which helps to improve other workplaces. I don't work against the system, but I work within my particular channel, making change, which I think is the general direction we're moving in as a society. In the next century, I believe more of us will be working independently on our own values and vision, and less against somebody else's.

Cynthia Wine
Toronto, Ontario

"Raising children was not a sideline as I originally thought. It was a very involving experience."

After graduating from university in the mid-1960s, Cynthia Wine became an editor, then went to work at the Winnipeg Free Press. *Since then, she has written for many Canadian newspapers and magazines and has also enjoyed a career as a broadcaster. Her first book,* Across the Table, *was published in 1985. She is currently the restaurant critic for the* Toronto Star.

I didn't expect to become a journalist. I expected to be a housewife and I really wanted to be a social worker or a doctor. At university, I worked on the newspaper, edited the football programme, went out with as many boys as I could and skipped classes. It didn't auger well for graduate school. If I'd been a better student, I probably would have gone into medicine.

After graduation, I went looking for a job and got hired as editor of a sales-promotion journal for a life-insurance company. Essentially, I did what was easiest. My next job, which lasted about four years, was at the *Winnipeg Free Press*. I started on what was then the women's section and later went into general reporting.

In 1966, I got married but didn't quit work, even though that was what you did in those days. I liked the idea of working a lot, although I've never worked as ambitiously as that statement might suggest. My husband enjoyed the idea of my working, too, maybe because his mother had always worked outside the home.

At some point, a couple of years before our daughter was born, I took a wonderful year off. I played solitaire, read Somerset Maugham from beginning to end, decorated the apartment, stared into the middle distance. I can't remember when I was happier and I don't know why I haven't done it again. I still think, "I have to go back to work, I have to go back to work," even when it isn't a financial issue.

Several months before my daughter was born, in 1971, I quit work at the *Free Press*. I consulted a friend who had never worked outside the home, like most of her generation, and she said, "Are you crazy, you can't work. You're not even going to have time to bake cookies."

I guess she's right, I thought. And you know how you get with a job. You start thinking maybe it's time to change.

One day, when my daughter was about six weeks old, I was sitting in the living room. The house was as clean as it needed to be, I'd baked cookies, and I thought, what aren't I doing? When my daughter woke up from her nap, I put her in her carriage, walked down to the *Free Press*, marched up to the editor and said, "I need to come back to work." That's when I began my weekly column on the city, "Cynthia Wine Says."

I researched and wrote the column from home and can't remember specifically what I did about child care. I know my mother and sister-in-law helped out a lot. Since my daughter was the first new child in the family for some time, there was no shortage of care givers.

I continued to work part time, but when you're a freelancer and you're working part time, you're really working full time because you're always at somebody's beck and call. You can't predict when you'll be working and children are unpredictable about when they'll need you, and the clash happens more often than you'd like. I've often thought, although I've never done it, that a regular 9-to-5 job is better than working at home because you can control it. You have a routine: when you're at the office, you're at the office.

During this time, I wrote my first book, *Parsley, Sage and Cynthia Wine: A Guide to the Restaurants of Winnipeg*. Obviously, a book nobody should be without. It sold 44,000 copies and was the phenomenon of the century. Believe me, this was no Pulitzer Prize winner. It sold because of marketing. I loaded up my car with books and drove to the northern United States where I sold it to stores. I also sold it to large companies, like the Hudson's Bay Liquor Company, who gave it away as gifts.

When my marriage ended in 1976, I moved to Toronto. I started broadcasting for CBC radio, where I really learned about deadlines. I also did a lot of stringing for *Maclean's* and a fair bit for "Morningside," which I had started doing in Winnipeg. I remember it as an unhappy time. I was lonely and frightened and wouldn't admit it. I was trying to live my fantasy of the single life which wasn't appropriate because I had two young children.

At some point, I interviewed the editor of *Homemaker's* for *Maclean's*, who wanted to do a story on this little magazine which was winning all kinds of awards. She asked me to become their food editor. It involved a lot of travelling across Canada and producing mega articles, which I did for a few years.

For most of my career, I worked out of an office—if you could call it that—carved out of a corner of my bedroom. I fantasized about having my own office since God knows when, but my attitude was that it was our house, not my house. Since this was just a little column I had to write, I didn't want to bother anyone. Of course I'd be furious if anyone walked into my space.

One day, I was talking to my life-long girlfriend who said, "You don't need to do this. You're a grown-up and you can have your own office." So, about two years ago, after I had started working at the *Toronto Star* as their restaurant columnist, I went out and rented an office.

It was a statement of how I was going to start finding what I wanted. If you're a writer, your surroundings are part of your head and you need that room of your own. I think it has a lot to do with womanhood and motherhood, because when you're responsible for young people, they're in your head, and if they're also physically in your space, it's hard to focus.

I kept that office for a year, but after my partner and I separated, it seemed redundant. I think it had as much to do with my need to be apart, as with my need for a professional space. Oddly enough, although I had been cursing it, the first month I was at home, working in my pyjamas, I thought I was in heaven. I couldn't believe I'd ever want to go out again.

The big problem with working at home is that you miss opportunities because your life gets so closely edited. The chances are you'll never see anybody you didn't expect to see and that's more of a drawback than we realize. Many of the jobs I've been offered have come about because I've been out and have run into somebody who said, "Oh, my God, her!" If I hadn't been out they might have thought of somebody else.

While I was working for *Homemaker's*, I lived in Nova Scotia for a year. It was another one of those enriching years off. During that time, I wrote a series called "Consuming Passions" for *Homemaker's*—it had to do with feelings about eating and nourishment—and I won a gold medal at the National Magazine Awards.

Winning that gold medal was a reminder of what you can do if you stop to listen to what's inside. I've begun to take violin lessons because the violin has always struck me as an instrument you play from the inside. You have to create the note—not like the piano where you hit the key. What comes out of you is what's really there and it's the best of you. It's like that gold-medal series. Those kinds of things are hard to do when you've got a million things bouncing off you.

While I was living in Nova Scotia, I became interested in the Jane Stafford story. She's the woman who murdered her husband, Billy, after he'd been abusing her. When I first heard about it, I phoned "Morningside" and said, "You've got to do something on this. This woman has just been acquitted of murdering her husband and everybody stood up and applauded." Then I contracted with a publisher to do a book on the case.

I loved working on that book because I found the story so fascinating. It was her story and the story of the community, Queen's County, where there had been about nine suicides that year. It was one of those troubling places that put the lie to the notion of the peaceful countryside where every kid has grandparents.

I was fascinated by Jane because, although I felt sorry for her, we were very different. I had been raised with every possible privilege and protection, and had different qualities and opportunities. I thought that could never happen to me, but I only needed two interviews with her to know exactly what she was talking about. She was a fascinating, smart, feeling person and I understood why she loved Billy. I could have imagined myself in her situation because I've been in situations with men where it's been like that. I don't mean the beating and the abuse, but I know the feeling she talks about: he's mad at me, he's mad at me, and there must be something I can say or do to make him like me. That's a woman's feeling.

I wrote a full draft of her story, but it was a difficult time in my life. My daughter was going through a troubled adolescence. Then, the former wife of the man I was living with died, and his two children came to live with us. Neither child was in terrific shape. Their mother had been sick for some time and it was a terrible loss. So there we were, suddenly with four kids. I didn't know what to do and I can remember wanting my mommy.

I couldn't focus on work, so I put the book aside for a while and, in that time, somebody else picked up the story and wrote it. I think about it from time to time, perhaps about turning the story into a novel. It's a whole book that I didn't write because of family responsibilities. It was the first time in my life I remember being overwhelmed.

That feeling lasted for a few years—it was like walking on a tightrope and trying not to look down. I remember thinking at the time that I had every resource imaginable to get through this: the support of a loving family, a very good relationship with my partner, financial resources, intelligence, education. I kept thinking about people who didn't have all these things and I didn't know how they managed.

The real help came from women. I could recall sitting around the table in Winnipeg, but those vigils weren't available to me in Toronto. When you move to a city like Toronto, people are here to work. They're not here just to be. The greatest help I got came from women who created the feeling of support I remembered from Winnipeg. I'm not the first to say this, but the community of women is a very big deal.

While I was going through this, I was working at TV Ontario, co-hosting a program called "Moneysworth." It was a good thing to do because it was one day a week. I went in to the studio Friday morning and shut the world out. I must have been writing books—*Across the Table* came out and I must have toured. I just can't remember. Then one day I noticed that nothing bad had happened for about a year and the sense of being overwhelmed disappeared.

My life has turned out quite differently from how I imagined it in my teenage years. In those days, I thought I'd be a wife and kids would be part of a household. I fantasized about my glorious romance with my husband. I never fantasized about children or work. The fantasy was love.

Now, looking back, I can see that my greatest rewards and joy have been through kids and work. And as far as that great romance—phph! That's been disappointing, though there have been rich moments.

I think the work that will come out of my experience with my children is yet to come. As I continue to be a writer, I'll write about the topics that are important to me and I'll draw on my feelings about my children—and that includes Ford's two boys whom I consider to be my family—because of the intensity and the truth of these feelings. You can't fool around with kids: you either are or you ain't.

Even so, I constantly struggled not to be as involved with the experience of children as I was. And part of that came from the feeling that my sisterhood didn't support it. I felt that many of my friends who were career women found raising children the lesser task and I took too much of that to heart, I'm sorry to say. Now, I realize there's no joy or commitment that can match children.

My child-rearing days are over. My daughter is at university in the States. My oldest son is moving out and he'll be back and forth. I'm only 49 and my life is mine, again, which I greet with mixed emotions.

12

The Arts

Frances Gage
Toronto, Ontario

"When I was younger, marriage and a career were an either-or situation. The people I knew who tried to combine both had made a mess of one or the other."

Frances Gage joined the navy after graduating from high school in 1944. After the war, she attended the Ontario College of Art on the veteran's programme. Throughout the 1950s, she established herself as a sculptor.

In 1944, when I was 18, I joined the navy, right out of high school. I worked in intelligence operations on the West Coast for the secret service, listening in on German and Japanese ships. Our work was so secret we didn't even know what we were doing.

I wasn't conscious of being discriminated against, although as women, we were certainly treated differently from the men. We had sheets on our beds and curtains on our windows and the men didn't. Also, the navy discouraged us from drinking. The men were given a tot of rum every day and the women were given seven cents.

The navy represented a great opportunity for a young woman like me, who couldn't afford to go to college. The Canadian veteran's programme was the best in the world, and I went to the Ontario College of Art courtesy of the Department of Veteran Affairs.

In those days, I didn't know there was such a thing as sculpture so I wanted to be a portrait painter. I was awarded a scholarship to study for nine months in New York, then Paris. When I came back, all the fun began because, of course, there was no work.

In 1956, I met Frances Loring and Florence Wyle, two women sculptors. When I got back from Europe, they gave me a job in their studio even though they couldn't afford me. They remained wonderful mentors as I began to get jobs of my own. It was my first experience of being accepted as an artist. They made me feel my work was worthwhile. They also gave me the courage to go on, because they lived on next to nothing for years.

Florence and Frances were very kind and warm. They helped everybody, particularly women. They had marvellous parties and made a point of introducing me to lots of people. I never had similar support from men.

In fact, the men in the arts community generally found women a threat and were very antagonistic. One well-known man put me down publicly and it hurt my career. I did what I did in spite of many of them. I'm only aware of one large job that I didn't get because I was a woman, but I'm sure there were more instances that I didn't know about.

I was raised to be ashamed of being a woman, because in my family, boys were much more highly valued. I was supposed to be a boy and that may have made me do things I wouldn't have done otherwise. I felt I had to prove I was as good as a man. With hindsight, I'd say the drive to prove that often kept me going.

I've always sculpted from the animal world. I feel very close to nature and for 12 years lived in the country by myself. It was an isolated location full of fascinating birds and wild creatures with which I've always felt a kinship. There seemed to be a force between us, particularly between me and the birds. Living in the country, alone, was kind of foolish, but it was something I had to do and there are things that people can't take away from me because of that experience. Finally, though, I realized I had to come back to the city. I was spending so much time on the chores associated with daily living, it was taking away from my work. Also, I wasn't able to promote and market myself.

One thing that's changed since my youth is that it now seems possible to have both marriage and a career—with the right partner. I didn't marry the one person I might have when I realized he perceived my work as a hobby, something to keep me occupied when I didn't have anything else to do. He had visions of me working in my little studio after the children were in bed.

I would have enjoyed having children. But I think if I'd had them, I probably would have stopped what I was doing as an artist. In the long term, I think it's most important to listen to what you feel is true, because if you have a gift, you must use it.

Helen Porter
St. John's, Newfoundland

"**B**ringing women writers to attention became a bit of a cru-
sade for me and several other women. Luckily we had each
other because there were always people who dismissed what
we said as individuals. 'Oh, that's just Helen and she's like that.'"

*Helen Porter worked as a typist and secretary in the early 1950s. She stayed home
for 12 years to raise her children, then returned to the work force in the mid-
1960s. In 1967, she began taking creative-writing classes and published her first
book,* Below the Bridge, *in 1979.*

I started working part time in the library in 1945 when I was 15. I needed
to make some money because I was the eldest of five children. Since I was
always at the library, it didn't seem like a job and I made 25 cents an hour.

In my early teens I read a lot of girl-detective books and thought I wanted to be a detective or policewoman, or even a reporter. After Grade 11 I
tried to get a job at both daily newspapers as a copy boy or a cub reporter.
I got a very straight answer: "We don't hire girls." It made me mad, but I
knew it was true. There were no girls working at either of the daily papers
in St. John's.

After I finished the commercial course, I went to work with the chief
of police as a shorthand typist which, I guess, was the next best thing. I was
18 when I started and I worked with four other young women in the junior
positions. We had to type police reports which came in from all over
Newfoundland, some of which we weren't allowed to see because we were
too young. That was when I got my first inkling of things like incest.

When I look back, I have trouble believing that we weren't bothered
by some of the things that went on. For instance, every morning the superintendent and his second in command would come over for a meeting with
the chief. They'd make oblique sexual references in front of us, which was
how people joked. I remember one morning when the captain and one of
the older women—she was about 38, but to us she seemed like 60—were
giggling about something in the paper and it turned out to be a Kotex
advertisement. It was very childish, but it was sort of a game that they could
laugh at this and exclude the younger, more innocent women.

Sometimes it got a little physical. If you were leaning over a table, they might give you a smack on the backside. One summer, for some inexplicable reason, I had a lot of boils, including one on my behind. The captain came in and gave me such a hard and painful smack that it broke. It's amazing to me, now, that we didn't mind it more. I guess it's all in the context.

After 1½ years I transferred to the Department of Justice and the rituals changed. At certain times of the year, the auditors arrived. One was a married man in his mid-30s, who would literally chase another young woman around the office. She'd be sort of laughing and panicky at the same time. I remember her saying to me, "Well, Fred is like that. He gets on your nerves, but there really isn't anything you can do about it."

Then he started doing it to me. I don't think I ever talked about it to my superiors, although I told my parents and my friends. You'd say, "Stop it. Don't do that," but he kept it up.

In 1953, while I was working at the Department of Justice, I got married. Women were supposed to quit when they got married, but I didn't see the sense. What would I do? I wasn't that interested in housework.

Anyway, I worked for a nice lawyer who didn't like to change staff. I told him I couldn't afford to quit work because my husband was going back to university. It was typical of the times, by the way, that my husband went to university and I didn't. So my boss wrote the Department of Finance every three months requesting permission to keep me on. That went on for 1½ years.

I didn't tell anyone when I got pregnant. They just saw me getting bigger and bigger. The feeling was that pregnant women should hide themselves away, but I just kept working. By the time I left, I was 7½ months' pregnant.

At one point the deputy's secretary went on holiday and I took over her work, as usual, part of which included getting tea for the deputy. One of the senior women called me aside and said she didn't think it was proper for me to be delivering the deputy's tray in my condition. I asked her if he had said anything, and she said he hadn't. "Well, I'll just continue until he tells me not to," I said.

After I left the Department of Justice, I stayed at home. I remember it as an enjoyable time because it wasn't my fault that I wasn't working. They wouldn't have me. I had seen my mother with babies and I had absolutely no illusions that it was going to be easy, so I relished the chance to rest. It was a good thing, too, because I had four children in 5½ years. That was before the pill.

After the first baby was born, I got a diaphragm. People think we didn't know anything about birth control in those days, but we did. The problem was, nothing worked. So the pill was a godsend. The big difference was that you could plan.

I stayed home for 12 years and some of it seems like a big blur. Everybody I knew was doing the same thing. I only felt out of place because I didn't like housework. I cooked because I had to. I think I would have been able to handle my life a lot better if I was at work, but it just wasn't done.

While I was at home I started to envy people for the first time—especially women, who were doing things like writing columns. I had always wanted to write, but I never saw it as a job. It was something extra, a hobby. I think that has to do with being from Newfoundland. E.J. Pratt was the only well-known Newfoundland writer and he left for Toronto when he was 19. I felt writers came from somewhere else.

In my last two years at home we were kind of desperate for money, so I started taking odd jobs. I worked for the town council for a couple of months doing specific jobs for $25 a week. By this time I was over 30 and a young fellow, who was 18, was hired at the same time. He got $50 a week compared to my $25. Although I was horrified, I didn't complain.

In 1967, I ended up back at the library as a half-day typist and eventually became a reference assistant. I had taken a creative-writing class in the early '60s and from 1967–74 was doing a lot of writing. I think it's more writing than I've ever done in my life. I was at that peak where you want to write so much that you devote every bit of time to it.

Sometime in 1974, I realized that I wanted to write a book, but I didn't think I'd get it done while I was working. So I got a small grant and when that ran out, I got UI. It's the only time in my life I've ever gone on unemployment insurance, but that's how I wrote *Below the Bridge*, a non-fiction book about growing up in a neighbourhood of St. John's that has disappeared because of industrial development.

I belonged to the Newfoundland Writers' Guild, which was established in 1968. There were several women members and we were all becoming increasingly conscious of how women writers were discriminated against. There was a real renaissance of writers in Newfoundland around this time, and most of them were men. Even though there was a tradition of female poets in Newfoundland, the men would always vastly outnumber the women in things like anthologies.

In 1975, International Women's Year, a few of us decided to apply for a grant to compile an anthology of women writers in Newfoundland. A prominent academic had recently compiled an anthology of Newfoundland writers that included one woman and something like 69 men. We found this very odd because we knew of lots of fascinating stuff by women. Anyway, we collected writing from 45 women, both dead and alive, from all over Newfoundland and Labrador, and put together a book called *From This Place*. It came out in 1977 and received very good reviews, but a couple of the male reviewers complained that they couldn't understand why anyone would feel it was necessary to do an anthology of women's work. These things galvanize you.

I was one of three women who had a story collected in a book called *Stories from Atlantic Canada*. When William French reviewed it in *The* (Toronto) *Globe and Mail*, he was quite upset because there weren't many stories about the sea. Obviously, he didn't realize that women's stories, in particular, are usually set inside the house.

The women's viewpoint was reflected in my first play, which was about the issue of resettlement. In the '60s, there was an unpopular move to bring people from tiny isolated places to what they called "growth centres." Several men wrote plays that addressed the issue from the perspective of a fisherman who never wanted to move. Most of the action was down on the wharf, and the female character would come down with lunch, or something similar.

I spent a lot of summers in isolated outports and I didn't feel this accurately reflected the situation. In every place I visited, the women wanted to move and the men didn't. So, even before I was conscious of feminism, I wrote my first play, *For Every Man An Island*. The story was told from the point of view of the woman who wanted to leave the outport, and it was a direct reaction to not hearing from women except as adjuncts to the men. That play is still studied in schools and it's been nice to have that kind of impact. Although I didn't set out to write about families, that's what most of my work is about.

Vina Sood
Vancouver, British Columbia

" There's a real limit—not to the roles I can play but to the roles I'm perceived as being able to play. And it's very frustrating."

Vina Sood's family immigrated to Canada from Kenya in the 1960s. She grew up in Calgary where she attended theatre school at the University of Alberta.

I don't feel that I experienced racism while I was growing up. When we moved to Calgary in the late 1960s, East Indians were such a novelty that *The Calgary Herald* ran a picture of my mother and father on the front page. Perhaps because there were so few people of colour in the community, we weren't perceived as a threat.

I don't think I really knew I was brown until I started to act. Only then did I begin to realize that my skin colour and looks were perceived as something different and this influenced how I got cast.

I suppose any actor is going to complain about the kind of parts they get, but being a person of colour can function both positively and negatively. Right now I believe it's an advantage in the theatre because the community has been influenced by the spirit of multiculturalism and is committed to non-traditional casting—being black or brown doesn't mean you can't play characters who may have originally been written as white.

My current struggle is in the film industry, which is still white oriented—make that white "male." As a woman of colour, I get to play hospital personnel, teachers, social workers and so on. People of colour are rarely cast in lead roles. We also tend not to play anything connected with a family. I'm never asked to play Mom—possibly because they feel they'd have to cast the whole family as brown, even though there are lots of racially integrated marriages. Unfortunately, film people won't take the necessary risks to educate the public. They just feed back into stereotypes and reinforce them.

Acting is also one of the few industries where you can get—or be refused—work on how men relate to you sexually. Usually you're auditioning for males and there's a big potential for sexual attraction that's easy to play into. Unless it's related to the part, I don't use my sexual energy in auditions, but if you don't relate sexually to the men you're auditioning for, on a subtle level you're rejecting them and, of course, that can influence whether or not you get the part.

Not surprisingly, when I audition for women, I'm always much better. Women see me and hear me beyond that superficial level of who I am sexually and, as a result, I'm willing to give much more of myself. I feel appreciated for my skills and abilities rather than just the external package.

Even so, not all my experiences with women have been positive. I was invited to perform my one-woman play, *Maharani and the Maple Leaf,* at a theatre festival in Calgary. The play reflects the positive experience of a woman of colour who is an actress. It was followed by a panel discussion, during which I said that although there are many problems in the theatre, for the most part things are moving in a positive direction. I really got raked over the coals by the other women who were very militant. They accused me of selling out, of not standing up for my own people or for women in general. I was very confused and hurt by the attack. It was very difficult for me to understand why I hadn't been heard.

The pendulum is swinging between two extremes right now: women who are really angry and militant, and men who are part of the old establishment. There's no middle ground.

Dora Wasserman
Montreal, Quebec

"People criticized me for needing to work. They said I was crazy."

Dora Wasserman was born in Ukraine in 1919, and studied at the Moscow Yiddish Art Theatre in the 1930s. She immigrated to Canada in 1950 and eventually began teaching drama to children at the Jewish Public Library. In 1956, she formed a Yiddish theatre, which is now the resident theatre company of the Saidye Bronfman Centre for the Arts. In 1993, she was awarded the Order of Canada.

I learned the craft of theatre in Moscow, but couldn't work there because I had applied to leave Russia during the war. My husband, daughter and I ended up in a transit camp outside Vienna, where my second daughter was born. When we sailed for Canada, we had no idea where we were going.

We arrived in Montreal in 1950 and found lodging in a house, with five other families. There were 10 children in all and it was awful. We had no money or government support, unlike immigrants today.

I was very depressed. My work meant everything to me and I didn't think I'd ever work again. Fortunately, I discovered the Jewish Public Library, where my credentials were enough to get me weekly performances, reading from Yiddish writers.

We lived in that rooming-house for two years and it was a very difficult time. My husband was an electrician, but it cost $300 to get certified so he became a tailor, instead. With two small children, there was no theatre for me.

For the first few years, things were very black. I only began to feel hope when I could organize a Jewish children's theatre at the library. It was very exciting. At that point I also started to perform in various organizations, playing guitar, singing and reciting.

It's very difficult to be an immigrant, to adjust yourself to a new system. Although we didn't have any money, we did have the language. We spoke Yiddish, as did the people here, which meant we could communicate. The immigrants who come from Russia today speak only Russian.

My husband and children were exceptional because they were always supportive. I never had to run to make supper. With so little money, we ate borscht, butter, bread and milk for years. I had one dress, which my older daughter ironed before I performed. Maybe because it was so difficult, we stayed together by helping each other. We had a lot of love.

Making a living was not on my mind. The important thing was to be able to do my work. Later, after some friends helped us to get a house, my great problem became what to do with the children while I worked. When my eldest daughter turned six, I started to leave them alone. Once there was a fire next door. That terrified me, so I started schlepping them to work with me.

Some of the neighbours criticized me for not being a normal mother, because I took the kids out at night and they got to bed late. They felt it would be easier for everyone if I got a job in a bakery or something. I knew if I gave in, I wouldn't be able to live. Maybe it was too much, but the main thing was that my family was together. If we were falling apart, I might not have been so stubborn.

For me, there was no choice. I had to do what I had to do. It may not have been normal, but I've never had any problems with my family. In fact, I think our struggles brought us closer together.

After the children's theatre, I developed a Yiddish theatre company that worked out of the schools. When the Saidye Bronfman Centre was built 25 years ago, we moved our theatre there. I was afraid we'd lose our freedom to boards, committees and directors, but that didn't happen, and with a permanent home, the group grew differently. Surprisingly, the Yiddish theatre has survived at the centre while the English theatre has not. I'm proud of what I've built, but now I'm thinking about retiring and looking for a replacement.

Sonia Smits
Toronto, Ontario

"**B**ecause the industry is controlled by men, most of the stories reflect their interests, and women's interests are not taken seriously."

Sonia Smits began working as an actor in the mid-1970s. Since then she has played many roles, including Carrie in the CBC series "Street Legal," which began it's eight-year run in 1986, and Morag in the film version of Margaret Laurence's novel, The Diviners.

I've been working as an actor for 18 years. I started theatre school when I was 18 and left after two years to work in small-town theatre. Then, I started getting jobs on CBC dramas.

In terms of popularity, "Street Legal" was my big break. The show made me a familiar face, probably because I came into people's homes for six seasons. The power of television is amazing. People still recognize me. They feel they know me and that I'm a friend.

In one episode of "Street Legal" my character was sexually assaulted. We were very careful about how we handled this, particularly the after-effect and how people responded to the rape. About a year later, I was in a restaurant and the waitress slipped me a note that said, "Thank you. You understood." It hit me in the stomach.

I've had a bit of harassment from fans—for instance, people writing about my physical attributes and pressing the pen so hard the paper is dented on the other side. But, basically, I've been fortunate, possibly because I've played fairly strong women. My real problems have revolved around people's perceptions of attractiveness. Most decision makers are men and they have a limited perspective on how women should look and behave. Often they're looking for their own image of the perfect woman.

For instance, when I was working in Los Angeles, a casting call went out for a big miniseries. A group of men were making the decision and my agent told me they didn't find me attractive enough. At a certain point, you must learn to detach. You are what you are, unless you get totally reconstructed.

About six months later, I was performing in a play in Los Angeles and the reviews referred to my physical attractiveness in glowing terms. The miniseries still hadn't been cast so they tracked me down and asked me to come in. I hadn't changed. But because other people had seen me in a certain way, my good looks were confirmed.

On the other hand, when I played Morag in *The Diviners*, some people thought I was too glamorous. They identified me with Carrie in "Street Legal" who was well groomed and wore nice clothes. In *The Diviners* I was playing an older woman not known for her attractiveness and there was an undercurrent of "Sonia drops her glamorous role."

Is she too attractive, not attractive enough? What the hell does this have to do with it? I was playing a woman who, in a 400-page novel, merits one paragraph of physical description. Her looks aren't important. Her interior life—her thoughts and emotions—and how she reacts with people is what matters.

I grew up in the country—not on the Upper East Side. I know where my sensibilities are. Plus, I'm a good enough actress to be able to play different characters.

Even so, looks are always an issue. Something starts happening on a production and my hair often becomes an issue. Hairdressers have been fired over my hair, even though I don't give a shit about it.

When I began to act, I had very long hair. People would stop me on the street and say, "Never cut your hair." I was identified as "you with the hair" at auditions. I started to get worried because I didn't want to be known just for my hair. I cut it off and didn't work for a year. I'd like to say that was a coincidence, but I don't think so.

Recently, I met with a director on an film project that seemed interesting. He told me I was too young and attractive for the role of the wife, which, when I think about it, may not be surprising because there's always a woman who's a monster in his work.

He wanted the audience to know immediately that the male character was in an unbearable marriage, and what's more unbearable to a man than being married to an older, not terribly attractive woman? The rest of the women in the film were, basically, innocent virgins. Right now, I'm caught in the middle. I'm not young and innocent enough to play the virgins, but not old and ugly enough to play the shrews.

Since men define what is interesting, on the basis of what interests them, the success of films such as *Thelma and Louise* is dismissed as a blip. The traditional wisdom is that women can't do action films and that that picture was the exception to the rule. Sigourney Weaver has had three very successful action films with the *Aliens* series. How many exceptions to the rule do you need? Also, her films are simply called "action pictures." She just happens to star in them. But Arnold Schwarzenegger films are called "Arnold Schwarzenegger" films.

Like most things, it starts at the top. Some of my best experiences professionally and creatively have been—not surprisingly—with women. "Street Legal" was created by a woman and executive-produced by a woman. I don't think it's a coincidence that it has strong female characters.

I got very involved with ACTRA, the performers' alliance, because about 10 or 12 years ago a lot of trash was being filmed in Toronto. It had become a dumping ground for, basically, soft-core pornography. I remember saying to my agent, "Something has to be happening."

"Sure, Sonia," he said. "Here's what's available." There were five parts and all of them involved things like getting raped, eaten by dogs or taking off your clothes. There wasn't one I could go out for because I just couldn't do it.

So you push yourself. You tell yourself, "You're an actor, you can do this." Then you have nightmares about it and you come to terms with the fact that you can't push your own instincts, ego and values that far. You can stretch them, but not that far.

Nudity hasn't been a big problem for me because I don't think I have the kind of body people want to see nude. But at one point, I began to see nudity as something I should do creatively. I was set up to do a nude bed scene with James Woods and Deborah Harry in *Videodrome*, a David Cronenberg film. I had drawn up a long agreement detailing who could be in the room, what body parts they would show, what angles, what shots and so on. I decided to do it because there was a creative need in the director's mind, but I wanted to have as much control as possible. Everything was agreed to, then David decided not to do the scene because a threesome wouldn't get past the censors.

There were love scenes in *The Diviners*, but no nudity. It was wonderful to work with a woman director on that picture. I've been accused of being a prude about sex, love or nude scenes. That's not true. My position is that people rarely explore sexuality or intimacy. The shots are about seeing two beautiful people making out and, most of the time, they reflect a kind of voyeurism.

In *The Diviners* it was wonderful to work on love scenes because the writer, director, producer and story editor were all women. The only man was Tom Jackson, the actor in the scene. We'd all had so many problems with so many bad love scenes and, finally, we were getting to do our version of it. It was a privilege, in a way, and very, very rare.

There's a difference between working with women and men on love scenes. Many men seem to be afraid of sexuality and intimacy. In a script written by a man, you'll usually find a full-page description of the character, for instance, rounding the corner and seeing the girl—chock-full of details. But you reach the love scene and it reads, "They make love."

Time is very limited in film so each moment should be informative and build towards something. A love scene is no exception. In fact, since it's so intimate, it provides an important opportunity to reveal character. But often, in conventional male screenplays, love scenes are just a thrill; there's no revelation.

To some extent this reflects the feelings men in the business have about women. Women have no identity of their own—they're roles rather than characters. That means that as an actor, you often have to fill in, take something that's very bareboned and work like hell to create any semblance of a full character.

You can't really blame the men because they don't know any better, but it's a problem for an actor because it limits you in your work. As I get older and become more experienced, I have less patience with this sort of thing. I think my craft has grown and developed. I've learned a lot in 20 years, but what I'm reading hasn't grown with me.

Acting is subjective. How people evaluate your acting ability is beyond your control. It also puts you in a passive position. Actors say they fight for a particular role. But what does this mean? That they kept going back until the role was given to them?

There's no basis of measure for accomplishment in acting. In other professions—for instance, athletics—you can measure your improvement because your times are better than someone else's. But acting—especially for women—is so tied in with your age, your looks and your physical presence. Your career goes up and down on the basis of factors other than ability. There's no logical build as you get better at your profession.

Statistics show that employment opportunities for women performers over the age of 40 drop by 100 per cent, and men's go up by something like 125 per cent. So just when you've become very solid in your craft, there's no work. On the other hand, very mediocre men often do well. My theatre-arts teacher once said there are 10 times more good actresses than actors, yet there are 10 times more jobs for actors. I don't think he's wrong.

Voice-overs—which is a good way for actresses and actors to make a living when they're not getting the good roles—are 95 per cent male. I know this stuff and soon it's going to be my reality. Why aren't the scripts and roles there? The CBC did "Dieppe," which had 400 roles for men and 1½ for women.

If it was personal, you could work on it. There would be hope, a possibility for improvement. But if you know the whole structure is stacked against you, simply because of your sex, it becomes very disheartening. People have been saying that things will change. They have: they've gotten worse.

The question is, how do I, as an artist, and someone who has developed my craft, continue to do what I feel is of value? If I stop acting and do something else, I've wasted my experience and craft. So I'm pushing myself into—and it's not my forte—trying to develop projects, mostly with other women because there are so many good women's stories that haven't been told.

It's easy to forget the power of media. The media has the power to make people feel horrible about themselves, or it can provide comfort. It isn't fair to be denied equal access to that power because you're a woman.

Peggy Thompson
Vancouver, British Columbia

"It's not hard to sell a picture with lots of action, violence and sex, but since women's stories don't tend to feature these elements, they're difficult to market."

Peggy Thompson started working in theatre in the mid-1970s on an Opportunities for Youth grant and, since then, has written extensively for radio, television and film, although she's also acted, stage-managed and produced. She has won two Genie Awards for her work as a screenwriter, most recently for The Lotus Eaters. *As a producer, she now works in close collaboration with Sharon McGowan. Their most recent film is* The Lotus Eaters.

Living in the West and working in Canadian film is a strange thing to be doing. Very few Western film makers have made it because so much is working against you. For instance, you have to have a distributor before you can get government financing, and there are no longer any distributors in the West.

Film is the most expensive of all creative expressions, so when you talk about making a film, you're talking about pulling together as much financial support as you can. Because central Canada is where the dollars are, you have to make major connections with eastern companies to raise your financing. It's difficult for all film makers. It's often more difficult for women because our stories tend not to fit the mould.

I've been working in film since 1985, but I've been involved in theatre all my professional life, which spans 20 years. I've written, produced, stage-managed and acted. In both film and theatre, I've done everything, as you do when there are few resources—I even did hair and make-up on the first film Sharon McGowan and I did together, as well as make the coffee and food. My line is, "I'll know that I've made it when I don't have to do the catering for the première."

For much of my professional life I worked independently with small budgets, in film and theatre. Making the leap to work with a higher level of financing was an adventure.

A Wimbledon tennis match was one of the odd things that helped to make *The Lotus Eaters* happen. I was watching a match—Billie Jean King was the broadcaster—and her analysis was that a particular player might win the game, but wouldn't win the tournament because he wasn't moving into the net, and you can't "move forward" until you move into the net. I thought, "We're not playing the net." So for eight months that became one of our operating principles. If we stopped moving forward, we were dead.

We planned a trip to Toronto to meet with distributors only to discover they were all going to Cannes. We said we'd be glad to meet with them when they got back. But from a couple of things that were said, we realized they were spending most of their money in Cannes. So we went to Toronto immediately, met with every distributor in four days and closed the deal.

Going to Toronto was like going to the net. We'd been talking to these people on the phone for six months and nobody said, "You have to come here." No one wanted to say, "You have to come to Toronto for $1,000 cup of coffee." But those are the kinds of things you have to do.

I also used a lot of methods to release the unconscious while I was working on the script of *The Lotus Eaters*. Dream analysis, self-hypnosis, the *I Ching*. I began to realize the power of these methods in preparing creative work when I saw a performance of the iconoclastic composer, John Cage, and attended one of his lectures. His non-linear approach was often helpful with business plans, as well.

When I teach screenwriting, I get the class to do an exercise called "Stealing Fire," which I learned from Linda Putnam, an alternative New York-based acting trainer. The object of the exercise is to identify your material. As you go through your day, wherever you are, if people catch your eye, you make a point of trying to figure them out—discounting people who are mentally disabled or schizophrenic because we all notice them, and this is geared more to you alone. These people "catch your fire." If you study people who catch your fire long enough, you'll be able to discover what they all have in common. At the same time, you're trying to figure out where you intersect with them. That place is the source for your material.

I did this exercise for a year when I was writing *The Lotus Eaters*. I realized I was connecting with people who looked dreamy and far away, like they wished they were living on a Gulf Island, which is what the film is about. The amazing thing was that whenever we screened it, these were the people who came. And they loved the film!

Wanda Kaluzney
Montreal, Quebec

"In conducting, we're still discovering the definitions for women. Women have difficulty fitting the mould because of the power and sensuality associated with the role."

Wanda Kaluzney began her professional career in 1965, at the age of 11, as a church organist. After studying piano performance at McGill University, she founded the Montreal Chamber Orchestra in 1974, when she was 20.

I'm 39 and had my first job as a conductor at the age of 11. I guess I was a child prodigy, although I hesitate to use the term. I played piano and organ and became an organist and director of two choirs at a Montreal church. I did that until I was 18 or 19. I don't think I realized it was such a big deal until after the fact.

The job required an audition, and when I won out over three men, I remember enjoying it. One of them hated me well into my teens. But when you're doing what you love, I don't think you consider things like gender and age. Other people may have thought these were issues. Choir members would do things like call my parents and say I was being rude in rehearsals, but I was just going after what I wanted.

My parents weren't musical at all. Music was something I wanted from an early age, and either they didn't take me seriously or they resisted because they never really did get behind me. I try not to let it bother me, but I may be suppressing my disappointment. Even when I was very young, they didn't come to recitals.

On the other hand, by starting to work so early, I was able to finance my own studies. I didn't have the pressure of parents pushing me to succeed, which some of my colleagues experienced. Whatever I wanted to do was fine with my parents, although they would have preferred a profession with more security.

In that sense, they're right. Security is non-existent in conducting. At the top levels, contracts are renewed every couple of years. There's nothing resembling tenure, except in universities, if you get into teaching. As a performer you're only as good as your last performance.

I started studying piano performance at McGill when I was 18. I quickly realized that performance was very lonely. You spend hours by yourself practising, and when you perform, you're alone. Even as a student, I tended to form trios, which I found much more satisfying. It was much more fun to share the experience of being on stage with other people.

I finally put two and two together and realized I liked working with people and being able to get the best out of them. Since this is basically what conductors do, it gradually dawned on me that I wanted to be a conductor, not a pianist. So, at the age of 20, a year before I got my bachelor's degree, I founded the Montreal Chamber Orchestra.

One of the reasons I founded the orchestra was that there aren't a lot of conducting opportunities for women. Even today, most of the women conductors started with their own orchestras. Conducting is still perceived as a position of strength and I think most boards of directors aren't ready to trust women with that role.

When I started, in 1974, Montreal's musical market was cornered and it was difficult for new graduates to break in. The only orchestras were the Montreal Symphony, the McGill Chamber Orchestra and a chamber music group called Camarata. By starting the Montreal Chamber Orchestra, I wasn't just giving myself the chance to conduct. I was also creating an opportunity for young musicians to get their first jobs.

I operate by getting a germ of an idea which seems to grow. Working as a volunteer for the junior committee of the Montreal Symphony, I had learned a bit about volunteerism and the business side of orchestras. I also watched male colleagues who had failed at starting groups and learned from their mistakes. I began by putting together a board of directors. Then, I started knocking on doors. I was lucky—I hesitate to say this because I think one creates one's own luck. The then-chairman of Royal Trust was quite taken with this 20-year-old with such fantastic ideas. He legitimized me by phoning a bunch of his friends and convincing them to take me seriously. We were also fortunate in that we were able to find a permanent performing space right off the bat.

Through much of my career I tried not to think about things like gender discrimination. It wasn't until I felt established that I could acknowledge some of the problems of being a woman. It's easy to say I would have gotten certain opportunities if I wasn't a girl. So I've tried, perhaps subconsciously, to ignore things that might be limiting.

I knew what I wanted to do and set out to do it. The sense that I could do anything I wanted, so long as I was willing to pay the price and put in the work, is one thing I got from my parents. I never got the sense that girls only do this and guys do that, possibly because I was an only child. My parents felt the world was wide open and education was the key.

But looking back, I recognize instances of discrimination. Little things, like people saying, "Montreal Chamber, that's that little girl's orchestra." At that time it didn't bother me. Because I was doing what I wanted to do, I didn't care if other people thought it was legitimate or not.

I suppose it's too simplistic to say I just want to be happy at what I'm doing. I've never married and have no children. I have an orchestra, instead. I didn't decide one day that one couldn't exist without the other. I just haven't found a situation where I could continue both, with the right person. I would love to have children, although I recognize that if I did, I'd compromise my career. On the other hand, if it doesn't happen, it won't torment me.

In the early days of the orchestra, there was so little happening in Montreal that it wasn't important to push for publicity and international acclaim. But with time, things became more competitive and I recognized the limitations to just being good where you were and satisfying yourself in those terms. I saw that we had to start playing the international game to be taken seriously at home, as well. That's true of the arts. You have to prove yourself elsewhere before people get excited about you at home. So we found a manager in New York and we started touring internationally,

I was allegedly the first woman guest conductor in Germany. I didn't do the research on that, I'm just taking someone's word for it. The reviews were interesting. One ran with the headline: "In Wanda Kaluzney We Have a Woman Conductor Equal to Any Man." The reaction from the guys at home was, "Way to go, babe!" The girls said, "It's a compliment, but we knew you were superior to most of the guys." It was interesting that the Germans felt this was the greatest praise they could bestow on me.

Working in Baden Baden is the only time I remember experiencing discrimination from a musician. The musicians can tell very quickly whether conductors know what they're doing, and as long as they're in good hands, they seem quite content. But there was one trumpet player who wasn't happy about taking orders from a woman. Although his professionalism won out and he played well, he made faces throughout the performance.

A while ago, I was talking to a Czech conductor who was thinking of inviting me to conduct an orchestra he worked with in England. But he warned me not to consider working with him in Prague, since there are only two women in the orchestra and he didn't think the men would tolerate a female guest conductor. People still make sweeping statements like that without realizing what they're saying.

On one occasion, a conductor in his 50s complained about the demands of a long tour. When I said I'd be happy to take over some of his work, he suggested I'd be much too tired because the men in the orchestra would keep me so busy after the concerts. He had definitely placed me in the category of orchestra playmate versus the person in charge. Still, he's the sweetest man and, surely, in his mind this was a compliment because he was implying that he found me attractive. On the one hand, I was furious, and on the other, I recognized he was on my side. But if this comes from an ally, you get an idea of the resistance within the profession.

I've been short-listed for many symphony positions. When you're short-listed, one of two things happens: either they interview you or they invite you to conduct the orchestra. In one of these instances, I was asked to conduct a pop concert, which is expected because when women are guest conducting, we're often given the lighter music programmes. Nobody trusts us with Mahler. That's infuriating, of course. One hopes the idea that it takes a man to do the job is gradually changing.

Anyway, I was conducting this pop concert with a wonderful trio of women singers whose arrangements often resembled the Andrews sisters. They had 12 songs, but when the programme was printed, one was omitted by mistake. We discussed the problem and I suggested we leave the 12th for an encore. The general manager objected. He said the audiences were so lukewarm that I shouldn't even expect a curtain call. I said we should take the chance.

There's an art to milking an audience and I decided to make this a true test of my abilities. We not only got to do the encore, we got a standing ovation. How ironic, I thought. The audience was jumping to its feet when the administration had warned me we wouldn't even get to do the last piece.

The next day, I had my interview. The same man asked if I felt I could handle a full symphony since my experience had been with a chamber orchestra. I was shocked. I had conducted a full symphony the night before and received a standing ovation.

I thought, this man's an idiot. Wasn't he there last night? But instead of confronting him I said, "Didn't you enjoy the concert?" In retrospect, I feel bad that I didn't say, "You wouldn't say that if I was a man." Now the lights go on more and I confront the issues, but in those days, it didn't even click.

When I was in my mid-20s, I applied for a position with a large choir. The short-list was down to two candidates and they chose the man. Before I was officially notified, a member of the board called me. He was a black man and he said he felt so strongly that I had been discriminated against, he was resigning. Having dealt with discrimination all his life, he felt confident he could recognize it, and he knew I was the better candidate.

That really took me aback, as did his comment that the many middle-aged women on the committee were the least supportive of my appointment. I guess some older women feel threatened because my generation, and women just a bit older than me, are the first generation to have careers, whereas they didn't have that option.

I spent eight summers in the States at the Pierre Monteux School studying conducting. Monteux had been dead for nine years when I started, but his family and some associates were still involved in the school and the students were always asking for Pierre stories, because we thought he was the greatest conductor.

Once we listened to a tape of a 1960 interview where he was asked if women would ever be conductors. He said, "Absolutely not." Pierre Monteux, my grandest teacher! I was devastated. Then the interviewer said, " Well, Nadia Boulanger was one of your students and she conducted the New York Philharmonic." His response was, "Ah well, it's not that women aren't capable of being conductors' it's just that they will never have the opportunity because, as we all know, symphonies are run by women's committees and they don't want women at the head."

In those days, it was probably true. Conducting contains a strong element of *machismo*. The physical image is related to the prowess of male conductors. I think the men in the orchestra can identify with that and the women can swoon over it. Once a woman tries to define herself in that role, it becomes problematic. It's like being a woman in business. Acting like a man just doesn't work. You have to be who you are, but that's not to say it's not as effective.

That also helps to explain why there are very few black or overtly gay conductors in mainstream classical music. It just doesn't fit with the image, which is the powerful male bending everyone to his will. Female conductors often start in opera, since the conductor is in the pit and the visual issue doesn't exist.

The first year I was at the Pierre Monteux School I was conducting Mozart's 39th. It was my first paid public performance as a conductor. I was the only woman out of a class of 12 and everyone was interested in what I intended to wear. This was 1974, when many people dressed like flower children and everybody assumed I'd wear a peasant-type blouse and long skirt.

Instead, I wore a heavenly gown. It was a sleeveless jersey knit with a décolletage and it fell from an empire waist. When I walked on stage I was immediately acknowledged by the brass section. The concert went very well, but as I was leaving the stage, I was met by Madame Monteaux, who was in her late 70s and very grand.

"My dear, do you know it took the men in the audience five minutes to realize you were doing Mozart?" she said. And she forbid me to ever wear anything quite so revealing again. But she had a point, insofar as conductors, male or female, are there to convey the music, not to distract from it.

When I started the Montreal Chamber Orchestra, my male teacher told me to get myself a suit and cut my hair. I said, "I'm a woman conductor and I'm going to make a statement." However, I changed my mind after seeing Eve Plummer conduct the Montreal Symphony in a dress. The dress moved every time she leaned into the orchestra, and there was an awful lot of distraction. I should say that I also find tails distracting, even on men, if they move around a lot. But when I realized I was watching a dress swoosh around instead of paying attention to the music, I switched to a tux because I do move around a fair amount.

Actually, I like women in tuxes. I think they look great. If I'm guest conducting and the orchestra is very formal, I wear tails.

If I remember correctly, somebody did a study about the most common fantasy related to conducting. Most people perceive it as a power trip: you wave your arms and this glorious sound comes out. For both men and women the issue of power has overshadowed the nurturing side of conducting. I think anyone will tell you, even an army general, that you really can't command with an iron fist. You have to get people into a position where they want to give you their best. Women have been doing this forever and we're much better at it than men.

Jane Rule
Galiano Island, British Columbia

"I hadn't anticipated being as public and as political a person as my writing turned me into."

Jane Rule began working in the early 1950s, as a teacher. Her first novel, Desert of the Heart, *was published in 1964. Since then she has written numerous novels and short stories as well as one non-fiction book,* Lesbian Images.

I finished high school in 1947 when I was 16, and since I couldn't get into college right way, I worked at Stanford University as a supply typist. That job was an eye-opener. At one point I was sitting next to a woman with a BA in creative writing from Stanford, which is what I thought I wanted to do.

I moved from department to department, which gave me a bizarre sense of how a big institution functioned. For instance, when I worked in the purchasing department, the boss told us that at the end of the day we should throw away the purchasing orders we hadn't finished typing. That's how we kept up with our work.

I ended up in the general secretary's office and typed my own rejection from Stanford as part of my job. I've often wondered if I could have gotten away with sending myself an acceptance.

Sitting next to someone who had a degree didn't dissuade me from going to university because I don't think I ever thought about working. I had no real need for money. My family was sufficiently well-off that if I wanted to go to college I could. I graduated from Mills, a small women's college in California, which I loved. Then I went to graduate school in England, which I loved, and came back for graduate courses at Stanford in the creative-writing department, which I hated. But all this time, I hadn't thought about making a living.

I suppose it never crossed my parents' minds because they thought I would marry. But one day I think they suddenly woke up to the fact that they had this youngster who seemed perfectly happy to go on and on in school, when what I really wanted to do, of course, was write books. Finally, they cleared their throats and said, "You can live at home and have all the time you'd like to write. But if you're going to live away from home, you'll have to support yourself."

This came as an extraordinary revelation. I certainly didn't want to live at home, because I'd been living on my own for a couple of years, so I decided I'd better get a job. I tried to get the jobs I had before I went to college —typing was still my only job skill—but now nobody would have me because I was overqualified. So my first experience with an education was that it disqualified me for earning a living.

I had a BA in English and some graduate courses. I had no ambitions for a higher degree. I knew I wanted to write fiction, but I also knew I wouldn't be able to make a living at doing this because I wasn't interested in writing stories to fit the formulas. My chief motivation in writing was to explain the world to myself—to pose certain circumstances, certain difficulties and certain climates and to explore them. Also, to explore language.

A friend, who had been teaching English at Concord Academy, in Massachusetts, was leaving her job and she asked if I would like to take it. It turned out it didn't involve teaching much English. I was an assistant in the biology lab and I also lived in and helped to look after the boarders. I was paid $300 a month and had two nights off a month, not on weekends. I stayed there for two years, then I came to Vancouver. It was the mid-'50s and there were jobs everywhere.

My first serious job was at UBC as assistant director at International House. The director was a male figurehead and I ran the place. It was interesting, but it was so demanding in terms of time that, after a year, I realized I wasn't getting any writing done. I worked seven days a week, often nights, and was paid a bit more than my secretary. When I resigned, the head of the board said, "You've done a terrific job and we desperately want you to stay on but, of course, we'll never be able to pay you what you're worth." And I said, "That's one of the reasons I'm quitting."

After I left, I went to work in the English department, part time, which is that wonderful way you get people to work terribly hard for not much money and pay them no benefits.

It took me until I was nearly 30 to figure out my relationship with the world in terms of dollars and cents. I think my attitude towards money had to do with being a girl. My brother certainly wasn't given the message that he could stare off into the fog until someone came along and said, "You have to get a job." Other friends had a sense that they should major in something practical, but I was very snobbish about that. I had the good liberal attitude that education wasn't utilitarian. It was about broadening the mind.

Although I loved teaching, I finally realized that I had to figure out how to earn a living so I'd have time for my own work. I decided to teach full time every other year, get a decent salary and then have real time off. And that's how I organized my life after that.

In those days, the pressure was on everyone to go for higher degrees. I had seen other people who wanted to write get sucked up into scholarship and didn't intend to do that. My plan was that by the time I was 40, I would have published enough that some writing department would give me a tenured position and, in fact, that's exactly what happened. When I was in my early 40s, UBC offered me a tenured position.

Around that time, something even more extraordinary happened: I started to make a modest living as a writer. In the end, I turned the job offer down and moved to Galiano Island to live a simpler life. I've made my living at writing ever since.

During the 10 years I was writing without being published, I wrote two novels and numerous short stories. *Desert of the Heart* is my third novel. I finished it in 1961 when I was just short of 30, but it wasn't published until 1964. The book was turned down by 25 publishers in the U.S., although it was accepted by the first Canadian and the first English publishers who read it. I got a $1,000 advance for it. At the same time, I wrote a short story for *Redbook* in one afternoon, for which I was paid a $1,000. That reconfirmed my belief that the relationship between my work and money is totally arbitrary.

When *Desert* came out I was teaching at UBC and one person on the faculty, a closet gay himself, raised the issue of whether I was acceptable as a teacher since I was writing about lesbians. The answer he got from another member of the faculty was that writers of murder mysteries are not necessarily murderers. That's how I was defended! At the same time, the head of the department pointed out that I wouldn't get any benefit from being a novelist in the English department. I should get a Ph.D. and stop fooling around.

I loved going into the classroom and shutting the door and having my own kingdom with the students, but as far as peers were concerned, the university was no place to find them. I think universities are really bad places for writers because in English departments, writers are, by definition, dead. If you're a live writer, you're a creative writer and you're very much below the salt. You're insanely arrogant to imagine that you can take your place among the published. I think a lot of people in English departments wish they were writers instead and, as a result, they're very snooty.

Once I knew *Desert of the Heart* was going to be published, I thought, oh my God. I need to come out to my parents. And that's what I did, in a very quiet way. I gave them the manuscript to read and my father's only comment was, "I think you're very courageous." There was no discussion of any sort, but there were repercussions in the family. I hadn't counted on my younger sister being very upset. She wished that I had used a pen name because her in-laws were embarrassed.

What I also hadn't anticipated was that I would be the only "out" lesbian in Canada. And there have certainly been times when I wished either there were other people out there with me, or that I could go away and be a recluse.

For instance, if somebody wanted to do a documentary on gays and lesbians in Canada, I was the only lesbian they knew to call. I'd say, "I know, you'll start with the drag queens on Hallowe'en and then there will be me." Their response was, "If you don't talk to us, where will we go?"

Since almost everyone interviews me ostensibly because I'm a writer, but really because I'm a lesbian, I have the choice of not being interviewed or taking public responsibility for educating people. So that's what I've done. In many ways, visibility is the job I have, and if I can do it well and be helpful to other people, then I'm happy. I know what it means to the community to have people who are willing to be visible and move things forward.

The political part of my life has been a by-product of my writing, and I didn't think of my writing as propagandistic or political. Now I joke about what happens to you after you reach 60. My American publisher recently called and asked if I was familiar with the Celestial Seasonings Company, which makes various kinds of teas. They put quotations on their boxes and they wanted to use a quote from one of my books. "They're willing to pay you $250 and send you a box of tea," she said. "What flavour would you like?"

About the same time, the university wanted to give me an honorary doctorate. If I were left to my own devices, I'd say, "Thank you very much, but no thank you." Receiving a degree I didn't work for, doesn't mean anything to me. But then I realized that some people within the university had been working very hard to get certain people honoured and that it would mean a great deal politically to have an open lesbian on the stage. It's not my idea of political timing—on a day that kids are graduating and their parents and grandparents are in attendance—so for me, there was an issue of how to do it in a courteous way that didn't offend people, but nevertheless do it.

It seems to me that the world reacts very peculiarly to writers. I've been asked to draw cartoons—and I can't draw—because one of the characters in *Desert of the Heart* is a cartoonist. I've been asked to lecture on Yeats because another character is a Yeats scholar. At one point, after *Memory Board* came out, the Canadian Medical Association asked me to address their annual meeting on the subject of Alzheimer's. I wrote back and said my character didn't have Alzheimer's and that I knew nothing about the illness. I thought it was hilarious that they had asked a novelist, but also sort of reassuring that they had been that imaginative.

In the range of my writing life, I've written about all kinds of people and all kinds of situations and, each time, people call on me to be an expert in whatever it is. Writers are thought of as experts on everything and we're not. We're good bluffers.

I wrote my first non-fiction book, *Lesbian Images*, very reluctantly at the request and urging of a young editor at Doubleday Canada. It was a move towards scholarship which wasn't where I wanted to go, but for the first time I read writers such as Willa Cather, whom I had never read before but should have. It made me realize that my whole inheritance as a gay person had been taken out of my education. I wonder what kind of writer I would have been if these writers had been the voices of my education? By the time I met them, I was a mature writer myself, so I met company rather than mentors. I think my resentment was the resentment of knowing that as they has been excluded, so I might be.

When schools tried to get her books out of the curriculum, Margaret Laurence wrote to me in great distress asking what I did when people attacked my work that way. I said, "I don't. I'm not in the schools."

This sense of being silenced, of being excluded from a curriculum, is angering. Now that women's studies and gay studies have come along, my books have begun to get into the curriculum. But I doubt you'd find much of them in the Can. Lit. sections.

I think it's changing, and part of that change comes from writing books like *Lesbian Images*. The English publishers begged me to change the title because they thought it would offend people. I said, "I'm putting lesbian in the title so that people can find it in the library."

When *Desert of the Heart* first came out, my agent was approached about film rights and I said no because I knew I wouldn't have any control over the kind of film they would make. If Hollywood had made a movie from the book at that point, one woman would have killed herself and the other would have gotten married—that would have been the happy ending. My agent said I should take the money and run, but my response was, "I don't have any place to run to."

When Donna Deitch came along in the late '70s wanting to make an independent film, things were different. I had seen every film she had made and I sat and talked to her for an entire weekend. After that, I thought, she can make a film I don't like, but she won't make a film that offends me. It took her seven years to raise the money, and even then she didn't pay the actors until a distribution company had picked it up. Helen Shaver, one of the stars, said, "We did it for love and all the peanut-butter sandwiches."

Of course, that film, *Desert Hearts*, gave the novel an entirely new life. Thirty years later, it's still my best-selling book. There's a movie option out on *Memory Board*, too.

I had my first extreme episode of arthritis when I was 45 and spent two months in bed. I was told, then, that I'd be in a wheelchair within five years. I'm now 63 and I'm only in a wheelchair when I have to stand or walk a distance, but I've essentially given up writing.

I don't miss not being able to write because I've said what I need to say. I've been lucky in that. A lot of people are so involved with earning a living that they don't get a chance to write until they're my age. I don't think most writers do their best work when they're old.

I met my partner, Helen Sonthoff, 40 years ago. I don't think I could have done the work I've done without her. She has an extraordinary sense of social responsibility and courage. I think anyone else in her social position would have said, "For God's sake, use a pen name. Don't get us involved in this." But Helen's sense has always been that we'll deal with whatever comes along and that fear should never stop us from doing anything.

The first house we bought had a suite in the basement that we used to rent to a student. Helen always said if we lost a job, we could live in the suite and rent the house upstairs to be financially independent. We've always had houses we could convert in that way.

It's always seemed to me important to carry my own weight financially. That always seemed silly to Helen. She felt that since she was making enough money to support us, I should stay home and write. I couldn't do that. I suppose because making a living has always seemed such a chore to me, I didn't want anyone to do it for me.

I feel very lucky. For someone who has been so little forethoughtful in how to shape a life to have figured out how to make a living and at the same time do what I wanted to do is really quite remarkable. I think it's as much matter of luck as choice. I suppose that's one of the positive things about being raised as a female: you pretty well know you have to roll with the punches. You don't get an early sense that you're in command of the world and that you order it around to your specifications.

I think it's difficult to know what you want until you get there. If Helen and I had been told, 40 years ago, that we'd end up living on a little island out in the drink in B.C., we would have said, "That's too bad. Can't we do something else?"

Jane Ash Poitras
Edmonton, Alberta

"I 'd say that the prerequisite for every great artist is to have a couple of kids around. If you can't have them, rent them."

Jane Ash Poitras was born in 1951 in Fort Chipewyan, Alberta. After graduating from the University of Alberta with a bachelor of science degree in 1977, she decided to pursue her interest in art. She earned her master of fine arts from Columbia University in 1985, the same year she had her first solo exhibition. Since then, her work has been exhibited widely in Canada and the U.S.

I carry an interesting Indian name in the Chipewyan language—Tchilekwiyusse, "little boy child." Perhaps that has something to do with the fact that I've never thought of myself as either a boy or a girl.

The Chipewyan are an Athapaskan Dene group from northern Alberta. I grew up there and in Edmonton. Mine is a familiar story for someone born in 1951. When my parents died of tuberculosis, I became a ward of the state and was placed in foster homes. Fortunately, for me, when I was about five or six, the Good Creator sent me an angel who rescued me from all the horrible things that should have happened. An elderly German lady found me sitting on a curb as I was being turfed out of my current home and that was the start of my new life.

She was a member of a Germanic/Shamanistic religious group, the Boehmeists, who aren't ruled by ego like most European traditions. They had a real connection to the supernatural and to dreams, which has probably influenced my work.

From the time I was a young child I can remember loving art. It was always a place to go to, a magical refuge. But when I got to university, I studied microbiology, with the intention of going into medicine. After receiving my degree from the University of Alberta, I decided to treat myself to two years of fine art before going to medical school. One thing led to another and here I am, sitting in my house, with everything paid for by what I do best: create visions. It really is a fairy tale. It must be all my good spirits.

While I was doing my fine arts degree, I got very interested in making prints. Even as a child, I had a great interest in stamping things and making collages. Printmaking is very shamanistic. There were some excellent print-makers at the University of Alberta and it became like a religion in the fine arts department. Because I had a lot of religion in my background, that fit with my personality. I realized I could deal with the turmoil and the hardship.

A tremendous amount of pain is involved in printmaking. The plates are very heavy and that, combined with the fumes and the long hours, make it one of the unhealthiest art forms. Sometimes, I'd be so wired on the fumes that I couldn't sleep for several days.

It also requires a lot of strength. I was lifting 100-pound rollers and cranking big presses. If you're making a print, you have to stay focused for about 10 hours because if you make one little mistake all your efforts will be lost. That takes a tremendous amount of energy. You can't just say, "I'm going for a beer now." Everything has to be done with precision and you give your life to it. Sometimes I'd go in at 9:00 at night and wouldn't leave until the next morning at 11:00.

While I was at university, I got in touch with myself as an Indian. For years and years I had been denying my Indianness. When I was growing up, no one wanted to be an Indian so there was always a little bit of lying to disguise your identity. You'd say you were anything but Indian, because it wasn't cool. I remember being worried that I wouldn't be admitted into university because of my race.

The first other Indian I saw at university was a girl in my painting class named Nora Yellowknee. I couldn't believe it! I was convinced that every door was shut to Indians. Nora asked me where my people were and I admitted I didn't know. I said I thought they were probably all dead. She advised me to call Indian Affairs and track them down, which I did. Through the treaty numbers, they were able to find my whole family.

That was exciting because it confirmed I wasn't an alien, which is some-thing I had often wondered about. I grew up feeling very alone and not knowing where I belonged. I knew I was Indian but the only Indians I ever saw were skid-row types who were in very sad shape and that's a scary image. I was afraid I'd end up like them. I think one of the things that drove me to be successful was the desire to distance myself from that image.

When I visited Fort Chippewyan, for the first time in my life, I real-ized it was okay to be Indian. I was so happy I went overboard. I started wearing fringes and feathers in my hair and painting my face and drum-ming and singing and speaking the language. It wasn't about trying to fit in. It was about celebrating the fact that I'd found my family, which was a very important step for me.

That gave me a tremendous sense of freedom, which spilled over into my art. As an artist, you don't want to be shackled by your identity. But before you can release yourself from your identity, you have to know what it is.

After I graduated with a fine-arts degree, my instructors recommended that I get a master's. That seemed like two more years of heaven. I didn't have any trouble getting into schools—in fact, they were all trying to recruit me. I decided to go to Columbia because New York was the centre of the art world.

It was a turning-point in my life. At that point I still thought I'd leave Columbia and go back to medical school. Then, while I was in graduate school, I discovered I was pregnant. I had met my husband, Clint Buehler, just before I went to New York. He was a journalist who came to do a story on me: Indian goes to New York on an art scholarship. He's not a native, but he's a well-known native advocate. Now he runs my life and makes sure it all keeps functioning. I probably could do it without him, but I'd have the whole country mad at me because I often don't pay attention to details.

I came back to Canada to have the baby, and the phone just started ringing. Curators, critics—everyone wanted to come and see my work and I hadn't even finished graduate school. I didn't have room to breathe. The response from the art world was terrific. I've come to believe that there's a moccasin telegraph in this country and it sure has kept me busy.

I have been fortunate enough to have been involved in a number of travelling solo and group exhibitions which have given my work great exposure and publicity across Canada and the United States. I have also been blessed with good commercial dealers. It's difficult keeping up with the demand.

My latest project is a book. A couple of years ago I started doing a blackboard series on letters of the alphabet. They were extremely well received and I thought it would be neat to put them in a book. Even before the letters are made, people are asking for them.

I think most success comes from working with others. Because I spent so much time in university, I have a group of people in the universities, from every profession, who buy my work. I sell half my art to people I have some kind of connection with. For instance, people I grew up with. They remind me that when we were kids hanging around the street, we used to talk about being successful when we grew up. We all came from poverty and have made something of ourselves, and we're proud of that.

I had my first son in January 1986 and my second in June 1988, and I really believe that having children has enriched my art. If I hadn't experienced the miracle of birth, I'd be way back in my evolution as a person. It was a moment of release from another shackle.

When the baby comes out of you and he's suckling, you realize this is what it's all about. It's not something you can read about. Then you take the baby home, and as it grows into a child, it is still more closely linked with the mysterious universe than an adult because it's more recently come from that world. When I think about the things my children have said to me, I realize that they lead me into the sacred-knowledge world that I, as an adult, have to struggle very hard to reach. By being there with them, I see and hear things that later appear in my art.

Yesterday, I was walking in the park with my youngest son. I said, "Eli, look at the trees, see this nice street with the babies and the dogs playing. Listen to the sway of the wind in the leaves, the birds singing and the laughter." All of a sudden it occurred to me that we could bring heaven down to earth, so I said, "Let's do that." He agreed, and for about two hours we were in heaven and we talked about what it was like.

Many people would love to be able to do that. They drink, smoke and eat too much to try to reach that euphoria. If they only stopped to see and to listen, they could do it themselves. If, as an artist, you can give your audience a bit of that euphoria because you've been able to experience it, then how can your art not be successful?

That's why Picasso said he had to learn to draw like a child. He wanted to get back to the freedom and truth that children have.

I stumbled into art. There are not that many artists who can make a living off their work. But I've come to believe there's been magic in my life —the magic of the old lady finding me, the magic of me just happening to be in a painting class with Nora Yellowknee, who opened the door to my family. If I hadn't met her, I might still not know who I am.

I guess the secret of my success is the ability to be open, and free. It's tough, because things are always entering your life and you're constantly trying to keep balanced. There are moments in synchronic time, and if you're stressed out and unaware, you'll miss them. I've always had a keen awareness and I've always questioned everything. When you have the ability to use seven or eight senses, things happen for you. Carl Jung talked about this, but Indian people have been talking about it since time immemorial. I think that's what I've done—grabbed those moments and hung on to them.

Mary Pratt
St. John's, Newfoundland

"Fortunately, I remembered my days at art school when I trained myself to find my own images—not the acceptable images of the art world."

After studying fine arts at Mount Allison University in the early 1950s, Mary Pratt married and produced four children. Although she continued to paint, she didn't show her work until 1967, when the art gallery at Memorial University in St. John's organized an exhibition of her paintings. In 1971, her work began to be shown outside Atlantic Canada and, by the early 1980s, she was an important figure in the art world, with major retrospectives and shows across the country.

I grew up painting. My father used to put me on his knee, tell me stories and draw pictures for me on the backs of envelopes and old legal documents. When I was 10 I contributed a picture to an international children's exhibition at the Luxembourg Museum in Paris. My parents decided, then, that I should become a painter.

My grades in school had always been fairly good—except in arithmetic. My father decided I'd never learn to play bridge and advised me to put my faith in the arts—"Otherwise you'll drive your husband crazy." There would, of course, be a husband.

When I registered at Mount Allison University, the official in charge was kind enough to exclaim, "With marks like this, Miss West, you don't *have* to take fine arts." I was somewhat taken aback. And, when Alex Colville, who was one of my teachers, asked me what sort of career I saw for myself, I replied that I wanted to be a painter—"but not just a Sunday painter."

"Then you won't be," he said. Later, when I doubted my ability—or my commitment—I remembered those words and they helped.

Christopher Pratt and I met at Mount Allison. We were in the same English class. I had heard he was E.J. Pratt's nephew, and since I admired the poet, I was curious about his relative. Although Christopher wasn't studying fine arts, he was obviously a very gifted young artist. We worked together making sets for plays and decorations for dances. We didn't take our relationship seriously for several years—we were just good friends.

When we did marry, Christopher finally went to art school, in Glasgow.

I already had a certificate from Mount Allison and was eager to play the wife. So I postponed enrolling at the school until I felt I'd mastered this other role. Long before I'd mastered much of anything, I was pregnant. I might have been allowed to enrol even then, but didn't. I made nightgowns for the coming baby.

Christopher excelled at art school. He learned more in six months than I had in three years. He not only showed promise, he indicated by hard work, and much talent, that he was an artist. By then I had two children—they were my degree. I also had a great case of jealousy and defeatism. I felt my dreams of being an artist were gone.

I even doubted I had learned much at art school but, fortunately, I'd learned something. Whenever the class was let loose to do a landscape, all my classmates hurried off to the marshes or woods to "find something to paint." Being somewhat cynical, I figured they were doing anything but painting or they were searching for a Group-of-Seven image. I realized that if I stayed on the steps of the school, I'd find something to paint, and though it might not look like everybody's idea of a painting, I'd find it myself and it would be mine.

When the Canadian art world recognized Christopher, I was bothered by the knowledge that although this painting thing had occurred to me first, he was the one who realized that success demanded a single-minded pursuit. With four small children, I was not single-minded. I was distracted. And, though I was genuinely pleased for Christopher and believed enthusiastically in his work, I knew that my lack of commitment would likely ensure a wretched and self-pitying future for me.

At one point, I despaired and decided to give up. I'd started working from photographs, which I didn't think was "correct" and my parents thought was immoral. I decided to stop painting altogether. My younger daughter who was about four years old, looked at me solemnly and said, "But if you aren't a painter, what can you be?" Suddenly I realized that I didn't want my daughter to see me fail and, I suppose, that was the beginning of the dedicated grind.

I painted every day. And the years of ironing children's clothes and washing dishes and stuffing chickens came to my rescue. Although I had no filled sketch-books, I knew about textures and weights: the shine of polished silver, the wrinkled skin of a raw chicken, the iridescent glint of fish scales. I was amazed to find that I loved to paint these things, but I was even more surprised when people wanted to buy the pictures.

In the middle of this discovery, Pierre Thélerge and Mayo Graham arrived from the National Gallery to visit Christopher. I hadn't been told about the visit, and when I let them into the house, my studio door was open. I'd been working on a painting of some cold fillets on tin foil, and Mayo, seeing the canvas through the open door, asked what it was. Weeks later, she phoned to explain that the trip east was a scouting trip to look for possible women artists to include in a National Gallery show marking International Women's Year. "Would you be interested?" she asked. I didn't believe stuff like that really happened. It was quite overwhelming. But having work shown in the National Gallery, a whole room to myself with six or seven paintings, all in new frames, and people making a fuss, was really okay.

It was necessary, of course, to have a Toronto gallery. I knew nothing about such things, but the generous Dorothy Cameron persuaded two young dealers to look at my work and I went to Toronto to confer.

Going to the big time was no small matter. I knew I had to pull myself together and make an effort to impress. I bought clothes quite unlike anything I'd ever worn: black boots, a black cape with a red silk lining, a pair of grey herringbone trousers, a black velvet jacket with leg of mutton sleeves and a zipper up the front. The lining had a black-and-white polka-dot design and the shirt matched the lining. I made myself a tie of gold lamé. There was a poor-boy cap to match the trousers.

I had never looked so unlike myself. I had never had such confidence. The young dealers and I came to terms that I had decided on before I left home, and, for several years, we enjoyed a relationship that I now look back on with pleasure.

The trick of being entirely myself when I'm at work and then stepping outside that person when I'm doing business isn't easy. For my first foray into the strange world, it's very likely the costume helped. I'm still not very good at business and only my suspicion that dealers hold most artists in contempt encourages me to make the effort.

Being entirely myself, on the other hand, isn't difficult, though it was a trick to begin with. Once I decided to take painting seriously, I kept to an intense schedule of housework. I got up at 5 a.m. and worked until 10:00. I'd have the bread baked early. The little ones were around, but they were never really any trouble because I let them help me.

One morning I was carrying all my cleaning stuff into our bedroom, which was in the east part of the house. It was autumn and the sun had just come up over the river. I opened the door and our bedroom was absolutely full of light, that bright, bright light off the water that you don't expect in the fall. The bed was all apart, the pillows were smashed together and the sheets were tumbled out. A red chenille bedspread I had dyed—not very successfully—was sort of dripping on the floor, and a matted old pink blanket that I had put in the dryer by mistake lay there, almost like a fold of skin on top of the bedspread. The other blankets were white and the bed was black with handmade posts. The image caught me, like someone had punched me in the gut.

I dropped everything and rushed over to Christopher's studio. I asked him for a square canvas and an easel. He told me to take what I wanted. I set it up and painted the bed. We slept on the sofa while I worked. I knew I had to keep this moment, this feeling, this amazing reaction. I thought of it as a sort of a miracle.

Once that happened, other things of no consequence, like a bottle of Windex against the window, shouted at me. Perhaps it happened because I was so lonely. I was off in the wilderness with four children and very little company. I didn't drive so I couldn't get into town. I think I was living in a state of hyped awareness. I suppose if I had told a doctor, I would have ended up on pills or in analysis. I didn't want to tell anybody, anyway. I just wanted to paint.

Fortunately, I still want to paint. Images continue to emerge from my own world, and though I've experimented with many approaches and various techniques through the decades, it is still my own personal world that informs and delights me.

Some people who hope to be artists think they must live differently from what they perceive to be the norm. I don't think it's wise to try to be different from the person you know yourself to be. It is wise, however, to be sensitive to the world you really know.

Index